On the History of Political Philosophy

Great Political Thinkers from Thucydides to Locke

W. JULIAN **KORAB-KARPOWICZ**

Anglo-American University

Boston   Columbus   Indianapolis   New York   San Francisco   Upper Saddle River
Amsterdam   Cape Town   Dubai   London   Madrid   Milan   Munich   Paris   Montreal   Toronto
Delhi   Mexico City   São Paulo   Sydney   Hong Kong   Seoul   Singapore   Taipei   Tokyo

Executive Editor: Reid Hester
Executive Marketing Manager: Wendy Gordon
Production Manager: Fran Russello
Project Coordination, Text Design, and Electronic Page Makeup: Vijayakumar Sekar,
    TexTech International
Cover Design Manager: Jayne Conte
Cover Designer: Suzanne Behnke
Cover Art: Fotolia: © Eishier

Library of Congress Cataloging-in-Publication Data

Korab-Karpowicz, W. Julian.
  On the history of political philosophy : great political thinkers from
Thucydides to Locke / W. Julian Korab-Karpowicz.
    p. cm.
  Includes bibliographical references (p.   ) index.
  ISBN 978-0-205-11974-5
    1. Political science–Philosophy–History.   2. Political
  scientists–History.   I. Title.
  JA71.K67 2012
  320.01--dc23

                                                                    2011037130

ISBN 10: 0-205-11974-3
ISBN 13: 978-0-205-11974-5

To my students for their inspiration.

BRIEF CONTENTS

CONTENTS

CHAPTER 6 St. Thomas Aquinas: Faith and Social Solidarity 91

CHAPTER 7 Machiavelli: How to Rule? 115

CHAPTER 8 Grotius: International Society 140

PREFACE

It can be argued that political philosophy begins with the question "What is justice?" raised by Socrates in Plato's *Republic*. The debate about justice that takes place in the dialogue leads to two opposing positions: the position represented by Socrates, according to which justice is a universal and timeless moral value that provides the foundation for order in any human society, and the position represented by Thrasymachus, according to which justice is purely conventional and relative to human laws that vary according to times and customs: "nothing else than the interest of the stronger." This debate, initiated by Plato, continues throughout the history of political thought. Already in the Republic, it inspires additional questions: Do moral values hold in politics? What is human nature? What are the origins and the end of the state? Can a war be just? What are the limits of governmental power? How much liberty should citizens enjoy? Who should rule? What is the best form of government? Answers to these questions, posed in a single work written more than twenty-four centuries ago, have served in one way or another as the basis upon which the main themes of political and international relations theory have developed.

This book provides a fresh, historical introduction to Western political philosophy from its beginning in ancient Greece to modern times. It is designed for students of philosophy, politics and international relations, and other fields, individuals taking courses in the history of political thought, and for general readers who have an interest in the subject. It is written simply and candidly, but without sacrificing intellectual depth. This book demonstrates the continuing significance of centuries old political and philosophical debates and problems. Recurring themes include discussions concerning human nature, different views of justice, the origin of government and law, the rise and development of various forms of government, idealism and realism in international relations, the distinction between just and unjust war, and the nature of legitimate sovereignty. It explores tensions between ancient and modern ideas and presents the history of political thought as a great debate about politics and ethics in which political thinkers of various eras expound on their views in turn.

Although my book focuses primarily on individual political thinkers, it is written so that each chapter develops a theme arising from a previous one. It is three-dimensional, with the first dimension being chronology. The second dimension is found in recurring themes, such as human nature, different views of justice, the origin of society and law, the rise and development of various forms of government, the role of idealism and realism in international relations, and the sources of public authority and the nature of legitimate sovereignty. The third dimension consists of topics, such as freedom, equality, power, authority, legitimacy, justice, sovereignty, happiness, natural law, and human rights.

Throughout this book, I have used parenthetical notes to keep bibliographical references as simple as possible. The works cited list at the end of the book contains the bibliographic information for the primary and secondary works referred to in the main body of the text. The primary works were written by the great political thinkers who are discussed in the various chapters, and are usually referred to by the title of the work in question, and then by numbers that indicate book, chapter, section, or line. The secondary works are usually referred to by author and page number.

To facilitate the reader's entry into the field of political philosophy, I have provided learning aids. Study questions at the end of each chapter can be used as topics for discussions or essays. Suggested readings are a guide to additional works on the subject of a given chapter. A glossary provides definitions of some of the main ideas discussed at much greater length in the text.

Three chapters of this book are revised and expanded versions of previously published articles. Chapter 1 is a revision of the article "How International Relations Theorists Can Benefit by Reading Thucydides," which was printed in *The Monist*, Vol. 89, Number 2 (April 2006). Chapter 2 is a revision of "Plato's Political Philosophy," which was written for *The Internet Encyclopedia of Philosophy*. Chapter 8 is a revision of "In Defense of International Order: Grotius's Critique of Machiavellism," which appeared in *The Review of Metaphysics*, Vol. 60, Number 1 (September 2006). I am grateful to the editors and publishers for permission to include these revised texts.

I would like to thank my family and friends for their support of the effort that went into the writing and publishing of this book. My special thanks are offered to Diane Ewart Grabowski, Deborah Peterson, Michael Shields, and Robin Turner for reading and checking the manuscript. I would also like to thank Professors C.D.V. Reeve, James V. Shall, and Ulrich Steinvorth for their helpful comments on individual chapters. Throughout the writing process, I was stimulated by class discussions with my students. I am grateful to them for being my source of inspiration.

It is my belief and hope that this book will enable readers to gain an essential knowledge of the history of political thought.

W. Julian Korab-Karpowicz

INTRODUCTION: WHAT IS POLITICAL PHILOSOPHY?

Perhaps the greatest contribution of ancient Greece to Western civilization is the discovery of autonomous reason. The early Greek philosophers asked questions about the universe, like other thinkers before them, but were the first to propose general, rational answers that were no longer based on religious considerations. The problem that confronted the Greeks, of finding what was really going on in the external world, which they considered rationally discernable and knowable, was extended to their political communities. It took the form of distinguishing between the often-confusing ways in which things *were* actually done and the way in which they *should be* done. The Greek thinkers engaged with essentially ethical, normative questions about politics. In this way, political philosophy was born.

Politics is a complex social phenomenon that includes the activities of governments, political parties and leading figures within them, lobbies and interest groups, and the general public, as well as other political actors. Whereas the study of politics can be confined, like much of today's political science, to empirical research, political philosophers have never limited themselves to observation and measurement. To be sure, they have never disregarded the knowledge of how things are, which can be regarded as the *descriptive* aspect of political philosophy. Their central concern, however, has been with the "ought." They have been explicitly prescriptive or *normative*, asking what is most desirable for society and most just. Ultimately, political philosophers have looked for the best social and political order.

From its very beginning, political philosophy has been essentially a normative theory that would identify sources of evil in a political community and prescribe a solution in the form of an ordering vision of what the community ought to become. Plato can serve us here as a paradigmatic example. The conflict and factional strife that he describes in the *Republic* were not inventions of his philosophical fancy, but the real stuff of Athenian politics. They were a result of establishing a democracy in Athens that increased political participation, but at the same time encouraged rival ambitions, eroded the city's traditions, destroyed its unity, and turned politics into an "incessant movement of shifting currents" (*Seventh Letter* 325e). This turbulent flux of political life, under the influence of which the best of characters could not remain uncorrupted, was for Plato a contradiction of any good political order, which could be based only on the rule of wisdom over mere opinion and of virtue over vice.

For Plato, political philosophy was a practical enterprise of the most serious kind. Its task was to restore order in both societies and human souls. For Aristotle, its task was to organize political communities according to reason and justice. This stress on practice, characteristic of classical political thought, would certainly still find modern adherents. For example, according to Fred

Dallmayr, "to the extent that it seeks to render political life intelligible, political theory has to remain attentive to the concrete sufferings and predicaments of people" (2). In much of today's political philosophy, often referred to as political theory, ideas are not formulated in vain. They are designed to offer us normative guidance on where to proceed and how to have an impact on day-to-day politics and policy making.

The main political theories today comprise a diversity of forms of liberalism, communitarianism, feminism, neo-Thomism, and post-Marxism. Their particular ideas rest on beliefs concerning human nature that have an extra-political, metaphysical character. Having established these foundational beliefs, current political theories attempt to show how political institutions and processes can be derived from them, thus making political life a more rational, just, or desirable form of existence.

Nevertheless, the modern era is not only marked by these new normative theories of politics but also by the decline of political philosophy as normative political theory into ideology. While the former is ultimately motivated by the desire to know reality (and this is related to its impartiality, reflective openness, and critical distance), the latter represents a limited, often dogmatic, partisan worldview that is intended to persuade and manipulate political actors. The chief motive behind ideologies is not really to search for truth, but to achieve definite goals. In them, political action overcomes rational investigation. Hence, in a sense, they represent a departure from rationality, one of the key elements of Western civilization.

The prevalence of ideologies in modernity has led some twentieth-century philosophical schools to dismiss the practice-oriented normative theory altogether. In logical positivism, for example, normative ethical and political propositions were deprived of the status of knowledge and were considered to express nothing but the emotional or psychological states of individuals. Under the influence of analytic thought, the main task of political philosophy has become conceptual analysis. In this view, political philosophy has little impact on politics. It is no longer the heroic enterprise of the great political thinkers, but instead is reduced to a "disciplinary enterprise." Its practice consists mainly in the training of oneself and others in the habit of clarifying concepts and examining arguments. The former involves trying to define or characterize political concepts such as justice or state; the latter involves evaluating the way people support their claims.

Surely even the best political ideas could not work if they were not clearly expressed and convincingly presented. Philosophers generally subject everyday convictions and foundational beliefs to careful logical scrutiny, exposing inconsistencies and misconceptions. Already, classical Greek thinkers, particularly Plato, distinguished knowledge of things from a mere opinion of them. To claim the status of knowledge, an opinion must be properly justified. There is thus a place for an analytic linguistic therapy in political philosophy—for clarifying concepts and examining arguments. Political philosophy cannot, however, be reduced to it.

Rather than being a mere "linguistic therapy," political philosophy is a "political therapy." Perceiving urgent problems around us, the great political thinkers have always aspired to move from where we are to where we might be. The study of their classic texts has become an established part of the discipline of politics. However, to really benefit from these writings, one should not study them merely for antiquarian interest, as if they were museum pieces. The texts might have emerged as a result of particular historical circumstances in which their authors found themselves, yet they transcend their own times and continue to provide us with questions and answers concerning our own political problems.

The great political thinkers that are introduced in this book regarded political philosophy as normative theory. In the classical tradition of moral and political thought, which was developed by Plato, Aristotle, Cicero, and other philosophers of antiquity and continued by Christian thinkers, this normative aspect of theorizing linked politics intrinsically with ethics. It was characteristic of the classics that they emphasized the importance of virtue for political life. The first notable critic of this tradition was Machiavelli, who separated morality and politics, and based his normative theory on considerations of power. As an admirer of the Roman republic, though, he was still to some extent under the influence of classical ideas. It was only Thomas Hobbes, the father of modern political philosophy, who at last completely parted company with them. However, despite of the challenge of modernity, the classical tradition of linking politics to ethics has survived to our times. It has equipped us with perennial ideas that at many turning points in the history of the West have proven to be an inexhaustible source of inspiration and renewal.

The classical tradition reminds us of virtues and their importance for politics. This book begins with Thucydides, often regarded as the father of realism in international relations and ends with Hobbes and Locke, the modern political philosophers, to whom we owe so much, but who have contributed to the weakening of the influence of this tradition.

Thucydides: War and the Polis

Often regarded as the father of realism in international relations, Thucydides was a historian and an original political thinker, best known for his description and analysis of the political events that occurred during the Peloponnesian War, which broke out in 431 B.C.E. between Athens and Sparta. Thucydides, an Athenian citizen, was a contemporary of these events. He was born around 460 B.C.E., and in 424 attained the rank of general. Because he was unable to defend the city of Amphipolis from the Spartans' attack, charges were brought against him. He was forced into a twenty-year exile, during which he spent most of the time at his home in Thrace, but he also visited the Peloponnesus and traveled to Sicily. He returned to Athens after the war ended, but did not live long enough to finish his *History of the Peloponnesian War*. The account breaks off in 411, seven years before the end of the war.

THUCYDIDES' WORK

Being a historical account, albeit one whose accuracy is sometimes challenged, and a literary landmark, which, although written in prose, resembles in some parts the best of Homer and of Greek tragedy, Thucydides' *History* is neither a work of political philosophy nor a sustained theory of international relations. Much of the *History* consists of paired speeches by personages who argue both sides of an issue. In these speeches and in Thucydides' own comments on the events that take place, we get a glimpse of a theory, but nowhere we do find it fully formulated or made explicit. Although Thucydides implies that his thought exemplifies universal truths about human nature, civil society, and interstate relationships, he does not directly present his point of view, and he never engages with other thinkers in a debate. Nevertheless, if the *History* is described as the only acknowledged classical text in the field of international relations, and if it has inspired theorists from Hobbes to contemporary international relations scholars, the reasons are that it is more than a chronicle of events and a theoretical position can be extrapolated from it. For some of its readers, the *History of the Peloponnesian War* represents an archetypal statement of power politics. Thucydides is viewed as a political realist who asserts that the pursuit of moral principles does not enter into the realm of international affairs. For others, this work is a sad and cautionary tale about failure and degeneration resulting from a war perpetuated by the actions of men unable to practice moderation in their ambitions. In this view, Thucydides is regarded as a moralist who explores the tension between the injunctions of justice and the requirements of power, and in the end finds repugnant imperial Athens' disregard for moral considerations in the conduct of its political and military affairs. Last but not least, we can discern in the *History* some principal themes and topics of political philosophy.

A BRIEF HISTORY OF THE PELOPONNESIAN WAR

Ancient Greece was divided into many city-states that differed in size and had a variety of political constitutions. Athens and Sparta, former allies who defeated the Persian Empire (479 B.C.E.) but subsequently became the main adversaries in the Peloponnesian War, were among the largest of them. By the middle of the fifth century B.C.E., they were the leaders of two contending alliances of Greek city-states: the Delian League and the Peloponnesian League.

Sparta, whose four-hundred-year-old constitution was attributed to the legendary lawgiver Lycurgus, was primarily a conservative land-oriented aristocracy, but it had a mixed constitution in which the distribution of power among social classes was remarkably balanced. The Spartan system of government was a model of stability. Its citizens constituted a professional army, which developed as a consequence of Spartans' subjection of a conquered people, the Helots, who greatly outnumbered them and on whom they relied as agricultural workers. Strict discipline prepared aristocratic youth for military service. The total population of Sparta was between 190,000 and 270,000, of whom only about 4,000 were male citizens of military age. Because of this fact, Sparta had to rely upon its allies in the Peloponnesian League for military assistance. Furthermore, as it was not able to enrich itself through the voluntary alliance it led, Sparta was relatively poor. Its chief source of wealth was agriculture.

In contrast, Athens was a thriving commercial center. The Athenians derived their wealth mainly from trade and natural resources. By defeating their rivals at sea, they turned the Delian League into an empire and grew rich. In exchange for keeping the Aegean Sea safe through the power of their navy, they collected payments from their allies. Moreover, the government of Athens was the paradigm of Greek democracy. The Athenian assembly and judicial service were open to all citizens. Most public officials were selected from among the citizenry annually by lot. Citizenship, from which women, foreigners, and slaves were excluded, was nonetheless accessible to a much wider class of people in Athens than in Sparta. A citizen was anyone, rich or poor, who could prove his Athenian ancestry. The total population of Athens was between 215,000 and 300,000, of whom about 40,000 individuals were citizens. Of these, approximately half could afford to purchase military equipment, enabling them to serve as members of the heavily armed infantry known as *hoplites*. Thus, for its fighting force, Athens relied on its citizenry complemented by a few thousand resident aliens.

In Thucydides' opinion, the true reason for the Peloponnesian War was "the growth of Athenian power, which put fear into the Lacedaemonians [Spartans] and so compelled them into war" (1.23.6). Sparta was driven to enter into war in order to restore the balance of power between the Greek city-states. But the war was also fueled by the ideological conflict between democracy and oligarchy that was endemic to ancient Greece. Athens aided democratic factions in neighboring cities, whereas Sparta aided oligarchic ones.

The first phase of the war began in 431 and lasted ten years. The second year of the war was disastrous for the Athenians. A plague broke out in the city, which was overcrowded by refugees from the countryside outside the walls. Still, the Athenians held out. Since Sparta had the superior army and Athens the superior navy, as long as Athens conceded land to Sparta and Sparta conceded the sea to Athens, neither side could hope to win. A truce declared in 421 proved to be fragile, and the war began again. In 416 the Athenians attacked the island of Melos, a Spartan ally. That same year, after the conquest of Melos, they immediately decided to undertake a more risky venture. Moved by ambition and a desire for further expansion, they invaded Sicily, an island that had among its settlements numerous colonies allied with Sparta. Their main target was Syracuse, the largest and most powerful of the Sicilian cities. This time, the Athenians badly underestimated the strength of their enemies. The result was a defeat from which Athens never fully recovered. Many of the Athenian allies rebelled. During the ensuing period of political instability, Athenian democracy was briefly replaced by an oligarchy known as the Four Hundred. Thucydides' *History* breaks off at this point, but the war continued. Following the destruction of the Athenian navy at the battle of Aegospotami in 405, the Athenians were compelled to sue for peace. They surrendered to the Spartans in 404 B.C.E.

FROM THE STATE OF NATURE TO POLITICAL SOCIETY

What would life be like in the state of nature, in a world before civilization? Would it be an idyllic existence in harmony with nature, or a "brutish" one? What would life be like without a government? Thucydides, whose influence on Hobbes in this respect cannot be overlooked, is the first political thinker who attempted to answer these questions by looking at the historical evidence available to him. In the opening pages of the *History of the Peloponnesian War* (1.2-19), he describes the emergence and growth of Athenian civilization. His portrait of the pre-political, archaic era shows us a world dominated by power relationships and characterized by insecurity. The Greeks of that time period lived a savage existence, merely satisfying basic needs. There was no trade, no farming, no permanent settlement. Human relationships were based on sheer force; everyone carried weapons. There was neither morality nor consideration of justice. Piracy and robbery were accepted ways of life. A commodious living, Thucydides implies, requires an authority capable of enforcing order and providing security. The advent of civilization comes with the establishment of the city-state, the Greek *polis*, and is recognizable by the presence of two interrelated factors: progress in physical security and growth in wealth. Due to its geographical location, on unattractive barren land and close to the sea, Athens escaped most of the early civil wars. Moreover, it was not self-sufficient and had to foster trading links with other cities. Athens was open to the world and would attract the most able refugees from other parts of Greece. Consequently, it developed and acquired wealth faster than other city-states. In Thucydides' description, the Athenians were the first to lay aside their weapons and put on long robes, symbolic of a more relaxed and luxurious way of life. Piracy was suppressed by the navy, and trade developed. The surplus of wealth allowed for the building of city walls for better protection. The population grew, and Athenian colonies were established on some islands and in Ionia.

These material factors—security and wealth—are, in Thucydides' view, the preconditions for the political and ethical achievements of civilization. These achievements are described in Pericles' "Funeral Oration" (2.35-46), one of the most famous speeches to have come down to us from antiquity. The Athenian leader Pericles gave this speech at a public funeral for soldiers who had lost their lives in various minor actions at the beginning of the war. As in his two other speeches recorded by Thucydides (the "War Speech" and the "Last Speech"), Pericles' aim in the "Funeral Oration" was to convince the Athenians that their cause was worth fighting for. However, in this case, he appeals to his listeners' virtue and the greatness of Athens.

In the years preceding the Peloponnesian War, Athens, governed by Pericles, was at the peak of its power and civilization. Even today, looking at the Athenian Acropolis, we can get a sense of the civic pride that led to the construction of the Parthenon, which, though now only a stone skeleton, remains glorious. The whole complex of grand temples, which was erected using funds taken illicitly from Athenian allies and finished only two years before Athens surrendered to Sparta, reminds us of Athenian imperial ambitions and perfected taste. "Our city is worth admiration and is a lesson for the whole of Greece," is the main message of Pericles' speech. He does not merely point out the material achievements of the Athenians or the city's political institutions, a democratic form of government and equality before the law. As he introduces different topics, it becomes clear that in his view the highest achievements of civilization are not buildings or works of art, or even institutions, but individual and public qualities, known as *virtues*, that contribute to the overall quality of a people. Athens is a great city because of the virtue and intelligence of its citizens. "We respect the law greatly and fear violating it." "We are not offended by our neighbor for following his own pleasure." "We have compelled all seas and all lands to be open to us by our daring." "We live in our city, open to all." "We alone think that a man who does not take part in public affairs is good for nothing." "We have provided many ways of giving our minds recreation from labor." "We are lovers of beauty with restraint and lovers of wisdom without any softening of character" (2.37-41). These words of Pericles anticipate the idea that political theory is about the good life. The "good life" is concerned with such normative issues as the best political order, respect for law, tolerance, openness, courage, moderation, prudence, fraternity, and prosperity. Periclean Athens at its highest development exemplifies a civilized community of citizens participating willingly and freely in public life—a political society based not only on individual self-interest, but also on the virtues of its members, who stand ready to support and defend the common good.

FRAGILITY OF CIVILIZATION

Thucydides is a master at depicting contrasting situations. Immediately after portraying the greatness of the Athenian civilization in the "Funeral Oration," he explores the theme of the vulnerability of a political community in his account of the plague that strikes Athens during the second year of the war (2.47-54). The city is overcrowded with refugees from the rural areas. This is a result of Pericles' war policy, namely, giving up the Athenian countryside to the Spartans and maintaining a stronghold over the sea and the urban areas protected by walls. The disease, which hits the overcrowded metropolis suddenly, soon becomes a disaster. The fear of a sudden and terrible death proves too severe for people to endure. Conventional restraints begin to break down. The Athenians return to a pre-political state of nature, so to speak, in which authority no longer holds sway. They begin to openly and publicly engage in actions that they would previously try to hide. They seek the pleasure of the moment. No institution is respected or held in awe due to fear of the gods or regard for the laws. Frightened at the thought of impending death, Athenian citizens become driven by individual egoism and exercise no self-restraint, but engage in lawless and impious acts.

Difficult times shape humanity no less than good times do, Thucydides implies. The events of the plague, and also scenes of outrage and violence that occurred at various points throughout the war (3.81-83, 7.29-30), show the fragility of the ethical achievements of civilization in the face of the ultimate struggle for survival. Thucydides expresses disapproval of, if not horror at, the destruction of most of the laudable qualities of individuals as well as of the moral bonds that hold communities together. He observes that morals easily deteriorate and most people cannot hold on to ethical values when their survival is threatened. Insofar as it strips away easy access to goods that satisfy daily needs, "war is a violent teacher" of vice, and justice one of its chief victims (3.82.2-3). War puts into jeopardy everything that has been achieved by civilization. Citizens' virtues and the community spirit are eroded and give way to wicked decisions, violence, revenge, private ambitions, and greed. The latter two are the chief reasons why Athens finally lost the Peloponnesian War.

The plague, which was the cause of Pericles' death two and a half years after the outbreak of the conflict with Sparta, was a crucial turning point in

Athenian history. From this time on, there occurred a marked shift from concern with the common good to individualistic self-interest, and hence gradual moral degradation of the city. In his last speech, Pericles does not appeal to virtue, but rather to necessity and enlightened self-interest. By saying that "it does not matter whether man prospers as an individual: if his country is destroyed, he is lost with it" (2.60.3-4), he tries to convince the Athenians that they have to see their own interests as inseparable from the larger collective interest of the *polis*. The language of virtue is not relevant to his compatriots anymore. In the speeches of those who succeed him as Athenian leaders, we find successive and increasingly blatant appeals to self-interest.

The story of the plague and other events he narrates suggest that Thucydides had a pessimistic view of human nature. To him, human beings are not naturally virtuous. Moral qualities, the product of the sustained work of education, are merely the surface beneath which lies a collection of egoistic passions. The emergence of civilization and the maintenance of its ethical achievements require insulation from them. When this fragile insulation, in the form of the security and prosperity that come with the establishment of civil government, is eroded by an extreme adversity, such as war or civil strife, and the restraints of law and justice no longer hold, then individual selfishness prevails and humans are reduced to a state of viciousness and conflict. But the fact that he makes such observations does not mean that Thucydides is a determinist. He recognizes that there are exceptions to the general trend, and that some people will stand up to adverse circumstances and will remain virtuous (2.51). These individuals can be thought of as the moral pillars of society. The idea that some people will remain unshaken in the face of misfortune is echoed in the concluding words of the "Last Speech" of Pericles: "The strongest cities and individuals are the ones that are least sensitive in their minds to calamity and the firmest in their actions to resist it" (2.64.6).

THUCYDIDES' REALISM

The task that Thucydides sets for himself is not just to describe the harsh events that occurred during the war "and will always happen as long as human nature remains the same" (3.82.2). As he says in its opening pages, the *History* is not a piece of writing designed to meet the taste of the immediate public—it is meant to last forever. He is not interested in merely reconstructing historical events on the basis of the best evidence available; he is also attempting to provide a general explanation for them. Thucydides' work is essentially a study of human and state behavior, in which a theory is implied and permanent characteristics of human affairs and international politics are revealed. Because of his pessimism about human nature, his emphasis on power, and his recognition that morality has little place in interstate relations, he is often credited with being the first writer in the tradition of political realism.

What is realism? Realism is a view of international politics that stresses its competitive and conflicting side. The principal actors in the international arena are states, which are concerned with their security, act in pursuit of their own national interests, and struggle for power. Thucydides seems to subscribe to this view. Distinguishing between the immediate and underlying causes of the Peloponnesian War, he does not see its real or underlying cause to be Athens' intervention in the conflict between Corcyra and Corinth, the siege of Potidaea, or the ban on trade with Megara—the events that immediately preceded its outbreak. He locates the root of the war in the changing distribution of power between the two blocs of Greek city-states, the Delian League and the Peloponnesian League. According to him, the growth of Athenian power made the Spartans afraid for their security, and thus propelled them into war (1.23.6). What he says resonates strongly with realist arguments on how the anarchic structure of the international system affects the behavior of states. The realists consider the absence of a ruler, literally *anarchy*, to be the defining element of international politics and the primary determinant of international political outcomes. They assert that lack of a common, rule-making, and enforcing authority means that each state is responsible for its own survival and is free to define its own power interests. In the words of the Athenian envoys at Melos, if there is no international government that can enforce order, "the independent states survive [only] when they are powerful" (5.97.2). International anarchy leads, in the realist view, to the overriding role of power in shaping interstate relations and causes all states to be motivated by fear and mutual distrust. To attain security, states increase their relative power and engage in power-balancing for the purpose of deterring potential aggressors. Wars are fought to prevent any competing nations from becoming militarily stronger.

The negative side of this emphasis on power is the realists' skepticism regarding the applicability of universal ethical norms to relations among states. National politics is the realm of authority and law, whereas international politics, unrestrained by any higher moral laws, is a sphere without justice characterized by active or potential conflict between states. A clear example of this position can be found in the "Melian Dialogue" (5.85-113). The dialogue relates to the events of 416 B.C.E., when Athens invaded the island of Melos. The Athenian envoys present the Melians with a choice between destruction or surrender, and from the outset ask them not to appeal to justice, but to think about their survival. In their words, "We both know that the decisions about justice are made in human discussions only when both sides are under equal compulsion, but when one side is stronger, it gets as much as it can, and the weak must accept that" (5.89). To be "under equal compulsion" means to be subjected to a common authority. Since such an authority above states does not exist, the Athenians argue that the only right in this world of anarchy is the right of the stronger to dominate the weaker. They explicitly equate right with might, and exclude considerations of justice from foreign affairs. Further, the right of the stronger to dominate is for them a natural law. "Nature always compels gods (we believe) and men (we are certain) to rule over anyone they can control" (5.105.2). Hence, in the Athenian speech there is implied not only a denial of international morals, but also a view of human nature that is essential to the realist view of international politics. International anarchy would not lead to conflict between nations if they were all populated by angels. The realistic theory is rooted in a conception of egoistic human nature. Human beings are perceived as self-interested and power-seeking, moved by the drive to dominate others, and not influenced by either compassion or any moral rules.

Realism is implied in the statements of the Athenian envoys at Melos and in the way Thucydides explains the cause of the Peloponnesian War. Moreover, the realist outlook of international politics is expressed in the very first speech of the Athenians recorded in the *History*, namely, the one given at the debate that took place in Sparta just before the outbreak of the war. The Athenians refer to the three motives that have led them to obtain and keep their empire: fear, honor, and self-interest (1.75.3; 1.76.2). A similar motivational triad can be found in Hobbes' *Leviathan* and in the writings of twentieth-century realists (Donnelly 9). Nearly all realists place fear at the core of state motivation. Fear is a defensive motive, based on the desire for self-preservation; in contrast, honor and self-interest, desires for recognition and gain, are fundamentally competitive and acquisitive. These three motives are paralleled in Pericles' "Last Speech," as safety, glory, and wealth (2.63-64). Athenian imperialism is thus justified on the grounds of security concerns, recognition, and expediency, but not on moral grounds. Further, the Athenians affirm the priority of power over justice in international relations and provide justification for this. They argue that morality cannot be put ahead of power because, as a rule, "the weaker are held by the stronger" (1.76.2). No one who can obtain something by power will be deterred from using it by moral considerations. To believe otherwise, they suggest, would be to mislead oneself about the nature of international politics.

The Athenians, then, give strong support to a realist position. The question is, however, to what extent their realism coincides with Thucydides' viewpoint. Is his realism the same as the realism of the Athenian envoys at Melos and of the Athenians at the debate at Sparta? Is he a realist at all? Thucydides' *History* provides numerous accounts of debates between groups and individuals who often hold opposite views. The political discourse that he describes is pluralistic, not single. Although fragments of the "Melian Dialogue" and other parts of the *Peloponnesian War* support a realistic reading, Thucydides' realism cannot be deduced from selected fragments, but must be assessed on the basis of the wider context of his book. The "Melian Dialogue" itself provides us with a plurality of contending perspectives.

REALISM VERSUS IDEALISM IN THE MELIAN DIALOGUE

Political realism is usually contrasted with idealism or liberalism, a theoretical perspective that stresses international norms, interdependence between states, and international cooperation. The "Melian Dialogue," which is one of the most frequently commented upon parts of Thucydides' *History*, presents the classic dilemma between idealist and realist thinking: Can international politics be based on a moral order derived from the principles of peace and justice, or will it remain the playground of conflicting national interests and power?

For the Melians, who employ idealistic arguments, the choice is between war and subjection (5.86). They do not wish to lose their freedom, and in spite of the fact that they are militarily weaker than the Athenians, they are prepared to defend themselves (5.100; 5.112). They base their arguments on an appeal to justice (5.86), understanding it as a universal moral principle. They associate justice with fairness, and regard the Athenians as unjust (5.90; 5.104). Further, they respect the gods and believe in honor, saying that their weakness will be compensated for by the aid of the gods, who will support their just cause, and also by the help of their allies, the Spartans, whom they trust and hold to be honorable (5.104; 5.112). Hence, in the speech of the Melians, one can identify such elements of the idealistic or liberal worldview as the beliefs that nations have the right to exercise political independence, that they have mutual obligations to one another and will carry out such obligations, and that a war of aggression is unjust.

The Athenian response is based on key realist concepts such as security and power, and is informed not by what the world should be, but by what it is. The Athenians urge the Melians to look at the facts—that is, to recognize their military inferiority, to consider the potential consequences of their decision, and to think about their own survival (5.87; 5.101). They exclude consideration of justice from their discussion, appealing instead to the identity of their interests (5.89; 5.91). They are concerned about their own security and express fear that independent Melos may endanger them (5.99). They argue that it will be better for both sides if Melos gives in. The Melians will save themselves from ruin, and the Athenians will reap profits from them (5.93). Melos, added to the Athenian empire, will increase the latter's size and strength, and will no longer be a potential security threat (5.97). Moreover, the Athenians describe the honor and justice of the Spartans, to which the Melians refer, as mere hypocrisy that masks Spartan interests. Considering Athenian power and the risk of military action, it is foolish, they claim, to believe that Sparta will go to war in order to aid Melos (5.105; 5.109). They advise the Melians not to be distracted by a false sense of honor, which, in the absence of strength, can bring them only disaster and the dishonor of defeat, and not to depend on mere hopes or place their faith in allies, but to think only about their own country and its survival (5.111).

In spite of these realist arguments, the Melians refuse to submit and decide to fight for their independence. After some initial successes on their part, however, the Athenian siege succeeds. The Melians pay the highest price for their choice. Melian men of military age are killed. Women and children are sold into slavery. Melos loses statehood after seven hundred years of its history. The island is repopulated by Athenian colonists. This tragic story shows that in the end a theory of international relations is not a merely academic matter, but "involves the ultimate experience of life and death, national existence and national extinction" (Wight, 1995, 33). It is a practical theory, the theory of survival. In the first recorded debate between idealism and realism, realism is the winner, if not by the strength of argument, then clearly by the force of the Athenian army. There are, nevertheless, reasons to believe that Thucydides does not accept the "radical realism" advocated by the Athenians at Melos. The Athenians do not act as his mouthpiece here. Equally, he does not identify with the "utopian idealism" represented by the Melians. Both positions reveal serious theoretical weaknesses.

The Melians greatly value courage and honor, and love their country. They have a sense of justice and respect political alliances. They are thus, in a sense, virtuous people. Some of their values resemble those of the Athenians from the earlier period. In his last speech, Pericles, who dies in the early stage of the Peloponnesian War, says that for the people who have a choice, going to war is always folly. Yet, when the choice is to either submit to enemies or face danger to preserve independence, it is better to fight (2.61.1). Contending that not to resist subjugation would be cowardly and shameful, the Melians make the same choice that Pericles suggests and that the Athenians once made themselves when, displaying great courage, they stood alone against the overwhelming might of Persia (1.73-74). The element that the Melians nevertheless lack, and that makes it impossible for them to be victorious, is what Pericles describes as a "strategy based on reality which affords predictable results" (2.62.5). Although they are courageous, the Melians lack resources and foresight. They are guided more by their hopes than by the evidence at hand or by prudent calculations. They make an appeal to justice, which is not listened to, and call for help from outside, which cannot be obtained. Ultimately, they are just and courageous, but politically naive. Because of their lack of good judgment, foresight, and intelligent planning, the kind of utopian idealism that they display leads to martyrdom: death for combatants, extreme suffering for civilians, and, in the end, destruction of their political community. Idealism on the part of those who do not have the ability to survive is, Thucydides suggests, of no use and is reported by him solely for the purpose of warning others against this sort of political wishful thinking. All of the noble aspirations of the Melians are ruined because they do not take into consideration the actual practice of states and do not make provisions for their own security.

The Athenians at Melos reveal themselves to be models of rational self-interested agents. They use all available means to realize their objectives. There is a seemingly powerful realist logic behind the Athenian arguments. Their position, based on security concerns and expediency, apparently involves reliance on rationality, intelligence, and foresight. However, upon close examination, their logic proves to be seriously flawed. Melos, a relatively weak state, does not pose any real security threat to them. Their slaughter of the Melians can be regarded as a regrettable act and a tragic error. The destruction of Melos does not change the course of the Peloponnesian War, which is lost by Athens a few years later. The Athenians argue that the international world, imperfect as it is, functions according to the law that the strong dominate the weak, and, therefore, moral values cannot be applied to it. They not only acknowledge the lack of justice in interstate relations, but also provide justification for acting unjustly and prescribe to states the way of domination. Consequently, their radical realism is not merely descriptive and defensive, but normative and offensive, and can be better termed as *realpolitik*. On the grounds of the purported selfishness of states and lack of universal moral standards in international politics, the Athenians glorify war and conquest, and act accordingly. They replace moral norms with *raison d'État*, the expediency of the state, as the highest norm. However, they do not recognize that self-interest and the rule of might alone cannot provide sufficient basis for a practical theory of international politics. In the *History*, Thucydides shows that, if it is unrestrained by moderation and a sense of justice, power brings about the uncontrolled desire for more power. There are no logical limits to the size of an empire. Drunk with the prospect of glory and gain after conquering Melos, the Athenians engage in the war against Sicily. They pay no attention to the Melian argument that considerations of justice are useful to all in the longer run (5.90). And, as the Athenians overestimate their strength and in the end lose the war, their self-interested logic is indeed very short sighted.

It is utopian to ignore the selfishness of states and to be blind to the reality of power in international relations, but it is equally blind to rely on power alone. Thucydides supports neither naive idealism nor cynical *realpolitik*. If he can in some sense be regarded as a political realist, his realism is neither *realpolitik*, in which international morality is denied, nor neorealism, in which moral questions are largely ignored. His realism is neither immoral nor amoral. In his realism, selfishness is recognized, but is not exalted and presented as a value. Indeed, he would claim that moderation and a sense of justice should keep states from becoming too opportunistic in defining and pursuing their interests. Thucydides' realism can thus be compared to that of Raymond Aron, Reinhold Niebuhr, and Hans Morgentau, twentieth-century classic realists, who, although sensible to the demands of power and national interest, would not deny that political actors on the international scene are subject to moral judgment. He is profoundly engaged in reflecting on ethical issues in domestic and international politics.

POLITICS AND ETHICS

While discussing the violent events that occurred at Corcyra during the civil war (3.82-85), Thucydides attributes the growing viciousness, not only at Corcyra but also in the whole Hellenic world, to factionalism and the deterioration of moral uprightness in the populace as a whole (3.83.1-2). Because it is ridiculed, modesty, the simple virtue found in noble natures, disappears. An excessive desire to control others for reasons of selfishness, greed, and personal ambition prevails (3.82.6). Society becomes divided into two opposing camps. Contending political parties promote their policies under fair-sounding slogans, like "equality for all" or "limited government," pretending thus to serve the public, but they are in fact merely struggling for power without any real consideration for justice and the common good (3.82.7). Both sides use any and all means necessary to win political battles, and they both commit the most horrible atrocities against one another. People go to every extreme. Oaths are not kept. There is disrespect for piety. Revenge is admired. There is even a revolution in language, with words taking on new meanings (3.82.4-5). Acts of thoughtless aggression are described as courageous. Moderation is considered a cloak for weakness. Plotting becomes a justifiable means of defense. Moreover, factionalism turns into the most overwhelming factor. The attributes of being a real man are now partisanship and violent fanaticism. Party membership becomes a stronger tie than that of family. Those who wish to stay neutral are destroyed (3.82.8). No argument is strong enough to convince the opposing sides to terminate their mutual hostility. In the opening pages of his *History*, in the section often referred to as "Archeology" (1.2-19), Thucydides shows that life in political society is preferable to living in the anarchic state of nature. An effective government can enforce order and provide security—both lacking in the state of existence before civilization, which is characterized by insecurity and individual violence. However, the events of the civil war in Corcyra show that civilization opens up a possibility for violence even more virulent than anything that may have preceded it because both political society and the international arena provide a setting for fierce partisan strife. The ideological motivations created by various factions make strife more uncompromising, fanatical, and cruel than the individual violence of uncivilized people.

The civil war in Corcyra is a paradigm of social disintegration. There are many similarities between the events that take place in Corcyra and the later revolution in Athens that leads to the overthrow of democracy and the establishment of oligarchy (8.65-71). In Athens, as in Corcyra, factionalism and violence gain the upper hand. The Four Hundred, the Athenian oligarchs, govern by terror. Their disregard for justice and emphasis on might is comparable to the earlier behavior of the Athenians at Melos. During their rule, which is based on unmitigated force and is, in effect, the extension of *realpolitik* to the domestic realm, people are terrified and become suspicious of one another. Social unity breaks down. Killings of political opponents occur. Pity and regard for justice disappear from everyday life. For Thucydides, the *polis* is not an abstract entity that has laws of its own. The state cannot be separated from the human beings composing the society. Even if a state can be regarded as a legal abstraction, it is not the state that makes decisions. Rather, decisions are always made by individuals. This is why most of Thucydides' ethical words and phrases are used interchangeably to describe both individuals and states. His ethical concerns, far from being an expression of abstract thinking, are related to the actual conditions in which states exist. A virtuous political society depends on the good qualities of its individual members, and above all on the quality of its leadership. A bad one is corrupted by vice. The disintegration of society that occurs in both Corcyra and Athens is described by words and phrases that have negative ethical connotations, such as *injustice, selfishness, greed, disregard for piety, faction, arrogance, envy, revenge, deceit, fear, cowardice,* and *cruelty* (Williams 24–25). The laudable characteristics of both individual character and a virtuous society, such as *respect for law, tolerance, openness, courage, moderation, justice, foresight, self-control, cautious deliberation, prudence,* and *fraternity,* mentioned in Pericles' "Funeral Oration," are absent.

In Thucydides' *History*, Pericles' Athens stands for the supreme achievements of civilization: material, political, and ethical. By contrast, the Athens of the revolution and the oligarchic rule that followed it is a model of political and moral decline. In his famous funeral oration, Pericles suggests that the Athenian democracy is a good constitution because it allows the admirable individual and public qualities that he mentions to flourish. He himself is known to have displayed such qualities of character as moderation, foresight, prudence, good judgment, independence of thought and action, and incorruptibility, and it is during his leadership that Athens reaches the peak of its greatness (2.65). Nevertheless, in Pericles' speeches there are also germs of vices that infect Athens and bring about her downfall. Since it produces immoderate individuals, Thucydides suggests, the excessive love of power in international politics removes all restraint from domestic politics as well (Forde 167). Pericles inspires the Athenians to harbor imperial ambitions and strive for glory, which ultimately leads them to excess (2.62-64). The ancient modesty or simplicity, which can be associated with a certain sense of limit, disappears not only from the Corcyran character, but also from the Athenian. The successors of Pericles do not follow his cautious and intelligent war policy; rather, they manage the state to fulfill their private ambitions and enhance their private gains (2.65.7). They are not, like Pericles, leaders and shapers of public opinion. Instead, they merely strive for popularity and so formulate policies to suit the whims of the people, regardless of whether those policies are actually good for the state (2.65.10). This ultimately results in the terrible defeat of the Athenians in Sicily and the oligarchic revolution that follows. The contrast that Thucydides outlines between Pericles and his successors, and between the Athens of Pericles and the Athens of revolution, suggests that the material and political achievements of a society are inseparable from its morals. Politics is not merely a matter of certain structural considerations, but is related to ethics. The state of different communities may range from one end, a supremely civilized community, based on virtue, to the other, a society degraded by vice and torn apart by civil strife.

Thucydides' *History* was meant by him to be a "lasting possession." It would be erroneous, however, to claim that what he wanted to convey to posterity was a narrow realist theory of international relations. His realism refuses to be confined to the narrow realm of security and power, for it takes into account the whole of political reality with its ideas, passions, and follies (Aron 599). He neither denies international morals nor, like today's neo-realists, ignores them in the name of pretended scientific objectivity. On the contrary, in the *History of the Peloponnesian War*, unlike in the writings of most of realists, we can find a deep reflection on the relation of ethics to politics. In much the same way as a physician who makes his diagnosis, Thucydides examines the causes of political disorder and studies the ways in which the ethical characteristics of a state, or the lack of thereof, affect its condition (Williams 41). Like other ancient Greek writers before and after him, such as Hesiod, Solon, and Aeschylus, as well as Plato and Aristotle, he considers the collective failure to recognize the need to adhere to moral principles to be a serious disease of the *polis*. In this respect, he is a part of the Hellenic moral tradition in which Western political philosophy is deeply rooted.

One of the main issues that Thucydides considers is the effect of power when it is not kept within the bounds of moderation and justice in both domestic and international politics. Although he never precisely defines *justice,* it is clear that for him this and other ethical concepts are neither culturally nor historically relative. The absence of justice as a universal moral value is always lamentable. A society that leaves no room for justice and moderation, that knows no law and no limit, Thucydides concludes, is doomed to fail. Humans are rational actors only in a superficial way. When they lack a sense of justice and moderation, they become fundamentally irrational, and their irrationality destroys their understanding of what is expedient for them. They learn moderation only by defeat. The Athenians finally lose the war because, moved by the love of power alone, they overestimate their strength, develop poor policies, and choose the wrong leaders. And, as numerous other examples from world history can show, no power is ever immune to such miscalculation.

In his final speech, Pericles says: "To be hated and to cause pain is, at present, the reality for anyone who takes on the rule of others, but anyone who makes himself hated for matters of great consequence has made the right decision; for hatred does not last long, but the momentary brilliance of great actions lives on as a glory that will be remembered forever after" (2.64.5). Athens was moved to war because of its desire for power, but was eventually exhausted and defeated, and its power diminished. If it is still remembered, it is not because of its hegemonic ambitions, but because due to the founding of Plato's Academy it eventually became the intellectual center of Greece. Sparta was victorious, but shortly after the war ended, its power was diminished as well because of a slave revolt and a conflict with its former ally, Thebes. If it is still remembered, it is because of its mixed and stable form of government and the civic virtues of its citizens. What is the goal of the state? Is it the pursuit of expansion and glory that Pericles proposes in the "Last Speech," the pursuit that makes citizens sacrifice their lives for the state's power? Can rule over others be an ultimate goal? Thucydides does not explicitly ask these questions, but they reverberate between the lines of his work.

QUESTIONS

- The state of nature, the human life that precedes the birth of the Athenian civilization, is described as *anarchic.* What do the words *anarchy, anarchic* mean?
- What is civilization? How do civilizations rise and how do they decline?
- Thucydides says that war is a "violent teacher." What does this mean? What happens to the morality of the Athenians because of the war and the plague? What happens to their civilization?
- What are *virtues*? Give some examples. Are virtues important in human life?
- Realists are pessimistic about human nature, and see human relations primarily in terms of conflict. Are there any good reasons for that pessimism?
- Realists place a great emphasis on security. Why? How important is security in international relations?
- Idealists are optimistic about human cooperation and prospects for peace. What are the reasons for that optimism?
- In the "Melian Dialogue," the Athenians say that "in fact the strong do what they have the power to do and the weak accept what they have to accept." What does this phrase mean? Do you agree with the view it implies?

- What argument are the Melians using in order to persuade the Athenians not to attack them? How convincing is it?
- How important is ethics in politics?

GUIDE TO FURTHER READING

Recommended Translations of Thucydides' Work:

Thucydides. *The Peloponnesian War*. Trans. Steven Lattimore. Indianopolis: Hackett, 1998.
Thucydides. *On Justice, Power, and Human Nature: The Essence of Thucydides' History of the Peloponnesian War*. Ed. and trans. Paul Woodruff. Indianapolis: Hackett, 1993.

Suggested Readings:

Boucher, David. *Theories of International Relations: From Thucydides to the Present*. Oxford: Oxford UP, 1998.
Cawkwell, George. *Thucydides and the Peloponnesian War*. London: Routledge, 1997.
Donnelly, Jack. *Realism and International Relations*. Cambridge: Cambridge UP, 2000.
Gustafson, Lowell S., ed. *Thucydides' Theory of International Relations: A Lasting Possession*. Baton Rouge: Louisiana State UP, 2000.
Rahe, Paul A. "Thucydides' Critique of *Realpolitik*." *Security Studies* 5 (Winter) 1995/1996: 105–141.
Russell, Greg. *Hans J. Morgenthau and the Ethics of American Statecraft*. Baton Rouge: Luisiana State UP, 1990.
Strassler, Robert B., ed. *Thucydides: A Comprehensive Guide to the Peloponnesian War*. New York: Touchstone, 1998.
Williams, Mary Frances. *Ethics in Thucydides: The Ancient Simplicity*. Lanham, MD: UP of America, 1998.

Plato: Who Should Rule?

Plato was born in Athens c. 427 B.C.E. Until he was in his mid-twenties, Athens was involved in a long and disastrous military conflict with Sparta, known as the Peloponnesian War. Coming from a distinguished family—on his father's side descending from Codrus, one of the early kings of Athens, and on his mother's side from Solon, the prominent reformer of the Athenian constitution—Plato cherished the hope of assuming a significant place in his political community, but he found himself continually thwarted. As he relates in his autobiographical *Seventh Letter*, he could not identify himself with any of the contending political parties or the succession of corrupt regimes, each of which was bringing Athens further into decline (324b-326a).

Plato was a pupil of Socrates, whom he considered the wisest and most honest man of his time, and who, although he did not leave any writings behind, exerted a great influence on philosophy. It was Socrates who, in Cicero's words, "was the first to call philosophy down from the heavens and . . . compelled her to ask questions about life and morality, and things good and evil." The pre-Socratic philosophers were mostly interested in cosmology and ontology; Socrates' concerns, in contrast, were almost exclusively moral and political issues. In 399, when a democratic court voted by a large majority of its 501 jurors for Socrates' execution on an unjust charge of impiety, Plato came to the conclusion that all existing governments were bad and almost beyond redemption. The immediate effect of Socrates' death on Plato was to make him look with a critical eye not merely on the political life of Athens, but also on the existing laws, customs, and constitutions of all cities. He considered that they were all corrupted. There was, however, one cure: philosophy, detached reflection on what is just and true. If humankind was to be saved, philosophy and political power must come together, he concluded. "The human race will have no respite from evils until those who are really philosophers acquire political power or until, through some divine dispensation, those who rule and have political authority in the cities become real philosophers" (326a-326b).

It was perhaps because of this opinion that, after a period of traveling, he retreated to his Academy, the school of higher learning that he founded in Athens in 385 B.C.E. He carried on much of his former teacher's work and developed his own philosophy. He visited the city of Syracuse in Sicily first in 389, then in 367–365, and again in 361–360, with the general purpose of moderating the Sicilian tyranny through philosophical education and establishing a model political rule. But this adventure with practical politics ended in failure, and Plato went back to Athens. His Academy, which provided a base for succeeding generations of Platonic philosophers until its final closure in C.E. 529, became the most famous teaching institution of the Hellenistic world and set an example for later European universities. Mathematics, rhetoric, astronomy, dialectics, and other subjects, all seen as necessary for the education of philosophers and statesmen, were studied there. Some of Plato's pupils later became leaders, mentors, and constitutional advisers in various Greek city-states. His most renowned pupil was, of course, Aristotle.

According to a tradition handed down by the ancient Platonists, Plato died in 347 on November 7, the same day of the month on which he had been born. During his lifetime, Athens turned away from its military and imperial ambitions and became the intellectual center of Greece. It played host to the four major Greek philosophical schools founded in the course of the fourth century B.C.E.: Plato's Academy, Aristotle's Lyceum, and the Epicurean and Stoic schools.

PLATONIC DIALOGUES

Plato was the first ancient Greek philosopher whose thought covered all of the fields—including epistemology, metaphysics, ethics, aesthetics, and political philosophy—that are today recognized as the basic subject areas of philosophy. His deep influence on Western philosophy is illustrated in Alfred North Whitehead's famous remark that "the safest characterization of the European philosophical tradition is that it consists of a series of footnotes to Plato." His writings, numbering more than thirty, are works of true artistry that express a wealth of ideas. They are not first-person monologues, like treatises in which the author speaks directly to the reader, but rather dialogues, and in most of these, Socrates plays the main part and Plato does not overtly appear. This raises the obvious question of how much the Platonic dialogues are expressions of Plato's own thought. Using the last and longest dialogue, the *Laws*, as the fixed point of reference, these dialogues are usually classified as "early," "middle," and "late."

While there is no perfect agreement among scholars concerning their chronology and selection, it is usually assumed that the early dialogues were composed after Socrates' death in 399 and before Plato's first Sicilian visit. They comprise the *Apology* and the *Crito*, which both pay tribute to Socrates, and others, such as the *Charmides*, the *Lysis*, and the *Laches*, in which Socrates examines the claims to virtue and knowledge of those who are reputed to possess them, and attempts to define various virtues. Because they present Socrates' method of teaching and put an emphasis on ethical issues, they are believed to be largely an expression of Socratic philosophy. The middle period dialogues include Plato's most well-known political work, the *Republic*; the *Symposium*, his work on love; the *Phaedo*, which gives an account of Socrates' last hours; and strictly philosophical works, the *Parmenides* and the *Theaetetus*. These writings are usually regarded as a result of the evolution of Plato's thought and his teaching within the framework of the Academy. In these dialogues, Plato uses Socrates largely as a mouthpiece for his own philosophy. Finally, the late dialogues, which were written after Plato's second visit to Sicily in 367, include the *Sophist*, the *Statesman*, the *Philebus*, the *Timaeus*, the *Critias*, and the last dialogue, the *Laws*. They are usually considered entirely Platonic. In these works, Socrates rarely appears as the main character and is replaced by another philosopher, usually enigmatically described as a stranger or an Athenian.

Plato's main works in political philosophy—the *Republic*, the *Statesman*, and the *Laws*—are all dialogues. Why did Plato choose dialogue as the main form for his philosophical writing? His writing of dialogues may be explained by pedagogical and political reasons. Plato's dialogues imitate the original Socratic conversations, based on questioning and answering, and present clarifications of concepts and critical evaluations of beliefs. The dialogues, which introduce a complex process of trial and error, conjecture and refutation, through which inquiry proceeds, are thereby effective in teaching critical reasoning and other basic skills to potential philosophers. One can also argue that by maintaining authorial anonymity in the dialogues, Plato could, through the mouths of his characters, express unorthodox views and escape the fate of Socrates. His dialogues thus provide a shield against possible political prosecution. Finally, and most importantly, there are philosophical reasons why Plato wrote dialogues, as opposed to treatises or essays.

The *Seventh Letter* contains an explicit critique of the written word as a medium for philosophy (341c-344c). A similar critique is also given in the *Phaedrus* (274e-276a). A written text, especially on an important and sophisticated topic, Plato claims, can always be misunderstood and misinterpreted and thus can excite unjustified contempt in some and blind admiration in others (341e-342a). The active experience of acquiring knowledge in conversation with oneself or with another person by presenting and then criticizing possible answers to important questions is replaced by a passive acceptance or rejection of what the author has written. This critique can be applied not only to the passive reading of texts, but also to the act of listening to lectures or speeches given in settings that do not allow the audience to enter into debate and present objections. For Plato, philosophy does not entail "dead" discourse that can put us to sleep, but dialogue—lively speech that can defend and justify itself, can explain its meaning, and "knows to whom it should speak and to whom say nothing" (276a). The dialogue, based on an interchange of conflicting claims, allows not only for authorial anonymity, but also for the possibility of readers themselves entering into the conversation by presenting their own objections to the thesis that is debated. In this sense the dialogue is not closed, presenting a limited scope of ideas, but is open for further examination. It is a living text that keeps us awake to philosophical questions, in contrast to the dead speech of treatises, which, as Plato notices in the *Phaedrus*, "speak as if they had intelligence, but if you ask them anything about what they say, wishing to be instructed, they always say just the same thing" (275d).

Like Socrates, who, by challenging the beliefs of his interlocutors tries to awaken them to philosophy, Plato does not make things easy for his readers. Often his words perform their function of guiding us to philosophical understanding only if we go beyond them. Otherwise, they present a collection of unsatisfactory assertions. Therefore, Platonic dialogues cannot be read merely as if they were essays or treatises, giving the author's meaning directly and presenting answers as final answers. Such readings are against the spirit of Plato and can lead to grave misinterpretations, such as that of Karl Popper, who in his book *The Open Society and Its Enemies* linked Plato's philosophy with totalitarian views. On the contrary, as an alternative reading of Platonic ideas can show, there is no thinker in the history of Western political thought to whom despotism is more foreign than Plato. Unlike modern totalitarianism ideologues, he does not attempt to control human beings totally, in their bodies and minds, but instead endeavors to liberate them from the subjugation of desires and lead them to the idea of the good. Further, because he is aware of the basic vulnerability of language, the possibility that ideas can easily be misunderstood, and the elusive ways of truth—which sometimes, as in the case of the vision of Love in the *Symposium* or the perception of the Good in the *Republic*, can be grasped only through a nonverbal experience— Plato, like Socrates, is always prepared to enter into dialogue and to examine his views again. His dialogues display a spirit of openness, which is a sign of a truly intellectual mind that remains aloof from all factionalism. Rather than presenting a dogmatic doctrine that "always says just the same thing," he stimulates his readers to think and guides the "few who are capable of discovering the truth by themselves or with a little guidance" (*Seventh Letter* 341e) to that understanding of reality that for him constitutes the foundation of philosophical knowledge.

THE TASK OF POLITICAL PHILOSOPHY

Although the *Republic*, the *Statesman*, the *Laws*, and a few shorter works are considered to be Plato's only strictly political dialogues, it can be argued that political philosophy was the area of his greatest concern. In the English-speaking world, under the influence of twentieth-century analytic philosophy, political philosophy's sole task is still often perceived as being conceptual analysis, the clarification of political concepts (Raphael 15). To understand what this means, it may be useful to think of concepts as uses of words. When we use general words, such as *table, chair,* or *pen,* and political terms, such as *state, power, democracy,* or *freedom,* by applying them to different things, we understand them in a certain way, and hence assign to them certain meanings. Conceptual analysis then is a mental organizational process, the clarification of concepts in their meaning. As such, it has a long tradition and was in fact first introduced in the Platonic dialogues. Although the results are mostly inconclusive, in the early dialogues, Socrates tries to define and clarify various concepts. However, in contrast to what it is for some analytic philosophers, for Plato conceptual analysis is not an end in itself, but only a preliminary step. The next step is critical evaluation of beliefs, deciding which of two incompatible ideas is correct and which is wrong.

For Plato, as for other classical political philosophers, choosing the right political order is, along with choosing between peace and war, the most important decision one can make in politics. Such decisions, he believes, cannot be left solely to the public, which in many cases does not have sufficient foresight and learns its lessons only *post factum* from the disasters recorded in history. In the twentieth century, beliefs of the common people, unsupported and unquestioned by political philosophy, and instead informed by ideologies such as fascism and communism, led to tragedies on a scale never seen before. In Plato's political philosophy, the clarification of concepts is a preliminary step in evaluating beliefs, and correct beliefs in turn lead to a right answer to the question of what the best political order is. The movement from conceptual analysis, through evaluation of beliefs, to determination of the best political order can be clearly seen in the structure of Plato's *Republic*.

WHAT IS JUSTICE?

One of the most fundamental ethical and political concepts, *justice,* is also one of the most complex and ambiguous. It may refer to individual virtue, or to the order of society, as well as to individual rights in contrast to the claims of the general social order. In Book I of the *Republic*, Socrates and his interlocutors discuss the meaning of justice. Four definitions that report how the word *justice* (*dikaiosune*) is actually used are offered.

The old man of means, Cephalus, suggests the first definition. Justice is "speaking the truth and repaying what one has borrowed" (*Republic* 331d). Yet, this traditional definition, which regards justice as a virtue, the excellence or perfection of an individual, and relates it to honesty and goodness (i.e., paying one's debts, speaking the truth, having good manners, showing proper respect for the gods and so on), is found to be inadequate. It cannot withstand the challenge of new times and the power of critical thinking. Socrates refutes it by presenting a counterexample. If we tacitly agree that justice is related to goodness, he suggests, to return a weapon that was borrowed from someone who, although once sane, has turned into a madman does not seem to be just at all, but in fact involves a risk of harm.

Cephalus' son Polemarchus, who continues the discussion after his father leaves to offer a sacrifice, gives his opinion that the poet Simonides was correct in saying that it was just "to render to each his due" (331e). He explains this statement by defining justice as "treating friends well and enemies badly"

(332d). Under the pressure of Socrates' objections that one may be mistaken in judging others and thus harm good people, Polemarchus modifies his definition to say that justice is "to treat well a friend who is good and to harm an enemy who is bad" (335a). However, when Socrates finally objects that it cannot be just to harm anyone, because justice cannot produce injustice, Polemarchus is completely confused. He agrees with Socrates that justice, which both sides tacitly agree relates to goodness, cannot produce any harm, which can only be caused by injustice. Like his father, he withdraws from the dialogue. The careful reader will note, however, that Socrates does not reject the definition of justice implied in the saying of Simonides, who is called a wise man, namely, that "justice is rendering to each what befits him" (332c), but only its explication given by Polemarchus. This definition is, nevertheless, found unclear.

The first part of Book I of the *Republic* ends in a negative way, with all parties agreeing that none of the definitions provided stands up to examination and that the original question "What is justice?" is more difficult to answer than it seemed to be at the outset. This negative outcome can be seen as a form of linguistic and philosophical therapy. Plato shows that popular opinions about justice involve inconsistencies; they are inconsistent with other opinions held to be true. The *reportive* definitions based on everyday usage of the word *justice* can help us perhaps to understand partially what justice means, but they fail to provide a complete account of what justice is. They have to be supplemented by a definition that will improve clarity and establish the meaning of justice. To propose an adequate definition, however, one has to know what justice really is. Plato rejects conventionalism, the view that all definitions are results of arbitrary linguistic impositions, agreements, or customs. A definition that is merely arbitrary, or too narrow or too broad, or based on a false belief about justice, does not allow for true communication.

Platonic dialogues are expressions of the ultimate form of communication that can take place between human beings; and true communication takes place only when individuals can share the meanings of the words they use. Communication based on false beliefs, such as statements of ideology, is still somewhat possible, but is inevitably limited and divides people into factions, ultimately leading them only to confusion. The definition of justice as "treating friends well and enemies badly" is for Plato not only inadequate because it is too narrow. It is also wrong because it is based on a mistaken belief of what justice is, namely, a belief grounded in factionalism, which Socrates associates not with the wise but with tyrants (336a). The way people define a given word is largely determined by the beliefs that they hold about the object referred to by this word. Therefore, in the *Republic*, as well as in other Platonic dialogues, there is a relationship between the conceptual analysis and critical evaluation of beliefs. The goals of these conversations are not merely linguistic, to arrive at an adequate verbal definition, but also substantial, to arrive at a right belief. The question "What is justice?" is not only about the linguistic usage of the word *justice,* but is in fact primarily about the thing to which the word refers. The focus of the second part of Book I is no longer clarification of concepts, but evaluation of beliefs.

PHILOSOPHY AND DOGMA

In Platonic dialogues, rather than telling his interlocutors what they have to think, Socrates is usually getting them to tell him what they think. In the discussion of the meaning of justice, the next stage is taken over by Thrasymachus, a sophist, who violently and impatiently bursts into the dialogue. In the fifth and fourth centuries B.C.E., the sophists were paid teachers of rhetoric and other practical skills, mostly non-Athenians, who offered courses of instruction, claiming to be the best qualified to prepare young men for success in public life. Plato describes the sophists as itinerant individuals, known for their rhetorical abilities, who reject religious beliefs and traditional morality, and he contrasts them with Socrates, who would refuse to accept payment and, instead of teaching skills, would commit himself to a disinterested inquiry into what is true and just.

In a contemptuous manner, Thrasymachus asks Socrates to stop talking nonsense and look into the facts. As a clever man of affairs, he answers the question of what justice is by relating justice to power and making it relative to the interests of the dominant social or political group. "Justice is nothing else than the interest of the stronger" (338c). However, although some commentators say otherwise, the statement that Thrasymachus offers as an answer to Socrates' question about justice is actually not a definition. The careful reader will notice that Thrasymachus identifies justice with maintenance and observance of law. His statement is an expression of his belief that in the real world, imperfect as it is, the ruling element in the state—or as we would say today, the dominant political or social group—institutes laws and governs for its own benefit (338d). The democrats make laws in support of democracy; the aristocrats make laws that support government by the well-born; the propertied make laws that protect their status and keep their businesses going, and so on. Thrasymachus' belief implies, first, that justice is not a universal moral value, but instead a notion relative to the expediency of the dominant group; second, that justice is in the exclusive interest of the dominant group; third, that justice is used as a means of oppression, and thus is harmful to the powerless; and fourth, that there is neither any common good nor harmony of interests between those who are in a position of power and those who are not. There is, instead, only domination by the powerful and privileged over the powerless. The moral language of justice is used merely instrumentally, to conceal the interests of the dominant group and to make those interests appear universal. The powerful "declare what they have made—what is to their own advantage—to be just" (338e). The arrogance with which Thrasymachus makes his statements suggests that he strongly believes that to hold a different view from his own would be to mislead oneself about the world as it really is.

After presenting his statement, Thrasymachus prepares to leave, as if he believes that what he said was so compelling that no further debate about justice was ever possible (344d). In the *Republic*, he exemplifies the power of a dogma. Indeed, he presents Socrates with a powerful challenge. Yet, regardless of whether Thrasymachus' argument sounds attractive to anyone else, Socrates is not convinced by the sophist's beliefs. Beliefs shape our lives as individuals, nations, ages, and civilizations. Should we in fact believe, as Thrasymachus claims, that "justice [obeying laws] is really the good of another, the advantage of the stronger and the ruler, harmful to the one who obeys, while injustice [disobeying laws] is to one's own advantage" (343c)? The discussion between Socrates and his interlocutors is no longer about the meaning of *justice,* but instead is about fundamental beliefs, and "concerns no ordinary topic but the way we ought to live" (352d).

Although in Book I Socrates finally succeeds in showing Thrasymachus that his position is self-contradictory and the latter withdraws from the dialogue, perhaps not fully convinced but still red-faced, in Book II Thrasymachus' argument is taken over by two young intellectuals. These are Plato's brothers, Glaucon and Adeimantus, who, for the sake of curiosity and playful intellectual exercise, push it to the limit (358c-366d). Thrasymachus withdraws, but his statement—moral skepticism and relativism, predominance of power in human relations, and non-existence of the harmony of interests—hovers over the Western mind. It finds its expression in the rhetoric of Carneades, the political theory of Hobbes, the revolutionary ideology of Marxism, and today's radical thought. Many generations of thinkers have struggled with Thrasymachus' and his followers' beliefs, and the debate still continues. After his exit, it takes the whole remainder of the *Republic* to present an argument in defense of justice as a universal value and the foundation of the best political order.

THE BEST POLITICAL ORDER

Although large parts of the *Republic* are devoted to the description of an ideal state ruled by philosophers and its subsequent decline, the chief theme of the dialogue is justice. It is fairly clear that Plato does not introduce his fantastical political innovation—which Socrates describes as a city in speech, a model in heaven—for the purpose of practical implementation (592a-b). The vision of the ideal state is used rather to illustrate the main dialogue's thesis that justice, understood traditionally as virtue, is the foundation of a good political order, and as such is in everyone's interest. Justice, Plato argues, if rightly understood, does not serve the exclusive advantage of any of the city's factions, but promotes the common good of the whole political community, and is thus to the advantage of everyone. It provides the city with a sense of unity, and so is a basic condition for its health. "Injustice causes civil war, hatred, and fighting, while justice brings friendship and a sense of common purpose" (351d).

In order to understand further what justice and political order are for Plato, it is useful to compare his political philosophy with the pre-philosophical insights of Solon, who is referred to in a few dialogues. Biographical information about Plato is fairly scarce. The fact that he was related through his mother to this famous Athenian legislator, statesman, and poet, regarded as one of the "Seven Sages," could be dismissed as merely incidental. On the other hand, taking into consideration that in Plato's time, education would have been passed on to children informally in the home and moreover was largely based on providing examples of honorable deeds from the past, it is highly probable that

Plato was not only well acquainted with the achievements and ideas of Solon, but that they deeply influenced him.

In the early part of the sixth century B.C.E., Athens was witnessing great tension between two factions, the poor and the rich, and stood at the brink of a bitter civil war. On one side, due to an economic crisis, many poorer Athenians were falling hopelessly into debt, and since their loans were often secured by their own persons, thousands were being put into serfdom. On the other side, lured by easy profits from such loans, the rich were standing in defense of private property and their ancient privileges. Partisan strife, which seemed inevitable, would make Athens even weaker economically, and defenseless in the face of external enemies.

The essence of the constitutional reform that Solon enacted as Athenian leader in 593, over one hundred and fifty years before Plato's birth, was the restoration of righteous order, *eunomia*. Appointed as a mediator between the two parties torn apart by conflict, he introduced a number of laws. He ordered the cancellation of all old debts, lowered the rate of interest, prohibited loans in which an individual served as his own security, and gave freedom to serfs. He acted so moderately and impartially that he became unpopular with both sides. The rich, deprived of what they regarded as their source of income, felt hurt by the reform. The poor, moved by excess, demanded a complete redistribution of landed property and its division into equal shares. Nevertheless, despite these criticisms from both parties, Solon succeeded in achieving social peace. According to Aristotle, by implementing new constitutional laws, he set up a "mighty shield against both parties and did not allow either to win an unjust victory" (*Athenian Constitution* 51). He introduced a system of checks and balances that would not favor any side, but instead took into consideration the legitimate interests of all social classes. In his position he could easily have become a tyrant, but he did not seek power for himself. After he completed his reforms, Solon left Athens in order to see whether they would stand the test of time, and returned to his native city only ten years later.

Even though as early as 561, Pisistratus seized power and became the first in a succession of Athenian tyrants, and in 461, the democratic leader Ephialtes abolished the checks upon popular sovereignty, Solon's reforms provided the ancient Greeks with a model of both political leadership and order based on impartiality and fairness. Justice did not constitute for him an arithmetical equality, giving equal shares to all alike irrespective of merit, as in the democratic concept of distributive justice, but it was equity or fairness based on difference, giving shares proportionate to the merit of those who receive them. The same ideas of political order, leadership, and justice can be found in Plato's dialogues.

For Plato, as for Solon, the starting point for the inquiry regarding the best political order is the fact of social diversity and conflicting interests that endanger society with a civil strife. The political community, he believes, consists of various social groups or classes, such as the noble, the rich, and the poor, each representing different values, interests, and claims to rule. This gives rise to the controversy of who should rule the community and what is the best political system. In both the *Republic* and the *Laws*, Plato asserts not only that factionalism and civil war are the greatest dangers to the city, more dangerous even than war against external enemies, but also that peace obtained by the victory of one class and the destruction of its rivals is not to be preferred to social peace obtained through the friendship and cooperation of all civic groups (*Republic* 462a-b, *Laws* 628a-b). Peace for Plato is not, as for Carr or Marx, a status quo notion, related to the interest of the privileged group, but instead is a value that most people usually desire. He does not favor war and the victory of one class, but rather peace in social diversity. "The best is neither war nor faction—they are things we should pray to be spared from—but peace and mutual good will" (*Laws* 628c). Building on the pre-philosophical insights of Solon and his concept of balancing conflicting interests, in both the *Republic* and the *Laws*, Plato offers two different solutions to the same problem of social peace based on the equilibrium and harmonious union of various groups. If in the *Republic* the main function of the political leadership of philosopher-rulers is to create the conditions in which civil strife will cease, in the *Laws* this mediating function is assumed by laws.

The best political order for Plato is one that promotes social peace in an environment of cooperation and friendship among different social groups and lasses, each adding to and benefiting from the common good. The best form of government, according to the ideas he advances in the *Republic*, is a philosophical aristocracy or monarchy. But in his last dialogue, the *Laws*, he advocates a traditional polity: a mixed or composite constitution that reconciles different factional interests and includes aristocratic, oligarchic, and democratic elements.

A CRITIQUE OF DEMOCRACY

It is generally believed today that democracy, "government of the people, by the people, for the people," as described in Abraham Lincoln's "Gettysburg Address" (1864), is the best and only fully justifiable political system. The distinct features of democracy are freedom and equality. Democracy can be described as the rule of free and politically equal people who govern themselves, either directly or though their representatives, in their own interest. Why does Plato not consider democracy the best form of government? In the *Republic*, he criticizes the direct and unchecked democracy of his time precisely because of its leading features (557a-564a).

First, although freedom is for Plato a true value, democracy involves the danger of excessive freedom, of each person doing as he or she pleases without regard for others, which leads to anarchy. Second, political equality, related to the belief that everyone has the right and equal capacity to rule, brings to politics all kinds of power-seeking individuals, motivated by personal gain rather than the public good. Democracy is thus highly corruptible. It opens the door to the demagogues, potential dictators, and can thus lead to tyranny. Hence, although it may not be applicable to modern liberal democracies, Plato's main charges against the democracy he knows from the political practice of ancient Greece are that it is unstable, leading from anarchy to tyranny, and that it lacks leaders with the proper skills and morals. Democracy depends on chance, but it can only function properly under competent leadership (501b). Without able and virtuous leaders, such as Solon or Pericles, who come and go by chance, it is not a good form of government. But even Pericles, who as Socrates says made people "wilder" rather than more virtuous, is considered not to be the best leader (*Gorgias*, 516c).

If ruling a state is a craft, indeed statecraft, Plato argues, then politics needs expert rulers, and they should not come to government merely by accident. They must be carefully selected and prepared through a course of extensive training. Making political decisions requires good judgment. Politics needs competence, at least in the form of today's well-educated civil servants. Who then should the Platonic experts be? Why does Plato, in the *Republic*, decide to hand the steering wheel of the state to philosophers?

In spite of the idealism with which he is usually associated, Plato is not politically naive. He does not idealize human beings, but in fact is deeply pessimistic about them. Most people, corrupted as they are, are for him fundamentally irrational, driven by their appetites and egoistic passions, and informed by false beliefs. If they choose to be just and obey laws, it is only because they lack the power to act criminally and are afraid of punishment (*Republic* 359a). However, human beings are not vicious by nature. They are social animals, incapable of living alone (369a-b). Living in communities and exchanging the products of their labor is natural for them, as are rationality and goodness. The human soul whose journey to the top of the heaven Plato describes in his dialogue *Phaedrus* is originally good and pure. It is desires amplified by demoralizing opinions and habits that obstruct its journey and lead to its downfall. Plato, as Rousseau does later, believes that once political society is properly ordered, it can contribute to the restoration of morals. A good political order, good education, and proper upbringing can produce "good natures; and [these] useful natures, who are in turn well educated, grow up even better than their predecessors" (424a). Hence, there are in Plato such elements of the idealistic or liberal worldview as a belief in education and progress, and a hope for a better future.

Nevertheless, unlike Rousseau, Plato does not identify the best social and political order with a democratic republic. In democracy, truth is overcome by the opinions of the majority. The lives of both individuals and communities are shaped by prevailing beliefs. If philosophers are those who can distinguish between true and false beliefs, who love knowledge and are motivated by the common good, and, finally, if they are not only master theoreticians, but also master practitioners who can heal the ills of their society, then they, and not democratically elected representatives, must be chosen as leaders and educators of the political community in order to guide it to proper ends. They are necessary to counteract the destabilizing effects of false beliefs on society.

THE GOVERNMENT OF PHILOSOPHER RULERS

To be sure, Plato's philosophers, among whom he includes both men and women, are not those who can often be found in departments of philosophy and who are described as the "prisoners who take refuge in a temple" (495a). Initially chosen from among the brightest, most stable, and most courageous children, they go through a sophisticated and prolonged educational process, which begins with gymnastics, music, and mathematics, and ends with dialectics, military service, and practical city management. They have superior theoretical knowledge, including knowledge of the just, noble, good, and advantageous, but are also no less capable than others when it comes to practical matters (484d, 539e). Being in the final stage of their education inspired with the idea of the good, they can see beyond changing empirical phenomena and reflect on such timeless values as justice, beauty, truth, and moderation (501b, 517b). Goodness is not merely a theoretical idea for them, but is instead the ultimate state of their mind.

Are philosophers incorruptible? In the ideal city there are provisions to minimize possible corruption, even among the good-loving philosophers. They can enjoy neither private property nor family life. Although they are the rulers, they receive only a modest remuneration from the state, dine in common dining halls, and have wives and children in common. These provisions are necessary, Plato believes, because if the philosopher-rulers were themselves to acquire private land, luxurious homes, and money, they would soon become hostile masters of their fellow citizens, rather than their leaders and allies (417a-b). The ideal city turns into a corrupt one, described as a *timocracy*, precisely when the rulers begin to gather wealth and become concerned with honor rather than with virtue (547b).

If the life of the philosopher-rulers does not include private property, family life, wealth, or even honor, and if the intellectual life itself seems so attractive, why then should they agree to rule? Plato's answer is in a sense a negative one. The philosophical life, based on contemplative leisure and the pleasure of learning, is indeed much happier than the burdensome role of ruling the state (519d). Nevertheless, the underlying idea of the *Republic* is not to make any one social group victorious over others and thus make it alone happy, but "to spread happiness throughout the city by bringing the citizens into harmony with each other . . . and by making them share with each other the benefits that each class can confer on the community" (519e). Plato assumes that a city in which the rulers do not govern out of desire for private gain, but instead are those least motivated by personal ambition, is governed in a way that is best and freest from civil strife (520d). Philosophers should rule not only because they are most morally and intellectually prepared for this, but also because if they do not, the city will no longer be well governed and may fall prey to economic decline, factionalism, and civil war. They should approach ruling not as really enjoyable, but as necessary (347c-d).

Some objections to government by philosopher-rulers have been made. First, because of the tight control of education and arts, and the restrictions concerning family and private property set forth in the *Republic*, Plato has been accused of totalitarianism. However, Plato's political vision differs from a totalitarian one in a number of important aspects. Especially in the *Laws*, he makes clear that freedom is one of the main values of society (701d). Other values that Plato espouses include justice, friendship, wisdom, courage, and moderation. He does not propose anything that in the least resembles the one-party rule or terror that can be associated with totalitarian states. His vision is far away from that of Hobbes' absolutism. The restrictions on individual liberty that he proposes apply mainly to the governors, rather than the governed.

Second, one can argue that there may obviously be a danger in the self-professed claim to rule of the philosophers. Individuals may imagine themselves to be the best qualified to govern, but in fact they may lose contact with political realities and not be good leaders at all. If philosopher-rulers do not have real knowledge of their city, they do not fulfill the essential condition that is required to make their rule legitimate— namely, that they alone know how best to govern. Indeed, at the end of Book VII of the *Republic* where philosophers' education is discussed, Socrates says: "I forgot that we were only playing, and so I spoke too vehemently" (536b), as if to imply that objections can be made to philosophical rule. As in a few other places in the dialogue, Plato throws his own political innovation open to doubt. Nevertheless, in Plato's view, philosopher-rulers do not derive their authority solely from their expert knowledge, but also from their love of the city as a whole and their impartiality and fairness. Their political authority is not only rational but also substantially moral, based on the consent of the governed. They regard justice as the most important and most essential thing (540e). Even if particular political solutions presented in the *Republic* may be open to question, what remains valid is the basic idea that underlies governance by philosophers and that can be traced back to Solon: the idea of fairness as the basis of the righteous political order. A political order based on fairness leads to friendship and cooperation among different social groups and classes.

For Plato, as for Solon, government exists for the benefit of all citizens and all social classes, and must mediate between potentially conflicting interests. Such a mediating force is exercised in the ideal city of the *Republic* by the philosopher-rulers. They are the guarantors of the political order that is encapsulated in the norm that regulates just relations of persons and classes within the city, and is expressed by the phrase: "doing one's own work and not meddling with what isn't one's own" (433a-b). If justice is related to equality, the notion of equality is indeed preserved in Plato's view of justice, expressed by this norm as the impartial, equal treatment of all citizens and social groups. In the Platonic ideal city, all persons and social groups are given equal opportunities to be happy, i.e., to pursue happiness, but not at the expense of others. Their particular individual, group, or class happiness is limited by the need of the happiness for all. The happiness of the whole city is not for Plato the happiness of an abstract unity called the *polis*, or the happiness of the greatest number, but rather the happiness of all citizens derived from a peaceful, harmonious, and cooperative union of different social classes.

According to the traditional definition of justice by Simonides, which is referred to in Book I and reinterpreted in Book IV as "doing one's own work," each social class receives its proper due in the distribution of benefits and burdens. The philosopher-rulers enjoy respect and contemplative leisure, but not wealth or honors; the guardian class, military honors, but not leisure or wealth;

and the producer class, family life, wealth, and freedom of enterprise, but not honors or rule. At the same time, the producers supply the city with goods; the guardians defend it; and the philosophers, attuned to virtue and illuminated by goodness, rule it impartially for the common benefit of all citizens. The three different social classes thus engage in a mutually beneficial enterprise, by which the interests of all are best served. Social and economic differences, that is, departures from equality, bring benefits to people in all social positions and are, therefore, justified. In the Platonic vision of the *Republic*, all social classes get to perform what they are best fit to do and are unified into a single community by mutual interests. In this sense, although each group is different, they are all friends.

POLITICS AND THE SOUL

It can be contended that the whole argument of the *Republic* is made in response to the denial of justice as a universal moral value expressed in Thrasymachus' statement: "Justice is nothing else than the interest of the stronger." Moral relativism, the denial of the harmony of interests, and other problems posed by this statement are a real challenge for Plato, for whom justice is not merely a notion relative to the existing laws instituted by the victorious faction in power. In the *Laws,* a similar statement about justice is made (714c), morality is denied, and the right to govern, as in the "Melian Dialogue" of Thucydides, is equated simply with might (715a).

For Plato the decisions we make about morals and justice are "no trifle, but the foremost thing" (714b). The answer to the question of what is right and what is wrong can entirely determine our way of life, both as individuals and as communities. If Plato's argument about justice presented in both the *Republic* and the *Laws* can be summarized in just one sentence, it would be: "Justice is neither the right of the strong nor the advantage of the stronger, but the right of the *best* and the advantage of the whole community." The best, as explained in the *Republic*, are the expert philosophical rulers. They, the wise and virtuous, free from faction and guided by the idea of the common good, should rule for the common benefit of the whole community, so that the city will not be internally divided by strife, but will be united as one in friendship (*Republic* 462a-b). Then, in the *Laws*, the reign of the best individuals is replaced by the reign of the finest laws instituted by a judicious legislator (715c-d). Throughout this dialogue, Plato's guiding principle is that the good society is a harmonious union of different social elements that represent two key values: wisdom and freedom (701d). The best laws ensure that all the city's segments—the democratic, the oligarchic, and the aristocratic—are represented in political institutions: the popular Assembly, the elected Council, and the Higher Council, and thus views of each social class receive their due expression.

Still, a "democratic skeptic" can feel dissatisfied with Plato's proposal to grant the right to rule to the "best," either individuals or laws, even on the basis of the tacit consent of the governed. The skeptic may believe that every adult is capable of exercising the power of self-direction, and should be given the opportunity to do so. He will be prepared to pay the costs of inevitable mistakes and to endure occasional civil unrest or even a limited civil war rather than be directed by someone who may claim superior wisdom. Why then should Plato's constitution based on rule by the best be considered preferable to democracy? In order to fully explain the Platonic position, the meaning of "the best" should be further clarified.

In the short dialogue *Alcibiades I* (little studied today, though held in great esteem by the Platonists of antiquity), Socrates speaks with Alcibiades. The subject of their conversation is politics. Frequently referred to by Thucydides in the *History of the Peloponnesian War*, Alcibiades, the future leader of Athens, highly intelligent and ambitious, and largely responsible for the Athenian invasion of Sicily, is at the time of the conversation barely twenty years old. The young Alcibiades of the dialogue, who is also, we learn, handsome and very tall, and from an eminent family, is about to begin his political career and to address the Assembly for the first time (105a-b). He plans to advise the Athenians on the subject of peace and war, or some other important affair (107d). His ambitions are indeed extraordinary. He not only wants to display his worth before the people of Athens and become their leader, but also desires to rule over Europe and Asia (105c). His dreams resemble that of the future Alexander the Great. His claim to rule is that he is the best. However, upon Socrates' scrutiny, it becomes apparent that young Alcibiades knows neither what is just, nor what is advantageous, nor what is good, nor what is noble, beyond what he has learned from the crowd (110d-e, 117a). His worldview is based on unexamined opinions. He appears to be the worst type of ignorant person, who pretends he knows something but in fact does not. Such ignorance in politics leads to mistakes and evils (118a). What is implied in the dialogue is that noble birth, good looks, and even intelligence and power, without proper knowledge, do not confer the entitlement to rule. Ignorance, the condition of Alcibiades, is also the condition of the great majority of people (118b-c).

Nevertheless, Socrates promises to guide Alcibiades, so that he may become an excellent leader, renowned among the Greeks (124b-c). In the course of further conversation, it is brought out that one who is truly the best not only has knowledge of political things, but also knows his or her own self and is a beautiful soul—perfect in virtue. The riches of the world can be entrusted only to those who "take trouble over" themselves (128d), who look "toward what is divine and bright" (134d), and who, following the supreme soul, God (the finest mirror of their own image), strive to be as beautiful and wealthy in their own souls as possible (131d). The best government can be founded only on beautiful and well-ordered souls.

In a few dialogues, such as *Phaedo*, the *Republic*, *Phaedrus*, *Timaeus*, and the *Laws*, Plato introduces his doctrine of the immortality of the soul. His ultimate answer to the question "Who am I?" is not an "egoistic animal" or an "independent variable," as today's behavioral researcher dispassionately might say (Sullivan 19), but an "immortal soul, corrupted by vice and purified by virtue, of whom the body is only an instrument" (*Alcibiades* 129a-130c). Plato believes that expert knowledge should include not only knowledge of things outside, but also knowledge of oneself. This is because those who are ignorant of themselves will also be ignorant of others, and will never become expert politicians (133e). They will go wrong, moving from one misery to another (134a). For them, history will be a tough teacher, but as long they do not recognize themselves and begin to practice virtue, they will learn nothing.

For Plato, a good society is impossible without an ongoing philosophical reflection on who we truly are. It is also impossible without transcendence, without a link to the perfect being who is God, the true measure of all things. He tries to show that God is the perfect being, the purest and brightest, always the same, immortal and true, to whom we should look in order to know ourselves and become pure and virtuous. Therefore, democracy would not be a good form of government unless, as Plato proposes in the *Laws*, the element of freedom is mixed with the element of wisdom, which includes ultimate knowledge of the self. Unmixed and unchecked democracy, marked by the general permissiveness that spurs vices, makes people impious, and lets them forget about their true selves, is for him only the second worst in the rank of imperfect regimes, after tyranny headed by a vicious individual.

Plato's great achievement arguably lies in the fact that, in opposing the sophists, he offered to decadent Athens, which had lost faith in her old religion, traditions, and customs, a means by which both civilization and the city's health could be restored: the recovery of order in both the *polis* and the soul. The political order that he advocates leads to the harmonious unity of a society and allows all the city's segments to pursue happiness, so long as it is not done at the expense of others. This order is described in the *Republic* in terms of four virtues: justice, wisdom, moderation, and courage. Justice is the equity or fairness that grants each social group its due and ensures that each "does one's own work" (*Republic* 433a). The three other virtues describe qualities of different social groups. Wisdom, which can be understood as the knowledge of the whole, including both knowledge of the self and political prudence, is the quality that should be possessed by the leadership (428e-429a). Courage is not merely military courage but also civic courage: the ability to preserve the right, law-inspired belief, and stand in defense of values such as friendship and freedom, on which a good society is founded. It is the main quality of the guardians (430b). Finally, moderation, a sense of the limits that bring peace and happiness to all, is the quality appropriate to all social classes. It encompasses the mutual consent of both the governed and the rulers as to who should rule (431d-432a).

The four virtues of the good society also describe the soul of a well-ordered individual. The rational part, whose quality is wisdom, is nurtured by fine words and learning. The spirited or volitional part is cultivated by music and rhythm. Together, they should rule over the appetitive part (442a). Under the leadership of the intellect, the soul must free itself from greed, lust, and other degrading vices, and direct itself toward the divine. The liberation of the soul from vice is for Plato the ultimate task of humans on earth. Nobody can be wicked and happy (580a-c). Only a spiritually liberated individual, whose soul is beautiful and well-ordered, can experience true happiness; only a country ordered according to the principles of virtue can claim to have the best system of government.

THE RELEVANCE OF PLATO

Most modern readers would regard Plato's critique of democracy as inapplicable to liberal democracy today. Liberal democracies are not only founded on considerations of freedom and equality, but also include other elements, such as the rule of law, multiparty systems, periodic elections, and a professional civil service. Organized on the principle of the separation of powers, today's Western democracy bears more resemblance to a revised version of mixed government, with its values of moderation and competence, than to the highly unstable and unchecked Athenian democracy of the fourth and fifth centuries B.C.E., in which all governmental policies were determined directly by the frequently changing moods of the populace. However, if Plato's political philosophy is still relevant for us, it is because he reminds us of the moral and spiritual dimension of political life. He argues that virtue is the lifeblood of any good society. He provides answers to the questions raised earlier by Thucydides.

Motivated by extreme ambitions, the Athenians, like the mythological Atlantians described in the dialogue *Critias*, became infected by "wicked coveting and the pride of power" (121b). Like the drunken Alcibiades from the *Symposium*, who would swap "bronze for gold" and thus prove that he in fact did not understand the Socratic teaching, they chose the "semblance of beauty," the shining appearance of power and material wealth, rather than the "thing itself," the being of perfection (*Symposium* 218e). "To the seeing eye they now began to seem foul, for they were losing the fairest bloom from their precious treasure, but to such who could not see the truly happy life, they would appear fair and blessed" (*Critias* 121b). They were losing their virtuous souls, the virtue by which they could prove themselves to be worthy of preservation as a great nation. Racked by the selfish passions of greed and envy, they forfeited their conception of the right order. Their benevolence, their desire to do good, ceased.

"Man and city are alike," Plato claims (*Republic* 577d). Humans without souls are hollow. Cities without virtue are rotten. To those who cannot see clearly, they may look glorious, but what appears bright is only the exterior. Plato argues that to see clearly what is visible (i.e., the political world), one has first to perceive what is invisible but intelligible: the soul. One has to know oneself. Humans are immortal souls and not just independent variables. They are often egoistic, but the divine element in them makes them more than mere animals. Friendship, freedom, justice, wisdom, courage, and moderation are the key values that define a good society based on virtue, which must be guarded against vice, war, and factionalism. To enjoy true happiness, humans must remain virtuous and remember God—the supreme soul and the perfect being. God, and not human beings, is the measure of political order (*Laws* 716c).

For Plato, the good of the city includes its moral health. He believes that there is a body of knowledge whose attainment can make it possible to heal political problems, such as factionalism and the corruption of morals, which together bring a city into decline. The doctrines of the harmony of interests, justice as the basis of the good political order, the mixed constitution, the distinction between correct and deviant forms of government, and the importance of virtue and transcendence for politics are all political ideas that can rightly be associated with Plato. They have profoundly influenced subsequent political philosophers.

QUESTIONS

- In the *Republic*, Socrates describes justice as "a thing more valuable than even a large quantity of gold." Why should be justice so valuable to us? Is justice beneficial to those who practice it?
- What are the meaning and implications of Thrasymachus' claim that "justice is nothing other than the advantage of the stronger"?
- Describe the qualities of a good political community that are presented in the *Republic*. Can we use those qualities to describe today's societies?
- Are you willing to abandon democracy in the face of Plato's arguments? Why or why not?
- What criticisms can we make of Plato's model of a just state? How do you think Plato might answer us back?
- Why should philosophers be rulers? Why should philosophers *not* be rulers?
- What is the goal of the state? Should politics focus on virtue and promote human goodness?

GUIDE TO FURTHER READING

Translations of Plato's Political Dialogues:

Plato. *The Laws.* Trans. Thomas L. Pangle. Indianapolis: Hackett, 1992.
Plato. *Republic.* Trans. G. M. A. Grube (revised by C.D.C. Reeve). Indianapolis: Hackett, 1992.
Plato. *Statesman.* Trans. J. B. Skemp and ed. Martin Ostwald. Bristol: Bristol Classical, 1987.
Pangle, Thomas L., ed. *The Roots of Political Philosophy: Ten Forgotten Socratic Dialogues.* Ithaca: Cornell UP, 1987.

The Complete Works in English:

The Collected Dialogues of Plato, Including the Letters. Ed. E. Hamilton and H. Cairns. Princeton: Princeton UP, 1989.

Suggested Readings:

Annas, Julia. *An Introduction to Plato's Republic.* Oxford: Clarendon, 1981.
Forde, Steven. "On the Alcibiades I." *The Roots of Political Philosophy: The Forgotten Socratic Dialogues.* Ed. Thomas L. Pangle. Ithaca: Cornell UP, 1987. 222–39.
Reeve, C. D. C. *Philosopher-Kings: The Argument of Plato's Republic.* Princeton: Princeton UP, 1988.
Zeitlin, Irving. *Plato's Vision: The Classical Origins of Social and Political Thought.* Englewood Cliffs, NJ: Prentice-Hall, 1993.

Aristotle: The Best Constitution

A ristotle was born in 384 B.C.E. in Stagira, an Ionian colony in eastern Macedonia (now part of northern Greece). His father, Nichomachus, was court physician to the King Amyntas of Macedon. Although his father died while Aristotle was still a boy, Nichomachus' profession would help Aristotle to establish a long association with the Macedonian Court. When he was seventeen, his uncle sent him to the Platonic Academy in Athens. He remained at the Academy for twenty years, initially as a student, and later as a researcher and teacher. His scholarly potential was soon recognized. In appreciation of Aristotle's intellectual powers, Plato would call him "The Brain." Yet, in spite of his great indebtedness to Plato and respect for him as a person, Aristotle decided to pursue his own philosophical path rather than following that of his mentor and friend. As he later said: "Friends and truth are both dear, but it is a sacred duty to prefer the truth."

After Plato's death in 348, Aristotle's research abilities should have made him a likely candidate to succeed his teacher as the head of the Academy, but philosophical differences between the two were apparently already too great to make this possible, and Plato's nephew Speusippus was chosen instead. Aristotle left Athens just as King Philip of Macedon was about to march on Greece and end the independence of the Greek city-states. At the invitation of Hermeias, the ruler of Atarneus and a patron of learning, he went to Assos in Asia Minor (now in Turkey). He stayed three years and, while there, married Pythias, Hermeias' niece. When subsequently Assos was invaded by the Persians, Aristotle fled to Mytilene on Lesbos, where he met Theophrastus, who was to become his closest associate and most devoted student.

In 343, Aristotle went to the Macedonian capital, Pella, upon the invitation of King Philip, to become the tutor of his thirteen-year-old son Alexander (later Alexander the Great). The tuition lasted until Alexander's appointment as regent in 340. After a brief stay in Stagira, Aristotle went back to Athens, where the Platonic Academy was flourishing under the leadership of

Xenocrates. In 335, apparently with some financial help from Alexander, who had by then, succeeded to the throne, Aristotle founded his own school in Athens, known as the Lyceum. The school took its name from "Lyceius," a cult title of the god Apollo, who was worshipped in a sacred grove nearby. When teaching at the Lyceum, Aristotle had a habit of strolling up and down. It was in connection with this and the *Peripatos* (colonnaded courtyard), which formed part of the school's buildings, that the students of his school became known as the *Peripatetics*, meaning "those who walk up and down."

In the same year that Aristotle established his school, Alexander conquered and destroyed the ancient city of Thebes. For the next thirteen years, Aristotle devoted all his energies to teaching and writing his philosophical treatises, while his former pupil, after bringing all the Greek city-states under his rule, went on to conquer the Persian Empire, carrying Hellenic culture all the way to the frontiers of India. Upon Alexander's sudden death in 323, the pro-Macedonian government in Athens was overthrown, and there was an increase in anti-Macedonian sentiment. A false charge of impiety was made against Aristotle. To escape prosecution, he fled to his relatives' house in Chalkis in Euboea. His motive, he said, alluding to the prosecution of Socrates, was that the Athenians might not "sin twice against philosophy." He died in Chalkis in 322 B.C.E.

ARISTOTLE'S WRITINGS

Aristotle was, next to Plato, the greatest mind produced by the Greeks. His intellectual achievement and influence were enormous. During the Middle Ages he was referred to as simply "the Philosopher." In his writings he covered all areas of knowledge of his times. His scientific work on biology, psychology, zoology, meteorology, and astronomy made a vital contribution to the development of these disciplines, while his philosophical treatises on logic, metaphysics, ethics, politics, and aesthetics continue to be the most profound studies ever written on these subjects. Although it is estimated that only about a quarter of Aristotle's texts have survived, in English translation the extant Aristotelian corpus still fills nearly twenty-five hundred closely printed pages.

The lost works of Aristotle were mainly popular philosophical studies. These writings, many of them dialogues composed under the influence of Plato, gave him a reputation as a writer with an elegant style. His extant works include treatises on logic, natural philosophy, metaphysics, and practical philosophy, written mainly between c. 335 and 323, when Aristotle was the head of the Lyceum and Alexander was engaged in his conquests. They lack the stylistic elegance of the earlier writings. Often terse and obscure, they occasionally contain passages that appear rough and unfinished. Their style suggests that rather than being finished works, they were originally drafts of lectures, which were then put together by Aristotle or his pupils to form treatises. Nevertheless, in their scope and originality, they represent a great achievement. Thus, while Alexander was away expanding his worldly empire, which quickly disintegrated after his death, Aristotle was in Athens mapping out, in his treatises, the territory of an intellectual empire that was destined to survive and to have an enduring influence on many generations. His main extant political works composed in that period are the *Nicomachean Ethics* and the *Politics*.

WHAT IS POLITICS?

During his lifetime Aristotle witnessed how Greek city-states, subjected to Macedonian power, were losing their old liberties and independence. He also experienced the effects of the ruthless way in which the Persian Empire ruled Asia Minor. Furthermore, he had the opportunity to observe the turbulent political life of Athenian democracy, characterized by the presence of demagogues and conflicting factions. It might be thought that on the basis of confrontation with these brute political realities, he would have arrived at the realist conclusion that power and conflict lie at the heart of politics. Further, if we accept the view of today's radical political theorists that "we do not see things as they are, but see as we are"—that is, that our view of the world is determined by our social and economic position in a society—then, by being so closely connected to the Macedonian Court, Aristotle should have had an interest in giving ideological support to the imperial policies of the kings of Macedon. Nevertheless, in spite of his experiences and position, he did not become a "theorist of the powerful." A close study of Books VII and VIII of the *Politics* shows that Aristotle was fully aware of the wicked ways of the world and in no sense naive, but he neither saw the world through a realist lens nor gave support to power politics. On the basis of some passages, a case can be made that he would not have objected to war against barbarian peoples with whom no relations based on trust and rules of justice could be established (*Pol.* 1333b37-34a1), but he neither identified the purpose of the state with militaristic aims nor supported expansionism. Although he was a tutor to Alexander, he did not see the hegemonic Macedonian monarchy as a model of government, but rather, admired the spirit of the independent *polis*. Notwithstanding the differences between the two thinkers, Aristotle, like his teacher Plato, was a political idealist who stood for universal moral values, and linked politics and ethics closely together.

It is often believed that power, the capacity to command or impose our will on others, is the essence of politics. This view of politics was clearly expressed in the *Politics Among Nations* of Hans Morgenthau, who emphasized that "all politics is a struggle for power" (25). Morgenthau regarded the struggle for power as a basic social fact. Under the influence of his book, first published in 1948, as well as the works of other realists, political realism, based on the central concept of power as the primary motivation or driving force of all political life, has become the dominant approach to the study of international relations and the intellectual creed of U.S. foreign policy. Realism, also known as power politics, became popular with many scholars and politicians because it encapsulated what they had previously taken for granted, namely, that politics was about power. However, if the struggle for power is seen not just as a fair competition, but, as in Morgenthau's writings, interpreted as seeking domination over others (31), then politics based on the concept of power can give rise to beliefs that Aristotle opposes in the *Politics*: namely, that the fundamental aim of the state is to rule its neighbors like a master, and only the state that masters others is a happy one (1324b2-4). From a descriptive position, originally intended to depict the political world as it is, realism moves to a normative position, *realpolitik*, a militaristic ideology of expansionism. Furthermore, if a decent human being cannot bear "to look the truth of politics straight in the face" (Morgenthau 13) because all politics is about power and domination—that is, inherently dirty and foreign to one who believes in the basic moral character of human beings—then such a view of political life can give ammunition to those uninvolved citizens who argue against participation in politics. They insist that domination is the greatest injustice and withdraw from being politically active, instead focusing on their private lives (*Pol.* 1324a25-38).

For Aristotle, happiness does not derive from exercising control over others, and politics, if rightly understood, is neither a dirty thing nor a means of domination. The opinion that politics is all about power is precisely the view he tries to counter. Not only is power a means rather than the aim of politics for Aristotle, but studying how to master one's neighbors and exploring power relations, the focus of today's radical political theorists, would appear quite absurd to him and could not be the subjects of his political science (1324b23-25).

Aristotle defends politics against both those for whom it merely concerns power and those who believe that all politics smacks of coercion and injustice (1324a35-24b4). Such beliefs, he contends, are founded on a shared, and mistaken, view of politics. While the former are attracted to government because they identify it with ruling over others, the latter reject it for the same reason. For Aristotle, politics is not domination, nor is it possible without citizen participation and freedom (1255b16-18). Politics, both domestic and international, is thus incompatible with despotism. Despotic rule, the autocratic and arbitrary rule of the despot or tyrant over his subjects that resembles the rule exercised by a master over his slaves, is different from *political rule*, in which citizens, all free, participate in the political process and "share in ruling and being ruled in turn" (1277b7-8). The phrase "ruling and being ruled in turn," describing political participation, may mean that the rulers and the ruled exchange their positions; however, it can also mean that while they are ruling in the interest of the ruled, the political leaders are limited by the latter's opinions and preferences. They are accountable to the ruled and do not exercise absolute control over them.

The Aristotelian concepts of politics and of political rule thus have no negative connotations whatsoever and can be associated with such features as elective government, justice, and moderation. Tyrants who rule absolutely and by fear, and do not give a share of ruling to their subjects, do not belong in politics. Aristotle argues further that if we accept that being dominated by others is unjust, whereas political rule is just, it is then inconsistent to seek a just rule for ourselves and at the same time pay no attention to justice in our dealings with others, especially where foreign relations are concerned (1324b35-36). In his view, politics cannot be identified solely with war or with security issues, and it does not consist in seeking authority over everyone, or in the despotic rule of one state by another.

In the realist picture of the world, military security is the dominant goal of states. Aristotle thinks otherwise. Non-military goals cannot be subordinated to the military one. To illustrate this point, he gives the examples of Sparta and other cities, which, preoccupied with power and security, develop a system of education that promotes only one virtue: courage. Instead of making them wholly virtuous, Spartans brutalize their youth through rigorous exercises, and stimulate warlike attitudes (1338b11-15). Although security issues are legitimate if they are subjected to the highest end of the state—a good life—they are not if they become ends in themselves (1325a5-7). Alluding to the conquests of Alexander the Great, Aristotle tries to show that the state's greatness does not depend upon its expansion (1326b7-25). Even a single city-state, isolated from others, can be happy if it is self-sufficient and well governed. Neither war nor domination are the essence of politics, nor are they needed for a state's well-being.

For Aristotle, politics (*politikê*) signifies both activities involved in the management of public affairs and a science of government. As science, politics is a practical and normative discipline whose aim is to shape the life of a political community and order it according to reason and justice. It deals with the questions of human well-being or happiness and of the best political order (1332a4-7). In his political works, Aristotle aims to discover in what mode of life happiness consists, and by what form of government and political institutions it can be secured. The former question requires the study of human character, which is treated in the *Nicomachean Ethics*; the latter, the study of constitutions, which is the main focus of the *Politics*.

THE STATE AS POLITICAL AND MORAL COMMUNITY

For Aristotle, as for Plato and other Greek political philosophers prior to the Stoics, the state is synonymous with the *polis* or city-state. In Book VII of the *Politics*, where he discusses the size of the best city-state, Aristotle considers a large state and concludes that it will not properly be a *polis*, but rather a nation, for it would not be easy for it to have a constitution (1326a1-4). He apparently believes that large states are difficult to oversee, and the way they are ruled may not be political since they would not promote "ruling in turn," that is, political participation.

By citizens' participation in the political process, Aristotle means not only the selection of public officials, but also direct citizen involvement in political institutions such as the judiciary and the popular assembly. To take an effective part in these activities, he argues, citizens must become familiar with one another. They must know what sort of individuals the other citizens are (1326a14-16). He fears that in a large state, the body of citizenry will remain largely anonymous and apathetic. Yet, in today's political context, because of technological and communication advances, overseeing a large territory is not an issue. Further, the modern conception of political participation, related to the model of representative government, is no longer based on direct and unmediated citizens' participation in political institutions. It encompasses all forms of activities by individuals that aim to influence the political process: election campaigns and elections, party organizations, protest movements, interest groups, community associations, and the like. Therefore, there is no need to limit Aristotle's theory of state to the city-state. Whether a state is organized at the level of a city or a nation, and whether it is based on direct or representative decision making by its citizens, it is still a state, which can be characterized by general characteristics such as wealth or poverty, income distribution, military capacity, form of government, domestic and foreign policy, and so on. In spite of the obvious differences between them, the overlap between the city-state and the nation state is so great that it is possible to move between them as long as these differences are borne in mind. Aristotle's conception of the state as a political and moral community is not an antiquated idea that is related solely to the Greek *polis*; rather, it has universal significance.

The concept of the state is ambiguous. It refers both to a territorially demarcated area inhabited by some people (*Pol.* 1276a33-35) and to a set of political institutions within this area. In today's usage, the word *state* is usually narrowly identified with government. This usage can be traced to the modern distinction between civil society and the state, which did not exist in ancient political thought. Although the concept of the state indeed implies government, to identify the state with government is misleading. The state is neither government nor society by themselves. It is rather a *political association* or *political community*, in the notion of which the unity of two concepts, community and authority, is expressed. Aristotle defines the state as a community that possesses a political organization, "a community of citizens sharing a constitution" (1276b1).

In contrast to the modern notion of the state as a political association that is organized for a specific task, such as providing security and protecting property, Aristotle's notion of political community (*koinonia politike*) suggests a core of shared tasks and values. For him, as for Plato, the state is a community that is self-sufficient with regard to material needs (*Republic* 369b-c, *Pol.* 1252b26-28). Unlike smaller social entities, such as a household or a village, which are not genuinely self-sufficient, the state is capable of producing and obtaining necessities of life (e.g., food, shelter, and clothing). In a famous statement, Aristotle asserts that the state "comes to be for the sake of living, but it remains in existence for the sake of living well" (1252b28-29). What is implied in this statement is that there are two fundamental aims of the state: survival and a good life. While the state, as a form of community, comes naturally into being because of our need to survive—in other words, for the sake of mere life itself—it exists having in view a good life, a complete life, the highest normative goal toward which it moves. It can contribute to the development of our rational character and morals. This implies that once the conditions of physical survival are met and basic prosperity is achieved, a political community becomes potentially an area of good living, an environment in which the mind can be enlarged and virtue can develop. The state is then for Aristotle a community that is not only political, but also moral.

Aristotle's conception of the state is related to his view of human beings. He regards the human being as by nature a social or political animal (*zôon politikon*) for, like Plato, he believes that humans are not self-sufficient as individuals and cannot ordinarily live alone (1253a3-4). Living in a community is required for a full human life. Only then can we satisfy our basic needs and exercise our capacities for reason and speech. Through language we can not only express pain and pleasure, as other animals do, but also enjoy conversation with fellow human beings and discuss what is just and what is unjust. Anyone who refuses to live in a political community, Aristotle claims, either lowers himself to the level of a brute beast or seeks to be, like a god or a superhuman, above law and justice (1253a29-30).

Reason and speech are then the capacities that distinguish human beings from other animals, and the exercise of them is essential for a truly human life. However, by the activity of reason (*logos*), Aristotle does not understand a mere instrumental or purposive rationality—the optimal use of available means of realizing objectives, maximizing benefits, and minimizing costs—but rather a rational deliberation about what is beneficial and harmful, just and unjust (1253a14-15). The complete exercise of reason cannot be reduced to its usage in obtaining something (e.g., objects of our appetites), but involves moral choice.

Consequently, human beings are for Aristotle both rational and moral agents, capable of deliberating about choices and distinguishing between right and wrong. In comparison with other animals, they are unique in having a moral sense: "a perception of what is good and bad, just and unjust" (*Pol.* 1253a15-17). Only in the human world does there appear a distinction between what is and what ought to be, in short, a sphere of norms and morals. Endowed with powers of speech and reason, humans are thus not only capable of the greatest good, but also of the greatest evil. The human being is the best animal when perfected by virtue, but when separated from law and justice, and engaged in vice, he may be the worst (1253a32-33). Left to mere chance, without moral guidance, individuals may choose wrong ends, unworthy of human beings. Led into the wrong direction, states can brutalize their citizens rather than make them virtuous (1338b29-33). Therefore, a task of the Aristotelian science of government is to endow a political community with a core of virtues or ethical values in order to guide it to noble ends. His political philosophy, which he calls the "philosophy of human affairs," is necessarily a moral philosophy as well.

WHAT IS HAPPINESS?

The ethical theory that is developed in both the *Nicomachean Ethics* and *Politics*—works that were originally intended to be read together—is called *eudaemonism*, from the Greek word *eudaimonia*, which means "happiness." Nearly all human beings agree, Aristotle argues, that happiness or well-being is the highest good that can be achieved by human activity (*NE* 1095a17). Not only individuals but also communities exist for the sake of the best possible life (*Pol.* 1328a35). However, there is a great controversy about what the best life for human beings consists of. Some say that happiness is pleasure, others identify it with wealth, still others think that it is honor. What then is happiness, the highest human good?

Living well or human flourishing, Aristotle thinks, can only be found in a life that is distinctively human, so it cannot be reduced to the life of pleasure that is shared by all animals. Pleasure is a component of happiness, but does not constitute its essence. Likewise, wealth or prosperity is certainly a precondition of human well-being, but making money cannot be the chief end for human beings, because it is only a means to obtaining other goods. Finally, honor is indeed an object of longing and a good for which many human beings strive, but it cannot be the highest good achievable through action because it is something bestowed on us by others, whereas happiness is something that should be achieved by our own efforts. Aristotle thus concludes his initial investigation into the chief end of, or highest good for, human beings by emphasizing the incompleteness of all three common views of happiness. He argues that happiness must lie in the flourishing of the most distinctive human capacities. Since activities that are distinctively human are those that are in accordance with reason (*NE* 1098a7-8), it follows that happiness consists in those activities involving the exercise of reason that are excellent, continued over the course of a lifetime. Furthermore, since activities that are excellent are virtuous, happiness is the activation or exercise of complete virtue (*NE*, 1101a15-17, *Pol.* 1328a37-38).

Aristotle's view that happiness cannot exist apart from virtue is built on traditional moral teachings. Hellenic education consisted primarily of studying Homer for moral lessons, and emphasized prudence, moderation, courage, self-control, piety, honesty, intelligence, and justice. All of these admirable qualities were together considered to make up the character of the virtuous individual. Like the traditional Greek moral teaching, the *Nicomachean Ethics* is directed to the task of the formation of character. In this work Aristotle systematically develops the ethical ideas of his time and provides an account of all the important virtues. He divides them into moral and intellectual, and describes the former as mental states or dispositions that establish in the individual a praiseworthy attitude toward emotions—for example, being courageous while facing danger or showing proper moderation when dealing with pleasure. In addition, he introduces new virtues, such as magnificence, gentleness, and wittiness, and designates magnanimity and justice as complete virtues, since they constitute for him the summits or crown of moral life and include all other virtues.

Aristotle's impressive account of moral and intellectual virtues allows him to reflect on the value of a good life based on virtue, and its superiority to other alternatives. However, he is also aware of the criticism of those who claim that happiness and complete virtues do not always fit perfectly together. As he observes himself, the virtue of magnanimity depends largely on fortune (the possession of a certain level of wealth and social position) and the virtue of justice is not one's own good but "the good of another" (*NE* 1130a3-4). Because of these objections, Aristotle introduces friendship as the third and most satisfying summit of moral life (Lorraine Pangle 172). Justice is concerned with the general order of the political community. Friendship provides a necessary supplement to justice, and holds the *polis* together. Whereas true friends do not have a need for justice, Aristotle argues, just individuals still need friendship to enjoy a fine life (*NE* 1155a28-29). He considers friendship to be essential for happiness because it contributes what is already good in life. In the activity of the intellect and the thoughtful conversation of individuals who are lovers of wisdom, friendship brings the natural human capacities for speech and reason to a complete realization.

FRIENDSHIP AND CONCORD

Friendship is classified according to whether it is based on utility, pleasure, or the good (1156a6-22). In the most complete type, friendship based on the good, friends are loved not just because they are merely temporarily useful or momentarily pleasant to be with, but because of who they are—the qualities they represent in themselves. This type of friendship is a relationship between individuals who are morally good and support one another, each for the sake of the other. It incorporates elements of the other types of friendship as well, because good individuals can also be useful and pleasing to one another.

On the political level, complete friendship is identified with concord among citizens concerning what is advantageous and just, and the way their country is governed (1167b3-5). Concord is a characteristic of decent persons who look out for the common good and act for the sake of what is equitable. Wicked individuals cannot be in concord, and are capable of friendship to only a slight degree. They oppress others by compelling them to do things that they avoid themselves (1167b10-15). They may enjoy relationships based on pleasure or utility, but they will tend to take advantage of others rather than pursue good for them. Their relationships will be neither perfect nor long lasting.

Friendship based on pleasure or utility, on nothing more than having fun together or exchanging favors, is characterized by frequent dissension (1156a20-21). On the political level, this results in *stasis* or civil conflict, in which the common interest of the political community is destroyed by a narrow and mistrustful preoccupation with self-interest on the part of the city's factions. Regardless of whether a state or an individual is concerned, Aristotle believes happiness or well-being can thus not be reduced to the level of amusement, exchange of goods, or mutual security. It must be based on complete friendship, an indispensable aid to the most perfect exercise of virtues. Therefore, promoting ethical education and the cultivation of friendship among citizens is for him a central task of the legislator (1155a24-28). Concord turns an aggregate of individuals, each seeking merely his or her own advantage, or the advantage of his or her faction, into a moral political community in which a good life can be enjoyed. A political community is grounded upon solidarity and friendship, and not upon the mere exchange of commodities or reciprocal protection (Viroli 146). Where there is no friendship, but only envy and contempt, no community can properly exist.

FORMATIVE LAWS AND THE MORAL ELITE

Human beings and their activities, Aristotle believes, differ in their decency or wickedness. The wicked individual does everything for his or her own sake; the more vicious he or she is, the more self-centered his or her actions are. The decent person, on the contrary, acts for the sake of what is fair and noble, and the better he or she is, the more true this will be (*NE* 1168a31-34). Since virtues and vices are not something we are born with, but are acquired by habit, the way we behave in our dealings with others makes us either good or vicious. This is why, Aristotle would say, even in a modern liberal state, where no moral standards were officially provided and the pursuit of moral improvement was considered to be an individual propensity, people would still develop some common morals. Their moral qualities would derive from obeying established laws and following existing customs, in which moral standards are always implicit. However, he would also add that it was wrong to rely solely on sheer luck, rather than on a deliberate choice, in such important matters as the excellence and morals of the political community (*Pol.* 1332a31-33). Whereas today we tend to regard laws as a neutral authority, Aristotle attempts to show that they are not morally value-free. Laws have formative power to shape citizens' characters. It follows that they should always aim at making citizens virtuous. All prudent legislators would choose to make citizens good by training them in good habits through properly framed laws (*NE* 1103b3-6). Furthermore, inculcation of correct habits distinguishes a good state from a bad one. "A *polis* is excellent because the citizens who participate in the constitution are excellent" (*Pol.* 1332a33-34). Citizens become excellent when they become habituated to right activities—those that develop their human capacities—and engage in practices of virtue.

Aristotle thinks that arguments alone are insufficient to make humans good. Moral discourse is incapable of establishing virtuous practice among so many individuals who are not habituated to good acts. Instead of cultivating virtue, most people who are deemed to be happy take refuge in pleasant amusements and identify happiness with pleasure (*NE* 1176b12-18). They can be deterred from wrong acts only by the fear of punishment. They have no real interest in and cannot be persuaded to cultivate nobility and goodness (1179b9-10). In this they not infrequently follow the example of those in positions of power. By identifying happiness with the life of virtue and the goal of virtue with the noble and fair, Aristotle addresses an audience of individuals who are beneficiaries of a decent upbringing, can accept certain moral standards, and have the capacity for virtue. In any actual state, virtuous persons tend to be a minority. To be moral, a political community must thus include a moral and intellectual elite. Morally good persons can furnish society with standards of propriety (1176a17-19). They will be able to recognize and sustain such basic moral distinctions as those between justice and injustice, gentleness and cruelty, respect and disgrace. Only such a group can oppose the potentially incorrect answer of the majority to the question of what happiness is, and, if needed, challenge the authority of the powerful. These individuals include among themselves potential virtuous political leaders, capable of bringing about a positive change in politics.

HUMAN NATURE AND THE NATURE OF THE STATE

The expression *human nature* is often understood as referring to permanent and universal characteristics of human beings: characteristics that are true at all times and are common to all societies. In this sense, modern political realists, following Machiavelli and Hobbes, refer to human beings as selfish and power-seeking. Further, by regarding states as "rational egoists," preoccupied chiefly with power and security, they attribute the individual egoism that they find in human nature to the level of state as well. Realists emphasize the constraints imposed on politics by the anarchic system of states that are subjected to no government above them, and by human nature, which, they believe, "has not changed since the days of classical antiquity" (Thompson 17). By contrast, when Aristotle uses the word *nature* (*phusis*) in reference either to human beings or to states, he means a potentiality rather than an actuality. His view of nature is *teleological*—that is, the nature of a living entity is for him what that entity becomes when it fulfills its natural purposes and its growth is completed. This is the end (*telos*) to which it moves as it develops properly (*Pol.* 1252b30-33). For example, the end of the oak tree is to be a well-grown tree, exercising fully its vegetable functions. Analogously, the end of the human being is to be a completely developed individual, exercising fully his or her capacities for reason and speech in virtuous acts.

Aristotle assumes that the world is intelligible, and that we have the possibility of knowing the nature of things. We can thus discuss rival theories of human nature and answer the question of whether the chief end of human existence consists in pursuing a life of egoistic pleasures, of wealth, or of complete virtue. The assertion that all humans are by nature selfish would appear questionable to him because of a lack of sufficient empirical evidence, and he also would regard such a claim as a statement pointing to a deviant end of human life, rather than a true description of human affairs. When he asserts that human beings are by nature political and that our nature is expressed in rational activity, he does not mean by this that the property of being political (or social) and rational applies to all actual human beings at all times, but rather that reason and speech are the natural capacities that are properly human and their complete exercise can take place solely in the environment of the *polis*. Humans derive the characteristics of being rational and political from their *telos*, the natural end for which they are striving: to be rational and to live in the most fulfilling social environment. Moreover, although Aristotle acknowledges that humans can fully develop their potential only in a community, he does not endorse the view of Marxists and today's critical theorists that human beings are completely dependent on their social or cultural conditioning. People become excellent by "nature, habit, and reason" (1332a39-32b7). They become what they are first through their inborn human capacities and natural qualities, second through the habits or ways of life they follow in society, and third through the guidance of their own reason, which sometimes, if they are persuaded that some other course of life is better, makes them act contrary to their own habitual ways. Therefore, since by using the faculty of reason it is possible for us to choose right things, we cannot blame our social environment for what we do and what we are. Society may have a considerable influence on us, but we are not reducible simply to products of society. Our choices are results of a process of deliberation. The ability to enter into a rational deliberation about what is advantageous or harmful, just or unjust, and to live the best possible life in accordance with virtue is for Aristotle what properly constitutes being human.

Even if the state, as is often the case, can be artificially founded, sometimes with the use of violence, the state as the form of community that is indispensable for a complete human life is for Aristotle not an artifact but a natural thing. When he says that "the state exists by nature" (1252b29-30), he does not mean that the state has a natural cause, but that it has a natural end, and that by striving toward this end it promotes the nature of human beings. The state allows the full realization of human potential. It fulfills the natural human impulse for society and the capacity for virtuous living. To be sure, like human beings who sometimes cannot live up to their nature, actual states are often imperfect and fall short of the end of realizing the good life. They are then mere associations united by the common interest of their members rather than by complete friendship and a deliberate choice to live together. They exist because they offer the benefits of sharing a common location, providing security, preventing mutual wrongdoing, securing property, and exchanging goods. While all these goals and functions of the state are necessary, Aristotle observes, they do not describe its essential nature and its chief end. Even when all of them are present, there is not a fully developed *polis* yet (1280b30-34). The chief end of political community is a good life. "Political communities must be taken to exist for virtuous actions, and not for the sake of [mere] living together" (1281a1-2).

The good life, the end of political community, is not the prosperity of some selected social group or class, or of the government elite. It is in fact something much greater: the well-being of all individuals who constitute it. The best and happiest life is a virtuous life, and the best state is the one whose citizens are excellent and cultivate virtue (1332a33-34). The cultivation of virtue requires the existence of a state, whose laws promote virtues and virtuous ends. A state that is less ideal is insufficient to inculcate virtue in the full sense, but is still better than states whose laws and customs have a demoralizing effect on their citizens. Since the state has in its political institutions an inner source of its own change, it can develop into the best state and eventually reach its end, but it can also undergo change for the worse and decline. Still, living in a state appears to Aristotle as, ultimately, better than living without a state at all. Outside political community, there are only beasts and gods (1253a29-30). Humans are by nature political animals.

CONSTITUTIONS

While the essential nature of the state is fully expressed in the political life of the best or ideal state—one that is perfectly constituted—real states differ with respect to their actual political practices and their less than perfect constitutions.

Aristotle puts great stress on successful political practice, aiming at the betterment of action. Discussing "what is best" on the one hand, and "what is easier and more attainable by all" on the other, is for him wholly consistent with his idea of a practical science of government (*Pol.* 1288b37-38). This is why he inquires into a number of different constitutions. He does not just consider the absolutely best one, but also examines which constitution is the best possible in given circumstances and which is appropriate for most political communities. He also inquires into the causes of revolutions that bring about changes of constitution, and tries to determine how constitutions can be improved, stabilized, and preserved.

The way in which Aristotle understands the word *constitution* (*politeia*) is broader than the idea of a legal document in which the structure and principles of a government are described. *Constitution* is synonymous with *political regime*. It designates not only the institutional arrangements of a society and its form of government, but also a political culture that corresponds to a form of government: a shared set of political beliefs and values. A political community consists of a plurality of groups and social classes, of which the most paradigmatic are the noble, the wealthy, and the poor. Since all of these groups make different claims to rule, there are a number of constitutions or political regimes. Aristotle arrives at six basic types of constitution by combining the number of those who constitute the ruling class—the one, the few, and the many—with two possible ends of their rule: the common good or the advantage of the ruling class. Each constitution can be characterized by a particular distribution of power (the way in which political offices are organized and distributed), the makeup of its ruling class, and its end or chief value (1289a14-18).

When one individual rules like a master in his or her own interest and disregards the interests of the rest of the society, such a regime is called *tyranny*. Its aim is the pleasure and private advantage of the tyrant. Since it lacks both justice and friendship, it is the least desirable of all constitutions (1289b1-2). When the few who are rich rule in their own interest, aiming at increasing their fortunes, the regime is called *oligarchy*. Its end or chief value is wealth (1294b10-11). When many poor citizens rule in their own interest, gaining authority over the rich and eventually dividing the latter's property among themselves or in other ways disregarding the interests of the wealthy class, the regime is a perverted *democracy*, which I will call "populist democracy," in order to distinguish it from today's liberal democracy in which there exists respect for private property. The chief values of populist democracy are equality and freedom, which is interpreted in its most extreme form of each one living as he or she pleases (1310a28-31). All these regimes are based on exploitative rule, that of the tyrant over the rest of society, the rich over the poor, or the poor over the rich. Further, since these regimes (with the exception of tyranny, which presupposes an arbitrary rule) are the product of some decision concerning a standard of political justice, they can be considered as superficially just, in the sense of being lawful, but there is no real justice in them. All three are in fact deviations from the three correct constitutions whose chief value is virtue: kingship, aristocracy, and polity.

Correct Constitutions	Deviant Constitutions
Kingship	Tyranny
Aristocracy	Oligarchy
Polity	(Populist) Democracy

The constitutional types can be further analyzed by reference to the concepts of friendship and justice. Each form of community, Aristotle suggests in the *Nicomachean Ethics*, has some sort of friendship and justice appropriate to it (1160a26-28). Complete justice and friendship are found only in correct constitutions, which are just because they aim at the common good and are based on rule that is not exploitative (*Pol.* 1282b16-17). Aristotle would strongly disagree with the view of Thrasymachus and also of Marx, that all rule is class rule, conducted only in the interest of the ruling class. Kingship is for him the rule of a person of outstanding virtue, who is materially self-sufficient and superior in virtue, and who rules for the benefit of the ruled (*NE* 1160b5-8, *Pol.* 1289a40-41). The sort of friendship implicit in kingship is that which exists between individuals who are on an unequal but amicable footing, such as that between a father and his children in a loving family.

Aristocracy is the rule of the few who are the best or who rule with a vision of the best (*Pol.* 1279a34-36). The type of friendship pertaining to aristocracy is that which exists between persons of similar status, one of whom is placed in a leadership position. It resembles the friendship of a husband and a wife in a traditional family, in which the husband is a leader, but not a tyrant (*NE* 1160b33-35).

The most complex of the correct regimes is called *polity* (*politeia*), which is also the generic name for the constitution itself, and which in the *Nicomachean Ethics* is referred to as *timocracy*. On the one hand, this is not as perfect as the other two correct constitutions because it does not aim at complete virtue. The many who rule in *politeia*, with a view of common good, are in Aristotle's view incapable of full virtue, which is the characteristic of the virtuous few, and can acquire only partial virtue, such as moderation or courage (*Pol.* 1279a36-79b1). On the other hand, polity is based on a more complete friendship than that found in other regimes: friendship among equals who are decent, such as between brothers or peers, who rule each other in turn (*NE* 1161a28-29). In this sense, polity, which can also be understood as a correct democracy, is the most desirable regime, even though it is not the best. Unlike the populist democracy in which the poor tend to oppress and exclude the rich, it is a mixed constitution in which there exist a number of social classes and parties representing them. At one point, Aristotle refers to it as a mixture of oligarchy and democracy (*Pol.* 1293b33-34), which can be interpreted as a type of regime in which the values of wealth and freedom are predominant. However, polity at its best is the rule of the whole people by the whole people equally represented. It is a constitution in which all of the key political values—freedom, wealth, and virtue—are present, and no social class or group is excluded.

JUSTICE AND THE DISTRIBUTION OF POWER

Having divided constitutions into correct and deviant types on the basis of whether the ruling class aims at the common good or only at their own benefit, Aristotle discusses the question of distributive justice in reference to competing claims to rule by different social classes. Distributive justice is for him the distribution of benefits and responsibilities according to worth or merit. Generally, he notes, people agree that justice consists of dividing things among equal persons in the same way, but although there is an agreement about equality concerning things, there is disagreement about equality concerning people (*Pol.* 1280a16-19). When equals receive unequal shares or unequals receive equal shares, such a distribution is a source of quarrels. This disagreement in politics is related to the correct standard of worth. "All agree that just distribution must accord with some sort of worth, but what they call worth is not the same; the democrats say it is freedom, the oligarchs wealth, others good birth, whereas the supporters of the best regime that it is virtue" (NE 1131a25-29). Each faction makes a claim to merit a governing position. The democrats, who place value on their status as free individuals, argue that all free individuals are equals, and therefore, they are all entitled to participate equally in deciding what is advantageous for the political community. They wrongly identify one aspect of equality, being born free, with equality in everything. The oligarchs, who associate worth with money, argue that, on the contrary, individuals are unequal with reference to wealth, and therefore, only the affluent should rule. They wrongly identify one aspect of inequality, inequality of wealth, with inequality in everything (*Pol.* 1279b21-23).

In Aristotle's view, not every kind of equality or inequality can make a claim to power. "It is not the case either that those who are equal in only one respect should have an equal share of everything or that those who are unequal in one respect should have an unequal share in everything" (1283a25-29). The error of both democrats and oligarchs lies in thinking that this kind of equality or inequality they represent constitutes the whole equality or inequality and entitles them to hold political offices. Neither faction offers satisfactory justification for the claim that either freedom or wealth alone gives one the right to rule. "They both put forward a plea that is partially just, but think that what they argue is completely just" (1280a21-22). A just distribution of political power, he argues, must be one that contributes to the unity of the community rather than causing its division into conflicting factions.

The deviant constitutions, oligarchy and populist democracy, arise because of different and erroneous views of justice. Both oligarchs and democrats demand justice and act as opposing factions due to their failure to grasp what is truly just. Sedition arises when either of the two parties, the oligarchic, representing the rich, or the democratic, representing the poor, becomes discontented with its respective share in ruling (1301a37-39). However, those who are most justified in setting up a faction are also those who, because of their moderation and small numbers, are least likely to do so: the community's virtuous persons. Because of their merit, they alone have a rightful claim to inequality. If the state existed solely for the sake of property, Aristotle contends, or solely for promoting social equality, then the arguments of either the oligarchic or democratic parties might perhaps be valid. However, the state exists for the purpose of making possible a complete life, which is a good life, and therefore, virtuous individuals, who can contribute to this life, should have a proper share of participation in public offices (1281a1-9).

By singling out the virtuous individuals and their rightful claim, Aristotle attempts to correct common misconceptions about justice on the part of members of both the democratic and oligarchic factions. Since there is inequality in virtue, the arguments of the democrats that all people are equal because all are born free, and that of the oligarchs that they deserve more because of their wealth, lose their force (Polansky 328). Virtue is the standard of worth according to which political offices should be distributed. Common people and wealthy individuals must be able to contribute to the life of the political community, but there must also be a contribution from those who represent virtue. If the political community cannot exist without the former two groups, it cannot be well governed without the latter. Nevertheless, Aristotle acknowledges that the best constitutions, in which public offices are distributed on the basis of virtue, fall beyond the reach of most states (*Pol.* 1295a31-32). If there are political communities in which virtuous persons can no longer be distinguished as a group, then both the rich and the poor can make reasonable claims to rule. Therefore, the next step in the Aristotelian inquiry is to determine the constitution that is the most appropriate for most actual political communities. In the course of doing so, he elucidates his concept of polity or mixed constitution.

THE MIDDLE CONSTITUTION

Aristotle derives his philosophy of human affairs from studying political reality. In the *Politics*, he acknowledges the basic fact that political communities do not merely consist of a number of people, but of people of different kinds (1261a23-24). Communities are composed of groups or social classes that represent different values and ends in life, and that have different notions of justice. Political life offers the possibility of cooperation between these groups, but it also has the potential for conflict. The strongest such conflict Aristotle envisions is that between the rich and the poor. He considers these groups to be polar opposites. The rich tend to be arrogant and unjust toward the poor. The poor tend to be malicious toward the rich and likely to engage in petty vice (1295b8-11). Both groups do not readily obey reason, but rather are moved by passions of either arrogance or envy where their mutual relationship is concerned. It is therefore difficult for them to form a community (1295b22-24).

Aristotle sees the solution to the potential conflict between the rich and the poor as twofold. He offers both an institutional solution: proper mixing, that is, combining democratic and oligarchic institutions in the constitution, and a social solution: the presence of a strong middle class. To begin with the latter, he argues that, in contrast to either the very rich or the very poor, those who are in the middle have a stabilizing effect on the community. They live in peace and relative safety. They tend to have neither too much nor too little, to neither oppress others nor to be oppressed, to neither desire other people's property nor to have other people desiring theirs. They have a moderate amount of goods and readily obey reason (1295b3-6). They live the middle life. And since individual virtues, such as courage or moderation, are defined in the *Nicomachean Ethics* as the mean between deficiency and excess, the middle life, namely, the mean that each decent person can achieve, is for Aristotle actually the best (1295a38-39). The middle class perhaps lacks magnificence, liberality, and other high aristocratic virtues, but it has the capacity for justice and goodness. It can provide the intellectual and moral elite Aristotle talks about in his *Ethics*, which is indispensable for any good political community. Famous ancient legislators, including Solon, Lycurgus, Charondas, and many others, Aristotle claims, have come from the middle class (1296a17-20). Accordingly, the political community that depends on a strong middle class, *de facto* the best element in the *polis*, can also be the best (1295b34-37). Moreover, in addition to the qualities of its members, the middle class is also valuable because of its aversion to radicalism. If members are numerous, this can prevent extremes from arising on either the right or the left. Aristotle describes the desirable size of the middle class as being, at minimum, larger than the rich minority, and, optimally, larger than the rich and poor added together. Thus, in the best polity, the middle class will constitute the majority of society. But if the middle class is small and weak, and there are large economic inequalities, then either people's democracy or oligarchy will arise, or even, as a result of both these excesses, tyranny (1296a1-3). In order to achieve a stable constitution, Aristotle concludes, those who are in the middle should be strengthened, and their strength should always be a focus of legislation.

The best possible constitution for most political communities is, in Aristotle's view, the mixed constitution based on the strong middle class. Polity, or the mixed constitution, can be defined as a political system in which different social classes, especially the rich and the poor, share in holding public offices, but it can also be understood at a more universal level as a regime in which different political values are represented. Since polity represents different values, such as wealth and freedom, which are expressed in its laws and the way its political institutions are organized, different parties may see it differently. When it is well mixed, polity is like the mean, Aristotle says, "for each of the extremes is visible in it" (1294b14-17). Democrats perceive it as a democracy and oligarchs as an oligarchy. Because they see in it values and institutions with which they can identify, they both are content with the regime. Since it includes different social classes in the government and tends to promote equality, polity is the constitution most conducive to friendship. Ideally, it also incorporates the element of virtue and insofar as it does, can be regarded as a form of aristocracy (1294a22-24).

Polity is then neither the best constitution in the unqualified sense nor a deviant one, but it is a decent one, lying in the middle rank of constitutions. It is a commonwealth, friendly to wealth and friendly to freedom, but not indifferent to virtue. Aristotle describes it as a "well-mixed harmony" (1290a25-26). If founded on a solid basis of the strong middle class, it can be stable and long lasting. Nevertheless, democratic and oligarchic parties usually do not grasp polity as it is, namely as a mixed constitution in which the interests of all are pursued, but rather see it only partially, as either oligarchy or democracy, and this contributes to its erosion. The democratic party's call for the "true" ideas of democracy—such as sharing wealth and rule based on numerical equality—to be put into reality leads to the exclusion of other parties, which under the implementation of the model of "true democracy" are no longer a part of the regime. The ideology of the oligarchic party that one's worth is related solely to money, if put in practice, excludes from politics those who do not meet the oligarchic criteria of property assessment for holding office. Although polity is the best possible constitution for actual states, Aristotle believes that it is rare, because under the sway of party politics it turns in the direction of a more extreme form of either democracy or oligarchy.

HOW TO PREVENT A REVOLUTION

Aristotle is aware of the danger that political change in the direction of extremes can bring about. Neither extreme democracy, which is ruled by decrees of the people and is headed by popular leaders, nor extreme oligarchy, where all wealth and power is in the hands of a few very rich individuals and their families, is favorable to the practice of politics as he understands it. Neither can contribute to a good life or to the full development of human potential. Much of the analysis of political change in the *Politics* is a consideration of how to prevent revolution and promote positive change that can transform an extreme regime into a more moderate one.

Political change encompasses several possibilities. The constitution can change completely, change partially, or become an either more or less extreme instance of the type it was to begin with (1301a5-24). Smaller changes take place steadily as the goals or desires of the population alter. The most radical political change is revolution, in which a community shifts from one type of constitution to another, such as from monarchy to democracy. The cause of revolution and other significant changes is usually factionalism, which arises when some class or group develops a sense of injustice as a result of its dissatisfaction with its respective share of political power in a community (1301a37-39). People engage in sedition in pursuit of equality. But sedition can also take place in situations of inequality, when unequals do not receive proportionately unequal benefits (1301b27-28). Aristotle discusses several situations in which revolution can occur and the ways by which various constitutions can be protected against it.

Democracies undergo revolutions because of their mistreatment of the rich and ambitious persons, which causes the latter to revolt against the regime (1304b20-34). They may be transformed into oligarchies, tyrannies, or more extreme forms of democracy. The remedy that preserves democracy is in each case not more, but less democracy. To prevent a revolution in a democratic *polis*, the wealthy must be made content with the regime. A moderate democracy at its best should resemble a polity. It is beneficial, Aristotle says, in both democracy and oligarchy to give preference to those who do not have a dominant position in the constitution: to the rich in democracy and the poor in oligarchy (1309a26-30). The democratic value of freedom should be combined with the oligarchic value of wealth. Democratic leaders should serve as spokespersons for the well off.

Polities may be overturned little by little through an erosion of the justice on which they are founded. This occurs when they no longer grant each social class its due, and by giving more value to either the rich or the poor, they shift polity into the direction of either oligarchy or democracy (1307a6-9). The remedy is to aim at the middle, by mixing democracy with oligarchy, and by balancing the multitude and the decent citizens, and the poor and the rich. Since injustice destroys polity, and illegality may creep in unnoticed, especially in a polity, justice must be well be protected, and there must be sufficient care taken to ensure that no one breaks the law, even in small matters (1307b30-33). In a polity, the head of the state cannot be a partisan of any faction, but should serve the whole community.

In oligarchies, revolutions may arise when the poor are treated unjustly and decent persons are excluded from government. Additionally, when oligarchies move into more extreme forms, they may be overthrown by rivalry between different factions of the rich. In the former case, they usually change to democracies, and in the latter, they change to other types of oligarchy (1306b16-20). The preservation of oligarchy requires that poor and virtuous people receive some form of public recognition, and their leading representatives get a share of power, so that the constitution becomes more democratic and less oligarchic (1308a2-10). Communities cannot survive without the existence of different social classes. Oligarchic leaders must therefore swear that they would never do any harm to the people (1310a6-11).

Just as polity or a mixed constitution is the goal of the positive changes recommended by Aristotle for both democracies and oligarchies, so kingship is the goal of the process of improving a tyranny. Tyranny is the worst type of regime, and the most harmful to those it rules. It combines the vices of both oligarchy and democracy (1311a9-18). Its destruction comes about due to the hatred and contempt it inspires in the populace. To protect themselves against their subjects, tyrants usually attempt to render them powerless, petty-minded, and mutually distrustful (1314a25-29). However, Aristotle insists that the tyrant should act in a quite different way to preserve his power. Instead of oppressing the people, he should pretend to act like a king and appear to serve the community. He should seem to take good care of public funds and act dignified and not harsh; he should be respectful to his servants and make his state beautiful by erecting imposing public buildings (1314a33-14b37). In this perhaps most Machiavellian part of the *Politics*, Aristotle does not refuse to give good advice to a tyrant. However, his strategy to protect tyranny removes most of its evil. A tyrant who takes his advice is no longer truly a tyrant, but becomes instead a steward of the state. Under some conditions, Aristotle suggests, if used to counter political extremism and great divisions within a society, even tyranny that is finally made moderate is worth preserving (1315a31-39), for it can be an alternative to civil war.

ARISTOTLE'S REALISM

Aristotle's attempt to reform tyranny shows that he recognizes the limits that are inherent in political life. He starts by seeking to give virtue the first place in politics. A large part of Aristotle's political philosophy is devoted to the arguments concerning what constitutes human well-being and the best life for a political community. Yet, while promoting ideally virtuous actions, he also considers the drawbacks and particular conditions of actual political communities. He is aware that the chances of decent individuals having the opportunity to dominate the political scene and guide others to virtue are not great (1301a39-40). The reasons are their being limited in number and in power, their reluctance to use force or fraud, their preference to stay away from politics, and finally to the tendency on the part of both the many and the powerful to go to extremes. Taking into consideration the slight prospect that virtue will prevail, Aristotle suggests that statesmen who aim to reduce social conflict and improve a state's conditions must not infrequently limit themselves to making the parties that compete for power more moderate and balancing them to create a better constitution. Changing ordinary regimes into polities or rendering tyrannies moderate and more royal is in most cases the greatest extent of the good that can be done by the virtuous leaders for whom he writes.

Living in political communities is natural for human beings, for they offer the only sphere in which human potential can develop fully. The deviant constitutions, especially their extreme versions, impede opportunities for virtuous action, while the correct ones foster them. Perhaps the greatest contribution of Aristotle is that, on the one hand, he advises us about true human goals, and, on the other hand, he points out our limits. By doing this, he shows the usefulness of both philosophy and the practical science of government in political life. Aristotle does not rise so high in his political vision as to speak about the immortality of the soul, as Plato does. He criticizes his teacher for disregarding the human love of diversity and for putting too much emphasis on the unity of his ideal *polis* (*Pol.* 1263b30-31). He reminds us that virtuous action always takes place in an actual political environment. And he suggests that only by recognizing both our true goals and our limits can we find our way to happiness in this world.

QUESTIONS

- What is politics? Is the Aristotelian view of politics still relevant for us today?
- Are human beings political by nature? What are the characteristics that distinguish them from other animals?
- What is a state? How do states come into existence? Can we regard them as "natural"?
- Do we expect states to sustain some values? If so, what are these values?
- Should we regard happiness merely as pleasure? What is happiness for you?
- Are solidarity and friendship important for political communities? Can we have solidarity and friendship in today's liberal democracies?
- What are moral and intellectual elites? Do we need them?

- What are the basic constitutions (forms of government)? Which of these does Aristotle regard as the best, and why? What are the worst and the best of the bad constitutions?
- If the best constitutions are not easy to obtain, what is the best possible constitution?
- Why is the middle class so important for Aristotle? Do you agree with his views concerning the role of the middle class in society?
- Can Aristotle be described as a realist? Why or why not?

GUIDE TO FURTHER READING

Translations of Aristotle's Political Works:

Aristotle. *Nicomachean Ethics.* Trans. Terence Irwin. 2nd ed. Indianapolis: Hackett, 1999.
Aristotle. *Politics.* Trans. C.D.C. Reeve. Indianapolis: Hackett, 1998.

The Complete Works in English:

The Complete Works of Aristotle. 2 vols. Ed. J. Barnes. Princeton: Princeton UP, 1984.

Suggested Readings:

Barnes, Jonathan. *The Cambridge Companion to Aristotle.* Cambridge: Cambridge UP, 1995.
Frank, Jill. *A Democracy of Distinction: Aristotle and the Work of Politics.* Chicago: Chicago UP, 2005.
Johnson, Curtis N. *Aristotle's Theory of the State.* New York: St. Martin's Press, 1990.
Keyt, David. *A Companion to Aristotle's Politics.* Oxford: Blackwell, 1991.
Knight, Kelvin. Aristotelian Philosophy: Ethics and Politics from Aristotle to MacIntyre. Malden: Polity Press, 2007.
Nichols, Mary P. *Citizens and Statesmen: A Study of Aristotle's Politics.* Savage, MD: Rowman and Littlefield, 1992.
Pangle, Lorraine Smith. "Friendship and Self-Love in Aristotle's Nicomachean Ethics." *Action and Contemplation: Studies in the Moral and Political Thought of Aristotle.* Ed. Robert C. Bartlett and Susan D. Collins. Albany, NY: State U of New York, 1999. 171–202.
Polansky, Ronald. "Aristotle on Political Change." *A Companion to Aristotle's Politics.* Ed. David Keyt and Fred Miller, Jr. Oxford: Blackwell, 1991. 323–45.
Tessitore, Aristide. *Reading Aristotle's Ethics: Virtue, Rhetoric, and Political Philosophy.* Albany, NY: State U of New York, 1996.
Thompson, Kenneth W. *Moral and Political Discourse: Theory and Practice of International Relations.* Lanham, MD: UP of America, 1987.

Cicero: The Idea of the Republic

M arcus Tullius Cicero, philosopher, statesman, and the most famous lawyer and orator of ancient times, was born in Arpinum near Rome in 106 B.C.E., six years before the birth of Julius Caesar. His father, a country gentleman who belonged to the class of *equites* or knights (those citizens who were originally required to equip themselves as cavalrymen in the Roman armed forces), saw to it that his son received a proper liberal education. Cicero was brought into contact with learning at an early age through his tutor at home, the Stoic Diodotus. As a youth, he attended the lectures of the Academic philosopher Philo of Larissa in Rome, and studied philosophy in Athens and rhetoric in Rhodes. After completing a course of studies in jurisprudence and establishing himself as a leading barrister in Rome, he embarked on a lifelong career of public service. His eloquence and other talents enabled him to obtain honors that were usually conferred only upon members of the senatorial aristocracy. In 76 B.C.E. he was elected to the office of *quaestor* (financial officer) in Sicily, which made him a member of the Senate; in 66 he gained the praetorship (the second most important magistracy); and in 63 he became consul (the joint head of state) at the youngest legal age possible, and was the first person in many years to assume the position without having consular ancestors. During his year-long tenure as consul, he put down Catiline's conspiracy against the Roman Republic and was awarded the title "Father of His Country." However, Cicero, champion of republicanism and enemy of autocracy, was no match for the growing political power of Caesar, Pompey, and Crassus (often referred to as the First Triumvirate), who aimed to change the constitution. In 58, Clodius, a popular tribune and supporter of Caesar, forced Cicero into exile, which he spent in Greece. His property was confiscated and his house was plundered and burned. Because of an amnesty, Cicero returned to Rome sixteen months later, but he could not return to politics. In the following years he practiced law and wrote. His major political dialogues, *On the Orator*, *On the Republic*, and *On the Laws*, date from the period 55–46. Cicero's writing

55

was briefly interrupted in 51–50 by his appointment as governor of Cilicia in Asia Minor.

During that period, the political situation in Rome became very unstable. Consular elections were suspended in 52. A sudden eruption of violence led to the burning down of the Senate House. Pompey became the sole consul and justified his dictatorial rule and the removal of his political opponents by citing the need to ensure security and restore order. Shortly after Cicero returned to Rome from Cilicia, Julius Caesar, then an opponent of Pompey, crossed the Rubicon River and entered Italy with his army. In 48 B.C.E., Caesar, after crushing Pompey's forces, became the first Roman emperor. Cicero, a member of the opposition, was given a pardon but was again barred from politics. In 45 he experienced a personal tragedy when his daughter Tullia died giving birth. Cicero's grief was expressed in a number of writings composed at that time, including the *Tusculan Disputations*, in which one of the questions discussed is about the immortality of the soul, and the *Hortensius*, which a few centuries later inspired St. Augustine's enthusiasm for philosophy. In 44, Julius Caesar was assassinated, giving rise to the possibility of the restoration of the Republic. Cicero returned to public life with vigorous public attacks on Mark Antony, who assumed the role of Caesar's successor. At the same time, he wrote the essays *On Old Age* and *On Friendship*, as well as his influential and final philosophical work, *On Duties*, composed in the form of a long letter to his son Marcus. However, his vigorous speeches (known as the *Philippics*) against Mark Antony, who was at that time associated with Caesar's adoptive heir Octavian, sealed Cicero's death warrant. He was murdered on the grounds of his villa at Formiae on December 7, 43. With his death, humankind lost a literary stylist without rival, a man of true integrity, and one of the greatest humanists and peace lovers of all time.

Cicero's influence on Western thought, although often not acknowledged, is comparable to that of Plato or Aristotle. Philosophy was for him a consolation in difficult times as well as a guide to living. Although he devoted most of his life to public service rather than to scholarly pursuits, he considered philosophy the most worthy human endeavor (*Duties* 2.5). His wide-ranging and curious mind led him to study Greek philosophers and make them accessible to Romans. But, like a typical Roman, Cicero studied them from a practical point of view. He disliked abstract speculations, and intended that his philosophy should educate his fellow citizens in useful matters. "My whole inquiry aims at making governments sound, establishing justice, and curing the ills of peoples," he said (*Laws* 1.37). Through both his political and his philosophical activities, he attempted to reverse the tide of decadence that finally led to the destruction of the Roman Republic.

THE CRISIS OF THE LATER REPUBLIC

From a small city-state, held to have been founded by Romulus in the eighth century B.C.E., Rome became the foremost world power over the course of the second century, after her defeat of both Carthage and Corinth. The vast territory under Rome's control eventually included all the lands around the Mediterranean Sea and a part of northwestern Europe. Roman supremacy was an outcome of the invincible combination of its military skill and might and its system of government. The Greek historian Polybius explained Rome's strength as being based on the fact that one could not describe its constitution as monarchy, aristocracy, or democracy, for it was a blend of all three forms. The Republic, which developed gradually over the course of the centuries after the expulsion of the corrupt king Tarquin the Proud in 509 B.C.E., was a mixed constitution. The result of this, Polybius wrote, was "a union strong enough to withstand all emergencies" (6.18). Indeed, republican Rome carefully guarded itself against extremism in politics. Roman strategy and diplomacy were guided by a cautious but determined group of nobles, backed by the Senate, whose members had the wisdom to know when moderation, and even generosity, best served the interests of the state. Rome's power rested on moral scrupulousness, which was evident to those nations that had dealings with Rome (Minogue 23). The Romans executed laws fairly and strictly. They gained the support of their neighbors by a system of privileges and alliances, which displayed a mastery of the art of statesmanship hitherto unknown in the ancient world (Adcock 33). They respected agreements and could be relied on to stand by their oaths. Although the Romans were a patriotic people who believed that the good of the *patria* had precedence over their private concerns, they were also unique in the degree to which they were open to the cultures of other nations, even those they had conquered, and eager to imitate what was best in them. They thus readily assimilated both the material civilization and the ideas of the peoples subjected to their rule. The most important influence on them was, of course, Greece.

Roman education had been based on imbibing family tradition, which was an important element in the formation of the character of the youth. Service to the state and reverence for the gods were learned through the same respect for tradition that was introduced at home. The second century B.C.E. saw the influx of teachers from Greece to supplement the old ways of upbringing. Conscious of their cultural superiority to the Romans, who at that time had neither philosophy nor science of their own, the Greeks taught them in their own language. They were introducing new ideas, which, in the view of more conservative individuals, appeared dangerous. Of the four philosophical schools centered in Athens—the Academy, the Peripatetic, the Stoic, and the Epicurean—the latter in particular presented a great challenge to traditional Roman values. The Epicureans rejected such commonly accepted social institutions as marriage and parenthood, undermined traditional religious beliefs, and recommended abstention from politics. Hence, there were sporadic attempts to minimize their influence. In 161 B.C.E. a decree expelling philosophers from Rome was passed, but it did not have a lasting effect, and philosophers and other Greek teachers were soon back in the city. In 155 the Athenians sent as ambassadors to Rome three distinguished philosophers: Critolaus the Peripatetic, Diogenes the Stoic, and Carneades the Academic. Their lectures, especially those of Carneades, who chose justice as his subject and argued first for justice and then against it, proved extremely popular among the youth and met with the general approval of their parents. This was a clear sign that the habits of the Roman upper classes were changing. It was now expected that the youth would have some knowledge of rhetoric and philosophy. As a result, by the time of Cicero's generation, the traditional Roman upbringing had become largely neglected. The austere virtues of the old Romans—frugality, industry, temperance, and simplicity—and the affirmation of a simple life based on love of family, country, and valor were fading away (Clarke 15). The youth were educated by professional teachers who were either Greek or strongly influenced by Greek ideas. On the positive side, however, philosophy proved by reason many things that the Romans of earlier generations had instinctively believed. At no other time had they been better educated and more keenly interested in intellectual pursuits. Cicero is the best example of a man of his time who combined philosophy and all-round culture with an active political life.

With Rome's rapid expansion, the prolongation of terms in office and military commands, and the changes in the Romans' habits, the later Republic years became a period of decay. Typical of the decadence of the Roman social order was the emergence of new social classes, whose power was based on wealth acquired through conquest and looting in foreign lands. Materialistic values were rising to a position of dominance. Along with the increase in wealth and prosperity came an increase in extravagance and luxury, along with a disrespect for things sacred. Members of the upper classes, which had originally relied on landed wealth, became increasingly interested in commerce and reaped the gains of colonial exploitation. The endless supply of enslaved war captives was used for cheap agricultural and urban labor. Slave revolts occurred in 134–132, 104–101, and 73–71 B.C.E., but were ruthlessly suppressed. The question of land distribution among returning peasant soldiers was a recurring political problem. Within this environment of profiteering and growing social antagonism, there was an attempt to move the Republic in the direction of a more popular government, initiated in 133 by tribune Tiberius Gracchus and continued by his brother Gaius, and also efforts to change it into a dictatorship, launched by ambitious individuals such as Pompey and Caesar. This unleashed a succession of civil wars. Cicero's action against the conspiracy of Catiline was the last significant effort to halt this process. Consequently, the crisis the later Republic underwent was not just a simple struggle between rich and poor, but a more complex phenomenon. Its source can be traced to the erosion of traditional republican institutions and the corruption of the morals of the Roman people. "It is because of our vices," Cicero says, "not because of some bad luck, that we preserve the Republic in name alone but have long ago lost its substance" (*Republic* 5.2a). His philosophy came as a response to this crisis. It was meant to be thoroughly practical. What he was really interested in were ethics and constitutional theory, the two elements on which he believed the strength of the Roman Republic was ultimately founded.

HUMAN NATURE AND DIVINE ORIGIN

Cicero's political philosophy is rooted in his conception of human beings and human relations. In both *De Legibus* (*On the Laws*) and *De Officiis* (*On Duties*) he presents his view of human nature. Unlike Hobbes or today's positivist social scientists, Cicero did not believe that one should assume humans to be merely egoistic and pleasure-seeking individuals, engaged in an endless struggle to dominate one another. Following the tradition of Greek philosophy, he identified the essence of being human with the ability to think and to make moral judgments. Although his ideas about human nature reveal the influence of the Peripatetic school, he thoroughly transformed whatever he borrowed from Greek thinkers, first, by freeing it from dependence on Aristotelian metaphysics and second, by expressing it in his own unique and beautiful style. Cicero, a great literary stylist, writes:

> Nature not only adorned the human being with the swiftness of mind, but also gave him the senses as servants and messengers . . . and a bodily shape that is both adaptable and suited to human nature. For although she made all other animals face the earth for grazing, she made the humans alone upright and roused them to look on the sky, as if on their former home . . . (*Laws* 1.26).
>
> The person who knows himself will first recognize that he has something divine and will think that his own reason within himself is a sort of consecrated image of the divine (1.59).

Cicero describes the rational soul as the divine and immortal element that was originally implanted in humans by God. There is within each individual, he claims, "a divine spark of genius and mental capacity" (*Republic* 3.1a). Because rationality is common to both humans and gods, there is a family relationship between them, so that they can be described as being of a common stock or origin (*Laws* 1.24). Insofar as they have reason, by which they "comprehend the chain of consequences, perceive the cause of things, understand the relation of cause to effect and the effect to cause, draw analogies, and connect and associate the present and the future," human beings are allied with the gods (*Duties* 1.11). They surpass all other animals. They do not merely busy themselves with the down-to-earth animal needs related to self-preservation and reproduction, but also look upwards to the world of thought and ideas. Human beings are the only creatures that have "a feeling for order, propriety, moderation in word and deed . . . and a sense of beauty, loveliness, and harmony" (1.14). They have invented musical notes, letters, and numbers, and can engage in the pursuit of truth. They can survey the course of their lives and reflect upon their conduct. They are thus both rational and moral animals.

By making references to God and the gods, Cicero introduces religion into his political philosophy. However, in fact, he does not refer to traditional Roman beliefs, but rather to "universally accepted views of all philosophers" (*Duties* 3.102). Gods exemplify for him morally perfect beings. They provide a paradigmatic standard for human perfection. Humans occupy the place between beasts and gods, and so hover between baseness and righteousness. They can be the source of the greatest good to one another, but also of the greatest evil. "What is uglier than greed, more horrible than lust, . . . and lower than sloth and stupidity?" (*Laws* 1.51). By indulging such ugly vices, people degenerate into beasts, for they completely lack moral restraints. Conversely, by cultivating purity of mind, honesty, kindness, generosity, goodness, justice, moderation, wisdom, piety, and other virtues inherent in a perfect human nature, they rise to the level of the gods, for they partake in moral perfection. "Virtue is the same in humans and gods and is found in no other species" (1.25). Cicero believes that every human being can become morally perfect or virtuous. "There is no person of any nation who cannot reach virtue with the aid of a guide" (1.30). Evil comes from improper training and bad examples, and not from nature. If humans were true to their original nature and thought nothing human alien to them, he argues, "then justice would be cultivated equally by all" (1.33). Our moral judgment, the ability to distinguish right from wrong, which Cicero calls "right reason," and our natural capacity for virtue are extinguished only by the corrupting influence of false beliefs, which misrepresent what is morally right and appropriate, and bad habits, which result from an excessive desire to experience bodily pleasures and avoid pain (1.46). We fall prey to vices, forgetting about our true nature and divine origin.

THE FELLOWSHIP OF HUMANS

Because reason exists as a portion of the divine in each human being, there is a similarity between humans and gods. Further, reason and speech make human beings similar to one another. Guided by his practical attitude, Cicero would find the problem of other minds raised by today's analytic philosophers—namely, that we can never know that there exist any other minds but our own—an artificial one. Externally observable behavior, he would say, most obviously the use of language, which individuals learn from one another, enables us to infer that other minds exist. "Trouble, happiness, desires, and fears pass equally through the minds of all" (*Laws* 1.32). Reasoning, sharing thoughts and feelings, learning and teaching, communicating ideas, and discussing them unite human beings in a sort of a natural fraternity (*Duties* 1.50). Consequently, on the basis of their similarity related to reason and speech, human beings can regard themselves as belonging to the family of humankind as a whole. As they search for truth and discuss universal ideas, they are not limited by their particular language, nation, or religion, but can view themselves as citizens of the entire world (*Laws* 1.61). In discussing moral questions in particular, Cicero argues, we are most closely bound together as humans and further removed from other animals. "For we admit that they may have courage (horses and lions, for example); but we do not admit that they have justice, equity, and goodness; for they are not endowed with reason or speech" (*Duties* 1.50). Deliberative rationality, the basis of morals, is the most comprehensive bond of fellowship uniting all human beings.

That we can identify with the whole human race and view all humans, regardless of their actual political affiliations, as belonging to one universal human clan does not mean for Cicero that we no longer have responsibilities to our nations, local communities, or immediate families. There is no mutually exclusive choice for him between love of humankind and love of one's country. The ideas of cosmopolitanism and patriotism are not contradictory for him, but in fact perfectly compatible. The statement, "I am a citizen of the world," does not signify a negative claim on the part of someone who, in the name of some notion of universal humanity, would refuse to render services to his own country and fellow citizens. In the context of Cicero's cosmopolitanism, this statement has a positive content. It informs us that because of our common humanity, we have moral obligations not only to our kinfolk, but to all humans.

The Ciceronian world is characterized by a traditional hierarchy of social relationships and responsibilities. Nature prompts individuals, Cicero says, "to acquire goods, not only for themselves, but also for others whom they hold dear and for whom they ought to provide" (*Duties* 1.12). As human beings, we are responsible for others. But since the number of people in need is infinite and our resources are limited, he argues, our obligations to others vary in accordance to their circumstances and the degree of social relationship we have with them (1.59). We should not refuse a glass of water or a meal to a person in need, or refuse to offer someone whom we do not know a piece of advice if he or she looks to us for direction (1.52). We should certainly do something if someone cries out for help, and indeed do everything that we can to prevent wrong (1.23). But we are not obliged to give our lives for others or to do anything else that may put our own resources in peril. If by helping others we impoverish ourselves, we may fail to take care of those for whom we have a primary obligation to provide, such as our families. The foremost bond of human fellowship for Cicero is that between husband and wife, the next between parents and children. The bonds of blood, family traditions, the same forms of worship, and the same ancestral tombs link humans tightly through goodwill and affection. Moreover, these common identities and widely shared values, which are referred to today as "political culture," are for him the true foundation of civil society (1.54-55). Beyond the family bonds, he claims, there is no other relationship among humans that is closer and dearer than the common history and ancient customs that connect each of us to our homeland. "Parents are dear, and children and acquaintances are dear, but our country has on its own embraced all the affections of all of us" (1.57). Therefore, he regards national responsibility, the obligation to one's own country, as being of the highest importance. Consequently, in order of moral obligations, our country and our parents, spouse, and children come first; next, come the rest of our family, and then our more distant kinsmen (1.58). Last but not least, after obligations to our country and our family are met, there comes the universal, cosmopolitan responsibility that we protect from wrong those upon whom it is being inflicted, and give value to each human being, irrespective of whether he or she belongs to our own political community.

COSMOPOLITANISM AND NATURAL LAW

The word *cosmopolitan* derives from the Greek word *kosmopolitês* (citizen of the world). Cosmopolitanism, the idea that all human beings, regardless of their actual political affiliation, belong to a universal moral human community, guides Cicero's political thought. This universalistic idea lies at the root of classical political philosophy. It is based on the concept of natural moral law that was foreshadowed in Plato's dialogues and later developed by the Stoics.

In Plato's *Republic*, Socrates defends the idea that there exist unalterable principles of morality and law. He contests the view that laws are merely conventional and justice is merely a matter of expediency. Insofar as he distinguishes what is naturally just from what is only legally or conventionally just, he defends justice as a universal moral value against Thrasymachus' ethical and legal relativism. He thus rejects a double morality—one toward those who belong to our community and another toward outsiders—and affirms a common morality and the same rights for all humans. The rejection of dual moral standards, which is characteristic of the cosmopolitan perspective, is clearly expressed by Cicero as follows:

> We are certainly forbidden by the law of nature to wrong our neighbor. For that is an absurd position which is taken by some people, who say that they will not rob a parent or a brother for their own gain, but that their relation to the rest of their fellow-citizens is quite another thing. Such people contend in essence that they are bound to their fellow-citizens by no mutual obligations, social ties, or common interests. This attitude demolishes the whole structure of civil society. Others again who say that regard should be had for the rights of fellow-citizens, but not of foreigners, would destroy the universal fellowship of humankind . . . and those who work all this destruction must be considered as wickedly rebelling against the immortal gods (*Duties* 3.27-8).

The natural law mentioned in this passage—a moral law that dictates principles of justice and morality, whose rules are discoverable by reason and are universally valid, constant, and eternal—had for many centuries been the predominant basis of Western political thought. This natural law determines what is right and wrong. We cannot be freed from its obligations by decrees of either the senate or the people, Cicero claims, and we do not need to look outside ourselves for someone to interpret it (*Republic* 3.22). It is written into the rational soul. It restrains the good from doing wrong, but it cannot restrain the wicked (3.33). The primary question regarding natural law is, what is right or just by nature.

The opponents of natural law, such as Carneades, whose views Cicero criticizes, "make self-interest the only standard and think that nothing is done for someone else's sake" (3.39a). They assert that nothing is right or just by nature, and that all justice is conventional and of human origin. Justice is derived from utility and is based only on calculation of the advantages of living together in a particular society. Conventionalism derives its support from the variety of laws that we can find in different human communities, a variety that seems incompatible with the idea of a universal norm of justice (3.21a). Conversely, advocates of natural law point out that major Western and non-Western cultures alike condemn murder, theft, and rape, and value benevolence, fairness, and certain obligations to others. These thinkers argue that there is a core of basic ethical norms that are always valid and can be universally recognized. They, like Cicero, say that it is as a matter of principle that "no man should be allowed for the sake of his advantage to injure his neighbor" (*Duties* 3.23). Hence, pursuing one's own benefit cannot be dissociated from the question of what is morally right (3.36).

In both *On Duties* and *On Laws*, Cicero develops arguments in defense of justice as a universal moral value and of the priority of reason, as opposed to the will, in lawmaking. "There is only one justice," he says, "which constitutes the bond among humans, and which is established by one law, which is the right reason in commands and prohibitions" (*Laws* 1.42). The main source of justice lies in the social nature of human beings. An unjust act, such as a violation of another's property, is destructive to the natural fellowship among humans. "If we are so disposed that each, to gain some personal profit, will defraud or injure his neighbor, then those bonds of society, which are most with accord with nature's laws, will be broken" (*Duties* 3.21). To the sphere of law, therefore, belong the rules that are intended to maintain the social order, such as the prohibition on taking something that belongs to another and the obligation to fulfill promises. Justice consists in doing what is by nature right. It is not established by opinion or by arbitrary will, but by nature (*Laws* 1.29). It is the dictate of "right reason." If penalties and fear of punishment were the only deterrents to criminal acts, Cicero argues, then no one would be unjust, and the wicked would simply be regarded as incautious (1.40). If justice consisted merely in obedience to the written law established by an opinion of a lawgiver, and if everything were measured by utility, he further argues, then whoever thought it advantageous to ignore laws would in fact break them. "Justice set up by utility is uprooted by the same utility" (1.42).

Cicero's central idea is that to be binding, positive or human-made laws must be founded on ethics. The universally valid natural law, whose principles provide unchangeable moral norms for all humans, is the foundation of all human-made laws. It cannot be annulled, and no act of human legislature can absolve us from obedience to it. "We can distinguish good from bad laws by the standard of nature" (*Laws* 1.44). Any positive law that contradicts the standard provided by natural law is therefore unjust.

Cicero was anything but a revolutionary, and yet the doctrine of natural law, which held that there existed a higher moral law providing a standard to judge government-enacted or positive laws, was embraced by individuals who in later centuries would challenge the established political order. The opponents of totalitarian regimes would justify their resistance upon Ciceronian grounds, by invoking universal moral principles. Without the concept of a higher law, neither the American Revolution nor the Solidarity movement in Poland would have taken place, nor would the ideas of freedom and social justice have found their way into people's hearts. When this law is disregarded, the bonds of human fellowship are destroyed and human goodness is eliminated.

INTERNATIONAL MORALS

By arguing that there was an absence of justice in the anarchic international system, the Athenians at Melos described in Thucydides' *History* provided foundations for political realism and posed a question that has persisted through the ages: What role should morals play in relations among states? In the dialogue *On the Republic*, Cicero explicitly takes up this question.

The case for injustice is entrusted to Philus, who takes the position that the faithful observance of the demands of justice runs counter to the human desire to be powerful and to rule over as many people as possible, and that it is seldom reconcilable with interests of the state, such as increasing resources and influence, and extending boundaries (*Republic* 3.24b). "There is no state so stupid that it would not prefer to rule unjustly than to be enslaved justly" (3.28) he says. The results of calculation, planning, and prudence are superiority, power, wealth, and resources. To act at all times in accordance with the rules of justice, he further argues, to look after the interests of all human beings and to refrain from seizing that which belongs to someone else, seems sheer folly. If Rome had always done so, it would have remained a poverty-stricken village instead of becoming a great imperial power (3.21b). Philus' argument in favor of injustice is then rebutted by Laelius, the oldest member of the group, who argues that justice is established by nature. Individuals who do not obey natural law scorn their nature as human beings, and in that they pay the greatest penalty for their injustice. Human actions, he claims, should be measured not by utility but by honor (3.33). The drift of the discussion makes it quite clear, however, that although Laelius' uncompromising moralism is preferable to Philus' cynicism, neither position can be regarded as fully adequate.

Like classical realists, Cicero insists on giving priority to the national responsibility over other responsibilities, and opposes conducting foreign policy without prior consideration of the national interest. At the same time, however, he emphasizes the importance of ethics in international relations. His vision of international politics resembles that of the Grotians in Martin Wight's threefold classification: Machiavellians, Grotians, and Kantians (Wight 1991). The similarity of Cicero's ideas to those of Hugo Grotius, the seventeenth century lawyer who is considered the father of international law, is not accidental. Grotius knew Cicero's works and frequently referred to them. By contrast to the Machiavellians, for whom international politics consists of anarchy and conflict between states, the Grotians describe international politics as both conflict and cooperation. In their view, states, although not subject to a common sovereign, can form an international society and enter into relations regulated by laws and mutual obligations.

International ethics addresses moral issues such as justice in war, armed intervention, or protection of human rights that are not confined by national boundaries. It is based on the assumption that we find in Cicero's writings, namely, that in addition to obligations to members of our family or to our fellow citizens, we have a cosmopolitan responsibility to humanity as a whole. Cicero grounds this assumption on his notion of universal human fellowship. He believes that acts of injustice destroy the natural fellowship among humans (*Duties* 3.21). The bonds of human society should be promoted by the cultivation of friendship and fulfillment of obligations to others, and thus made stronger rather than weaker. This does not mean for him that humans should be selfless and abstain from what benefits them. "We are not required to sacrifice our own interests, and surrender to other persons what we need for ourselves" (3.42). Further, we may engage in fair competition against others and devote all our strength to winning. But we may pursue what is beneficial to us only so far as this may be done without injustice to others (3.22). This rule applies to the actions of both individuals and states. "The same thing is established not only in nature, that is in the law of nations, but also in the laws of individual peoples, through which the political community of individual states is maintained: one is not allowed to harm another for the sake of one's advantage" (3.23). States may follow their national interests and increase their power in relation to others, but only within the framework of international norms for which the ultimate reference is natural law.

There are many examples of interstate relationships in which what seems to be expediency appears incompatible with moral rectitude (3.47). Yet to be just, Cicero argues, is not only moral but also expedient in the long run. While they may not be enforceable by any government, international norms that are based on natural law cannot be ignored with impunity. Respecting rules of justice in international affairs may seem to be against the narrow, short-term interest of a given state in a particular case, but it brings about long-term advantages: It encourages cooperation among nations and gives them a sense of peace and security, and it prevents the state's own demoralization and eventual destruction. Hence, "what is morally wrong can never be expedient" (3.49). Without denying the importance of national interest, Cicero secures a place for morality in international relations. He limits his discussion of international morals to two issues: the moral restraints that states should observe at war and the exercise of hegemonic power.

MORAL RESTRAINTS IN WAR

Disputes between humans can be settled either by discussion or by violence. Since violence is characteristic of wild beasts, while rational dialogue is characteristic of humans, Cicero argues that war should always be the last choice. "We must resort to force only in case we may not avail ourselves of discussion" (*Duties* 1.34-35). Cicero can be considered the father of the just war theory. No one before him so strongly insisted on the maintenance of justice in war. "In undertaking, waging, and ending wars both justice and good faith should be as strong as possible, and there should be official interpreters of them" (*Laws* 2.34), he says. Further, no one before him categorized wars on the basis of just and unjust causes or set forth standards for judging military action (*Republic*

3.35a). It is in the phenomenon of war that the difference between domestic and international politics is most clearly seen. In the international context, there is no sovereign that can impose order. International politics, unlike the domestic variety, is anarchic. Hence, it is politics without a ruler. Cicero's just war theory represents a way of thinking about international relations in terms of right and wrong without an institutional basis in the form of a common sovereign. It implies the conception of a society of states that uphold international law.

War can be judged in two ways. First, it can be judged on the basis of its causes. Second, it can be judged on the basis of the way it is conducted. Medieval writers described this difference by introducing the notions of *jus ad bellum* (justice of war) and *jus in bello* (justice in war). Cicero discusses the issue of the just war by considering these two aspects. It is a characteristic of an upright person to be unwilling to begin a war, he argues: "A good man is one who helps all whom he can and harms nobody, unless provoked by wrong" (*Duties* 3.76). Hence, the only justification of war is self-defense. The only reason for which we go to war, Cicero says, "is that we may live in peace unharmed" (1.35). The defensive war, which has a reasonable chance of success, is permissible. Cicero acknowledges, however, that wars are in fact fought not only in self-defense, but also for supremacy and glory (1.38). Whatever its cause, war has to be formally declared and conducted in a lawful way: "No war is just, unless it is entered upon after an official demand for satisfaction has been submitted or warning has been given and a formal declaration made" (1.36). He is the first to propose a limit to the intensity of combat as well as rules that set certain classes of people outside the permissible range of warfare. Bitterness in war should be avoided (1.38) and cruelty is to be abhorred (3.46). Promises made to the enemy should be kept, even if they were made under the stress of circumstances (1.40). In addition, prisoners of war should not be killed or tortured. If they on their part do not break rules and behave like savages in warfare, the enemy combatants who lay down their arms should be spared and protected (1.35). Cicero derives these rules from old Roman customs. It was the Roman reputation for justice in war, he claims, that in the past had caused the enemies of Rome not to fight to the bitter end and, once defeated, to submit to Rome's power and to enjoy its protection.

Militarism finds glory in war and fighting. Subscribing to the cosmopolitan worldview, Cicero was not a militarist. But neither was he a pacifist. He shared the pacifist belief that the ideal world is one of peace, but he did not condemn all wars. In his view, not all use of violence is prohibited, only that which is in conflict with the principle of human fellowship. The social order must be maintained. Just as civil society has to be protected, by force when necessary, against wicked individuals who destroy human fellowship, so also a country must protect its citizens against external enemies. Waging a defensive war can thus be justified. Cicero believes that in the anarchic system of states, marked by the absence of a common sovereign, peace can be promoted by laws that outlaw aggressive war and limit the right of independent states to engage in warfare. However, the view that international law upheld by a society of nations can contribute to interstate peace is an idea that was only foreshadowed in his writings. It was developed by Grotius, but did not find its full practical expression until the creation of the United Nations in the twentieth century. Another alternative to the conflict that pervades international relations, which was already well known to the ancient world, is dominance by one nation with sufficient power to keep all other nations in check and to defeat aggressor states. In other words, interstate peace can also be created by a hegemonic power.

ETHICS OF HEGEMONIC LEADERSHIP

A hegemonic leader is a state with preponderant influence and authority over all others. The Greek word *hegemonia* was originally used to describe the paramount position assumed by Sparta (404–371 B.C.E.) among Greek city-states after it emerged as the victorious power in the Peloponnesian War against Athens. The exercise of hegemony can be regarded as actions taken by a single predominant state in pursuit of its own national self-interest, which also provide benefits, such as order and security for other nations. In more contemporary terms, hegemony refers to the domination of a leading nation over others—guided by that nation's self-appointed mission to defend the world against rogue states, to maintain peace, and to promote commerce, economic stability, and cultural exchange on a global scale. Cicero's ethical reflections on hegemonic leadership are a part of his larger argument, namely, that human cooperation is secured by virtue and affection, but destroyed by injustice and fear.

Cicero argues that people hate those whom they fear. Any despotic regime that inspires fear and keeps subjects in check by force poisons them with hatred. No amount of power can withstand the hatred of the many for long. Therefore, "fear is but a poor safeguard of lasting power; while affection, on the other hand, may be trusted to keep it safe for ever" (*Duties* 2.23). Furthermore, Cicero compares those who have the chance to live in a society of equals but instead choose to put themselves in a tyrannical position to the "maddest of the mad" (2.24), for by this act of oppression, they destroy freedom and natural fellowship among humans. Those who put themselves in a position to be feared must in fact be afraid of those whom they intimidate (2.25). Thus, fear reinforces fear; hate produces hatred; violence leads to more violence. This rule refers to situations in both domestic and international politics. To illustrate, Cicero uses the examples of Sparta and Rome. After they won the Peloponnesian War, the Spartans tried to impose their will on Greek cities in a much more arrogant way than the Athenians had done earlier, exercising their supremacy tyrannically (2.26). As a result, they lost practically all of their allies. The Theban commander Epaminondas was thus able to defeat the Spartan army at the battle of Leuctra in 371 B.C.E., and the Spartan hegemony ended. In contrast, the early Romans exercised their supremacy benevolently. The Roman hegemony maintained itself through acts of service and justice rather than oppression. For instance, Rome provided a safe haven for political refugees and nations. "Wars were waged in the interest of our allies or to safeguard our supremacy; the end of our wars was marked by acts of clemency or by only a necessary degree of severity" (2.26). The benevolent hegemony of the Roman Republic was "a patronage over the world rather than an empire" (2.27), and the values of justice and honor on which it was based eroded only during the succession of civil wars in the later period.

Consequently, Cicero acknowledges the potentially beneficial, but also corrupting effect of dominant power. The Spartans were drunk with their passion for dominance. But when one strives to surpass all others, he notes, "it is difficult to preserve the spirit of fairness which is absolutely essential for justice" (1.64). The result is that instead of promoting the value of justice and the spirit of cooperation, which are the foundations of any society, a hegemonic power may no longer feel constrained by either rational argument or lawful authority. Arrogance can lead a hegemonic power to attempt to be superior through force rather than to be satisfied to remain an equal through international law. It may even use bribery, deceit, and propaganda to further its interests (1.64). However, "reason demands that nothing be done with unfairness, with false pretense, or misrepresentation" (3.68). If through acts of injustice a benevolent hegemony turns into a tyrannical one, it becomes a potentially terrifying concentration of power. A tyrannical superpower inevitably invites opposition. A self-conscious bid for global hegemony that is no longer based on respect for law and affirmation of moral values frightens away allies and impels foreign rivals into open hostility. However, no power is strong enough to last if it relies solely on inspiring fear (2.25-26). In contemporary terms, to be a true hegemon and not invite opposition, the leading nation cannot solely rely on its "hard power," its ability to get others to do what it wants because of its superior military and economic capacities; the nation needs "soft power" as well. It must influence others by its values, ideas, and policies. Therefore, Cicero argues, hegemonic leadership must be based not only on the leading nation's terrifying might, but also on its moral worth. Successful leadership must be established through justice, and through service to others that earns their affection, confidence, admiration, and esteem (2.31). In promoting the spirit of cooperation, a benevolent hegemon does not need to make sacrifices in the international interest. Cooperation is needed for its own advantage as well, and thus can be pursued even by narrowly self-interested states (2.17). It is through safeguarding of values and benefits for other nations that the hegemonic state can secure their cooperation to forward its own benefit.

Although the benevolent hegemonic state has dominant strength, it keeps itself open to the opinions of allies in order to guide its actions in such a way that they are not outraged. By vindicating the principles of peace and justice in the international forum and serving other nations, it earns their loyalty and support. However, if a hegemon no longer follows ethical principles and refuses to listen to international public opinion, it turns into autocracy, with its dominance based on terror and military force alone (*Republic* 2.41). Unchecked power may always be misused, and hence, "no one should be allowed to grow used to power" (2.23). Therefore, hegemony is not the best solution for international politics. This realistic view that underlies Cicero's discussion of hegemonic leadership also supports his concept of a mixed constitution.

THE ROMAN MIXED CONSTITUTION

The idea of polity or mixed constitution, already introduced in the writings of Plato and Aristotle, is one of the most important legacies of ancient political theory. It had an impact on the development of constitutional theory in the Middle Ages and in the early modern period, and influenced such diverse thinkers as St. Thomas Aquinas, Machiavelli, Montesquieu, and the American founding fathers. This idea was further developed by Cicero. Like Polybius, he attributed the greatness of republican Rome to its morals and its mixed form of government. However, unlike the Greek author, he did not describe the Roman mixed constitution merely as a defensive system of checks and balances, which strives to balance the interests of various social groups, but rather as a harmonious mixture through which the qualities and virtues of each basic form of government (*potestas, consilium,* and *libertas*) could be best promoted (*Republic* 1.69). He judged it to be by far the best type of organization for a state.

The dialogue *De Re Publica* (*On the Republic*), in which the idea of the Roman polity is discussed, begins with a famous statement: "*Est . . . res publica res populi*" (1.39a). Its literal translation—"The public thing (*res publica*) is the people's thing"—does not express its full meaning. The expression "*res publica*" has a range of uses. It can mean "public affairs," "the common good," "the shared property," "the commonwealth." The word *populi* ("people") is not just any assemblage of individuals; for Cicero; it signifies the nation as a whole or the entire society, which is united by "an agreement with respect to justice and a partnership for the common good" (1.39). The statement can thus be more accurately translated as: "The commonwealth is the wealth of the whole people." The commonwealth (*res publica*) is then any form of government in which a shared sense of justice and a community of interests are present. In a more specific sense, however, this statement expresses the normative idea of the republican form of government: The republic is the government of neither the rich nor the poor, nor of any other faction or party for its own benefit; rather, it is the government of the whole people by the whole people for the benefit of all. This idea of the ancient republic is based on the concept of a mixed and well-balanced constitution (1.69). In such a form of government, no social class is reduced to political insignificance. The rights and responsibilities of each are balanced in an equitable fashion (2.57). There is power (*potestas*) for magistrates, the deliberative function (*consilium*) for senators, and liberty (*libertas*) for the common people. The mixed constitution amounts to a harmonious blend of dissimilar elements, represented by upper, middle, and lower orders (2.69). In the Roman Republic, two consuls (joint heads of state elected for a term of one year) embodied the monarchic element of the government; senators, the aristocratic element; and tribunes and popular assemblies, the democratic element.

In contrast to the Spartan mixed constitution, which was designed at a particular point in time by the famous ancient legislator Lycurgus, the Roman constitution developed over many generations and was the product of the intellect of many outstanding individuals (2.1). It was not based on any abstract theory couched in the form of a blueprint for remaking society, but rather was founded on the concrete political experience of the Romans. Cicero criticizes Plato for constructing a model of state that was "totally alien to human life and customs" and stands against all abstract theorizing in politics that suppresses the empirical and historical treatment of political themes (2.21). He employs an empirical approach to trace the unfolding of the Roman constitution to its ideal mixed and balanced form, going back to the origins of the Roman people and looking at various developments over the course of Rome's history. Using the great statesman Scipio as a spokesman in *On the Republic*, he argues that none of the basic forms of government can remain stable. Sooner or later, each turns into its undesirable counterpart. Monarchy, in which the entire ruling power is entrusted to the discretion of a single person, becomes tyranny; aristocracy, based on the authority of the few ablest citizens, becomes oligarchy. Although conducive to freedom, democracy, seeking to place ever more power in the hands of the people, leads to the erosion of authority and results in anarchy and tumult, characteristic of a populist regime (1.69). In contrast, a mixed and well-balanced government prevents these perversions. It prevents the concentration of power by one social class or group. In the case of Rome, it was only after a considerable passage of time from its founding, when the demands of the plebeians for the selection of popular tribunes to offset the power of the consulate were met, that the mixed constitution approached a fair balance (2.58).

It is misleading to describe Cicero's mixed constitution as a mere "device for stabilizing and conserving lordly domination" and see it as "entirely compatible with an authoritarian, elitist, and inegalitarian political society" (Neal Wood 175). The criticism that is implicit in such an account overlooks the timeless value of the idea that Cicero advances and the spirit of fairness on which it is built. "Those who care for the interests of only one part of the citizens and neglect others," he says, "introduce into political life the ruinous condition of dissension and factional strife" (*Duties* 1.85). The normative idea of the republic requires that justice and the common good be kept clearly in view. The government should "care for the welfare of the whole body politic and not serve the interests of some one party to betray the rest" (1.85). When the affairs of the state are conducted in such a way that they are no longer the affairs of the entire society, but only those of the ruler or some party (as in a tyranny, oligarchy, or populist democracy), then there is no community of interests and no *res publica* at all (*Republic* 3.43–3.45). Referring to democracy, Cicero believes that in the well-balanced and mixed constitution, people's freedom to vote, elect magistrates, and manifest their views publicly should be protected. However, he is opposed to the view that the power of the common people over the state's affairs should be unlimited, and that consequently there should be no constraints whatsoever on their individual liberty (Schofield 76). When unrestrained, liberty degenerates into license, resulting in the erosion of all authority and traditional values of life, and ultimately leading to tyranny. The people become the "masters of the laws and the courts, of war and peace, of treaties, and of the status and wealth of all individuals" (*Republic* 1.48). The people's rule, which is not based on respect for justice and the protection of private property, is in comparison to other tyrannical forms of rule "all more disgusting because there is nothing more awful than the monster which pretends to the appearance and name of the people" (3.45). In making this remark, Cicero warns us against the rise of totalitarian people's democracies.

During the seventeenth and eighteenth centuries, the study of Cicero lay at the heart of the school curriculum in both Britain and America. For John Adams, Thomas Jefferson, James Madison, and many other Americans at the time of independence, his idea of the mixed constitution provided the model of how a government should be structured (MacKendrick 294–304). Like Cicero, most American supporters of a mixed constitution anticipated that senators would be composed of an aristocracy of merit—the ablest and wisest members of the community. However, when the role of two legislative chambers in the American system of government was discussed in the late eighteenth century, the Senate was justified as a device to check the otherwise unrestrained legislative power of a single assembly, but was not regarded as being an embodiment of aristocracy. The Americans found it difficult to distinguish those individuals who had the most wisdom, experience, and virtue. Inequalities and distinctions certainly existed among them, but real differences of rank were believed to be increasingly insignificant in a country where education and commerce had diffused knowledge and wealth among so many.

"All the people were at one time plebeians and at another senators" (*Republic* 3.48), Cicero could say in response. In contrast to the American republic, the Roman one was not a democracy. It was founded on existing divisions of birth, wealth, and abilities. The liberty of the plebeians was expressed in their participation in one branch of the government, but not in their supreme power. Deliberation and policy making were allocated to the aristocratic senate. Power was divided among the upper, middle, and lower social classes. The Roman Republic thus represented the classical ideal of an integrated and ordered world. Its success depended on the continued existence of virtuous leaders, free from dishonor and able to serve as positive models for the rest of the citizens (*Laws* 3.32). With the decline of Roman mores, a succession of civil wars, expansion over a great territory (which resulted in the prolongation of terms of office and military commands), and finally, the establishment of the Empire and of what was in effect the rule of one man, republican Rome came to an end. Free and open debate no longer stimulated political life, nor did individuals compete freely for office. But although the Republic no longer existed, the memory of it survived, and the classical ideal of mixed government continued to inspire many thinkers. The idea that the only effective way to promote freedom was by separating power and distributing it into different hands was resurrected in the modern doctrine of the separation of powers.

REPUBLICAN VALUES

In commenting on the poet Ennius's saying that "The Roman Republic stands upon the morals and men of old," Cicero expresses the view that the institutions of republican government add a moral dimension to political life (*Republic* 5.1).

There is a reciprocal interaction between the quality of people and that of their institutions. Republican institutions and ancestral values reinforce each other. Good institutions promote political and moral values in society. Without those values, established in the minds of the people and continuously reinforced by the example of outstanding individuals and political leaders, institutions lose their substance and become republican in name alone (5.2a).

Looking at Cirero's political writings, it is possible to enumerate nine key political and moral values that, according to him, are fundamental to successful republican government.

First, *legitimacy based on justice and service*—the conviction that political power must derive its legitimacy from justice and acts of service. It cannot be based on force or fear. The government is like a trustee (*Duties* 1.85) and must work for the benefit of those entrusted to its care rather than for its own benefit. The function of government is to care for the welfare of the people as a whole, not promote the welfare of one party.

Second, *limited and divided political power*—the idea that no one should grow used to power and that unbalanced power is always a dangerous weapon in any hands (*Republic* 2.23). The method of government must be based on a reasoned balance that leads to the harmonious concord of different social groups (2.69a).

Third, *freedom and responsibility*—the belief that all citizens should have the freedom and responsibility to acquire knowledge and skills that can make them useful to society, to express their opinions, and to participate in political life, as exemplified by the right to vote and assemble (*Republic* 1.33, *Laws* 3.27).

Fourth, *justice and cooperation*—the idea that cooperation based on justice is essential for the common benefit of society (*Duties* 2.18). What is just is advantageous, and it is wrong to disassociate private advantage from the question of justice (3.36). Neither individual nor group benefit should be pursued at the price of harm to others.

Fifth, *leadership and loyalty*—the conviction that the loyalty of the people and the country's allies are the result of benign and competent leadership (*Republic* 5.5, *Laws* 3.5). The prerequisites of successful leadership are learning, prudence, and justice.

Sixth, *rationality and knowledge*—the belief that human beings are able to recognize rationally what is good, true, and real, and can study things by looking into their causes and consequences (*Duties* 1.11). There exists a body of practical and moral wisdom, as well as factual and formal knowledge, to be learned. Learning must be based on liberal education (*Republic* 1.29). Knowledge divorced from the right is cunning rather than wisdom.

Seventh, *human fellowship*—the conviction that family traditions, along with a common history, ancestry, and form of worship keep people together and create strong bonds of fellowship (*Duties* 1.55). These bonds can be strengthened by cooperation and are destroyed by acts of injustice.

Eight, *openness to other peoples and cultures*—the idea that all human beings have a common cultural and intellectual heritage. All members of the human race are bound by reason and speech. To obstruct access to cultural and intellectual interchange is contrary to the idea of universal human fellowship (*Duties* 3.47).

Ninth, *moderation and peace*—the belief that excess should be avoided, and that the well-being of society can best be achieved through order, tranquility, and the promotion of peace (*Republic* 2.26, *Duties* 1.35). Force and fraud are bestial (*Duties* 1.41). Laws of war must be observed, and the sanctity of treaties should be respected.

The basic question that Cicero asks in his writings can still be considered ours: How can we maintain and improve our commonwealth? "There is no possibility of living well in the absence of a good government," he says, "nor is there anything more blessed than a well-ordered state" (*Republic* 5.7). A republic will last as long as it remains a government based on some essential moral and political values. It cannot survive without the preservation and continual affirmation of the home-grown virtues that have been implanted in it by its founders and the following generations. It is not preoccupation with power alone, Cicero believes, that either makes nations great or ultimately destroys them, but the character and spirit of the people. States die not as a result of invasions, but because of decay from within. Frugality, industry, honesty, courage, temperance, and simplicity make a people strong. Obsession with comfort and enjoyment, on the other hand, eventually weakens them and makes them a soft, dissipated mass, easy to manipulate, and unfit and unwilling to serve the public interest. "When a state is removed, destroyed, extinguished, it is something similar to the death of the entire cosmos" (3.34b). The punishment for moral decline is death. But "the states ought so to be established as to be eternal" (3.34b).

The Roman people were in the habit of calling Rome the "Eternal City." Although no longer a republic, the "eternal" Rome survived until the fifth century C.E.—a total of approximately twelve hundred years from the time of its legendary foundation by Romulus in 754 B.C.E. Cicero's thought has survived longer. He succeeded in bequeathing to later generations the heritage of moral and political ideas and values that are fundamental to the continuous existence of Western civilization.

QUESTIONS

- What does it mean to be human?
- Why do we have obligations? Are we responsible to some people more than to others?
- Can we be "citizens of the world" and at the same time love our country?
- Why, for Cicero, is increasing one's own property at the cost of another more contrary to nature than death, poverty, or pain?
- Are moral values merely conventional, or are they universal?
- What is natural law? How can we know it?
- Is morality important in international relations? Can a hegemonic power pay no attention to justice?
- What is the mixed constitution? Is this concept still relevant for us?
- Can the ancient model of the republic be modified to be acceptable from our point of view, or is it hopelessly anachronistic?
- What are the key republican values? Do we need them?

GUIDE TO FURTHER READING

Translations of Cicero's Selected Political Works:

Cicero. *On Duties*. Ed. M. T. Griffin and E. M. Atkins. Cambridge: Cambridge UP, 1991.

Cicero. *On the Commonwealth and On the Laws*. Ed. James E. G. Zetzel. Cambridge: Cambridge UP, 1999.

Cicero. *On the Good Life*. Trans. Michael Grant. London: Penguin, 1971. (Contains fragments of *Tusculan Disputations*, *On Duties*, *On Friendship*, *On the Orator*, *On the Republic*.)

The Complete Works in English:

Cicero. *Works*. Loeb Classical Library. 28 vols. Cambridge: Harvard UP. (Latin texts and English translations by various scholars.)

Suggested Readings:

Bellamy, Alex J. *Just Wars: From Cicero to Iraq*. Malden: Polity Press, 2006.

Clarke, M. L. *The Roman Mind: Studies in the History of Thought from Cicero to Marcus Aurelius*. New York: W. W. Norton, 1968.

Everitt, Anthony. *Cicero: The Life and Times of Rome's Greatest Politician*. New York, Random House, 2003.

Fuhrmann, Manfred. *Cicero and the Roman Republic*. Oxford: Blackwell, 1992.

MacKendrick, Paul. *The Philosophical Books of Cicero*. London: Duckworth, 1989.

Minogue, Kenneth. *Politics: A Very Short Introduction*. Oxford: Oxford UP, 1995.

Polybius. *The Rise of the Roman Empire*. Trans. Ian Scott-Kilvert. London: Penguin, 1979.

Powell, J. G. F. *Cicero the Philosopher: Twelve Papers*. Oxford: Oxford UP, 1995.

St. Augustine:
The City of God

S aint Augustine, theologian, philosopher, and father of the Western Church, was born in 354 C.E. in Thagaste, in Numidia. At the time of his birth, this North African province was one of the most prosperous parts of the Roman Empire. Barbarian raids along the European and Asiatic frontiers injured neither Italy nor North Africa. The Empire, whose center of power was now Constantinople, seemed still to be destined to last forever. With the conversion of the emperor Constantine in 312, Christianity became the dominant religion. Augustine's mother Monica was a devout Christian; his father Patricius accepted baptism on his deathbed, when Augustine was seventeen.

After receiving his basic education in his native town and nearby Madaura, in 371 Augustine went to study rhetoric at Carthage, a wealthy metropolis with half a million inhabitants. As he later described in his *Confessions*, the only thorough autobiography of ancient times, he became seduced there by "unholy loves" and, after some adolescent adventures, established a more permanent relationship with a woman who lived with him for fifteen years and gave him a son, Adeodatus.

At the age of nineteen, Augustine was awakened to the love of wisdom when he read Cicero's *Hortensius*. This book altered his way of thinking. He began to take a serious interest in philosophical and religious issues. The questions raised by Cicero, especially about the quest for happiness, moved him to begin reading the Bible. However, Augustine was initially not impressed by its style and obscure content. His intellectual curiosity led him to instead investigate the Manichaean religion—which was based on the idea of a conflict between the forces of good and evil—and he was associated with the Manichees for the next decade.

Augustine completed his studies at the age of twenty-one and returned to his home town to take up a career as a teacher of rhetoric. Soon after, he moved back to Carthage, where he gradually earned a reputation as a formidable scholar and orator. In 383 he went to Rome and one year later to

Milan, where, with the help of influential Manichaean friends, he was appointed municipal professor of rhetoric. During this period, familiar questions and perplexities again rose to plague him. He had tried Manichaeism, and then Skepticism and Neo-Platonism. None of these systems of thought or belief provided more than temporary satisfaction, however. Christianity began to appeal to him in a new, more intellectually attractive light. He began to study the Bible again, and came under the influence of bishop Ambrose of Milan, who, like Augustine, was later designated a father of the Church.

One day, when he was resting in the garden of his house in Milan, overcome by conflicting thoughts about the purpose of his life, he heard a child's voice coming from a neighboring house repeating, *tolle lege*—"pick it up and read it." It seemed to him a sign from heaven. He opened the Epistles of Saint Paul at random and found the passage: "Let us walk honestly as in a day, not in revelry and drunkenness, not in debauchery and licentiousness, not in quarreling and jealousy" (*Romans* 13:13–14). This extraordinary experience led him to the decision to embrace Christianity. However, his conversion was not a sudden flash, but the end of a long process of painful gestation of thought and questioning. He and his son were baptized by Ambrose on Easter eve in 387. His mother, who had joined him in Milan, rejoiced at this answer to her long-held hopes and prayers. She died soon afterwards.

Augustine, intending to break wholly with his former life, gave up his professorship and decided to return with a few of his friends to North Africa, where he still had a small property at Thagaste, to live in Christian retirement, praying and studying scripture. Two years after his return, he sold his inheritance and founded a monastery and a clerical school in nearby Hippo Regius. In 391 he was ordained a priest; in 395, auxiliary bishop; and in 396, when Valerius, the bishop of Hippo, died, Augustine was chosen to fill his place. He would remain at this post until his own death thirty-four years later.

This was a time of growing political instability. With the crossing of the Danube by the Goths, the fortunes of the Empire had steadily deteriorated. In 395, the Goths, led by their king Alaric, reversed their previous role as allies and became the source of disturbances. They plundered Greece and then, during 401–403, turned against Italy. Their initial successes had also encouraged similar attempts. As a result, masses of Vandals and other barbarian tribes invaded Gaul and Spain. This was also a period of theological unrest. Schism and heresy threatened the church. As a bishop, Augustine fought incessantly against heretics, denouncing their doctrines in numerous treatises and in homilies on several books of the Bible. His first expressly theological works were devoted to attacking Manichaeism. Besides combating the Manichees, whose teachings he knew so well from his youth, Augustine engaged in two other great theological debates. One was with the Donatists, who were essentially purists and wanted Catholics to live up to their own ideals more stringently. The other was with the Pelagians, followers of a British monk, who denied the doctrine of original sin. In the course of these debates, Augustine developed his doctrines of the human fall and divine grace, divine sovereignty, and predestination.

In 410 Augustine shared in the universal shock at the sack of Rome by the Goths under the leadership of Alaric. A number of wealthy Romans fled the city to country estates in Campania, Sicily, and North Africa. The more intellectual among them began to wonder aloud whether their new religion might not be to blame for the disaster they had suffered. Their argument was that Rome had been immune from capture for eight hundred years, but just two decades after the formal end of public worship of the pagan gods (commanded by the emperor Theodosius in 392), it fell to the barbarians. Augustine was invited by a friend, the imperial official Marcellinus, to refute these charges. His response, *The City of God*, written between 413 and 426, was a masterpiece of Christian apologetics. Its first chapters, in which Augustine argued convincingly that the fall of Rome was not the Christians' fault, were published quickly. But the work as a whole, in which many political and philosophical issues were included, continued to appear in installments over the next years, revealing a broad vision of history and Christianity.

In 429, a band of barbarians found its way to Africa. The Vandals, who came from Germany into Gaul in 406 and then passed through Gaul into Spain, had been invited into Africa by Boniface, a Roman governor, in rebellion against the emperor. They proved to be untrustworthy allies. In the summer of that same year, they were besieging the city of Hippo, as the aged bishop lay dying within. Augustine died on August 28, 430. In 432 Boniface fought his last battle against the Vandals and then fled to Italy, taking on his ships most of Hippo's remaining citizens and Augustine's library, including many precious manuscripts. The barbarians burned Hippo, and then in 439 they took Carthage, turning the devastated city into a pirates' lair; from this base they raided Rome in 455. In 476 the Germanic chieftain Odoacer overthrew the last of the Roman emperors, Augustulus Romulus. Ancient Rome was no more. The western part of the Empire was divided among barbarian invaders. What survived its ruin was Christianity, which, during the several centuries known as the Middle Ages, provided Western Europe with religious and cultural unity across its new frontiers.

FAITH AND REASON

For Augustine, Christianity was not a mere love of wisdom, just one more philosophy that would replace other philosophies and be replaced in its turn, but instead was a way to salvation by faith in Christ. Early Christians like him stood in an ambiguous relationship with classical philosophical ideas. They were products of classical education, and though they were dedicated to subverting ancient philosophy, they could not escape its influence. Accordingly, the early Christian thinkers, especially Augustine, were influential agents in the transmission of classical learning. They would frequently employ the concepts of ancient Greek and Roman philosophy to illustrate their own arguments. Moreover, they felt that philosophy could be helpful in the defense and exposition of Christian teachings. There were ancient philosophers, Platonists in particular, Augustine declared, who conceived of God "as the author of all created things, the light of knowledge, and the Final Good of all activity" (*City of God* 8.9). Hence, like other Christian thinkers who saw harmony between faith and reason, Augustine believed that through their study of natural phenomena, logic, and ethics, the ancient philosophers anticipated and closely approximated the Christian position.

The prevailing characteristic of the philosophy that originated in Greece and extended to Rome was its rationality. From the first to the last, the thinkers of antiquity believed in the power of human reason to ask general questions about the world and discover the truth of things by its own unaided effort. Even the rejection of certitude by the ancient sceptics was based on rational argument. This approach did not, however, lead ancient philosophers to agnosticism. The main current of speculation in antiquity guided philosophy in the direction of a theistic interpretation of the world. Plato posited "God, the perfect being," Aristotle, the "Unmoved Mover, the pure Form," and Cicero, following the Stoics, the "Divine Mind." In the words of St. Paul, "the invisible things of Him were clearly seen" by the best minds of Greece (*Romans* 1.19f).

Christian thought added to the rationality of ancient philosophy a new element—revelation as an indispensable auxiliary to reason. Like other Christian thinkers, Augustine regarded the exercise of reason unaided by revelation as valid up to a certain point, but he would also point out that between the ancient philosophers and him and his contemporaries, "the Christian revelation has intervened, and profoundly modified the conditions under which reason has to work" (Gilson 5). Although he believed that there were profound truths that could be discovered by reason alone, Augustine maintained that none of ancient philosophers had arrived at a complete understanding of the world. "They were ignorant of the end to which all these [truths] were to be referred and the standard by which they were to be assessed" (*City of God* 18.41). Their understanding was incomplete because it remained unsupported by beliefs, such as those concerning God's true nature and the existence of an everlasting life beyond the present life, that were obtainable only through the revelation of the Christian scriptures. Consequently, Augustine argued that reason needed the support of faith, but that faith also needed reason, because it was reason that showed what one should believe in. In his intellectual and pastoral endeavors he aimed to demonstrate that both reason and faith had to work together to bring people to see the whole truth. His saying, "Understand that you may believe; believe that you may understand" (*Sermons* 43.9), became the basic formula of mediaeval Christian philosophy. Under his influence, classical political ideas underwent a dramatic shift to a God-centered direction.

CHRISTIAN PESSIMISM

Augustine is often regarded as a political realist, and even the "first great realist in Western history" (Niebuhr, 1995, 120). His pessimistic view of the human condition and critique of classical political idealism follows from his acceptance of the Christian doctrine of original sin. He claims that the original sin, which can be understood as self-love or pride, led the first humans to disobey God, and to their fall. This "fall away from the godly and heavenly, and the turn towards the human and earthly," is the source of all the evil deeds of human beings (*City of God* 14.11). The fallen "man regards himself as his own light, and turns away from that light which would make man himself a light if he would set his heart on it" (14.13).

Despite of his pessimism, it is however misleading to suggest that for Augustine human nature is evil. "No one is evil by nature, but anyone who is evil is evil because of a perversion of nature" (14.6). Like angels, humans were originally created good. In a Ciceronian mood, Augustine declares that "God made man also upright, with the same power of free choice, an animal of earth, yet worthy of heaven" (22.1). The origin of evil, which is a defect or perversion of nature, is for him human apostasy from God. The miseries that afflict humankind are the result of following human ends rather than the true end, which is God, and of living according to earthly standards rather than godly ones. As they follow earthly ends and seek to satisfy their desires, fallen individuals attempt to exploit and dominate others. Only subjection to rulers and coercive institutions can restrain them from plunging into evil. Education and law must be used to suppress vice (22.22). Consequently, for Augustine, the state, an outgrowth of human sinfulness, performs a more limited function than it had for the thinkers of classical antiquity. Rather than being identified with a benevolent community in which individuals can develop friendship and achieve virtue, the state is a coercive institution whose main purpose is to keep order.

The concept of original sin was unknown to ancient philosophers and would almost certainly have been discarded by them. The classical political ideal was a rationally ordered political life, based on respect for norms and values that could contribute to the well-being of the whole community. Political society was regarded as an area of good living, an arena in which individuals could pursue happiness. Augustine challenges this ideal as illusory. He thus becomes one of the most penetrating critics of the ancient philosophical tradition to which he himself owed so much. All ancient philosophers, he says, "have wished with amazing folly, to be happy here on the earth and to achieve bliss by their own efforts" (19.4). They sought a perfect resolution of all conflicts. What they overlooked were the miseries of this life and the unceasing confrontations with evil that human beings face. "The world is full of a vast mass of evils" (19.8).

To put Augustine's view in more modern terms, history is for him just the same damn thing over and over again: wars, bloodshed without cause, suspicion and competition among states, and ultimately, the rise and fall of great powers. Conflict prevails within the city, as well as between states: "The larger the city, the more it is filled with civil lawsuits and criminal trials" (19.6). By accepting the revealed truth about the human fall, Augustine believes that it is an illusion that humans can achieve happiness here and now by themselves and without God. Human beings are all subject to pain, disease, and disaster. It is impossible to arrive at finality and permanent harmony in the world of contingency and discord. Neither prudence nor self-control, nor any other ancient virtue can permanently remove the temptations that plague individual human beings or the conflicts that exist in society (19.4). While serving to further human glory, the virtues of ancient philosophers—an expression of an unaided human attempt at the betterment of the self—are also not free from pride. Therefore, as long they are not brought into relation with God, they are regarded by Augustine as vices rather than as true virtues.

Augustine's realism, with its stress on the disordered and conflicting character of human life, is corrective to a political idealism, characterized by belief in norms and ideals, delusions about human behavior, and the tendency to hide selfishness behind the facade of values. However, his realism is not cynical. It does not serve to justify evil deeds. Although Augustine thinks that something radically and abidingly wrong remains present in the human condition, he does not regard evil as normative, but as a defect of human nature, a result of the self's abandonment of God as its true end. True justice exists when "God rules and man obeys" (19.27), and in the ultimate state of peace to which such justice leads, human morals will be restored and there will be no more moral perversion. This is the eternal peace of the City of God.

TWO LOVES AND TWO CITIES

According to Cicero's definition, which Augustine cites, the people who constitute a political community are not simply any assemblage whatsoever, but "an association united by a common acknowledgment of right" (19.21). For Cicero, a political community must be united by a shared sense of justice and a community of interests. Where there is no justice, in the sense of a good political order, and one part of society oppresses another, as in tyranny, oligarchy, or extreme democracy, there is properly no community at all; and where there is no community or people, but rather a kind of a mob, there is no commonwealth, or "weal of the people." However, if people do not obey God, Augustine argues, they have no proper control over their vices. When people fail to give proper due to God through obedience and worship, and fail to recognize the higher order provided by God, they in fact know no true justice, the virtue that assigns to everyone his or her due; instead, they seek glorification of their own desires. What holds them together is not justice, but "a common agreement on the objects of their love" (19.24). If we use true justice as the criterion, he claims, then "there never was a Roman commonwealth" (19.21).

The analysis of political community following Cicero's definition leads Augustine to replace justice with love as the cornerstone of human societies. To discover the character of any people, he claims, we must observe what they love or what their ideal is. There exist two loves that from the beginning of history have classified humankind into two basic paradigms of human society or two cities: "the self-love that reaches the point of contempt for God" and "the love of God carried as far as contempt of self" (14.28). The former love creates the *earthly City* that "looks for human glory" and glorifies itself;

the latter founds the *City of God*, which "finds its highest glory in God" and whose life is based on faith.

The two cities are the outcome of two different loves and two different standards applied to life, and hence are utterly distinct. The impious inhabitants of the earthly City identify themselves as mere bodies. They "live after the flesh." They choose to live by human standards and with the view of enjoying earthly happiness (14.1). Since they do not conduct their lives with a view toward the purpose for which they were created, they live in falsehood (14.4). By contrast, the inhabitants of the City of God, or the heavenly City, consider themselves to be spiritual beings. They "live after the spirit." They conduct their lives according to God's directions, loving God and their neighbors, and with a view toward happiness to come. They have no attachment to earthly things and make use of them as would pilgrims on their way to heaven, sojourning in this world as in a foreign land (19.17). They remember God as their Father and thus live in truth.

Consequently, the City of God differs from the earthly City as widely as "the sky from the earth, life eternal from temporal joy, substantial glory from empty praises, the society of angels from the society of men" (5.17). The earthly City, a state which is organized for power and wealth, comfort and pleasure, praise and glory, is something far apart from the heavenly City, which is organized for eternal life. In the earthly City there is only human wisdom, which exalts itself under the domination of pride; in the City of God, there exists not mere human wisdom, but rather the revealed knowledge of the beginning, the middle, and the end of creation. In the former, princes rule in the love of domination and, although they are ruled by vice, each of them desires to be the world's master; in the latter, princes and their subjects serve one another in love (14.28). The one city aims at earthly peace and "limits the harmonious agreement of citizens concerning giving and obeying of orders to the establishment of a kind of a compromise between human wills about things relevant to mortal life"; the other city, whose citizens are on a pilgrimage in this world, makes use of earthly peace also, but relates it to the eternal peace that is "the perfectly ordered and completely harmonious fellowship in the enjoyment of God, and of each other in God" (19.17).

Augustine's *City of God* is not a systematic work on politics after the manner of Plato's *Republic* or Aristotle's *Politics*. Nevertheless, his vision of two cities implies an important criticism of classical political thought. Augustine does not disagree with the ancient philosophers about the need to think about a good political order and to formulate the outlines of the ideal state in which there is justice and peace. He does not consider philosophy either useless or false. But his rejection of the ancient philosophical tradition follows from his conviction that it was unable to produce the kind of society that was essential to human well-being.

Augustine argues that for Plato and other ancient philosophers—whom, in spite of their search for God, he associates with the earthly City—the main goal of the state is to promote social well-being based on earthly peace and security. While Augustine's ideal community, the City of God, enjoys such peace, it ultimately aims at the enjoyment of peace that is everlasting and can be obtained only through faith (19.27). By living according to the spirit, this community looks beyond this world to the timeless world of blessed joy and silence. It aims at salvation, such as it will be in the world to come, as the ultimate happiness—a happiness that the philosophers and earthy politicians, in their attempt to fabricate for themselves a delusive earthly contentment, refuse to believe in (19.4).

In addition, for Augustine the classical ideal state is not only inadequate, but also doomed to fail. This ideal, he claims, was in fact never realized, not even in the Roman Republic (19.24). At best it exists only in speech. In this respect, Augustine's critique of the ancient philosophical tradition is similar to that of the early modern philosophers who implied that it was impractical. Yet he is anything but a Machiavellian or a Hobbesian. It does not occur to him to lower politics by divorcing it from ethics. The standards of human conduct that he derives from Christianity are even more stringent than the standards of virtue provided by the ancient philosophers. In his view, ancient political philosophy failed, not because it expected too much of human beings, but because it was ignorant of the true end to which all human actions were to be directed and by which all truths should be measured. Having no conception of original sin, it did not apply the proper remedy to the disordered and conflicting character of human life. This remedy for Augustine consists in following God, who reveals the true goal of human existence and gives "instructions for the promotion of the highest morality and the reproof of wickedness" (2.25).

In this way, although pessimistic about the human condition, Augustine also displays some optimism. He believes that a genuine improvement of the world is possible. His answer to the classical question of the best political order is that the City of God does in fact exist and is the destiny of humankind. Indeed, it is better and more real than the purely speculative solutions provided by the philosophers. Only in the City of God is true justice to be found. Only it aims at the true common good, which is salvation and eternal life, and only it is based on a kind of rule that is not exploitative. It is an actual city, but one unlike any earthly city. Although it may have an impact on politics, it is not a political institution, and thus cannot be identified with any existing state. It is, rather, a universal community of true believers: the locus of happiness and destiny for those human beings, who born in earthly cities and coming from all nations set their hearts on the Supreme and become its citizens by grace (15.1, 22.24).

A CHRISTIAN COMMONWEALTH

The distinction between the two cities, the City of God and the earthly City, which can be identified by the distinction between the two spheres of power, the one directing humans to their spiritual end and the other to their earthly or temporal ends, is often regarded as Augustine's main contribution to political philosophy. And yet, if his task were merely to contrast a religious community that loves God and an earthly society that loves itself, assigning to each of them a different realm, he would be unable to present a successful argument against the pagan intellectuals who accused Christians of pacifism and withdrawal from public affairs. He would be unable to prove that Christianity did not contribute to the fall of Rome. It is a part of Augustine's argument to demonstrate that Christians can, in fact, make good citizens and soldiers because they love God. He shows that despite the consequences of original sin, a state whose citizens are animated by religious values can be improved, even though it will never be identical with the City of God. It is thus evident that he relates the improvement of society to the betterment of individuals rather than to the reform of political institutions. In his view, the real significance of Christianity for political life lies in its transformation of basic human values.

In a letter to Marcellinus, composed not long before he began writing the *City of God*, Augustine says:

> Let those who say that the teaching of Christ is incompatible with the well-being of the commonwealth give us an army of soldiers such as the teaching of Christ commands. Let them give us such provincial subjects, such husbands and wives, parents and children, masters and servants, kings, judges, and finally, such tax-payers and tax-collectors as the Christian religion has taught that humans should be; and then let them dare to say that it is adverse to the well-being of the commonwealth. Rather, let them no longer hesitate to confess that this teaching, if it were observed, would be a great benefit of the commonwealth (*Letter 138*).

By using writings of the Roman historian Sallust (86–34 B.C.E.) as authority, Augustine shows that the Empire prior to Christianity was highly corrupt. The integrity of Roman morals had somehow been maintained in the initial period of the Republic. The first Romans preserved a certain sort of uprightness that could suffice for founding, enlarging, and preserving their earthly city. They brought riches to the public treasury while living in relative poverty and austerity in their own homes. "But it was by a mere handful of men, good men in their way, that the great public interests were managed; and it was thanks to the foresight of the few that the domestic ills were rendered tolerable" (*City of God* 5.13). The rise of luxury and extravagance in the later period brought about the subsequent advance of the worst vices. "Through wealth a horrible wickedness, worse than any enemy, breached not the walls but the mind of the city" (*Letter 138*). Augustine thus argues in his letter that Christianity, turning human attention from external things to the cultivation of the inner life and exhorting people to "voluntary poverty, continence, benevolence, justice, concord, true piety, and other bright and powerful virtues of life" (*Letter 138*), did not contribute to the deterioration of the Empire; on the contrary, it saved Rome from sinking into even greater moral and political decline. It allowed new spiritual shoots to grow amid the decay of Rome's civil and military power. A similar argument is presented in the first five books of the *City of God*.

The Romans of old strove for glory, honor, and power by merit, not by deceit. They increased their lands assisted by the wickedness of those against whom their just wars were waged (4.15). Although they lived in an earthly city, they were patriotic people working for the common good and acting for Rome's safety and well-being with disinterested concern (5.14). They were the virtuous few, who contributed to Rome's advancement and were granted the earthly glory of an empire that surpassed all others (5.15). But the later Romans started to rejoice in the extent of their empire. They became corrupted by the love of domination. Moved by their desire for power alone, they sought supremacy by means of hidden or open crimes and exceeded the beasts in their cruelty and self-indulgence (5.19). According to Augustine, there is thus a kind of a "slippery slope that leads from the extensive love of human praise to the burning passion for power" (5.19). If they are unable to pursue their earthly goals in a virtuous way, humans may end up despising virtue and desiring only power and domination. The erosion of their morals follows from a failure to relate earthly goals to something higher than themselves. Therefore, it is better to resist the love of human praise and not to make glory a high goal of life. Merely human virtue is as deceitful as it is proud (19.4). What is lacking in it is precisely the connection with the true end of human beings. There are no real morals and there is no true virtue "without piety, that is without the true worship of the true God; and the virtue which is employed in the service of human glory is not true virtue" (5.19). Piety is needed to oppose the consequences of the human fall. The love of human praise must be overcome by the love of justice, and human justice is fully realized only if it is supplemented by the love of God.

Augustine acknowledges that the citizens of an earthly city are more of a service to their city when they at least possess human virtues, deficient through they may be, than if they lack them. However, he also says that there is no more beneficial situation for political communities than when those "who are endowed with true piety and lead a good life, if they are skilled in the art of government, . . . wield power" (15.19). Thus, he lays the foundation for the idea of an earthly Christian state. The inhabitants of the City of God, guided by central Christian virtues of faith, hope, and charity, live for the sake of everlasting happiness, but by "living this life most properly," they also contribute to the "most harmonious unity in the earthly city" (*Letter 138*). Enduring patiently the malice of those whom they seek to make morally good, they cause the number of the good to grow, rather than adding themselves, by returning evil for evil, to the number of the wicked. Their reign is "a blessing for themselves, and even more for the whole of human society" (*City of God* 4.3). In their humility and selflessness, they "attribute to the grace of God whatever virtue they may be able to display in this present life" (5.19). Those of them who find themselves in positions of authority may be considered happy if they govern with justice, and if surrounded by voices praising them on all sides, "they are not inflamed by pride, but remember that they are merely humans," whose goal is to serve (5.24). They rule not from the love of power, but from the sense of duty they owe to others; not because they are proud of their authority, but because they are willing to assume the responsibility of taking care of others (19.14).

Guided by his realistic bent, Augustine anticipates deep sources of disorder in the earthly City, even when it is populated by Christians. The City of God, in which a few individuals will choose to live, is a community of true believers, pious and morally good individuals, who can be identified neither with the visible church nor with any actual state. From the miseries of this life, which are the common lot of good and evil people alike, there is no liberation save through God's grace (22.22). Until such time, then, as humans are delivered from their wretched condition, they must accept the constraints of the present life and endure their current situation, which may be better or worse according to circumstances, but never as perfect as they would wish it to be. Although Augustine recognizes the possibility of acting positively to create a more humane earthly city in the form of a Christian commonwealth, he does not thereby intend to substitute Christianity for political life. Christian virtues and temporal power may occasionally coexist in the persons of good and pious administrators, but even in that case they remain distinct. Augustine would have been greatly astonished by those later medieval writers who interpreted his idea of a Christian commonwealth as a theocracy, an empire run by bishops with the pope at their head (Chadwick 105). Yet he would have been equally astonished by the doctrine of quietism put forward by more modern interpreters of his works who, referring to his distinction between the two cities, insisted that the Christians should always obey earthly rulers and give them unchecked temporal power.

OBEDIENCE AND WAR

Even if some are more decent than others, earthly cities never represent a perfect political order. True justice, by which humans recognize a higher reality and guide their lives according to it, is found only in the City of God (*City of God* 2.21). But, Augustine rhetorically asks, if justice is removed from the relations among nations, "what are kingdoms but gangs of criminals on a large scale?" (4.4). The immorality of societies pursuing their own interests at the cost of others is for him evident. This leads us in turn to the question of obedience in unjust regimes. If human societies are necessarily imperfect, if each one is to a greater or lesser degree a "compact of wickedness," should a citizen of the City of God, a moral human being, obey the rules of an immoral society?

For Augustine, the primary goal of the state is to settle and prevent conflict. Insofar as the earthly city protects law and order and provides for earthly peace, its goal is not fundamentally opposed to that of the City of God, which aims for the attainment of eternal peace. Augustine equates earthly peace with harmony among humans concerning the giving and obeying of orders. Since, as a community of believers, the City of God is an actual community of individuals who share with the inhabitants of the earthly city the condition of mortality, it "needs to make use of this peace also" (19.17). Being on a pilgrimage in this world, the religious community supports earthly peace by seeking compromise between humans concerning the things that are relevant to mortal life. It obeys laws and customs by which this peace is achieved and preserved "so far as may be permitted without detriment to true religion and piety" (19.17).

Hence, however much the City of God might cooperate with the earthly city in promotion of earthly peace, there is a limit to this cooperation. It is unable to share with the earthly city any legislation that obstructs worship. Suppression of Christianity and religious prosecutions by the public authorities are sufficient reasons for civil disobedience. Furthermore, Augustine states that citizens of the City of God cannot allow themselves to be forced by any civil authority into impious and wicked acts (5.17). Although he makes it clear that salvation is an individual matter and does not depend on living in any particular regime, the moral condition of the government can make a difference. The reign of the morally good, through their worship of God and upright lives, is "for the benefit of all, of the subjects even more than the rulers" (4.3). In contrast, the rule of the wicked is harmful to all, and constitutes a true test of virtue for the good. There is thus unity between religion and morality (Burnell 179). If the state attempts to force them into wicked acts, Christians, guided by the precepts to love God and their neighbor, can disobey a civil authority on moral as well as on strictly religious grounds.

There is perhaps nothing more miserable and evil than war. The gravest evils in war are the "love of violence, revengeful cruelty, fierce and implacable enmity, wild resistance, and the lust of domination" (*Against Faustus* xxii). In the absence of any rules that put limits on warfare, a war can easily turn into mass murder. Far from considering all human beings in terms of total depravity, when discussing war, Augustine makes a normative distinction between the good and the wicked. He says: "To make war and extend the realm by crushing other peoples is a good fortune in the eyes of the wicked; to the good it is stern necessity" (*City of God* 4.15).

Augustine condemns imperialism, but he also rejects pacifism. War is a tragic necessity to which Christians must at times resort. It can be legitimate, but whether it is permissible or not depends primarily on its cause. The war of aggression that aims at territorial gain or other worldly goods is a crime. As a general rule, Augustine argues, it would be a great injustice if the unjust who invade others should thereby rule over the just (4.15). What justifies military action is therefore the enemy's injustice, and so, it is right to conduct a war of self-defense. The warrant to wage war grows out of the need to defend oneself and the obligation to allot punishment for wrongdoing. Wrongful acts by another state can be punished, just as can wrongful acts by private individuals. But if a war does not have a just cause, good individuals should not engage in it (19.7).

In an idealistic twist, Augustine thus gives war a moral dimension. For it is precisely the aggression of the other side that is to be deplored and, provided that it can be practically opposed, imposes on morally good and prudent human beings the duty to wage war. But equally, Augustine suggests, the injustice of their own earthly city against another would give Christians the right to engage in civil disobedience. To ask individuals to participate in an unjust war is not for him a legitimate demand of political society.

Because human beings are tainted by original sin, they readily grasp at power, cloaking personal ambition in righteous rhetoric. To avoid this snare, politics must be limited. Foreign adventures are to be avoided. Christians can disobey their government when coerced to take part in a war they believe is unjust. They must remain skeptical toward the state and be ready to warn it against transgression of its legitimate limits.

THE IDOLATRY OF POLITICS

Unlike modern political realists, Augustine does not lower politics by separating it from ethics, but rather implies that politics is limited and circumscribed. Politics is incapable of completely satisfying the human longing for happiness, and it is unable to rescue individuals from the miseries of the present life. Political ideas can fail utterly when societies are driven into turmoil, while individual human beings who in times of crisis turn to God can succeed in preserving their own integrity. True happiness is to be found in salvation that does not come from this world. Therefore people should seek God first. This priority limits politics. To look for salvation and the resolution of all human problems through politics, and consequently to assign politics the highest place in human life, is precisely what political idolatry means. To substitute the state for God is to idolize the state. A politics that does not confine itself to matters within its own competency is a politics that rivals the divine. A perverted attempt to imitate God results from human pride.

The way to salvation is constructed not by impious pride, by which humans reject God, but by humility, by which they set their hearts on the Supreme (22.24). Augustine identifies the biblical Babel with the ancient Babylon. He uses the image of the towers of Babylon, intended to reach to the sky in their challenge to God, to illustrate the futility and self-annihilating character of all worldly achievements (16.4). Babylon symbolizes a great power, preeminent among all nations, driven by the idea of earthly peace. This city has its "lovers who look for peace in this world and hope for nothing beyond" (*Comm. on Ps. 136*). However, as long as human beings pursue their aims by themselves, separated from God, instead of seeking eternal peace, they only arrive at confusion. The language of those who built the towers was confused and they were dispersed all over the earth, leaving their constructions unfinished. Babylon, dominated by the lust for power, thus represents the ultimate confusion of humankind that lives according to human standards. The waters of Babylon symbolize all the earthly things that humankind has loved, but which have passed away. When we look at the ends to which humanity has devoted its life, forgetting about God as the true end, and which have all ultimately resulted in failures—for example, at false political dreams, futile ideologies, and utopian designs—we can see the waters of Babylon flowing away. We should not enter these waters, Augustine warns. We should not enter into the mist of confusion. The trees growing by these waters are barren. They are indeed "watered by the waters of Babylon and bring forth no fruit" (*Comm. on Ps. 136*). At best, we can sit down by these turbulent waters, look at them, and weep, either for those who are being carried away by them, or for ourselves who have been brought captive to Babylon.

Rome is for Augustine a new Babylon, a great worldly power, which is not free from vices. He challenges the views of classical writers who idealized Rome. He notes that in *On the Republic*, Cicero presents a most vigorous argument on behalf of justice against injustice. While underestimating the human inclination to self-interest, Cicero defends the imperial rule of Rome as just on the grounds that servitude is in the interest of the conquered in cases where they were in a worse condition before subjugation (*City of God* 19.21). The same idea of Rome as a righteous empire can be found in Virgil's *Aeneid*. Throughout his epic, Virgil reiterates the ongoing mission of Rome to "beat the proud" and become a universal empire of peace and justice, leading history to its final destination, a new Age of Saturn in which there will be no more war. In the *City of God*, however, Augustine seeks to undermine these claims. To defeat the proud is God's prerogative and not Rome's (1.0). It is a mission that Rome has falsely claimed as its own. To invest a state with a task that belongs to God alone is, in Augustine's theological analysis, nothing less than idolatry (Richard Gamble 5). No nation can claim that it is morally superior to others and identify its political aspirations with some universal morality. The pride of powerful nations, convinced of the righteousness of their missionary impulse to extend the fruits of their own culture to others, and ready to build their empires through conquest, only proves to him the power of human self-deception. Wars, and the evils brought on by them, are rationalized as the manifestation of a dominant power's concern for the well-being of other peoples. The real history, however, is far more complicated than such a rationalization allows. Instead of glorifying the Roman Empire, Augustine demythologizes the history of Rome (19.24). The ancient Romans had never been as innocent as they thought themselves to be. They were positively ambitious and their virtues enabled them to arrive at their power. Yet, "they loved the glory of men rather than the glory of God" (5.14). As "the slaves of human glory," their ideas of righteousness and justice, like those of the Athenians or the Assyrians, or other nations that in the past exercised imperial rule, were but a moral facade for their expansionist political policy.

Augustine connects the rejection of God as the true end with the attempt to set up fabricated ends for human beings. To assert the priority of the Supreme is for him the only real defense that human beings may have to protect themselves against regimes that, by denying spiritual salvation and assigning primacy to politics, attempt to enforce complete control over the individual.

THE *CITY OF GOD* AND TRADITION

Few thinkers have had such a great influence upon posterity as Saint Augustine. For more than eleven centuries after his death, the *City of God* provided intellectual and spiritual sustenance to the West. The importance of his fundamental work was accentuated by the contingencies of history. The *City of God* was inspired by the sack of Rome in 410. The fifth century witnessed the collapse of the remaining structure of the Roman Empire in the West. The ravages of the barbarian invaders engulfed Europe in almost half a millennium of devastation. Yet ultimately, the conversion of the pagan successor kingdoms to Catholic Christianity and their gradual withdrawal from Byzantium's sphere of influence resulted in the conception of Western Europe as a unified Christian state or Christendom, as it came to be called in the ninth century (Morrall 22). The irruption of the Muslims into the Latin West also served to strengthen its sense of religious and cultural unity. When, from the ruins of the ancient world, the pioneering architects of western Christendom began their task of reconstruction, "the monumental *City of God* shone to them across the intervening dark abyss somewhat after the manner of the proverbial city upon the mountain" (Ferrari 340). From the *City of God* grew the idea of universal papal authority, which culminated in the omnipotent papacy of medieval Europe. Later, when the thinkers and writers of the Reformation set forth their remedies for all they thought wrong with medieval Christendom, they were no less guided by Augustine's masterpiece.

Augustine was a theologian rather than a systematic political writer. He wrote so much and so diffusely that he became a source of misunderstandings and great controversies. The bitter struggles of the Reformation and Counter-Reformation, producing a number of wars, were largely disputes over different interpretations of Augustine. Under his influence, Luther and other reformers of the Church criticized medieval Catholicism for too much emphasis on the human efforts to overcome sin and too little on the role of divine grace. They regarded humans as so helpless and corrupted that they were willing to grant unqualified power to the state, and to accept all governments as legitimate. On the other hand, Catholic writers, in their emphasis on human perfectibility through faith and the moral value of good conduct, developed moralistic illusions about human beings. Focusing on the love of God and one's neighbor, they failed to account for the persistence of human self-love.

As a political thinker, Augustine himself supported neither the idea of total human depravity nor a moralistic simplicity. He believed that limited improvement of society was achievable, but also warned about possible problems. He saw potential dangers in both the persistent egoism of citizens and the selfishness of rulers. He was convinced that the demoralizing effects of original sin would persist as long the world lasted (Burnell 188). He thought that norms regulating political life were essential, but he did not think that they would always be obeyed. Thus, despite the defects and inconsistencies that gave rise to the widely differing views that have been justified under his name, he has proven himself to be a reliable guide to the complexity of this world (Niebuhr, 1995, 133). He stands between cynical political realism and naive idealism. To those thinkers who attempt to construct a vision of an ideal political union on the basis of reason alone, he offers a warning that without God, humanity cannot save itself, and human beings cannot be truly happy. He reminds us of the true end of human beings.

QUESTIONS

- In the "Funeral Oration," Pericles referred to democracy, equality before the law, tolerance, beauty, and wisdom as the basic values on which the Athenian civilization was based. What would Augustine find missing in Pericles' famous speech? Under which conditions could the Athens of Pericles be a city worthy of admiration for Augustine?
- Why are ancient virtues for Augustine vices rather than virtues? Does his critique apply to all virtues? Does it make sense today?
- What is justice for Augustine? What are international relations like without justice according to his political theory?
- Is the United States or Canada an earthly city or the City of God? Give reasons and explain the difference between the two cities.
- In what way can a City of God cooperate with an earthly city? Is there any limit to their cooperation?
- What do "Babylon" and "waters of Babylon" symbolize? Can we find equivalents of these symbols in modern politics?
- How would human life look if there was no God? Does the existence of God make any difference?
- What is the idolatry of politics? Is it possible to have politics that is not idolatrous?

GUIDE TO FURTHER READING

Translations of St. Augustine's Political Works:

Augustine. *The City of God*. Trans. Henry Bettenson. London: Penguin, 1984.

Augustine. *Expositions on the Psalms* (vol. 6). Trans. Maria Boulding. New York: New City Press, 2004. Contains the "Commentary on the Psalm 136" cited above.

Augustine. *Political Writings*. Ed. Ernest L. Fortin and Douglas Kries. Indianapolis: Hackett, 1994. Contains fragments of *The City of God* and a selection of letters and other works including the "Letter 138 to Marcellinus" and "Against Faustus the Manichaean XII" cited above.

Suggested Readings:

Bathory, P. D. *Political Theory as Public Confession: The Social and Political Thought of Augustine of Hippo*. New Brunswick, NJ: Transaction Books, 1981.

Chadwick, Henry. *Augustine*. Oxford: Oxford UP, 1986.

Donnely, Dorothy F., ed. *The City of God: A Collection of Critical Essays*. New York: Peter Lang, 1995.

Fortin, Ernest L. *Political Idealism and Christianity in the Thought of St. Augustine*. Villanova, PA: Villanova UP, 1971

Gilson, Etienne. *The Spirit of Medieval Philosophy*. Trans. A. H. C. Downes. New York: Charles Scribner's Sons, 1940.

Morrall, John B. *Political Thought in Medieval Times*. Toronto: U of Toronto P, 1980.

Schall, James V. (1984). *The Politics of Heaven and Hell: Christian Themes from Classical, Medieval and Modern Political Philosophy*. Lanham, MD: UP of America, 1984.

St. Thomas Aquinas: Faith and Social Solidarity

S aint Thomas Aquinas, a thirteenth century Dominican friar, theologian, and philosopher, was born in Roccasecca in 1224 (or at the beginning of 1225). He was the seventh and the youngest son of Landulf, Count of Aquino, and Theodora, Countess of Teano. At the age of five Thomas was placed in the Benedictine monastery at Monte Cassino for elementary and religious schooling. He remained there until 1239, when he enrolled at the University of Naples (founded in 1224 by Emperor Frederick II) to study liberal arts. There, he was first exposed to the newly rediscovered physical and metaphysical works of Aristotle, and also came into contact with members of the Dominican order, the Order of Friars Preachers.

The Dominicans were a religious order that made devotion to study one of their main objectives. They opened schools at the emerging universities in Western Europe to promote studies in philosophy and theology, and at the same time engaged in their mission of evangelization through preaching. At the age of nineteen, Thomas decided to join the order. His noble parents were not pleased with his choice, primarily due to the friars' extreme poverty and itinerant lifestyle. When his mother set out for Naples in order to retrieve Brother Thomas from the clutches of the Dominicans, the friars sent him to Rome. On the way there, however, he was captured by his brothers, who were soldiers under the Emperor Frederick. He was taken to a family castle at Roccasecca and imprisoned for a year, during which time his mother, sisters, and brothers tried to dissuade him from becoming a Dominican.

While imprisoned, Thomas continued his studies, and when finally released, he professed his vows in the Order of Friars Preachers. At the age of twenty, he was sent first to Paris and then to Cologne, where he was placed under the instruction of the scholastic philosopher Saint Albert the Great. Because of his large stature and quiet nature, his fellows at first called him a "dumb ox," but when Saint Albert heard him in disputation, he prophetically declared: "The bellowing of this ox will one day be heard throughout the world." In 1248 he obtained a bachelor's degree, and at the age of twenty-five he was ordained to the priesthood.

In 1252, the master general of the Order sent Thomas Aquinas to fill the office of bachelor (instructor) in a Dominican college in Paris. His teaching and discussions of theological topics soon attracted the attention of both professors and students. His duties consisted principally in explaining the *Sentences* of Peter Lombard—a compilation of the opinions of the Fathers and the teachers of the Catholic Church, which was used as a standard theology textbook for more than two centuries. Over the next few years he composed his *Scriptum Super Sententiis* (*Commentary on the Sentences*), which was completed in 1256 and prepared the way for his main theological work, the *Summa Theologiae* (*The Summa of Theology*), a masterpiece of medieval scholasticism, which he began in 1266.

The years from 1257 to 1273 comprised Thomas Aquinas' most prolific period of writing, teaching, and preaching. He is said to have been able to dictate several different treatises to various scribes at the same time. He received a master's degree in theology at the University of Paris, became a professor, organized many seminars and academic debates, and produced over one hundred works, including philosophical essays, theological treatises, and commentaries on a range of works from Aristotle to the Bible. Moreover, he became an advisor to popes Alexander IV and Urban IV, and taught theology at pontifical residences in Anagni, Orvieto, and Viterbo. In 1264, while in Orvieto, he completed his *Summa contra Gentiles*, which was intended to serve as a guide to Christian missionaries. In 1265, he opened a new house of study in Rome, where he began his unfinished political work *De Regno* (*On Kingship*), also known as *De Regimine Principum* (*On the Governance of Princes*). However, in 1268, he went back to the University of Paris to help quell a controversy that had arisen there regarding the use of Aristotle by Christian scholars. Following the argument of the Muslim philosopher Averroës, Siger of Brabant, a professor on the Faculty of Arts, was asserting that Aristotle had proven that there was one common intellect for all human beings and that the world was not created but eternal. Concerned with the threat to the Christian faith posed by such propositions, Aquinas wrote *On the Unity of the Intellect against the Averroists* and *On the Eternity of the World*, arguing that they could not be supported by reason. In 1272, he went to the University of Naples, where he was appointed head of the Faculty of Theology.

On December 6, 1273, Thomas Aquinas laid aside his pen, as a consequence of a mystical vision he had experienced. "Such secrets were revealed to me," he later reported, "that what I have written seems but straw" (Parkes 255). He started to prepare for death. Called to the Council of Lyons by Pope Gregory X in February 1274, he traveled as far as Terracina in Central Italy, and then collapsed. He was taken to the Cistercian Monastery of Fossa Nuova, where he died on March 7, 1274, at the age of fifty. He was canonized by Pope John XXII on July 18, 1323. Pope Saint Pius V proclaimed him a doctor of the

Church in 1567, and over three centuries later, in 1879, Pope Leo XIII, in the Encyclical *Aeterni Patris* recommended Thomism as the model and norm of Christian philosophy, the culmination of a long series of pontifical commendations of Thomas Aquinas. Considered a master voice of the golden age of scholastic thought, his teachings have also attained the status of an official doctrine of the Catholic Church in modern times.

THE GOLDEN AGE OF SCHOLASTICISM

The period extending from the beginning of Christian theological and philosophical speculations to the time of Saint Augustine is known as the Patristic era. In general, the era was inclined toward Platonism, placing a lesser value on the ideas of Aristotle. It was marked by the advancing disintegration of ancient society and culture, and ended with the fall of the western part of the Roman Empire and the decline of scholarship in the Latin world. After Boetius (ca. 480–524), often described as the last of the Roman philosophers and the first of the scholastic, philosophy lay dormant until the king of the Franks and Lombards, Charlemagne, was crowned emperor by Pope Leo III in 800 and decided that the expansion of his realm should be paralleled by a revival of learning.

With the Carolingian revival began a period of educational activity that resulted in a new era of Christian thought known as Scholasticism. Charlemagne's greatest contribution to the advancement of knowledge was the establishment of schools. In a famous declaration, the Emperor of Rome and the West proclaimed: "In every bishop's see, in every monastery, instructions should be given in the psalms, musical notation, chant, the computation of years and seasons, and in grammar" (Knowles 72). The curriculum of the new schools, which were founded by palaces, cathedrals, and monasteries, was modest by today's standards. Besides the Bible and the writings of the Church fathers, students studied the liberal arts, which were divided into two courses: the *Trivium*, embracing grammar, dialectic, and rhetoric, and the *Quadrivium*, comprising arithmetic, geometry, astronomy, and music. From the eleventh century on, dialectic or logic, which at that time was the only branch of philosophy studied systematically, became a central subject and exercised considerable influence on theology. It was usually taught by the master of the school. Great emphasis was laid on dialectical and critical reasoning. Theses, objections, and answers to objections were usually presented in the discussion of a given problem. The word *scholasticism* is derived from the manner of instruction that grew out of the curriculum of the medieval schools, specifically, from the dialectical method used by their masters (*scholastici*).

Although the revival of learning continued, particularly in schools at Benedictine monasteries, wars and the decline of the Carolingian dynasty were not conductive to the further development of Charlemagne's educational vision. After John Scott Eriugena (ca. 810–877), the first of the major scholastics, no significant philosopher or theologian was to appear until Anselm of Canterbury

(1033–1109), known for his ontological argument regarding the existence of God. In the eleventh and twelfth centuries, the major philosophical problem was the problem of universals: whether genera and species exist only in the mind or in reality. This seemingly abstract problem led to a revitalization of philosophy. The twelfth century witnessed the rise of Peter Abailard and other advocates of reason, who contributed to both the discussion of the problem of universals and the development of the scholastic method, and insisted that any thesis should be reasonably examined. Their ideas triumphed in the cathedral and monastic schools, but brought a reaction from Bernard of Clairvaux and other champions of mysticism, who expressed a reverence for the mysteries of faith and condemned the potential abuse of reason. There was also the school of Charles, a great center of Platonic studies, whose members tried to give to the Scholastic movement a broader spirit of toleration, and imparted a sort of humanism, so to speak, to Christian philosophy. The revival of learning and revitalization of philosophy, the introduction of Arab, Jewish, and Greek authors into the Christian schools, the growing availability of the works of Aristotle in Latin translation, and the rise of universities were the movements that finally led to the extraordinary intellectual activity of the thirteenth century, centered at the University of Paris, and regarded as the golden age of scholastic philosophy.

The turning point of the twelfth and thirteenth centuries falls within the period when the cathedral and monastic schools, with their curriculum of the seven liberal arts, were giving way to more diversified educational institutions: a *studium generale* (school of general studies) and a *universitas studiorum* (university). The life of Saint Thomas is contemporaneous with the rise of these new institutions. With their corporate privileges, fixed curricula, and formally certified levels of attainment, these corporations of professors and students had no exact ancient prototype, but made a vital impact on the subsequent development of Western culture. Although the Italian universities in Padua and Bologna were founded somewhat earlier, the University of Paris, which received its charter in 1200, at about the same time as the University of Oxford, became the intellectual center of Europe. Concurrent with the rise of the universities and the building of great cathedrals at this time was the rediscovery of Aristotle, whose many works, lost for many centuries, reached the West through Latin translations of Arabic texts and commentaries.

After the closure of the Academy in Athens by the Byzantine Emperor Justinian in 529 C.E., some ancient scholars had moved with the works of their masters, Plato and Aristotle, to Edessa in Syria, and from there to Persia and Egypt, establishing new centers of Greek scholarship. The works they brought with them were then translated, first into Syriac and later into Arabic. With the emergence of Islam in the seventh century, military conquests rapidly expanded the Muslim world from the deserts of Arabia to the borders of India in the east, and North Africa and Spain in the west. From the early eighth century on, most of Spain was under Islamic rule. The crusades to recover the Holy Land from the Muslims and the reconquest of Spain brought Christians in contact with Arab learning. A translation center was established in Toledo after it was recaptured in 1085 and became the Spanish capital.

The early translators of Arabic texts in Spain were interested almost exclusively in the natural sciences. In the course of the twelfth century, however, the metaphysical works of Aristotle became the center of translators' attention. The most famous of the Islamic Aristotelians in Spain was Ibn Rushid (1126–1198), also known as Averroës. Although his commentaries on Aristotle's works were tinged with what seemed to be theological errors, such as the denial of personal immortality and of the divine creation of the world, he gained faithful disciples among Jews and Christians. Because of his great influence, many translations of Aristotle's works from Arabic were in circulation at the emerging universities. Aristotle became "the Philosopher" and Averroës his "Commentator."

Thus, the works of Aristotle initially became available in Latin translations from Arabic, and often contained commentaries by Muslim philosophers. This new philosophical literature had far-reaching consequences for intellectual life. The Christian world was suddenly presented with a system of thought that was intellectually stimulating and rationally persuasive, but in some of its doctrines directly antithetical to Christian revelation. The reacquaintance with Aristotle reached its first critical point in 1210, when a group of bishops met in Paris and prohibited instruction on Aristotle's scientific works. Subsequent prohibitions came in 1215 and 1231. Nevertheless, the advance of Aristotelianism was not to be halted in that manner. The secular Aristotelians, delimiting in the Scholastic fashion the respective domains of faith and reason, pursued philosophical studies without regard to Christian teachings, and from the 1240s on, the prohibitions seemed to be forgotten. Aristotelian studies flowered at Paris and Oxford. New translations made from the original Greek texts obtained after the Latin conquest of Constantinople in 1204 revealed an Aristotle free from the theological errors attributed to him by Averroës.

Above all, however, it was Saint Thomas who made a vital contribution to the reception of Aristotle, by harmonizing Christian faith and Aristotelian thought. He responded to the challenge that was posed to medieval Christianity by the rediscovery of Aristotle's works. He argued that although there was a distinction between theology and philosophy, there could not be a fundamental disagreement between them. His conviction that it was impossible that what was true in philosophy could be false in theology contradicted the theory of two-fold truth of Averroës, namely, that the truth knowable by natural reason and the revealed truth could be different. Under Thomas Aquinas' influence, the Church moved away from the Platonism of the Fathers and turned to the Aristotelian tradition. Still, Thomism did not immediately win official approval. In the condemnation in 1277 of 319 propositions derived from Aristotle, not only Averroist propositions were condemned but also three Thomistic propositions. As far as political philosophy is concerned, the accurate translation of Aristotle's *Politics* and *Nicomachean Ethics* from the original Greek texts by Thomas Aquinas' Dominican colleague, William of Moerbecke, was crucial. It marked a new beginning for systematic and rational reflection on political ideas. The thirteenth century saw the emergence of the works of Thomas Aquinas, who moderated the pessimism of Augustine with an element of optimism streaming from both Christian revelation and the Aristotelian view of politics.

CHRISTIANITY AND SOCIAL THEORY

It would be artificial to treat Saint Thomas Aquinas' political philosophy as a field of study separate from theology. There was no tension between secular and spiritual issues in his mind. He was first of all a theologian, carrying out his studies in the service of God and the Church, and guided by the medieval ideal of a unified Christian society. Apart from the nineteen brief chapters of his major political work, *On Kingship*, and his commentaries on the *Nicomachean Ethics* and the *Politics* of Aristotle, he did not write at length on politics. His political ideas have to be extracted from a number of theological writings, and particularly from his monumental *Summa of Theology*. These ideas, however, when put together, give us a social and political theory that represents the most balanced presentation of the medieval political tradition following the Aristotelian revival (Morrall 72). Aquinas carries out an impressive synthesis of Aristotelian philosophy and Christian faith, and develops a central theme that is common to both Aristotelianism and Christianity, namely, that of rationality and the purposive order of nature. However, his synthesis involves more than a Christian version of Aristotelianism. He incorporates into it Neoplatonic ideas of the hierarchical structure of the universe, Roman legal thought, and the Stoic conception of natural law. Moreover, he relates his political vision to concepts unknown by Aristotle and introduced by Christianity, such as the idea of the human person, whose eternal goal transcends the purpose of the state, and of God's providence, the "order of things towards an end" (*Summa Theologiae* I, q. 22, a. 2).

To understand Aquinas' vision, it is important to grasp the centrality of the concept of hierarchy in it. For Saint Thomas, the universe was brought into being to manifest God's perfection. Since divine perfection cannot be represented by a single creature alone, the world consists of many and diverse creatures, and is marked by distinctions and inequalities. It is hierarchic, starting at the top with rational creatures and descending through irrational animals and inanimate plants to minerals, inorganic substances, and simple elements (I, q. 47, a. 2). Every creature is intended to acquire its own perfection or fulfillment, which is the likeness of divine perfection and goodness (I, q. 44, a. 4). Because of the various forms of their existence, in all created entities there is some similarity to God, who is the perfect existence. However, in the rational creature, the human being, this is not merely a likeness in the form of a trace, but a likeness in the form of an image (I, q. 93, a. 6).

In Aquinas' view of the fall, reason—the image of God impressed on the human mind—was vitiated but not destroyed by original sin. God made man righteous. This rectitude consisted in human reason being subject to God, lower powers being subject to reason, and the body being subject to the soul. In the state of innocence, the human being possessed all virtues (I, q. 95, a. 1, 4). The original sin resulted in the loss of grace and the erosion of the original order whereby the lower powers were subjected to reason. Through the mission of Christ and of the Holy Ghost, grace has been restored. Grace does not destroy nature but perfects it (I, q. 1, a. 8). Its effects consist in the illumination of the intellect and the kindling of love and affection. It joins human beings to the highest good, which is God. Hence, although prone to error, human beings are capable of searching for truth and practicing virtue. Endowed with intellect and free will, they are not merely made more like God than any other creature in the universe, but they exist to imitate God's image, in a movement leading them to perfection (I, q. 35, a. 2).

Aquinas draws a sharp distinction between the rational nature of human beings and the sub-rational nature of animals, plants, and the rest of nature. All beings are governed by God's providence and in some way participate in it by moving toward perfection and goodness (I-II, q. 16, a. 4). However, since humans, as rational creatures, have through their free will control over their actions, they are subject to divine providence in a more profound way than other beings (I-II, q. 91, a. 2). They are not mere parts of creation, indistinguishable from the rest; they control it and take care of it. Through their liberty and intelligence, they are principal agents in the fulfillment of the end of the universe. They have a natural aptitude for the cultivation and development of their faculties, and for understanding and loving God (I, q. 93, a. 2). As masters of their own actions, they are not merely moved, but can move themselves to the final end, that is, to God and perfection. This leads them to occupy a special place in the created world. In Aquinas' view, it is a uniquely human prerogative to be "persons," subsistent individuals of a rational nature (I, q. 29, a. 3). Furthermore, human personality implies dignity. All humans, being rational and thus the most excellent things in all nature, possess a peculiar dignity of their own (III, q. 2, a. 2). This dignity consists specifically in humans being autonomous and existing for their own sake, and not as means for something else. By striving toward a supernatural end—understanding and loving God—they are elevated to their highest dignity.

The belief in the inherent dignity of the human person, which can be traced to the writings of Aquinas, is the foundation of Catholic social teaching. It is the starting point for a moral vision of society. Such a vision resists any attempt by political programs or social movements to treat humans merely as means to an end. It points to the attainment of divine likeness as the end of human life, which transcends the goals of a state. It regards each individual human being as something unique, for which no substitute can be conceived.

For Aquinas, human beings are not only rational, and therefore capable of self-perfection and assimilation to God, but also social. Following Aristotle, he claims that living in society is necessary for them to obtain all that is required for their livelihood and to develop their personalities (*De Reg. Prin.* I, 1, 4–7). Individuals can achieve perfection not only in regard to their own individual selves but also in regard to the whole community in which they live (*Summa Theologiae* III, q. 65, a. 1). Therefore, they ought to participate in society, assisted in life by the fellowship of others and aiming at the common good

(II-II, q. 58, a. 9). The Christian obligation to "love God and one's neighbor" has an individual dimension, but it also implies a broader social commitment. Whatever their social or economic differences, human beings need to understand the value of social solidarity. They must try to contribute to the well-being of each individual, as well as to that of all members of society.

PRIVATE PROPERTY AND POVERTY

Aquinas' social and political theory is a part of his wider vision of human nature and the true end of human life. The essential nature of human beings is what is proper to them as humans (II-I, q. 94, a. 3). It signifies their perfection or fulfillment. Since intellect and free will are the most essential marks that distinguish human beings from other animals, humans are by nature rational and free. They are free in that they exist for their own sake and have free choice by which they can direct themselves to their final end (I, q. 83, a. 1). They are free insofar as they are rational. Whatever is contrary to the order of reason is contrary to human nature (II-I, q. 71, a. 2). Through activities that are both rational and free, humans can to some degree attain fulfillment of their potentialities. Yet, only by contemplating truth can they fully satisfy their human potential (*Contra Gentiles* III, 37). In contrast to activities that do not transcend the limits of this life, Aquinas claims the contemplation of truth—the preeminent human activity—begins in this life, but is consummated in the life to come (III, 63). Our true happiness consists in this perfect activity of the intellect, which is proper only to humans, and fulfils them (*Summa Theologiae* I-II, q. 55, a. 2). An imperfect happiness obtained during this life is called *felicity*; the ultimate and perfect happiness, attained after this life as a vision of God, is *beatitude*.

The contemplation of truth, which ultimately consists in reflection on God and divine things, is for Aquinas the supreme activity and the end to which all other human activities ought to be ordered. It demands freedom from both internal disturbances caused by passions and external disturbances caused by misgovernment of public affairs. It requires that bodily needs be fulfilled (*Contra Gentiles* III, 37). External goods are needed insofar as they are conducive to the end that transcends the use of material things. Riches, bodily well-being, and sensory pleasures are not the ultimate end of human life; they should serve only as an instrument to happiness (*Summa Theologiae* I-II, q. 4, a. 7).

Since in a right order of things, lower elements in nature are subjected to higher ones, humans have a natural *dominium* over the use of material things for their own benefit (II-II, q. 66, a. 1). External goods have been given for the use of all humankind. Therefore, regarding the use of material things, Aquinas thinks that property is natural to human beings. It is justified by the end of human life and is thus a part of natural law. However, the institution of property does not imply any particular form that it may assume in different ages or regions. The justification for private ownership is not found in the natural conditions of humankind, but in specific social conditions of a developed society.

Aquinas argues that private property can best serve the purpose of satisfying human needs for three reasons: first, human beings generally take more trouble to care for things they privately own than for things that are held in common or by many; second, human economic affairs can be more efficiently organized in private hands; and third, when people are content with their own private tasks, they tend to live more peacefully than they do when holding things in common (II-II, q. 66, a. 2). Still, the right to use external goods is grounded in the essential purpose of the human being, and therefore takes precedence over the right of private ownership that is derived from the power to care for them.

Aquinas recognizes that the world's resources are not unlimited. It is impossible, he says, for one individual (or state) to enjoy an overabundance of goods without someone else suffering want (II-II, q. 118, a. 1). States may enact laws justifying a surplus of wealth on the part of one individual, but there is no such justification in natural law, except when such wealth is put to social or philanthropic use. Therefore, to the extent that private possessions exist in excess of the needs of the owner, they should be distributed to serve the needs of others. "Whatever certain individuals have in superabundance," Aquinas claims, "ought to be used to the purpose of helping the poor" (II-II, q. 66, a. 7). But since the poor are many and they cannot be supported from one source alone, the decision should in the end be left to wealthy individuals as to how to manage their property so as to support those in need (Ibid.). Thomas Aquinas thus attempts to balance the right of private ownership with the right of the use of external goods for the benefit of all. Still, because the latter has precedence over the former, in a situation of hunger and extreme scarcity, where people are in immediate danger and cannot be helped in any other way, everything becomes common property. "It is not a sin for someone to take property of another that has become a common property by necessity" (Ibid.). Consequently, Aquinas contends that the division and appropriation of property under the authority of human-made laws does not prevent its being used by those who are in need in times of scarcity. Private owners have freedom to acquire and exchange property and make a profit, but when the common welfare is at stake, their property must be regulated in the interest of the whole community.

According to Saint Thomas, the surplus of wealth that is accumulated as profit is not in itself inevitable or necessary, nor does it confer any particular dignity. Neither is such wealth, however, inherently vicious or contrary to nature (II-II, q. 77, a. 4). It can be directed to a necessary or honorable goal, and in this way, becomes socially and morally justified. Profit must be governed by the principle of the primacy of social use over superfluities. Hence, business conducted for profit that is used for the support of one's family, or for helping the poor, or for any other socially beneficial purpose is licit (Ibid.). In private ownership there also lies the guarantee, not only of greater security regarding the material conditions of existence but also of greater personal freedom. "That is free which is its own master" (I, q. 21, a. 1). Whoever has no property and depends exclusively on daily wages can all too easily become a tool in hands of others. This implies a normative obligation to organize a given society in such a way as to make possible for everyone to acquire the minimum amount of private property necessary for a stable and secure existence. The pursuit of wealth that is not motivated by greed for money that would eclipse the final end of human beings, but is regarded as a just reward for honest labor, is thus socially beneficial and legitimate.

Nevertheless, Aquinas admits that the acquisition of external goods, especially in the form of money, can cease to be a means and can become an end to be enjoyed in itself. Someone who has made wealth his goal may come to desire wealth without limit, rather than merely the limited amount of wealth necessary to support life (I-II, q. 30, a. 4). In other words, an avaricious person may desire to be as rich as he or she possibly can be. By transforming the means into an end and thus reversing the right order of things, avarice dehumanizes the human being. When the accumulation of property becomes the end of human existence, an erosion of the moral and social order occurs. Hence, issues regarding private property and the surplus of wealth have to be regulated in the interest of society as a whole. Inequalities in wealth and private possessions, Aquinas argues, are a dangerous source of social disorder (I-II, q. 105, a. 2). The moral obligation to share a surplus of wealth with those in need should be reinforced by a legal obligation imposed by civil authority.

THE ORIGIN, PURPOSE, AND LIMITS OF AUTHORITY

According to social contract theory, which was developed in the eighteenth century by Hobbes and Locke and became one of the foundations of modern thinking about politics, human beings are not social by nature, but exist naturally as isolated individuals. Society arises through a pact known as a *social contract,* by which individuals agree to come together in a political community. The social contract, which represents a secular and human ordering of society, is held to be the origin of civil authority. In contrast, Thomas Aquinas holds that society and authority have divine origins rather than secular. The theory that the people are the ultimate source of authority in the state is for him incorrect. Following Aristotle, he develops a theory of authority postulated on the social nature of human beings, but that takes also the divine into account.

Aquinas believes that God created humans to live in communities (*De Reg. Prin.* I, 1, 4). No individual can adequately provide for himself on his own. Individual human beings are linked by the obligation to love one another and to practice social solidarity. Only by living in society can they survive and develop their potential. Hence, even though the actual historical forms of different communities may be the products of cultures of human origin, their initial impulse comes from nature and hence from God. God is thus the foundation of society. Consequently, Saint Thomas departs from the Augustinian tradition of regarding political authority as merely coercive. Subjection is of two kinds, he argues (*Summa Theologiae* I, q. 92, a. 1). There is subjection of the slave, in which masters use people subject to them for their own benefit; this kind of vicious subjection is the result of sin. Then, there is subjection of the citizen, in which leaders guide people to what is beneficial or good for them. In the state of innocence, a human being would not execute rule over another in the first sense. But even in the state of innocence, Aquinas claims, there would necessarily have been inequalities: inequality of knowledge, bodily disparity, and differences of sex and age (I, q. 96, a. 4), and some individuals would have been better qualified than others to be leaders. Thus, in its original and primary sense, authority implies leadership rather than coercion. Authority in society would exist even if human beings had never sinned.

Further, since any society requires authority, then it follows that the concept of civil authority has its origin in God (*De Reg. Prin.* I, 1, 8). This does not mean, however, that those who are actually in authority receive their powers and faculties immediately from God (the so-called "divine right" theory that was developed by James I and other early modern advocates of absolutism), but rather that the very existence of authority derives from God's disposition of things, that is, from the norm of natural law. The consequence of Aquinas having associated authority with divine creation rather than with original sin is that politics is vindicated in Catholic thought. Political community is no longer identified merely with the earthly city of Augustine, the place of sin, but becomes a value in its own right. The way is thus open to the improvement of social conditions and to political leadership whose chief aim is to promote the common good.

The distinction between right and wrong exists in politics. For Aquinas, to govern is to lead a thing to an end (*Summa Theologiae* I, q. 103, a. 1). Endowed with free will, individuals are essentially free to shape their own lives, yet they must be directed. Without the right direction, any group activity can eventually degenerate into the irrational impulse of a mob, operating blindly and moving by impulse. A thing is rightly directed when it is led toward a proper end, and wrongly when it is led toward an unbefitting end (*De Reg. Prin.* I, 1, 10). Any direction to a proper end must take into account the nature of the being so directed; otherwise, violence is done to it. This is presupposed by the perfect model of authority, divine providence, which guides each creature to its end according to its nature (Rzadkiewicz 114). Since the common good, which the human being could not enjoy through individual effort, is the social end of each individual person living in political society, the purpose of civil authority is to lead members of society to this end. The ultimate reason for the existence of government is thus direction to the common good. The government that guides citizens to the common good is right, just, and suitable for free individuals (*De Reg. Prin.* I, 1, 10). If, however, a government aims not at the common good but at a private good of the ruler or a ruling faction, Aquinas argues that it is unjust and perverted (Ibid.). The exercise of authority is thus based on a moral order and is regulated by natural law. It has a form of justice that it must observe and cannot be arbitrary. If it deviates from the common good, it constitutes an abuse of power.

The power of authority is not absolute because society is not an end in itself. In the human personality there lies the guarantee of human liberty.

While forming a community, human persons are at the same time above it by virtue of their ordination to the final end of life that transcends any goal of social life. Therefore, the demands of society cannot consume an individual's entire scope of activity. Freedom to pursue activities related to personal self-perfection must also be allowed. This prohibits the total absorption of the individual by the state, and limits the power of authority (*Summa Theologiae* I-II, q. 21, a. 4). A government that infringes on citizens' essential liberties under the guise of promoting the common welfare is transgressing its proper limits. Consequently, although obedience is due to superiors within the sphere of their authority, such obedience is not unlimited. The individual is obliged to obey government in things that have to be done externally, by means of the body, but not in matters that refer either to the nature of the body or to the soul, which retains its liberty (II-II, q. 104, a. 5). The citizens are thus free to decide whom they wish to marry, how they wish to support themselves, and how they should raise their children. In the matter of forming and holding opinions, they are obliged to obey God alone. Moreover, obedience to government extends only so far as is required by justice (II-II, q. 104, a. 5). If the authority is usurped rather than legitimate, or if it commands what is unjust, the citizens are not bound to obey it, except in cases where it would be expedient, for instance, to avoid scandal or reprisal.

MONARCHY AND THE MIXED CONSTITUTION

Because all human beings have the same rational nature, an essential equality exists among them. This means that they all have equal worth and dignity, on which solidarity and basic rights common to all are founded (II-II, q. 104, a. 5). This essential equality of human persons does not, however, mean that accidental inequalities and functional differences between them do not exist at the same time. There are for Aquinas some areas of social and political life that pertain to everyone, but there are other areas that require a distribution of different functions, and a diversity of missions and activities. A good political order would be lacking, he believes, "if some [individuals] were not governed by others wiser than themselves" (I, q. 92, a. 1).

What distinguishes one political community from another is its form of government. The question of the best regime or the best constitution thus emerges as the central theme of political philosophy. Aquinas approaches this question through examining the three basic forms of government, which he designates as monarchy, aristocracy, and democracy. The greatest political evil for him is partisan strife and the division of society through party dissension. Private concerns divide the community. The dissension that results from the division of society into rival political parties works against social peace. When there are too many individuals or groups involved in the government, it is likely that some of them will fail to be concerned with the common good. Without a single controlling force, a body politic can easily disintegrate.

A single individual can advance political unity and promote virtue better than a plurality can do it (*De Reg. Prin.* I, 2, 17–18). Therefore, in his earlier and unfinished work *On Kingship*, Aquinas considers monarchy in the form of kingship, the government of one person for the common good, as the best constitution. He compares it to the divine rule of the universe. "The king should recognize," Aquinas says, "that he has a duty to act in his kingdom like the soul in the body and God in the world" (I, 12). If kings acknowledge this, they will then observe justice. By showing that they are genuinely devoted to the cause of the common good, they will gain the love and support of the multitude (I, 7, 78–79). In this way, a monarchic government will be stable and long-lasting.

Yet, despite its excellence, the unconditional rule of one virtuous individual also poses to Aquinas the danger that it may degenerate into a tyranny. Just as a united force serving the good is more effective than a force that is scattered or divided, so also a single force operating for evil is more harmful (I, 3, 23). In contrast to kingship, which is the best regime, tyranny, the rule of one who governs society unjustly by seeking private benefit at the detriment of the common advantage, is the worst. The more a tyrant departs from the common good, the more injustice and harm he or she can bring about. Tyrants do not merely oppress their subjects in corporal things; they also hinder their spiritual growth (I, 3, 26). They are more suspicious of the good than of the wicked, and are always afraid of virtue. They promote dissension, and prohibit gatherings that foster mutual trust among human beings. They seek to prevent their subjects from becoming virtuous and developing a public-spiritedness that would not tolerate their unjust domination (I, 3, 27). Aquinas acknowledges that tyranny is more likely to develop from the rule of the many than from the rule of one person (I, 5, 37–39). Further, he believes that tyranny resulting from the corruption of kingship may be a lesser evil than that arising from the corruption of democracy. Nevertheless, in his later discussion of the best regime in *Summa Theologiae*, Aquinas gives priority to the mixed constitution rather than monarchy.

While discussing the mixed form of government in the *Summa*, Aquinas departs from both the Aristotelian and the Roman traditions. In relation to polity or the mixed constitution, a concept he introduced in the *Politics*, Aristotle's main concern was to balance the potentially conflicting interests of the different social classes, represented paradigmatically by the reduction of society into the rich and the poor. He emphasized the desirability of mixing the elements of oligarchy and democracy, which he identified with the dominant values of wealth and freedom, respectively. Unlike Aristotle, Aquinas does not include the oligarchic element in his model of the mixed regime. He is not interested in balancing conflicting interests, but rather in promoting virtues associated with different social groups against their corresponding vices. He considers monarchy, aristocracy, and democracy as being the parts of the mixture (*Summa Theologiae* I-II, q. 105, a. 1). Further, in contrast to Cicero and other advocates of Roman republicanism, Aquinas gives separate political institutions to only the monarchic and aristocratic parts of society. He does not envision anything like the Roman institutions of tribunes and popular assemblies. His fear of anarchy and tyranny, both of which he associates with an excess of democracy, leads him to allow only a limited role to the democratic part of society (Kayser, Lettieri 210). He restricts this role to the opportunity to vote in wide-based popular elections and participate in government through elected representatives. Thus, while minimizing the influence of other groups in society, Aquinas elevates the importance of its monarchic and aristocratic elements, which he associates with virtue.

The critique of the Roman republican tradition is expressed in Aquinas' dismissal of Rome as the actual ideal republic. He believes that history shows us the ideal of the mixed constitution in the divinely ordained regime of the ancient Hebrews. This regime satisfies his criteria for the best mixture in having both a wide popular basis and a ruling element composed of a blend of monarchy and aristocracy. To begin with the latter, by governing the people "as sole rulers over all," Moses and his successors represented a monarchic element (*Summa Theologiae* I, q. 105, a. 1). But under God's dictates, this monarchical element was supplied with an aristocratic element, the seventy-two "elders in virtue." The democratic element was present due to the elders, the "wise and honorable men," being selected from among all of the people. In such a manner, Aquinas presents the classical idea of the best regime within a new framework. He replaces the ideal of the Roman Republic with an ideal mixed regime sanctioned by Scripture. Aquinas' mixed constitution is no longer the embodiment of the individual wisdom of a single brilliant legislator, nor of the collective wisdom of a particular people. Instead, as the outcome of the divine will, it is in accordance with the divine plan for the universe and exists in a timeless dimension.

Aquinas argues that "all should have some share in the government" (Ibid.). The monarchic element, represented by "the one who is given the power to preside over all," supplies the unity and wisdom that are necessary to all regimes (Kayser, Lettieri 216). The aristocratic element, present in the regime "insofar as a number of persons are set in authority," provides the enlightened counsel of prudent and honorable persons (*Summa Theologiae* I, q. 105, a. 1). The democratic element, which exists "insofar, as the rulers can be chosen from the people, and the people have the right to choose their rulers," contributes to social peace and helps to ensure the endurance of the regime (Ibid.). If they do not have a share in power, the people may not be sufficiently attached to the regime, and may become rebellious. This is no less true in the case of the government of one virtuous person for the sake of the common good than in the case of any other governmental form. Further, if not safeguarded through enlightened counsel and popular elections, the kingly rule of one individual, which gives unity to the state, can turn into tyranny. These considerations lead Aquinas to conclude that the mixed constitution, involving monarchic, aristocratic, and democratic elements, is the best actual regime.

It was through Aquinas' political writings that the ideas of the mixed constitution and citizen participation in government entered the medieval milieu. Through these ideas, he contributed to the development of the tradition of Western republicanism.

CHURCH AND STATE

The Church fathers handed down to the Middle Ages the concept of two authorities, spiritual and temporal, ecclesiastical and secular, coexisting in political society. Although this dualism was generally accepted, it led to many different conclusions about the position of the Church. In his writings Thomas Aquinas shows considerable detachment from contemporary events. However, he lived during times that were profoundly affected by disputes about the proper relationship between the ecclesiastical and secular authorities. The possible positions varied from *hierocracy*, the subjection of the state to the Church, to *ceasaropapism*, the subjection of the Church to the state; in both, the dualism of two autonomous authorities existing in society was rejected in favor of a unity based on the supremacy of either the ecclesiastical authority or the civil authority. Aquinas identified himself with neither of these extreme positions. But he also did not advocate a radical separation between Church and state along modern lines. The scope of the Church's activities was for him not merely individual private life, but rather the whole fabric of social, economic, and political relations. In his discussion of the relationship between the ecclesiastical and secular authorities, he achieves a remarkable balance that respects the precedence of the spiritual order without infringing on the autonomy of the temporal one (Fitzgerald 517).

In his early work *Commentary on the Sentences*, Aquinas already asserts a formal distinction between the ecclesiastical and secular authorities, both of which he derives independently and directly from God (*Scriptum* II, d. 44, q. 2, a. 3). Neither of these powers is absolute; rather, both are relative and limited by their proper areas of competence. In other early writings as well, he separates the spheres of Church and state, and is careful to safeguard the authority not only of the Pope but also of the civil power. In his *Commentary on the Epistle to the Hebrews* he says: "Just as the leader or ruler has chief authority in the city, so does the Pope in those things which pertain to God" (*Comm. Hebraeos* c. V, 1). Furthermore, by considering human beings as naturally social, he arrives at the idea of a natural dimension in political life that has a value in itself and is the proper domain of lay authority (*De Reg. Prin.* I, 1, 8). He thus contributes to the development of the concept of the secular state, which can be regarded as a major innovation of late medieval political thought. Nevertheless, the dualism of the two powers, which are autonomous in their own spheres and have distinct competencies and jurisdictions, is for Aquinas conditioned by another principle, namely, that of the superiority of the spiritual order. The end of civil government, the well-being of the political community, remains for him only a means to the final end. And the final end of Christian society is not merely a good life, but "through a life of virtue to attain the enjoyment of God" (*De Reg. Prin.* I, 14, 108). Since "the one to whom it pertains to achieve the final end commands those who execute the things that are ordered to that end," the ultimate moral authority belongs to the Pope, God's vicar, to whom all Christian rulers should be subjected, as to Christ himself (Ibid.). The Church holds complete authority in spiritual matters, but in temporal matters its power is restricted. It can interfere in them only insofar as the events occurring in the temporal sphere may in some way jeopardize the final end (*Summa Theologiae* II-II, q. 60, a. 6).

The separation between ecclesiastical and secular authorities, which is so clear in the writings of Thomas Aquinas, does not mean for him that Church and state should not cooperate. Their proper relation is not neutrality, but mutual support. Since the end of civil government is only a means to the final end, the separation between Church and state cannot be understood as the denial of a connection between Christian faith and the conduct of public affairs. Such a denial, grounded in the belief that religion is a merely private affair, would not be acceptable to Aquinas. For him, the need for religious pluralism would not be a justification strong enough to secularize a Christian society. The grace that comes with faith in Christ, he claims, does not eradicate human nature, but rather elevates and perfects it (I, q. 1, a. 8). It turns human beings toward their true end and the right order of things. Evil is the privation of limit and order. It indicates the absence of some good. In a corrupted state, without the healing power of grace, humans cannot perform all the good natural to them (II-I, q. 109, a. 2). Without the redeeming link to God, social life turns into moral and political disorder. "When the wicked reign it is the ruination of men" (*De Reg. Prin.* I, 3, 29). Unless they are of great virtue, those who are under the jurisdiction of the wicked can easily be moved to follow their commands. Therefore, Aquinas argues, the Church should not permit unbelievers to be placed in authority over the faithful, or to acquire domination over them (*Summa Theologiae* II-II, q. 10, a. 10). If it is already in existence, such domination can be tolerated only as a matter of expedience in order to avoid a greater evil. The human union with God also encompasses human solidarity, based on the dictate to love one's neighbor. Cooperation between Church and state is indispensable for maintaining a morally healthy society.

THE NATURE OF LAW

Aquinas is the foremost exponent of the natural law tradition, and in his writings derives human-made laws from natural law. He opposes two propositions that are characteristic of the positivist or voluntarist view of law, namely, that whatever pleases the prince, or any other lawmaking agency, has the force of law; and second, that the existence of a law is one thing, but its merit or lack thereof is another (Golding 239). He argues that arbitrary legislation does not result in any genuine law at all, and that laws cannot be detached from morality.

Aquinas identifies four kinds of law: eternal law, natural law, human law, and divine law. His theory of law rests upon his view of a rational and purposive order that exists in the universe, and of the human being as a part of this order. Everything that exists is from God and is governed by divine providence. Since law is an ordinance of reason, God's rational governance or ordering of all things toward proper ends (which humans can know only incompletely and uncertainly) has the quality of law (*Summa Theologiae* I-II, q. 91, a. 1). Further, since divine governance is not limited by time, the kind of law that corresponds to it is called "eternal." The eternal law thus describes an ideal, rational, and purposive order of the universe. All laws, insofar as they partake of right reason, derive from the eternal law (I-II, q. 93, a. 3). All things in the universe, insofar as they have inclinations to their proper actions and ends, are regulated and measured by it.

Since human beings are not mere parts of creation, but, in their ability to become aware of their proper ends and the means of attaining them, share in the action of providence themselves, they participate in the *lex aeterna* in a more complete way than do other creatures. Endowed with reason and free will, they can choose good instead of doing wrong. By virtue of their rationality, the imprint of the divine light in them, human beings can discover the most general principles of human action. As they discover and follow these principles, their participation in the eternal law assumes the form of "natural law" (I-II, q. 91, a. 2).

Natural law, the human being's participation in the eternal law, is law in the proper sense: a rule and measure of acts that proceed from free will and that rational individuals alone are capable of, so they can fulfill their potential. It is not a physical compulsion or a rule to be blindly followed. It refers to the understanding by which humans are directed to perform their activities and is found only in rational creatures making decisions by means of their reason. Its counsels and precepts provide directions for individual conduct and standards for positive or human-made laws. Its first, most basic precept is that "good is to be done and ensued, and evil is to be avoided" (I-II, q. 94, a. 2). From this precept, there follow other general principles of human action, such as "give to everyone his or her due" and "do not harm any person" (I-II, q. 95, a. 2). In spite of the original sin and the human fall, these moral principles or judgments of conscience can never be entirely blotted out from people's hearts. They are immutable and valid for all human beings at all times and in all places (I-II, q. 94, a. 4–6).

Because some individuals have their reason distorted by passions or evil habits, human beings stand in need of clearly prescribed norms suited to the actual circumstances of their lives and emanating from an authority. Such norms, devised by human beings, are called "human" or "positive laws." They are truly laws, however, only to the extent that they conform to natural law. A positive law that in any way differs or opposes natural law is "no longer a law, but a perversion of law" (I-II, q. 95, a. 2). Enforcement of such a perverted or unjust law by the authority would therefore be an act of violence. There is thus for Aquinas a distinction between the obligation to obey and the coercive force of law. Enforceability, an important feature that distinguishes a positive law from a moral counsel, is not sufficient to make laws binding (I-II, q. 96, a. 5–6). After all, one can be forced to do almost anything, including immoral acts, but such a coercion does not imply obligation. It does not bind in conscience, and therefore cannot make a law effective. The obligatory nature of a law is related to its moral content and resides in its directive power. What is fundamental to the nature of laws is that they direct human acts. Law is "an ordinance of reason for the common good, promulgated by the authority which is in charge of the community" (I-II, q. 90, a. 4). Insofar as it conforms to natural law, any positive law is ordained with a view to the common good, the common benefit of all citizens. When it fails to be directed toward promoting the common welfare, it loses its binding power (I-II, q. 96, a. 6). It cannot be divorced from justice, that is, "from being right, according to the rule of reason" (I-II, q. 95, a. 2). Nevertheless, Aquinas thinks that even an unjust law may sometimes be obeyed in order to avoid social disorder (I-II, q. 96, a. 4). The possibility of civil disobedience is acknowledged, but Thomas Aquinas is not a revolutionary. In his view, lawlessness should be avoided.

The responsibility of law making belongs either to the whole people or to a public personage who has care of the whole people (I-II, q. 90, a. 3). Since it is to be directed at the common good, law cannot be arbitrary. Reason alone can grasp the relationship of actions to one another and to an end. This activity of reason precedes the will, the converting of deliberation and judgment into an act. Law making is therefore a rational and purposive activity that cannot be divorced from general human purposes. Although it owes its positive existence to a volitional act of the lawgiver, law is reason and not will. "Law is the dictate of practical reason" (I-II, q. 91, a. 3). As "a rule and measure of acts whereby any person is induced to act or restrained from acting," law presupposes a rational being possessed of free will as the addressee or subject of the legal norm (I-II, q. 90, a. 1). Its enactment is not an act of will or power, but rather of rational discovery, searching for what is right. "In order that the volition of what is commanded may have the nature of law," Aquinas says, "it needs to be in accord with some rule of reason ... otherwise the will of the sovereign would savor of lawlessness rather than law" (I-II, q. 90, a. 1). He affirms the priority of the intellect over the will and thus opposes legal positivism, which gives the primacy to will. Law is for him not a matter of a mere convention. It cannot consist in a command that would not conform to reason. Even divine law, consisting of God's commandments, has for him a fundamentally rational character. It supplies the human intellect with additional guidance, in the form of the precept of charity (I-II, q. 107, a. 1). By following it, Christians share fully in the eternal law, the ideal rational order, and are thus directed to a supernatural end (I-II, q. 91, a. 4).

There were certainly theological reasons why Aquinas, a defender of Christianity and the Western civilization, rejected the view of divine law as absolutely authoritative simply because it was divine. This was in contradistinction to other religious traditions. According to the Koran, the universe is governed not by laws of nature, which humans can hope to decipher, but by an inscrutable divine power. Such a view of the universe gives incentives neither to independent rational investigation nor to individual moral effort, but leads the adherents of Islam to a total subjection to the divine will (Parkes 114). There is also no moral natural law, but only the law of God, in classical Judaism. It is through God's revelation, mediated by prophets, that people know what is right and wrong. The divine commandment is the main source of law. In the hundreds of injunctions and prohibitions found in the Old Testament, there is nothing that suggests that human reason could know them independently (Fox 77).

In contrast, by following the natural law tradition that developed from Plato and through the Stoics entered the epistles of St. Paul, Aquinas grounds the fundamentals of morality and law in reason. He argues that moral rules do not need to be derived solely from divine commandments. They are also clearly not established on the basis of a mere preference or of the interest of whoever is the stronger, that is, whoever is in power. They are a result of rational argument and demonstration. "Since human morals depend on their relation to reason, which is the proper principle of human acts," Aquinas says, "those morals are called good which accord with reason, and those are called bad which are discordant with reason" (*Summa Theologiae* I-II, q. 100, a. 1). He introduces a principle of selectivity into the interpretation of the Old Testament, on the basis of which he retains moral precepts while rejecting the rest of the older biblical legislation. In his view, the precepts of divine law, which are supernatural, must harmonize with the precepts of natural law, which are rational in character (I-II, q. 98, a. 5). Human beings, Christian or not, are essentially rational creatures, and, insofar as they follow reason in establishing what is right, they are also moral. Further, they can live in a well-ordered society only insofar as they follow natural law in establishing their own laws.

NATURAL LAW AND OPEN SOCIETY

Natural law is not a code of immediately evident or logically derived, detailed rules that fit every concrete situation of actual life. Regarding general principles, Aquinas believes natural law remains immutable and the same for all. But when it comes to secondary precepts, agreement and immutability cease. Natural law can at this level be blotted out from the human heart by vicious persuasions or evil customs, such as would be the case among those people who do not consider theft or sexual perversion to be sinful (I-II, q. 94, a. 6). Reason advances toward true norms slowly, step by step, and often only after starting down many wrong paths. This is because of uncertainty in practical matters, which are singular and contingent, and pervaded by conflicting interests, in contrast to those that are studied theoretically by reason (I-II, q. 91, a. 3). One cannot therefore construct a body of positive law derived from natural law as a rational deductive system, valid for all humans in all ages; one must, on the contrary, continually consult experience and custom.

Nevertheless, natural law includes a definite material content (Rommen 203). It is based on the assumption of the rational and social nature of human beings endowed with free will, who, in order to be true to this nature, must continually strive, individually and socially, to advance toward an ever higher degree of intellectual and moral perfection.

Aquinas insists on a close relationship between law (*lex*) and right (*ius*). Right is the object of justice. Through an act of justice, we give a person what is rightfully his or hers. Law is reason ordaining what must be done to bring about justice, that is, what is right or fitting (Gelinas 157). To natural law, then, belong human inclinations toward what is by nature right or appropriate to human beings. Since being rational is naturally proper to the human being, humans have a natural inclination to act according to reason. However, humans also share part of the same nature as non-rational creatures and thus partake of the eternal law not only by the way of rational knowledge but also by the way of passion and action (*Summa Theologiae* I-II, q. 93, a. 6). The order of the secondary precepts of natural law thus follows from the order of natural human inclinations that are apprehended by reason as being good. Aquinas lists these as self-preservation (an end that humans share with all substances), the union of male and female and the raising of children (the ends that are shared with all animals), and living in society in peace with others, avoiding ignorance, and knowing God (the ends of rational creatures) (I-II, q. 94, a. 2). All these inclinations, insofar as they are ruled by reason, belong to natural law and can be derived from its first precept. The precepts of natural law advise actions that are in line with natural inclinations and prohibit actions that defeat the purpose of a natural inclination, or render it difficult to carry out.

Aquinas thus derives the secondary precepts of natural law from what is right, and in doing so lays also the foundations for the concept of human rights. Human rights are determined by their relation to a natural moral order. It is justice that creates law and rights, and not the opposite. For example, it is naturally right or fitting, and therefore just, that a male should unite with a female for the procreation of offspring, and that parents should care for their children. From this right or rightness (in the primary sense), one can infer that adult men and women have the right (in the secondary sense of a moral claim) to marry and found a family, and children have the right to parental care. The more essential a good is to the perfecting of a person, the more essential is the right to this good. Consequently, we can arrive at the idea of the basic rights of the individual, of which no one can be deprived: to preserve life, to marry, to rear and educate children, to associate with others, to develop intelligence, to express opinions, to search for truth, to believe in God. Rights such as these are found in the American Bill of Rights and the Universal Declaration of Human Rights of the United Nations. Recent times have seen the proposal of additional rights, that, rooted in the notion of pure subjective will, are often incompatible with Christian and natural law teachings (Schall 47). In contrast to these "new rights"—subjective claims in which the notions of good and evil lose their moral connotations and become effusions of desire and aversion—human rights based on natural law presuppose a moral order. They guarantee individual liberty and define its range. People need a sphere of liberty in order to procure things that are by nature proper to human beings, so that they can attain fulfillment of their potentialities as members of the human species. Liberty exists for an end and must be proportioned to this end (*Summa Theologiae* I-II, q. 96, a. 1). Natural law guarantees the pursuit of goods required in life, but not the indiscriminate pursuit. It deprives humans not of freedom, but of license. It puts freedom and order in harmony.

For Aquinas, natural law is *ratio iuris*, the understanding of what is commensurate. This understanding cannot be complete without knowledge of the true end of human life. Public opinion by itself is not entitled to create rights. What is contrary to right reason cannot become right by any human legislation or public will. Positive laws, being a determination of natural right, cannot be arbitrary and the product of whim (I-II, q. 97, a. 1). To conform to natural law, positive laws must be just, honest, suitable to the time and place, useful, and clear. Their proximate purpose is to direct citizens to the common good. However, as human conditions constantly change and it is natural for human reason to advance from the imperfect to the perfect, human laws are also not unalterable. In Aquinas' vision, society is not governed by fixed rules, but is open to change as long as that change is directed to the common welfare. Nevertheless, mere changes in the law without good reason are prejudicial to the common good, and are a serious offense. Since the end of laws is the common welfare, which comprises many things that may not be immediately evident, Aquinas argues that positive laws should always depend on the historical experience and customs of the country (I-II, q. 96, a. 6). They should rely on what in the British and American legal tradition has been identified as common law—law founded upon national customs and precedent. Stable government grows out of laws, rather than laws growing out of government. If the authorities decree positive laws without reference to customs, those laws may be evaded or defied, and respect for the law will diminish. Therefore, human laws can be changed only insofar as change is clearly conducive to the common good, and if any potential loss is compensated for (I-II, q. 97, a. 2). In establishing new laws and changing old laws, there must be clear evidence of the benefit to be derived.

Natural law is only an ideal norm for positive laws. It does not give a concrete norm applicable to a particular situation. It does not, for example, determine a specific form of property, but rather judges systems of property in terms of justice and their applicability to individuals' proper ends (II-II, q. 66, a. 2). Further, natural law does not determine the particular form of government, but only asserts that just as living in society is natural for human beings, so also is having a government, and that no nation can achieve much, or even survive long, without a body of able and virtuous leaders (I-II, q. 91, a. 1). Moreover, it tells us that government should aim toward the common good, and one that departs from justice and does not recognize the fundamental human rights turns into a tyranny. To give an instance drawn from the contemporary world, natural law would not say, for example, that the Security Council of the United Nations is, in its concrete present form, good and efficient. But natural law would forbid that the independence of a small nation be sacrificed on the basis of expediency, for the sake of the security of a greater power (Rommen 235–236). This unvarying quality of the natural law, which elevates it above changing positive laws, makes a good political order possible. The peaceful coexistence of individuals within a society, as well as of nations within the international community, depends on the acceptance of such a higher law.

Politics for Aquinas is not merely a technique of achieving and maintaining political power for some selfish end. Rather, politics is an art by means of which human beings build their institutions for the more perfect realization of a good life. It remains part of a moral universe. The main function of politics is to achieve an order and unity among individuals in such a way that, at the same time they are pursuing their individual and group interests, they also are capable of realizing the common good under the rule of law.

AQUINAS' LEGACY

The political thought of Thomas Aquinas conveys a way to avoid extremes. Papal theocracy, divine right monarchy, absolute popular sovereignty, and modern totalitarianism are all in complete opposition to Aquinas' thought (Sigmund 71). His synthesis of Aristotelian philosophy and Christian teachings has been of profound importance in the development of the concepts of the modern state, democracy, and the rule of law. He has inspired a number of political thinkers from the fourteenth century onwards. His legal ideas influenced Francisco Suarez and Hugo Grotius, and provided the foundation for international law. His natural law teachings were adopted by Richard Hooker, who influenced John Locke. His views of property, the family, and sexual morality have been widely cited in papal encyclicals. His political theory provided the conceptual framework around which were constructed the pontifical critiques of the ideologies and programs of both the extreme right and the extreme left. Encyclicals *Rerum novarum* of Leo XIII and *Quadragesimo anno* of Pius XI placed the social teaching of the Church in an intermediate position between liberalism and collectivism. Drawing from his natural law teaching, twentieth century Catholic writers criticized legal positivism. They opposed the view that human law is but a projection of will— the will of a leader, a commissar, a party, or even a sovereign people—that is not bound by a body of moral values. Inspired by his thought, Catholic intellectuals, such as Yaves Simon, Erich Vogelin, Jacques Maritain, and Heinrich Rommen (who after Hitler's rise to power emigrated to the United States) tried to show that the erosion of constitutional democracy was a result of a disordered positivist philosophy based on relativism and agnosticism. Aquinas' statement on the invalidity of unjust laws was cited by Martin

Luther King Jr. in his *Letter from Birmingham Jail*. Although Thomism is no longer regarded as the dominant school within Roman Catholicism (following the Second Vatican Council in 1968), it is still an important source of inspiration for solutions to social and political problems—solutions that are universal in scope, and not only Roman Catholic or Christian.

In spite of the presence of Catholic universities and colleges, Thomistic thought in the United States can still be regarded as a neglected inheritance. The ideas of Thomas Aquinas initially were passed on to Americans only indirectly through Richard Hooker and his *Laws of Ecclesiastical Polity*. The country's founders, along with a large part of the American Protestant public, tended to think of the Middle Ages as an era of the Catholic Church's supremacy that represented ideas that were seemingly alien to the newly emerging republic. They failed to distinguish the ignorance characterizing the period immediately following the fall of the Roman Empire from the high cultural achievements of the medieval world of the twelfth and thirteenth centuries. Nevertheless, their views were pervaded by Christian conceptions of human nature and the state. They were adherents of the doctrine of natural law, which held that a higher moral law existed above the ruler and the sovereign people (Corwin 5). They also believed in public virtue, that is, the willingness of the people to work for the common good, and in a close connection between politics and ethics (Gordon Wood 69). The American political order, though pluralistic and partially secularized, would thus owe much of its roots, to medieval Christianity. "The worth of the person, the equality of all persons before the judgment-seat of God, the limitations placed upon all earthly authority—such Christian convictions as these would shape the American Republic" (Kirk 175).

The questions that Aquinas raises concerning issues such as the relationship between church and state, the nature of law, the function of property, or the purpose and limits of authority continue to be important in the present day. His treatment of natural law is by far the most influential discussion of the subject in the history of political philosophy. His idea that the foundation of society is ultimately a moral and rational order, and that the force, validity, sanction, and binding power of authority derive from this order, is worthy of exploration. And his belief that human beings can perceive a purposive order in the universe and organize a political society in such a way that the requirements of both order and freedom can be reconciled is one that has attracted political thinkers for ages.

QUESTIONS

- What is human dignity? What does the belief in human dignity imply?
- Why and under which conditions is the pursuit of wealth socially beneficial?
- Should rights of private ownership be always respected?
- Why and when may citizens disobey their government?
- What are the advantages and disadvantages of monarchy as a form of government?
- Should state and religion be separated?
- Why do we have laws? Which laws do not bind us in our conscience?

- What is the role of reason in Aquinas' conception of law?
- Aquinas views human rights as preconditions for developing human potentialities. Do you agree?

GUIDE TO FURTHER READING

Translations of St. Aquinas' Political Works:

Aquinas, Saint Thomas. *Political Writings.* Ed. and trans. R. W. Dyson. Cambridge: Cambridge UP, 2002.

Aquinas, St. Thomas. *On Politics and Ethics.* Ed. and trans. Paul E. Sigmund. New York: Norton, 1988.

Aquinas, St. Thomas. *Selected Political Writings.* Trans. J. G. Dawson. Oxford: Blackwell, 1959.

Basic Works in English:

Pegis, Anton C., ed. *Basic Writings of Saint Thomas Aquinas.* 2 vols. New York: Random House, 1945.

Suggested Readings:

Davies, Brian. *The Thought of Thomas Aquinas.* Oxford: Clarendon Press, 1993.

Burns, J. H, ed. *The Cambridge History of Medieval Political Thought c. 350-c. 1450.* Cambridge: Cambridge UP, 1988.

Corwin, Edward S. *The "Higher Law" Background of American Constitutional Law.* Ithaca: Cornel UP, 1979.

Finnis, John. *Aquinas: Moral, Political, and Legal Theory.* Oxford: Oxford UP, 1998.

Kretzmann, Norman and Eleonore Stump, eds. *The Cambridge Companion to Aquinas.* Cambridge: Cambridge UP, 1993.

Morrall, John B. *Political Thought in Medieval Times.* Toronto: U of Toronto P, 1980.

Pieper, Josef. *Guide to Thomas Aquinas.* San Francisco: Ignatius Press, 1986.

Parel, Anthony and Thomas Flanagan, eds. *Theories of Property: Aristotle to the Present.* Waterloo, Ontario: Wilfrid Laurier UP, 1979.

Pieper, Josef. *Guide to Thomas Aquinas.* San Francisco: Ignatius Press, 1986.

Rommen, Heinrich A. H. *The Natural Law: A Study in Legal and Social History and Philosophy.* Trans. Thomas R. Hanley. Indianapolis: Liberty Fund, 1998.

Schall, James V. "Human Rights as an ideological Project." *American Journal of Jurisprudence* 32 (1987). 47–61.

Machiavelli: How To Rule?

Niccolò Machiavelli, a diplomat, historian, playwright, poet, and political theorist, is one of the most controversial figures of political philosophy. He was born on May 3, 1469, in Florence to a middle-class family whose members had traditionally filled responsible positions in the Florentine government. Outwardly a republic, since 1434, Florence had been ruled by the powerful Medici clan. In the year of Machiavelli's birth, Lorenzo di Cosimo de' Medici, known as Lorenzo the Magnificent, a great patron of arts and a humanist scholar, succeeded to the leadership of this Tuscan city.

According to the custom of his times, Machiavelli received a humanistic education. As the main part of his classical training—a requirement for those entering a public career—he learned Latin, studied rhetoric, and read texts of ancient history and moral philosophy. At that time, Florence had become the center of the European Renaissance, the scene of an incomparable artistic flowering as well as the seat of the Platonic Academy established in 1462 by Marsilio Ficino. The city hosted distinguished scholars and great artists, such as Leonardo da Vinci and Michelangelo. In 1469, after completing a new translation of several Platonic dialogues, Ficino wrote his commentary on Plato's *Symposium*. In 1472, Leonardo finished his apprenticeship and was listed in the register of Florentine painters.

As a cultural movement that can be properly called "humanist," the Renaissance brought a revival of arts and letters, and an interest in classical culture. With its stress on rationalism and individualism, the Renaissance was an outcome of the scholastic ideas of human rationality and personhood. However, many Italian humanists did not consider the Renaissance to be a logical sequel to the medieval world, but rather a revolt against it (Parkes 309). These humanists rejected the prevailing Augustinian assumptions about man's fallen nature and insisted that humans did in fact have the power to attain the highest excellence (Skinner 93). They studied the classics for their intrinsic value, rather than merely for the inculcation of rhetorical rules, as they had been used in medieval schools. They derided the scholastics for engaging in petty dialectical reasoning and largely trivial inquiries, instead of paying sufficient attention to such practical questions as how one ought to behave or how to attend to affairs of state. They attacked scholastic theology as a barren distortion of the original Christian piety. Above all, they looked to classical antiquity as their admired model in thought and literature, replacing scholastic commentaries and summas with elegant treatises, essays, and dialogues (Kristeller 26).

Machiavelli's father, Bernardo, who earned his living as a lawyer, was an enthusiastic student of the classical poets, orators, and historians. He had read several works of Cicero, regarded by Renaissance humanists as one of the greatest geniuses of antiquity, and acquired a copy of Livy's *History of Rome*, the book that some years later served as a framework for his son's *Discourses*. In spite of the large expense involved, he provided the boy with an excellent grounding in the *studia humanitas*. Niccolò Machiavelli completed his education at the University of Florence. In his final years there, he was a student of Marcello Adriani, who later became Chancellor of the Republic of Florence.

The cultural and political environment of the independent state, governed by its own citizens rather than by some remote authority—of which Florence was the best example— had stimulated the unfolding of creative artistic and intellectual powers. It was thus no accident that the Renaissance developed initially in Northern Italy, which as early as the middle of the twelfth century had in practice lost its political unity and become divided into city-republics. Among those, Florence was the champion of both independence and self-government. Throughout the thirteenth and fourteenth centuries, it succeeded in defending its liberty from the encroachment of both the Church and the Holy Roman Empire, and until the rise of the Medici dealt successfully with all internal attempts to introduce a hereditary government. A prolonged conflict between Florence and Milan, which started in 1390, came to an end in 1454, and afterwards Florence enjoyed a period of peace. However, the increasingly powerful French monarchy had become interested in extending its influence in the Italian peninsula and begun to interfere in the affairs of the independent city-states. King Charles VIII entered the Italian peninsula in 1494, forced Florence and Rome into submission, fought his way to Naples, and allowed his armies to pillage the countryside. His successor, Louis XII, mounted three further invasions, repeatedly attacking Milan and generating endemic warfare throughout Italy.

In 1494, Piero de' Medici, the oldest of Lorenzo's three sons, made a political mistake in hastily surrendering a major Tuscan fortress to the French forces. As a result, the Medici family was banished from Florence. The city fell briefly under the control of Girolamo Savonarola, a member of the Dominican order and an implacable critic of the corruption of the clergy and the vanities of the Florentines. During his rule, the artistic life of the city stagnated, and the center of the Renaissance moved to Venice.

Savonarola's unremitting challenges to papal authority finally led to his excommunication in 1497. His political adversaries arranged for him to be arrested and executed. Upon the change of government in 1498, Marcello Adriani became Chancellor and Machiavelli became the Second Chancellor and Secretary to the Council of Ten for War, a government agency dealing chiefly with foreign affairs.

It still remains unclear why Machiavelli, an inexperienced twenty-nine-year-old from a distinguished but impoverished family, should have been elevated to one of the state's key offices. It is possible that while Adriani was filling vacancies in the chancery, he remembered his pupil's scholarly achievements at the university. Despite his youth, Machiavelli was routinely commissioned to undertake sensitive diplomatic missions to other Italian cities, as well as to the courts of King Louis XII in France and Emperor Maximilian I in Germany. He assisted Piero di Tommaso Soderini, who had been instrumental in the downfall of the Medici, and who in 1502 received a life appointment as *gonfaloniere* or Head of State.

The lesson Machiavelli learned from his diplomatic missions to France was that to foreign eyes, his own city's sense of importance seemed ridiculously disproportional to the realities of its financial and military power. His later writings are full of warnings about the folly of political thinking that loses touch with the facts. However, Machiavelli's contacts with Cesare Borgia, Duke of Romagna, were the most instructive for his development as a political theorist. His mission to Borgia's court in 1502 lasted nearly four months, in the course of which the duke, who launched a series of hostile campaigns against neighboring city-states, explained to him his political ambitions and policies. Machiavelli saw in Borgia's rise the emergence of a new leader in Italy, and admired his courage and a sense of purpose. He described the duke as one who made use of every means and action possible to lay the foundations of future power. Yet, Borgia's career came to a sudden end after the death of his father, Pope Alexander IV, in August 1503, and the subsequent election to the Chair of Peter of Cardinal Giuliano della Rovere, who took the name of Julius II. Within a few months, Cesare Borgia was arrested and banished to Spain, where he was killed while serving as a mercenary.

After reclaiming Romagna and reasserting authority over Bologna and Perugia, territories previously held by the Church, Pope Julius II started to form a coalition, the aim of which was to drive Louis XII's forces from Italy. During his diplomatic missions, Machiavelli was present at several audiences with the Pope and admired his remarkable ability in political affairs. On October 4, 1511, Pope Julius II signed the agreement forming the Holy League with Ferdinand of Spain. While Machiavelli strongly recommended that Florence become a member of the Holy League, Soderini insisted on a policy of neutrality in the conflict. To punish Florence for its lack of support of his crusade, Julius II deployed the coalition's forces against the city and compelled the Florentine citizens to accept the return of the Medici. Cardinal Giovanni de' Medici, the second oldest son of Lorenzo the Magnificent, entered Florence on September 14, 1512, and assumed control of the government. Soderini went into exile in Siena, and Machiavelli was dismissed from his office two months later. On February 23, 1513, he was falsely accused of being part of a conspiracy to restore the republic, and was arrested. Released twenty-two days later, as the result of an amnesty, he moved with his wife and children to his ancestral villa at Sant' Andrea, a village near Florence.

Although denied any further political career and living in relative poverty, Machiavelli still managed to exercise his intellectual faculties. He was a frequent guest at the Oricellari Gardens, owned by Cosimo Rucellai, where a circle of Florentine intellectuals met to discuss political and literary matters. Later, he also became a friend of Francesco Guicciardini, one of the greatest Renaissance historians. His premature retirement from public life at the age of forty-three gave him the opportunity to write literary, historical, and political works. It was during this period that he composed his major political treatises, *The Prince* and *The Discourses on the First Ten Books of Titus Livy*, which were published after his death, in 1531 and 1532 respectively.

In 1519, shortly after he completed *The Discourses*, a sudden turn of fortune brought him patronage from the Medicean government. Cardinal Giulio de' Medici, the Florentine governor, commissioned Machiavelli to write *The History of Florence*, and entrusted him with some diplomatic missions and administrative tasks, including inspection of the fortifications of Florence. A final turn of fortune came, however, in 1527. Giulio de' Medici had become Pope Clement VII in 1523. However, his political mistakes led to the sack of Rome in May 1527 by mercenaries employed by the Holy Roman Emperor Charles V. This led to a four-day massacre of Roman citizens, which horrified the Christian world. The Florentines took the opportunity to drive the Medici out of the city and re-establish the republic. For Machiavelli, with his republican sympathies, the restoration of the republican government in Florence ought to have been a moment of joy. The new government was, however, suspicious of his ties to the Medici and thwarted his hopes for advancement under the restored republic. This was more than Machiavelli could bear. Disheartened by his country's internal strife and disillusioned about his own future, he fell ill, and died on June 21, 1527.

Although *The Prince* had borne the imprimatur of Pope Clement VII when it was first published in 1531, in 1559 it was placed on the Index of Prohibited Books, along with other works by Machiavelli. The Index was created by Pope Paul IV in 1557, and was designed to ban dissemination of any book that was deemed morally damaging to the Catholic faith. As a result, some Italian and Spanish members of the Jesuit order published treatises devoted to exposing the evils of Machiavellism. Toward the close of the sixteenth century, Machiavelli was further denigrated in a book by Innocenzo Gentillet published in France and was held responsible for political corruption and contribution to moral vices. Gentillet's interpretation of *The Prince* as advocating statecraft based on ruthlessness and immorality was subsequently disseminated throughout Britain in the works of such popular dramatists as William Shakespeare and Christopher Marlowe. Although Machiavelli's writings would also slowly receive public approval, they were not removed from the Index until 1890. Yet, in spite of their controversial nature, they have over centuries influenced philosophers as diverse as Francis Bacon, Thomas Hobbes, Benedict Spinoza, Jean-Jacques Rousseau, Georg W. F. Hegel, Karl Marx, and Friedrich Nietzsche, as well as modern political theorists including Vilfredo Pareto, Gaetano Mosca, and Robert Michels.

THE NEW TEACHING OF POLITICS

In the introduction to *The Discourses*, Machiavelli boldly declares that he has "determined to take a path which has not yet been taken by anyone." In chapter XV of *The Prince*, he announces that in departing from the teachings of his predecessors, he seeks "the effectual truth of the matter rather than the imagined one." He clearly sees himself as a political innovator, breaking with established tradition. The novelty of his approach is sometimes seen in his critique of ancient and medieval political thought as unrealistic, and in his lowering of the standards of politics from what human affairs ought to be to what they are in reality (Parel 153). Machiavelli, it has been argued, changed the aim of politics from the pursuit of virtue to the pursuit of power. While some scholars believe that Machiavelli's originality lies in his redefinition of the aim of politics, others emphasize his contribution to a new, more scientific methodology. He is considered the first modern political thinker, and even the first modern political scientist, a morally neutral analyst who seeks an objective understanding of human society.

Although Machiavelli's contribution to the development of modernity cannot be denied, it is, nevertheless, largely misleading to call him a modern thinker. He kept one foot in the ancient world. Like other humanists, he regarded the Roman Republic as the greatest achievement in the political history of the world, and a model to be imitated. His methodology is "wholly new" only insofar as it yields a number of interesting generalizations made through reflection on personal experience and the study of worldly affairs, and supported by selective use of historical evidence. Yet he presents us neither with general laws based on observation nor with hypotheses subject to falsification. His writings are filled with maxims and advice drawn from ancient history. Moreover, his work is painstakingly normative rather than descriptive. He is not a dispassionate observer; he is a committed partisan whose studies are thoroughly impregnated with value judgments (Boucher 91). If there is any scientific aspect of Machiavelli's approach, it is akin to the medicine of his day, which he describes as a record of "experiments, carried out by doctors of old, upon which the doctors of our age base their prescriptions" (*Disc.* I, intro.) Like other traditional political writings, Machiavelli's works are in fact replete with medical analogies: "In those sicknesses that concern the state, there is no time, and unless they are cured by a prudent man, they bring the state to ruin" (*Disc.* III, xlix). Princes and statesmen are likened to doctors called upon to cure political diseases.

Machiavelli says that "anyone wishing to see what is to come should examine what has been, for all the affairs in the world in every age have their counterparts in ancient times" (*Disc.* III, xliii). In his view, human beings have always had the same passions and, in spite of the flow of time and the introduction of new ideas, they have not essentially changed. Machiavelli is thus a traditionalist who believes that we can learn more about politics by means of historical study than we can by abstract theorizing. However, what is really new in Machiavelli is that he departs from both ancient and Christian moral traditions. He separates morality and politics. It is a part of his project to undermine the tradition of virtue in favor of *virtú*, ability or vigor, a quality displayed by successful leaders but also by the body of citizens as a whole. He removes from his political philosophy any trace of natural law teaching, whether in its Stoic or Christian versions. The "effectual truth" is for him the only truth worth seeking. It represents the sum of the practical conditions that he believes are required to make both the country and the individual free, prosperous, and strong. As a prophet of *virtú*, he promises to lead both nations and individuals to earthly glory and power.

POLITICS AND CHANGE

It was perhaps his turbulent life that led Machiavelli to the firm conviction that everything is in constant flux and motion. Change is the essence of human affairs. There is no permanent tranquility. A political community is an unstable universe of passions, for it is inhabited by real human beings who love and hate, have ambitions and desires, and want to be recognized, esteemed, and rewarded (Viroli 168). The process of political corruption can not only dissolve the original constitution of a state but also destroy the very spirit of the people by which it is ultimately sustained. Further, the permanent threat of political instability is posed not only by human weakness and corruptibility but also by *fortuna*, fortune or fate, an unforeseen and unpredictable element in political life. Political leaders should thus always be prepared to encounter unexpected events and face challenges. Machiavelli values *virtú* in rulers because it is the quality that is indispensable to establish and successfully maintain the state. Insofar as they display *virtú*, political leaders are able to suppress *fortuna* or use it for their own advantage or the benefit of their states. But as they generally display little ability and rely completely on fortune, they come to ruin as soon as *fortuna* changes (*Prince* XXV). Consequently, all political formations and systems are fragile. States move from order to chaos, and then from chaos to order again.

St. Augustine and other Christians viewed history as essentially a linear development, a gradual unfolding of God's purposes for the world. Like many other Renaissance humanists, Machiavelli reverts to the view advanced by Polybius and other ancient thinkers, namely, that the course of human events can be shown to proceed in a series of recurring cycles. In his view, all states go through a cycle in which the basic forms of government—monarchy, aristocracy, and democracy—give rise to their corrupt forms of tyranny, oligarchy, and anarchy (*Disc.* I, ii). Because things have a tendency to deteriorate and the pursuit of the common good can be perverted by factional interests, a monarchy easily becomes tyrannical, an aristocracy may turn into an oligarchy, and a democracy can produce licentiousness leading to anarchy, "where neither the individual citizen nor public official is feared, and each individual lives according to his own wishes, so that every day a thousand wrongs are done" (Ibid.). A prudent legislator can reverse the process of decline and set the state on the right path again by means of appropriate laws. However, no state is likely destined to survive for very long the process of transformation from one form of government to another and complete the full cycle. What prevents this is the presence of egoistic states that are driven by their ambitions to dominate their neighbors. Once a state's correct form of government is replaced by a corrupted one, resulting in a weakening of the state, the cycle is likely to be broken by its subjugation to a stronger and better-organized state.

In his version of realism, Machiavelli believes that the "desire to acquire is truly a very natural and normal thing" (*Prince* III). It is true that not every state is inclined to follow this impulse; the nations concerned with the preservation of their status quo may desire to maintain their freedom rather than pursue their expansion. Nevertheless, since human affairs are in constant flux, a state that is run in such a way as to merely preserve its status quo will sooner or later be forced to change its policy. "It is impossible for a state," Machiavelli says, "to remain forever in the peaceful enjoyment of its liberty within its own narrow confines, for, though such a state may not harm other states, it will be harmed by them, and when thus harmed, there will arise in it the desire and the necessity for expansion" (*Disc.* II, xix). Everything that is weak arouses the greed of a stronger neighbor. Even if a state does not need to expand, idleness will weaken it and invite an aggressor.

Since internal welfare cannot be realized without outward security, and civil institutions without military backing are subject to disorder (*Art of War* Pref.), Machiavelli puts an exceptionally strong emphasis on military affairs. He argues that the necessary foundations of all states are "good laws and good armies" (*Prince* XII). To maintain military skills and keep itself strong, a state should prevent its citizens from being corrupted by idleness and luxury, and should be organized in such a way that it can always wage war (*Disc.* III, xvi). As a matter of prudence, it should gain power by enriching its treasury, increasing its population, making allies, supporting military training, and even by profiting from war. And if these methods of gaining power are not found pleasing, the state should consider the fact that merely preserving the status quo may lead to its ruin. Weak states become the hunting grounds of strong states. The state cannot make itself secure without power (*Disc.* I, i), and without security, its liberty is in jeopardy.

A substantial part of Machiavelli's political teaching is devoted to the issue of how to deal with change and corruption in politics. Once the state's security is guaranteed by power, it has to develop stable political institutions. Since they can easily be corrupted, all basic forms of government are defective. History has shown us that "those who were prudent in establishing laws recognized the fact and, avoiding each of these forms in themselves, chose one that combined all of them, judging such a government to be steadier and more stable" (*Disc.* I, ii). Machiavelli praises the concept of the mixed constitution, which, put into practice in Sparta and the Roman Republic, enabled those states to last for many hundreds of years. In his view, the Athenian democracy had only a brief existence because "Solon did not mix democracy with the power of the principality and with that of the nobility"(Ibid.). Furthermore, Machiavelli recognizes the value of a natural aristocracy, based on merit and devotion to the state. It is obvious to him that states cannot survive without citizens of outstanding ability and character (*Disc.* III, xxviii). The stability of the commonwealth requires that the citizens who distinguish themselves by their talents and public service occupy the highest ranks regardless of their wealth or social position at birth. If the people are moderate and content to share power with such outstanding individuals, by their example they gradually acquire the same ability (*virtù*). If ability increases in society, states grow in power (*History of Florence* III, i). But if ability and discipline are lacking, then laziness, license, anarchy, and ruin follow. It is evident to Machiavelli that, because of envy, people have little esteem for individuals of worth in times of peace (*Disc.* III, xvi). However, once such individuals are deprived of office, ability in arms and boldness of spirit are extinguished in society, for these qualities are hard to find among the ordinary people (*History of Florence* III, i).

The main aim of the mixed constitution of a republic is to prevent any part of society from dominating the political scene. By giving seats in the senate and the highest magistrate to the most capable citizens, the mixed constitution promotes ability. By establishing a popular assembly, it provides a means by which the common people can express their concerns and ambitions (*Disc.* I, iv). But although Machiavelli supports the classical idea of the mixed constitution, he denies the classical ideals of civic concord and the harmony of interests between different social classes. The two chambers effectively contain individuals of different social standing, and embody different inclinations: the people desire to be free from oppression, the upper classes desire to dominate them; the former promotes license, the latter servitude. The presence of different inclinations and conflicting class interests may produce disunity and consequently threaten the well-being of a state. In real life, however, "one cannot remove one inconvenience without causing another to arise" (*Disc.* I, vi). Politics does not offer ideal solutions. One has to choose between alternatives, neither of which is perfect. Hence, to preserve ability and to maintain the state, any quarrels or conflicts that may arise between different social classes must be tolerated. Their net effect is a tensely balanced equilibrium, which ensures that neither group can dominate the other, or ignore the other's interests (Skinner 181). Moreover, the laws and institutions that benefit political liberty, namely those that establish a system of constitutional checks and balances, and preserve the mixed constitution, are born precisely of such conflicts (*Disc.* I, iv). Since they serve to cancel out all partisan interests, the conflicts between social classes serve at the same time to guarantee that the only motions that pass into law are those that benefit the community as a whole. They are thus not the solvent but the cement of the commonwealth.

MACHIAVELLI'S REPUBLICANISM

Machiavelli gives strong support to the idea of mixed rule and thus subscribes to the classical republican tradition, whose roots can be traced to the writings of Cicero, Livy, Sallust, and other Roman writers, and that was continued during the Renaissance by the Florentine humanists Coluccio Salutari, Leonardo Bruni, Braciolini Poggio, and their followers. Like other republican theorists, he gives his allegiance to the ideal of liberty, which he understands in a traditional way. His discussion of political liberty is in clear contrast to today's emphasis upon freedom as a system of legal protections of individual rights. By "political liberty" he means the liberty that pertains to a free state. Free states are those "which are far from any external servitude and are able to govern themselves by their own judgment" (*Disc.* I, ii). They can enjoy the privilege of making their own laws and are not under the rule of foreigners. Their pursuits and chosen ends are determined by the public will, and not by despotic power. For Machiavelli, then, "political liberty" denotes both political independence and self-government—"liberty in the sense of being free from external interference as well as in the sense of being free to take an active part in the running of the commonwealth" (Skinner 77). In many passages of his works, he suggests that such liberty can be best secured in an independent republic.

Contrary to popular opinion based on a selective reading of *The Prince*, Machiavelli does not approve of tyrannical rule. Tyranny, or even princely rule, is antithetical to liberty in his view. People who are ruled absolutely by princes, he claims, do not know how to live in freedom (*Prince* v). There are definite advantages that can be related to living in a free state: "All countries and provinces living in freedom make very great progress" (*Disc.* II, ii). To gain power and wealth, a state must be independent and self-governed: "When a tyranny replaces a free self-government, the least amount of evil that results in cities so affected is that they no longer advance or increase in power and riches, but in most cases—in truth, always—they decline" (Ibid.). Machiavelli distinguishes between monarchy and absolute rule, and includes constitutional monarchies and republics among the states capable of freedom (*Disc.* I, xxv). Under conditions of freedom, ability is usually rewarded, whereas under despotism it is feared; accordingly, it is in self-governing states that great deeds and achievements are encouraged. Furthermore, they are the only states that can guarantee citizens their individual liberties (namely freedom from any elements of constraint or servitude), protect their individual legal rights to security of person and property, and give them the opportunity to pursue their own chosen ends. It is in free states that individual citizens "can be assured that they will be born free, and not slaves, and that they may, through their ability, become great men" (*Disc.* II, ii).

Machiavelli believes that Europe has been fortunate to have so many independent republics and other self-governing states, and argues against European unification. "Where there are more states there are more able men" (*Art of War* II). The environment of a free state is conducive to ability. When the Roman Republic became an empire and destroyed all the independent city-states of Europe and Africa, it left no path for ingenuity to flourish other than Rome. All ability was concentrated in the Roman Empire. Thus, when Rome was corrupted, almost the entire world became corrupted as well. The empire destroyed the abilities of nations and was incapable of maintaining its own.

Monarchs or other single rulers can promote the cause of liberty by prudent legislation, by which the animosities between factions may be calmed and individuals restrained from evil doing (*History of Florence* IV, i). In the longer run, however, the simple governmental form of monarchy is inconsistent with freedom, for it has a tendency to degenerate into tyranny. Since both ability and liberty are best maintained under a mixed form of a rule, the republic is thus the best form of government. As republics come in both more aristocratic and more democratic forms, there is still a question as to whether most political authority should belong to an élite, which can furnish the people with leadership, or to the majority. Machiavelli discusses this issue by raising the question of how liberty can be best protected. Since in every republic there is an upper and a lower class, it may be asked, he says, "into whose hands this protection may best be placed" (*Disc.* I, v). His answer is not free from ambiguity. Ruled by small and close-knit groups of nobles, Sparta and Venice lasted longer than the more democratic Roman Republic. Aristocratic republics thus last longer, for they are more interested in maintaining the status quo and "prohibit the restless minds of the plebeians from thinking about power; a cause of infinite conflicts and scandals" (Ibid.). Once the common people become thirsty for power, they are no longer satisfied to participate in government only through their assembly. Ready to suppress the power of nobility, they demand to be placed in all ranks of authority. As they are always looking for change and can be easily deceived by ambitious individuals, they bring their country into a decline. However, because "the fear of losing generates in them the same desires that those who want to acquire possess" (Ibid.), disturbances are often caused by those who have rather than by those who do not. Privileged groups can also effect changes. Their ambitious behavior kindles greed in other segments of society. Therefore, if it is only the protection of the status quo that is being sought, the care of the republic's affairs should be entrusted to the nobility. But since it is safer to organize the state for expansion, Machiavelli argues, it is better to follow the Roman republican model, even if this will bring unending civil disturbances. The government should have a large popular basis and the people should be made the guardians of liberty (*Disc.* I, vi).

Machiavelli provides a possible counterargument to the democratic peace theory, which assumes that democracies are less war-prone than non-democratic states because they are governed by their citizens' true interests. He argues that republics whose governments have a broad popular basis are less status quo oriented than those ruled by the nobility, and therefore they are more likely to engage in international conflicts. Even if governments of democratic republics must indeed answer to their citizens, who eventually pay for a war in blood and treasure, people can be easily manipulated and inspired by a false sense of glory or of what is good, and can therefore be persuaded to go to war (*Disc.* I, liii). Furthermore, Machiavelli is perfectly aware that a combination of factional conflict and prolongation of military authority destroyed the Roman Republic. Having expanded over a great territory, Rome was forced to concentrate on military matters, and this resulted in the extension of the terms of military commands, and consequently in the rise of Julius Caesar and the loss of republican government (*Disc.* III, xxiv). By recommending both the policy of expansion and the Roman model, Machiavelli thus ultimately sacrifices liberty to the pursuit of greatness. He focuses on the expansionist aims of the state and the role of a mass citizen army in attaining such greatness (Osmond 423). He upholds the traditional republican theme that the highest offices should be open to the most able citizens, but he often associates ability narrowly with military quality (*Disc.* III, xvi). Hence, he departs from the classical republican tradition, and puts republicanism into a new conceptual framework provided by his political realism and militarism.

HUMAN GOODNESS AND CORRUPTION

There are reasons to believe that Machiavelli had a low view of human beings. He describes them, indeed, as "ungrateful, fickle, simulators and deceivers, avoiders of danger, greedy for gain" (*Prince* XVII). On the other hand, he does not regard people as wholly and incurably evil. He thinks that "the world has always been in the same state and that there has been as much good as evil in it; but this evil and this good changes from country to country" (*Disc.* II, intro.). He observes that in Germany of his time, "goodness and religion are still strong among people," and this is why German cities flourish (*Disc.* I, lv). There once was also much goodness in ancient Rome, where ability was honored and the public interest was more valued than private interests, but, according to him, there is not much left of it in libertine Italian republics, where "there is no observance of religion, laws, or military discipline, and all is stained with every kind of filth." In an environment of moral decline, which could affect any state, individuals "never do good except out of necessity" (*Disc.* I, iii).

If *virtú* is the quality that a political leader needs to establish and successfully maintain the state, *necessitá*, necessity, another key term in Machiavelli's writings, is a means to compel human beings to goodness. People tend to be corrupt when, by giving priority to their own particular interests, they ignore the claims of their community. The condition of "necessity" or compulsion can occur "naturally," when, for example, the whole community is endangered by a common enemy and is forced to work together for the sake of self-defense, or it can be imposed on people by means of laws, and such "laws make them good" (Ibid.). Laws can prevent the dominance of partisan interests and can institute liberty. Good laws and the education that follows from them inculcate public spirit, which animates the community (*Disc.* I, iv). Consequently, a good social order depends on the sagacity of the legislators. Successful management of political affairs is not a product of the spontaneity of an "invisible hand," but requires prudence and skillful leadership.

Providing a state with a constitution is not a communal activity for Machiavelli. He argues that the truly great states have always been the products of great minds. Their judicious founders or able-minded reformers were distinguished individuals, who were able to formulate their laws and govern them for the common good, and were also wise enough to leave what they founded in the care of the many (*Disc.* I, ix). Machiavelli praises Lycurgus, the famous legislator who provided Sparta with a constitution that survived for more than eight hundred years. "A republic can, indeed, be fortunate," he says, "if it produces a man so prudent that he gives it laws organized in such a manner that it can live securely under them without need to revise them" (*Disc.* I, ii). Generally, however, republics and other states are not so fortunate as to be able to bring forth prudent founders or to give birth to reformers who can see clearly their defects. Nearly all human beings, deceived by false appearances, allow themselves to be led by those who deserve more blame than praise (*Disc.* I, x). Even if well-qualified individuals were to be found, they would not easily be able to persuade the populace by peaceful means to, first, accept them as leaders and, second, follow their policies (*Disc.* I, viii). Therefore, most countries are unfortunate. Unable to find prudent organizers, they are forced to constantly reorganize themselves by continually changing their constitutions and undergoing frequent unrest. The most unfortunate and furthest from order is the state whose citizens are so licentious that setting them on the right path is an all but hopeless task.

A good social order does not depend only upon political institutions, Machiavelli argues, but must also be sustained by goodness, or what might be called public spirit or civic virtue: moral strength, vigor, respect for law, and above all devotion to the commonwealth. "Where this goodness does not exist, nothing good can be expected, as nothing good can be expected in regions that are evidently corrupt" (*Disc.* I, lv). All states at the time of their origin must have possessed some goodness, he asserts, by means of which they gained their initial reputation and accomplished their first growth. Since over the course of time this goodness becomes corrupted and countries decline, "the means of renewing them is then to bring them back to their beginning" (*Disc.* III, i). This return to the original condition is accomplished either by external events or as a result of foresight. The increasing moral corruption of a state's citizens may lead them to bad political choices and ultimately into war or other events that threaten the country's very survival. Therefore, there is "nothing more necessary in a political community than to restore it to the reputation that it had at its beginnings and to strive to see that there are either good laws or good men to produce it without having to resort to external forces." Thus reborn, it "takes on new life and new strength and adopts once more the observance of religion and justice" (Ibid.). Far from approving a rigid segregation of church and state, Machiavelli considers religion to be the most important ally of a well-constituted republic. Factionalism and neglect of religious practices are for him the greatest sources of corruption. "There is no greater indication of the ruin of a country than to see its religious worship not respected" (*Disc.* I, xii). Whenever extravagance, dissipation, and the satisfaction of private wants are encouraged, factions become outlets for private ambitions, and religious practices are abandoned, the state's ruin is at hand (*Disc.* I, xi).

Machiavelli would strongly oppose the view, based on the negative concept of liberty as freedom from restraint, that political life can be reduced to the mere enjoyment of personal independence and the pursuit of private interests. "It is the common good and not private gain that makes cities great" (*Disc.* II, 2). In a corrupted state, where citizens give priority to their own private interests, no political life can properly exist. There are certain tasks, such as defending the community and participating in the political process, that citizens need to undertake in common in order to preserve both the freedom of the state and their individual liberties. During the early period of the their history, the Romans attained a high level of civic virtue, expressed in their concern for the common weal, and this virtue enabled Rome to withstand many challenges, including a brief term of rule by wicked leaders. The early Roman Republic could return to order and self-government because its citizens were still uncorrupted (*Disc.* I, xvii). In the later period of Rome's history, however, when moral corruption spread among the citizenry, laws, institutions of government, and other republican remedies were unable to reverse the process of decline.

Even if it embodies the best form of government, a state cannot be considered a republic, nor can it long remain free, if its citizens become corrupt and lose their interest in upholding the common good. To bring a state back to order is therefore the most glorious political aim (*Disc.* I, x). This requires such a high degree of prudence and ability to foresee dangers that it could belong only to an extraordinary individual. If a state recovers from a decline, "this happens because of the ability of a single man living at that time and not because of the ability of the people supporting its good institutions" (*Disc.* I, vii). Like other political writers of the humanist tradition, Machiavelli thus praises the political man (*politicus vir*) who displays his talent by promulgating laws, bringing back order, and saving his country from corruption (Viroli 163–164). According to traditional republican sources, such a prudent organizer and morally good person (*uomo buono*), who is devoted to the public welfare and is capable of restoring social order, must be wise, love truth and justice, and not be crafty. There are no circumstances in which he would be justified in ruling as a despot or imposing injustice. To fulfill his duty, he must cultivate the full range of Christian and moral virtues (Skinner 131). Machiavelli rejects this conventional image. "A man who wants to be good under all circumstances," he writes in a famous chapter of *The Prince*, "will certainly come to ruin among so many who are not good." Therefore, the prince or any one else whose goal is to reorganize a state needs to learn "how not to be good, and to use this knowledge or not to use it according to necessity" (*Prince* XV).

Machiavelli does not discard the republican idea of politics or the concept of the political man. Like other humanists, he stresses the importance of civic virtues and the common good, and emphasizes the intimate connection between self-government and political greatness. However, by giving his morally ambiguous advice to the prince, he challenges the traditional humanist moral and political thought.

THE RULE OF PRINCES

Machiavelli considered *The Discourses* his most important and comprehensive political work, although he interrupted his writing of this text in order to complete his shorter treatise, *The Prince*. He dedicated the former to two young friends of his, while the latter was dedicated to two successive Medici princes. Since the two works focus respectively upon a republic and a principality, it may asked how the same author could advocate two entirely different forms of government without being guilty of intellectual dishonesty. This in turn raises questions about Machiavelli's character, intentions, and convictions, which have been the subject of investigation and speculation on the part of many scholars.

Without inquiring into the intentions or motives Machiavelli may have had in writing *The Discourses* and *The Prince*, it is, nevertheless, possible to discern a link between the two works on the basis of their texts. In chapter xviii of Book I of *The Discourses*, Machiavelli contends that it is impossible to maintain a free government in a state whose citizens are totally corrupt. In such a state, the people cannot be controlled by laws; they will disobey them. "For just as good customs require laws in order to be maintained, so laws require good customs in order to be observed." In a highly corrupted state, where good customs and habits are lacking, the people's "insolence may be checked in some manner by a kind of regal power; and to make them to become good by any other means would be either a most cruel undertaking or completely impossible" (*Disc.* I, xviii). Thus, although Machiavelli clearly prefers the republican form of government, he believes that a principality can play an important historical role under certain circumstances. In a country that is so "clearly corrupted, as is Italy" (*Disc.* I, lv), he says, a country that is "disordered, beaten, despoiled, ripped apart, overrun, and prey to every sort of catastrophe" (*Prince* XXVI), an absolute princely or monarchic government is imperative to end corruption and create conditions for an orderly political life.

In Machiavelli's view, "different institutions and ways of living must be instituted for a bad subject than for a good one" (*Disc.* I, xviii). In deprived and corrupt circumstances, when so many people engage in robberies and similar crimes, and good citizens are excluded from public offices, a wise ruler's first obligation to his or her country is to survive, so that he or she can reestablish in it the conditions of lawful civility. One of the main issues in *The Prince* is thus how to maintain oneself in power in a corrupted state. Machiavelli is concerned with those qualities that rulers need in order to acquire and hold power, and to promote peace, order, and security. In chapter XV he lists some of the virtues that humanists generally regarded as praiseworthy for a prince to exhibit. He acknowledges that liberality, mercy, honesty, courage, kindness, chastity, and tolerance are qualities that the people usually admire. Yet, contrary to the humanist tradition, he asserts that no ruler can possess or fully practice them. He thus mounts a direct attack on the moral and political theories of his contemporaries (Skinner 129). His main thesis here is that "taking everything into account, one will discover that some qualities that appear to be virtue, if the prince pursues them, will end in his destruction; while other qualities that look like vices, if he pursues them, will result in his safety and well being" (*Prince* XV). In chapters XVI–XVIII he supports this thesis. He argues that morally good actions may lead to undesirable consequences, and evil actions can be beneficial. The prince must then learn how not to be good and yet escape gaining a bad reputation. He does not need to be virtuous all the time, but only to pretend to be virtuous, so that he can please the public opinion. However, "he needs not to be concerned [with public opinion] if he acquires a reputation for those vices without which he would be unlikely to save the state" (*Prince* XV).

Having set out a canonical list of virtues, Machiavelli proceeds to undermine them point by point. Liberality is a classical virtue, but its practice in politics may be damaging, he claims, when by generous spending (such as providing citizens with lavish social services) a state uses up all its resources. A liberal prince may in the end be forced to burden the people with extensive taxes and make himself hateful to them. However, a miserly prince may be able to carry out his enterprises without overburdening his people with unpopular taxes. Thus, as a miser, he actually "comes to be generous with all those from whom he takes nothing" (*Prince* XVI). Machiavelli employs a similar paradox in his discussion of mercy. Sparing a few scoundrels or allowing the loosening of military discipline brings ruin upon society. Too much mercy permits social evils to flourish and results in frequent crimes, which affect everyone, whereas cruelty to individuals who deserve punishment promotes obedience to rules and peace in society. A cruel prince would thus actually be more compassionate than the ruler who, in order to escape being called cruel, fails to put down disorders, which result in murder and plundering (*Prince* XVII). Machiavelli does not deny that both liberality and mercy are virtues, but argues that in the context of politics, the vice of miserliness is preferable to liberality, and similarly, the vice of cruelty is preferable to mercy. When reforming a corrupted state, a prince should not worry that he might be considered either miserly or cruel. However, although he might be feared, he should not go so far as to make himself hated. To be successful, Machiavelli adds, a prince would do well to be generous only with wealth that does not belong to him or to his subjects, but rather that rightfully belongs to others, in particular, property obtained through war.

As for moral obligations in general, Machiavelli sees them as varying according to the circumstances. When one is dealing with corrupt, as opposed to honest people, one is in effect dealing with beasts, and so a prince must know how to act in a beastly way, unrestrained by conventional morality (Kocis 118). Although it is praiseworthy to keep one's word, "a wise ruler, therefore, cannot and should not keep his word when such an observance of faith would be in his disadvantage and when the reasons which made him promise are removed" (*Prince* XVIII). "This rule would not be good," Machiavelli says, "if humans were all good," but since they are "a sorry lot and will not keep their promises," there is no reason to keep one's word to them (Ibid.). Hence, a prince should never lack legitimate reasons to break his promises, but he should also know "how to disguise his nature of a great hypocrite and a liar." The underlying "morality" of *The Prince* and *The Discourses* is the same (Skinner 183). The guiding norm is the survival of the self or of political community. Even immoral means are justified when they are necessary for the preservation of the state. Breaking promises and established agreements is not a glorious thing, but "when the entire safety of one's country is at stake, there should be no consideration of just or unjust, merciful or cruel, praiseworthy or disgraceful; on the contrary, putting aside every form of respect, that decision which will save her life and preserve her liberty must be followed completely" (*Disc.* III, xli).

In Machiavelli's realism, echoed later in the writings of Hans Morgenthau, the supreme virtue of politics is prudence, that is, the ability to "consider where the fewer inconveniences are and choose the path as the best one, because a choice that is completely clear and without uncertainty can never be found" (*Disc.* I, vi). Unlike more radical realists, Machiavelli does not abandon the traditional moral vocabulary. He does not dissociate politics from moral considerations. He is aware that political decisions often carry moral implications. Yet he is also "aware of the ineluctable tension between the moral command and the requirements of a successive political action" (Morgenthau 9). He establishes politics as a sphere autonomous from ethics, and separates the two. His notion of prudence as an autonomous, amoral skill used in pursuing the good of the state is alien to classical and Christian moral thinkers, for whom prudence cannot be separated from morality (Coll 78). He judges political actions by their consequences and subordinates all other considerations to political success.

Because of his love of paradoxes and ambiguities, it is ultimately not easy to discern Machiavelli's moral position. When advising his prince that "he should not stray from the good, if that is possible, but he should know how to enter into evil when necessity commands" (*Prince* XVIII), he does not seem to abandon conventional morality. He retains the customary view that there is a difference between good and evil. He suggests that moral principles cannot be disregarded, but also maintains that they cannot be universally applied to political actions. Rather, they must be filtered through the concrete circumstances of place and time. Nevertheless, Machiavelli also suggests that although good qualities such as mercy, liberality, frankness, or piety may be admirable in themselves, there is little place for them in politics, and "it is not necessary for a prince to have all of the above-mentioned qualities, but it is very necessary for him to appear to have them" (Ibid.). To rule a political community that embodies conventional morality, and at the same time to prevent moral corruption of citizens and to escape a bad reputation, it is above all necessary for a prince to be hypocritical and "to seem to possess" (Ibid.) certain qualities, especially that of being religious. The prince may disregard moral principles, but should refuse to admit to others that he is doing so. Machiavelli thus appears as a mastermind of deception, who has himself stepped outside the bounds of conventional morality. He could be speaking of himself, as well as of the prince, when he says: "Everyone sees what you seem to be, few perceive what you are" (Ibid.).

According to Machiavelli, ordinary people are always deceived by appearances and "in the world where there is nothing but ordinary people, there is no room for the few, while many have place to lean on" (Ibid.). By denying a place in society to the few who can recognize hypocrisy and correctly distinguish right from wrong, he marginalizes the very moral and intellectual elite that Plato and Aristotle, and the classical tradition following them, attempted to put at the core of the political community.

A CRITIQUE OF THE MORAL TRADITION

In spite of its traditional republican elements, Machiavelli's thought runs counter to the humanist intellectual current that was dominant during his time. For the Renaissance humanists, as well as for the ancient and Christian political philosophers before them, political theory was a part of ethics. They were a part of the classical tradition of moral and political thought, represented by Plato, Aristotle, Cicero, Seneca, and other ancient thinkers. It was characteristic of the classics that they emphasized the importance of virtue for political life. This tradition of virtue was never put in opposition to Christian religious doctrine; rather, attempts were made to harmonize the two. Individual virtues would thus include not only the four cardinal virtues of antiquity—wisdom, courage, moderation, and justice—but also the fundamental Christian virtue of faith (Skinner 92). It is true that by arguing against the Augustinian view of human nature as corrupt, the humanists cultivated individuality and rehabilitated the idea of human glory. However, they also maintained that there was no real glory and worldly fame except what springs from virtue and good deeds. One of the favorite Renaissance themes was that the mere vigor and fury of a barbarian like Hannibal could never match the kind of virtue the Roman general Scipio displayed in his final and overwhelming campaign against Carthage. This lesson, like other humanist and classical moral teachings, was explicitly rejected by Machiavelli.

Cicero's *On Duties* was read and copied more frequently than any other single work of Roman philosophy during the Middle Ages and the Renaissance. It played an important formative role for the Florentine humanists, and served as one of Machiavelli's classical sources (Colish 82). In this work, Cicero says that "if supremacy is sought for the sake of glory, crime should be excluded for there is no glory in crime" (*Duties* 3.87). He contributes to both the natural law and just war traditions, and defines universal moral standards by which individuals and states should always judge their actions. Cicero condemns a morally wrong action. According to him, expediency must always be "measured by the standard of moral rectitude" (*Duties* 3.83). "No cruelty can be expedient," he argues, "for cruelty is most abhorrent to human nature" (*Duties* 3.46). In his view, wrong can be done in either of two ways, by force or by fraud: "fraud seems to belong to the cunning fox, force to the lion; both are unworthy of man" (*Duties* 1.41). But of all forms of injustice, he believes, "none is more flagrant than that of the hypocrite who, at the very moment when he is most false, makes it his business to appear virtuous" (Ibid.). It is against these moral views, widely disseminated among the Renaissance humanists, that Machiavelli directs his arguments.

In chapter XVII of *The Prince*, Machiavelli discusses the question of whether it is better to be loved than to be feared, and asserts that the inhuman cruelty of Hannibal and the fear he inspired helped to keep his army united and prepared for combat. He contrasts him with Scipio, whom he criticizes for his tolerant nature, and in *The Discourses* ends his comparison of the two military leaders by saying that "it matters little what method a general follows, provided that he is skillful and that his ability makes him highly regarded by his men" (*Disc.* III, xxi). He celebrates Hannibal's "outstanding *virtú*," and adds that Scipio and Hannibal achieved the same results, the former by praiseworthy means and the latter by despicable ones. He thus implies that to achieve glory in war, it is enough to be successful. He separates expediency from moral rectitude. Consequently, Machiavelli approves of acts of political violence that may bring glory to the state and is silent about natural law. He undermines the just war tradition and removes any limits to the conduct of war. In chapter XVIII, he recalls the images of the fox and the lion to convey a message completely different from that of Cicero. He acknowledges that there are two ways of fighting, one according to law, which is proper to humans, and the other with force, which is proper to beasts, "but because the first, in many cases, is not sufficient, it becomes necessary to have recourse to the second" (*Prince* XVIII). To maintain their position, and to conduct successful foreign policy, his princes must know how to be half beast and half man. They must use force (like lion) and fraud (like fox).

Machiavelli's criticism of the applicability of universal moral standards to politics is not directed solely at Christianity. He does not present us with a hard choice between two different moralities, Christian and ancient, as Isaak Berlin suggests he does. The dilemma—either Christian values or "a noble and glorious society in which humans grow strong, proud, wise, and productive" (Berlin 58)—cannot be attributed to Machiavelli, and is deeply flawed. Although he is not concerned with any human ends beyond this life, he recognizes the utility of religion in society and regards it as one of the foundations of a good state. For instance, he considers the "goodness and [Christian] religion" practiced by the people of Germany as making cities "flourish there with liberty" (*Disc.* I, lv), while the concurrent disrespect of religious worship in Italy as bringing "countless evils and countless disorders" (*Disc.* I, xii). Machiavelli's critique is in fact directed equally at the classical and Christian moral traditions. He parts company with both ancient and Christian defenders of natural law, and looks skeptically at both classical and Christian virtues. His concept of *virtú* does not refer to traditional virtues, but to the qualities that the prince must have in order to maintain his state and achieve great things, such as firmness of purpose, presence of mind, an ability to see more clearly than others, and fortitude in adversity (Skinner 138). Such qualities are neither moral nor immoral. They can appeal to the sentiments of most "strong" individuals, regardless of whether they are Christian, ancient Roman, or totally without morality and religion (Plamenatz 177).

Although Machiavelli can be accused of separating politics and ethics, and he often seems to suggest an immoral course of action to benefit the state, he in fact works within the framework of a single morality. The concept of a double morality, comprising a conventional Christian morality applicable to the lives of private individuals and a "higher" public morality applicable to the actions of political leaders, is nowhere overtly expressed or even clearly implied by him. Nevertheless, it is this latter interpretation of his thought that has, in the form of the doctrine of *raison d'État*, exerted the most profound influence on posterity.

THE POLITICS OF *RAISON D'ÉTAT*

In the noteworthy statement Machiavelli says that "many writers have imagined for themselves republics and principalities that have never been seen nor known to exist in reality, for there is such a gap between how one lives and how one ought to live" (*Prince* XV). He is thus in fact making a critique of the classical tradition of moral and political thought which, by formulating universal moral standards, has placed restrictions on the means of action. He implies that the idealistic view of human nature, and of interstate relations regulated by moral norms, is based on wishful thinking and that "anyone who abandons what is done for ought to be done learns his ruin rather than his preservation" (Ibid.). What ultimately counts for Machiavelli is thus not moral scruples or norms, but *raison d'État*: whatever is good for the state. Departing from the way marked out by the classical tradition, he lays down a path which, by shifting attention from God to man and abandoning the goal of the eternal life, elevates the state and worldly glory to the highest value.

Machiavelli never uses the phrase *ragione di stato* (reason of state) or its French equivalent, *raison d'État*. Nevertheless, the contention that in order to maintain and protect the state, it is appropriate for a prince to engage in a morally reprehensible course of action is central to his political theory. Under his influence, this view of princely conduct became the main theme of an entire genre of political writings in sixteenth-century Italy, the most notable contribution being Giovanni Botero's work *Ragione di Stato* (Skinner 248). It was, however, in seventeenth-century France, in the policies of Cardinal Richelieu that were directed toward the furthering of the Catholic faith and the benefit of the Christian state, and later in Germany that Machiavellian political ideas came to prominence and contributed to a significant evolution of the doctrine of *raison d'État*. With the breakdown of the unity of western Christendom caused by the Reformation, the rise of the modern state system, and the expanding secularization of European culture in the course of the eighteenth and nineteenth centuries, this doctrine lost its connection with any religious ends and devolved into materialistic calculation of what was necessary to promote the interest of the state (Russell 41). *Raison d'État* became the main principle of European interstate relations and served as a justification of the methods that a number of statesmen felt obliged to use in their practice of foreign policy. Such methods, earlier outlined in *The Prince*, involved conquering by force or by fraud, destroying cities, putting to death anyone who could do harm, moving populations from one place to another, establishing colonies, and seeking the maximum extension of the state's territory and power at the expense of rivals. The question of morality, in the sense of norms restraining states in their mutual relations, either did not arise or was subordinated to the competitive struggle for power.

In sixteenth-century German cities, organized according to traditional Germanic jurisprudence and enlivened by Christian religion, Machiavelli's ideas were unthinkable (Meinecke 392). Although the doctrine of *raison d'État* had been introduced to Germany already during the course of seventeenth century, up until the time of Kant, prevailing German ideas on the subject of the state remained un-Machiavellian. However, the struggle for independence and power carried out by the rulers of Prussia in the eighteenth century, and especially by Frederick the Great, who called Machiavelli the enemy of mankind but closely followed his advice, led to a greater acceptance of Machiavellian methods. The politics of *raison d'État* was carried even further in the nineteenth century, as embodied in the ruthless policies of Bismarck. His "blood and iron" method of unifying Germany interpreted *raison d'État* as reliance on armed strength for national ends. By claiming that the state derives its norms primarily from itself, and emphasizing the state's interest as a primary value, he established a pattern of thought that came to be known as *realpolitik*. Moreover, the spread of this doctrine received an additional impulse from the ideas of the philosophers Fichte and Hegel, and the historians Ranke and Treitschke. The earlier doctrine of *raison d'État* had admitted the possibility of conflict between politics and morality. It became a specific task of German thought to resolve this conflict through some sort of justifying synthesis. By asserting that "the state has no higher duty than of maintaining itself," Hegel gave an ethical sanction to the state's selfish interest and advantage (Meinecke 357). Leopold von Ranke coupled the concept of state egoism with the idea of a moral purpose that the state must fulfill (Russell 44). The good of the state was interpreted as the highest moral value. Referring to Machiavelli, Heinrich von Treitschke declared that the state was power and that the supreme moral duty of the state was to foster this power. He considered international agreements to be binding only insofar as it was expedient for the state (Meinecke 397). The idea of an autonomous ethics of state behavior was thus introduced, as well as a notion of double morality, one private and one public. Power politics was associated with a "higher" type of morality. These concepts, along with the belief in the superiority of German culture, served as weapons with which German statesmen, from the eighteenth century to the end of the Second World War, justified their policies of conquest and extermination.

The doctrine of *raison d'État* had until recently very little impact on America. The United States was created by people who "believed in a sacred Covenant, designed to restrain the human tendencies toward violence and fraud" (Kirk 29). The American founders were adherents of the doctrine of natural law and believed in universal moral values. Although Machiavelli's ideas were available to them through the medium of the seventeenth-century English political thinker James Harrington, they looked for the principles of republicanism primarily in the writings of classical authors, such as Cicero, Sallust, Tacitus, and Plutarch (Gordon Wood 51). The American political soul was thus thoroughly permeated by idealism. Nowhere was this idealism more clearly stated at the international level than in President Woodrow Wilson's *War Message* of April 2, 1917: "Our object now, as then, is to vindicate the principles of peace and justice in the life of the world as against selfish and autocratic power and set up among the really free and self-governed people of the world such a concert of purpose and of action as will henceforth ensure the observance of these principles." American idealism, based on the belief in the international rule of law and collective security, led to the creation of the League of Nations, and, after the Second World War, to the founding of the United Nations.

The ideas of power politics were introduced to America by a realist academic community that emerged only in the 1940s, and in particular by Hans Morgenthau, who had immigrated to the United States in the 1930s. Morgenthau published a series of books in the 1940s and 1950s, the most influential of which was *Politics Among Nations*, a work that became the standard textbook on international relations for a generation (Brown 32). However, in contrast to the continental theorists of *raison d'État*, the leading twentieth-century American realists—Morgenthau, Niebuhr, and Kennan—recognized but did not exalt state egoism, and were unwilling to set forth any separate ethics of state behavior (Russell 241). They acknowledged the importance of national interest, but they were willing to adjust it to international norms. It was the behavioral revolution in social sciences that produced neo-realism and other scientific approaches and led to the gradual removal of ethics from research on international relations. The role played by Hans Morgenthau in his generation was filled by Kenneth Waltz in the 1980s. In Waltz's neo-realism, *realpolitik* dominates international behavior (Harbour 35). "The ruler's, and later the state's interest provides the spring of action; the necessities of policy arise from the unregulated competition of states; calculation based on these necessities can discover the policies that will best serve a state's interests; success is the ultimate test of policy, and success is defined as preserving and strengthening the state" (Waltz 117). Waltz theory of foreign policy concerns itself with the purely materialistic matter of calculating what is necessary for the interest of the state; it does not consult international ethics. Because of the rise of positivist social science, which excludes studying values from the domain of research, Machiavelli has thus entered America through the back door, so to speak.

Perhaps the greatest problem with political realism is that it has a tendency to slip into its extreme version, *realpolitik*, in which any policy that can benefit the state is accepted, no matter how morally problematic it may be. In this extreme version, realism, motivated by a state's security and self-interest, can develop a violent tendency. In the case of Germany, this led to the affirmation of the doctrine of *raison d'État*, and subsequently to two world wars. Even if they do not explicitly raise ethical questions, in the works of Kenneth Waltz and many other today's neo-realists, a double morality is presupposed as a basic assumption, and Machiavellian ideas and words such as *realpolitik* no longer have negative connotations. The decline of classical education, the inability of positivistic political scientists to deal with ethical issues, and the secularization of American life have led to a situation in which Americans have become less and less immune to Machiavellism.

MACHIAVELLI AND MACHIAVELLISM

Machiavelli's bad reputation rests primarily on a single treatise, *The Prince*. This book is the source of his image as a proponent of the doctrine that the end justifies the means. Certainly, *The Prince* presents a critique of the classical moral and political tradition, which embraces the ideas of such thinkers as Plato, Aristotle, Cicero, Augustine, and Aquinas. Nevertheless, a close reading of the works of Machiavelli (especially *The Discourses*) reveals a more complex political theory, from which much can still be learned. His dedication to the ideas of republicanism and political liberty leads him to explore the phenomena of political and moral corruption, which pose a threat to republics in any era. His emphasis on prudence in international politics is a vital contribution to political realism. His view of the state as an autonomous political entity points to the theories of sovereignty later formulated by Bodin and Grotius. Yet, not surprisingly, Machiavelli's main concern remains the achievement of order and stability in the climate of corruption, lawlessness, and conflicts that characterized Italian city-states in the early sixteenth century. In the concluding chapter of *The Prince*, he urges the Medici to unify Italy and liberate it from foreign domination. Accordingly, his political vision was a source of inspiration to Mazzini and Garibaldi, who in the nineteenth century led the movement for Italian unification.

Glory is an important concept for Machiavelli (Price 588). To achieve glory, either military or political, means to be recognized for outstanding deeds and achievements in serving the good of the state. Military glory is gained by performing valorous actions and being victorious in battle (*Disc.* III, 42). Founding a new state and "strengthening it and adorning it with good laws, good arms, good friends, and good examples" brings political glory (*Prince* XXIV). Inspiring the desire for glory is for Machiavelli a means of transforming individual selfishness into group, and, particularly, state egoism. The Romans, devoted to their Republic, sought domination and glory, and were not content with tranquility as their goal (*Disc.* II, 9). In contrast, most Italian states were governed by mediocre and slothful rulers who, rather than pursuing glory, preferred to live in comfort and security, or at most to increase their wealth (*History of Florence* I, 39). In chapter XXIV of *The Prince*, Machiavelli criticizes these rulers severely, noting that they all suffered the shame of losing their states. Analyzing the reasons for their downfall, he finds that they lacked prudence and displayed idleness and lack of spirit. *The Prince* can thus be seen in part as an attempt on Machiavelli's part to turn the personal ambition of the Medici into a desire for political and military glory. The recurrent theme of his advice to the princes is to seek glory suited to modern times, and to lay the foundations for security, prosperity, and freedom.

While the values of national security, prosperity, and freedom are legitimate and can be related to Machiavelli's overall goal to unify and liberate Italy, they justify the cultivation of military strength only to a point. Because of his extreme emphasis on military matters and celebration of glory, Machiavelli can rightly be accused of having "crossed the thin line to militarism" (Kocis 214). Although it is ultimately aimed at the good of the state, his liberation of politics from the restraints of morality can be interpreted as an invitation to conquer. Furthermore, his design to transform individual selfishness into a love of glory and devotion to national greatness may be regarded as his contribution to the idea of nationalism. Nationalism and militarism mixed together form a deadly poison that destroys the body of common humanity. In his penetrating study of Machiavellism, Friedrich Meinecke observes: "On the introduction of universal military service [in modern Europe], militarism grew deeply involved with the life of the people, and thereby acquired incommensurable physical and moral powers…War, which was based on universal military service, came to be characterized as a people's war, a national war. The instincts and passions of entire peoples now flowed into war and politics" (418–419). The effects of Machiavellian ideas could be seen on the battlefields of modern Europe, as mass citizen armies fought against each other to the deadly end without regard for the rules of justice.

Machiavellism has come to be associated with a certain kind of political behavior, in which expediency is placed above morality. This kind of behavior existed long before Machiavelli, and had been debated by political philosophers since long before his time. The arguments of the Athenian envoys presented in Thucydides' *Melian Dialogue*, that of Thrasymachus in Plato's *Republic*, and that of Carneades, to whom Grotius refers—all of these challenge the classical and Christian view of the unity of politics and ethics. However, before Machiavelli, this amoral or immoral mode of thinking had never prevailed over the dominant moral tradition of Western thought. It was only the Machiavellian justification of resorting to evil as a legitimate means of achieving certain political ends that would persuade so many thinkers and political practitioners after him. This justification was extended by the theorists of the doctrine of the *raison d'État*. The tension between expediency and morality lost its validity in the sphere of politics. The concept of a double morality, private and public, was invented. Ethics was subjected to politics. The good of the state was interpreted as the highest moral value. The extension of national power was seen as a nation's right and duty. In the Marxist version of this doctrine, a superior type of morality was attributed to the revolutionary cause. In the name of such a "higher" morality, identified with the interests of the proletariat or of the state, or of an elite nation or race, the gravest crimes against humanity have been committed. Actions that employed violent, cruel, or otherwise conventionally immoral means have been regarded as legitimate to exigencies of "progressive change."

Machiavelli himself justifies immoral actions, but never refuses to admit that they are evil. His writings retain the traditional meaning of immorality in the sense of a suppression or violation of morality for the sake of expediency, either of the individual or of the state. He cannot be held responsible for the extreme Machiavellism of double ethics or for the crimes it has produced. Nevertheless, by giving rulers the license to disobey moral norms whenever the interests of the state are at stake, he projects to humanity a false dream that the state can become prosperous and the world "better" by means of an evil action. He sanctions the commission of ethically repugnant acts on behalf of "higher" political goals, and thus contributes to the climate that enabled followers of such militarists as Frederick the Great, Otto von Bismarck, Benito Mussolini, Adolf Hitler, and Joseph Stalin to condone the evil policies of their leaders. In this sense he can be rightly charged with literally demoralizing Europe. It came only after experiencing the painful lessons of history, in the form of the centuries of wars, that Europeans came to the realization that "it is only within the family-like community of states that the individual state can prosper in the longer run" (Meinecke 431). By distancing itself from Machiavellian advice, promoting the spirit of international cooperation, and integrating nation-states into a community, Europe has at last returned to a place where the counsels of wisdom may prevail.

QUESTIONS

- What are Machiavelli's *virtú* and *fortuna*, and how is *virtú* different from virtue?
- What are the potential advantages and disadvantages of the mixed constitution?
- Machiavelli argues that, for the sake of their safety, states should adopt the policy of expansion. Do you agree?
- What does Machiavelli suggest about goodness and corruption in politics? How can corruption be prevented?
- What must the prince "who wishes to maintain his position" learn and why?
- Is the kind of vicious behavior Machiavelli is advocating to the princes truly vicious?
- What is old and new in Machiavelli's thinking? In what sense does his philosophy no longer represent the classical and Christian moral traditions?
- What is the doctrine of *raison d'État*, and what are its moral implications?
- What kind of politics do we commonly associate with the adjective "Machiavellian"?

GUIDE TO FURTHER READING

Translations of Machiavelli's Political Works:

Machiavelli, Niccolò. *The Prince*. Trans. Harvey C. Mansfield, Jr. Chicago: Chicago UP, 1985.

Machiavelli, Niccolò. *The Prince*. Ed. Quentin Skinner and Russell Price. Cambridge: Cambridge UP, 1988.

Machiavelli, Niccolò. *The Discourses*. 2 vols. Trans. Leslie J. Walker. London: Routledge, 1975.

Bondanella, Peter and Mark Musa, eds. *The Portable Machiavelli*. London: Penguin, 1979. Contains *The Prince*, *The Discourses* (abridged), fragments of *The Art. of War*, *The History of Florence*, and a selection of private letters and literary works.

The Complete Works in English:

Machiavelli, Niccolò. *The Chief Works and Others*. Ed. Allan Gilbert. Durham, NC: Duke UP, 1995.

Suggested Readings:

Bock, Gisela, et al., eds. *Machiavelli and Republicanism*. Cambridge: Cambridge UP, 1990.

King, Ross. *Machiavelli: Philosopher of Power*. New York: Harper collins, 2009.

Kocis, Robert A. *Machiavelli Redeemed: Retrieving His Humanist Perspectives on Equality, Power, and Glory*. Bethlehem: Lehigh UP, 1998.

Ledeen, Michael A. *Machiavelli on Modern Leadership: Why Machiavelli's Iron Rulers are as Timely and as Important today as Five Centuries ago*. New York: St. Martin's Press, 2000.

Mansfield, Harvey C. *Machiavelli's Virtue*. Chicago: Chicago UP, 1998.

Mc Alpine, Alistar. *The New Machiavelli: The Art of Politics in Business*. Danvers: John Wiley & Sons, 2000.

Meinecke, Friedrich. *Machiavellism: The Doctrine of Raison d'État in Modern History*. Trans. Douglas Scott. New Brunswick, NJ: Transaction, 1998.

Paret, Peter. *Makers of Modern Strategy: From Machiavelli to Nuclear Age*. Oxford: Oxford UP, 1986.

Skinner, Quentin. *The Foundations of Modern Political Thought*. Vol. 1. Cambridge: Cambridge UP, 1978.

Skinner, Quentin. *Machiavelli: A Very Short Introduction*. Oxford: Oxford UP, 2000.

Grotius: International Society

ugo Grotius (Huigh de Groot in Dutch) is often hailed as the father of
international law. Because of the scope of his interests, he was truly a
humanist. A jurist and diplomat, he also gained recognition as a political thinker, theologian, historian, playwright, and poet. He was born in Delft,
Holland, on August 10, 1583, to a patrician family distinguished by its long
tradition of public service, with connections by marriage to many of the principal families of the Netherlands. His father, Jan de Groot, was burgomaster
of Delft and later rector of the University of Leiden. Hugo was a child prodigy,
writing Latin poetry at the age of eight, and he entered university when he was
twelve, one or two years earlier than was usual at the time. At the University of
Leiden, he studied classical languages, law, and theology, completing his studies at the age of fifteen.

The conclusion of his studies may have been accelerated by the opportunity offered him to accompany Johan van Oldenbarnevelt and Justin van
Nassau on a diplomatic mission to the court of France. Oldenbarnevelt,
the *Landsadvocaat* (chief justice) of the States of Holland, later the Grand
Pensionary (prime minister), was a statesman of immense prestige. During this
mission, Grotius was presented to King Henry IV, who hailed the young Hugo
as "the miracle of Holland." He remained for some months in France, in the
course of which he received a doctorate in law from the University of Orleans.

Back in Holland, Grotius was admitted to the Bar at the end of 1599 and
settled in The Hague. However, his work as a lawyer seemed only to act as a
stimulus to his literary activity. Any free time left over from his legal practice
was devoted to the study of literature and history. A collection of his poems
published in 1601 included a tragedy entitled *Adamus exul*. On the death of
Dousa in 1604, he succeeded to his position as historiographer of Holland,
and subsequently wrote *Annales et Historiae de Rebus Belgicis* (*A History of
the Dutch Republic*). In addition, during 1604 and 1605, he wrote *De Jure
Praedae* (*On the Law of Prize*) in connection with a case in which he served as

a legal adviser for the Dutch East India Company. The book did not appear in its entirety during his lifetime, but the chapter *Mare Liberum* (*Freedom of the Seas*), in which he argued that the seas should be free for the use and mutual benefit of all, was published in 1609.

Social status, education, and family traditions and connections all enabled Grotius to advance swiftly in his career. Toward the end of 1607, when he was twenty-four, with Oldenbarnevelt's support, he was appointed Advocate-Fiscal (public prosecutor) at the Court of Holland, Zealand, and West Friesland, an important post that also strengthened his social position. The next year he married Marie van Reygersberch, the daughter of the burgomaster of Veere. She became a very important influence in his life and would give him four sons and three daughters. The few years during which he held the office of Advocate-Fiscal were perhaps the most fortunate in his life. But the course of events was hastening toward a catastrophe that was to bring him to prison and exile.

Grotius was born during one of the most turbulent times in Dutch and European history, a period of religious wars in which politics and religion were inextricable. In the course of the sixteenth century, the Protestant Reformation swept over the Low Countries, which at the time were under Spanish (i.e., Catholic) rule. Calvinism was the driving force behind the movement, which aimed at both religious domination and Holland's political independence. In 1568, violent resistance to Spain led by the Calvinists triggered the Eighty Years' War (or Dutch Revolt). On January 6, 1579, the southern states (most of which are in today's Belgium) signed the Union of Atrecht, expressing their loyalty to the Spanish Crown. In response, on January 23, 1579, the leader of the Dutch rebellion, William I, Prince of Orange, united the northern, predominantly Protestant states of Holland, Zealand, and Utrecht, and the province of Groningen in the Union of Utrecht. In 1581, less than two years before Grotius' birth, this union declared independence from Spain, forming the United Provinces of the Netherlands (also known as the Dutch Republic).

By stimulating shipping, colonial expeditions, and the development of financial institutions in the Netherlands, the Dutch War of Independence turned gradually from a religious conflict into one in which commercial interests seemed far more important. The war led the Dutch to develop a shipping empire so extensive that for the greater part of the seventeenth century they largely dominated European foreign trade. At the beginning of the seventeenth century, the increasing war debt and the demand to safeguard the commercial gains made strengthened the position of those who wanted peace. These people ranged themselves behind Johan van Oldenbarnevelt. On the opposite side stood Prince Maurice of Nassau, William's son, who, after his father's assassination, became the commander-in-chief and the stadtholder (head of state). Against his advice, Oldenbarnevelt, acting on the behalf of the States General, signed the Twelve Year Truce with Spain, which lasted from 1609 to 1621.

The war against Spain and the hostility between Protestants and Catholics were not the only sources of trouble during the turbulent times in which Grotius lived. There were also tensions among the Protestants themselves. The

Dutch Reformed Church was predominantly Calvinist. The ideal of Calvinism was theocratic: It aspired to make the Calvinist church and the state coincide, and to rule the state through the church. To some degree, Calvinism was able to realize this ideal in Geneva, but it never succeeded in Holland, where it encountered a powerful and able opposition in the form of most members of the wealthy and educated elite to which Grotius belonged. To such an elite, the idea of replacing the previously ascendant Catholic Church with another dominant church was repugnant (Geyl 5). Inspired by the ideals of liberty of Erasmus and other northern humanists, and afraid of the populism of Calvinist radicals, members of this elite controlled the Provincial Assembly and protected Catholics and non-Calvinist Protestants alike from persecution by the Calvinist clergy and their followers. Many of the liberal Protestants, called "Arminians" (or Remonstrants), were aligned with *Jacobes Arminius*, Professor of Divinity at Leiden. Educated at Geneva in the principles of Calvinism, he later began to question some of those principles. As a professor, he was constantly embroiled in argument with his strict Calvinistic colleague Francis Gomarus and the latter's followers, the "Gomarists" (or Contra-Remonstrants). Their dispute would divide into two hostile camps not only the university but also the whole country.

With the conclusion of the truce with Spain in 1609, this internal religious dispute intensified. On the one side were the Gomarists, who demanded that the government impose a religious uniformity based on the Reformed Church and suppress the influence of Catholics and non-Calvinist Protestants. On the other side were the Arminians, who argued that matters of religion should be controlled by the secular power, which would impose tolerance. The quarrel also widened the division between Oldenbarnevelt and Prince Maurice. After 1609, Maurice increasingly sided with the strict Calvinists, while Oldenbarnevelt leaned toward the Arminians.

In 1613 Grotius went with a diplomatic mission to England to negotiate problems related to freedom of navigation and commerce in the Indian seas. However, conducting commercial talks was not his only objective. Grotius tried with some success to persuade King James I to take a more favorable view of the policy of enforcing religious tolerance that had been adopted by the Netherlands. After returning to his country, he entered a new phase of life. He was appointed the Pensionary (chief magistrate) of Rotterdam and the town's representative to the Provincial and National Assemblies. At about the same time, his book *Ordinum Hollandiae ac Westfrisiae Pietas* (*The Religiosity of Holland and West Friesland*), defending freedom of belief and the policy of tolerance, appeared. While some praised the book, many more condemned it. This was just the beginning of the storm that swept him and Oldenbarnevelt from power.

In spite of Calvinist opposition, the Province of Holland was prepared to take further steps to ensure religious tolerance. Early in 1614, a "Resolution for Peace in the Church," drafted by Grotius, was passed by the Provincial Assembly (R. Lee 239). The resolution urged tolerance and moderation, and prescribed some limits concerning what might be taught in the churches. Since the law had little effect, further measures against radical Calvinists opposing it, involving the prohibition of religious gatherings, were implemented. The Calvinists in turn appealed to Prince Maurice, who, although largely indifferent to issues of faith, saw in the quarrel an opportunity to get the better of Oldenbarnevelt, a man whom he hated.

The situation worsened when in 1617 the Provincial Assembly, facing growing social unrest and fearing that the army of the Dutch Republic might be used to compel the holding of a national synod in which the Arminians would be condemned, accepted the "Sharp Resolution," which stated that all army personnel should only obey those who paid their salaries and disregard any other orders. This was a direct attack upon Prince Maurice, the commander-in-chief, and accelerated the Calvinist *coup d'état*. On August 29, 1618, supported by the army and acting on a secret resolution of the States-General (National Assembly) that empowered him to take any measures necessary in the public interest, Maurice arrested Oldenbarnevelt, Grotius, and two other prominent statesmen, and started to purge town councils of Arminian supporters. The principles of Arminius were condemned in the Calvinist Synod held at Dort. The court proceedings that followed in 1619 against so-called "Remonstrant heresy" were held in secret. The judges were selected extralegally, and the captives were tried before an ad hoc court. Oldenbarnevelt was executed, while Grotius received a life sentence and lost all his property.

Grotius was taken to Loevestein, the state prison. His wife was allowed to visit him, and he was provided with writing materials and books. It was during his imprisonment that he wrote a book on the jurisprudence of Holland, as well as some theological works. In 1621 his wife concealed him in a chest for books, and organized an escape that would become legendary. Grotius went to Paris, where he spent nearly the entire remainder of his life. Barely surviving with his family on a small pension from King Louis XIII, Grotius began in 1623 to write his great treatise, *De Jure Belli ac Pacis (On the Law of War and Peace)*, which was published in 1625. Although France, caught up in the Thirty Years' War, was dominated by the policies of Cardinal Richelieu, and the politics of *raison d'État* were in fashion, the influence of this work nonetheless spread.

While in exile, Grotius cherished hopes of returning to his native country. After the death of Prince Maurice in 1625, his successor Frederick Henry, who became stadtholder, attempted to effect a reconciliation between the contending religious factions. As a result, in 1630 the City of Delft compensated Grotius for his confiscated property with a payment of sixty pounds, and he came back to Holland for a brief period in 1631. However, because of hostilities directed against him, he had to leave the country again. He fled to Hamburg, which, like some other parts of Germany at that time, was under the control of Sweden. There, he established a close friendship with Salvinus, Vice-Chancellor of Sweden. It was on his recommendation, and because of the support of the Chancellor Oxenstierna, that Grotius was appointed Swedish ambassador to the French court. He returned to Paris in this capacity in 1635. However, his experience as ambassador brought him little but disillusionment.

Annoyed by quarrels about rules of precedence and other manifestations of diplomatic vanity, Grotius withdrew into the privacy of his study and composed works of theology. Like his earlier and very popular book (*De Veritate Religionis Christianae*) *On the Truth of Christian Religion*, published in 1627, these works focused on essential Christian teachings rather than on the issues that divided Christianity. They were an expression of Grotius' grand idea of the reunification of all Christian churches.

In 1645, after serving in Paris longer than any other ambassador, Grotius was recalled by a letter from Queen Christina. He left France in March and traveled to Sweden by way of Holland. Reaching Stockholm in June, he was received by the Queen with due honors, but no offer of future employment was made. He boarded a ship for Lübeck, apparently to join his wife and daughter there. But a storm came, and the vessel was wrecked on the Polish coast near Gdansk. Grotius continued his journey for eight days in an open carriage, but got no further than Rostock. Exhausted and ill, he died at Rostock on August 28, 1645. His body was brought back to Delft, but a plan for a monumental tomb had to be canceled because of the opposition of his political and private enemies. The Nieuwe Church contains a simple monument that was erected only in 1781, at the expense of his descendants.

THE JUST WAR TRADITION

The age in which Grotius lived was one of almost continuous warfare. The emerging sovereign and mutually independent states of Europe were incessantly fighting over territorial, dynastic, and commercial matters, as well as differences in religion. The Thirty Years' War, arguably one of the most cruel and lawless wars in European history, broke out in 1618 as a result of religious disputes. Disgusted with these wars among Christians, Grotius wrote in the *Prolegomena* to the three books of *On the Law of War and Peace*: "Throughout the Christian world I observed a lack of restraint in relation to war, such as even barbarous nations should be ashamed of; I observed that men rush to arms for slight causes, or no cause at all, and that when arms have once been taken up there is no longer any respect for law, divine or human; it is as if, in accordance with a general decree, frenzy had openly been let loose for the committing of all crimes" (*Prol.* §28). At a time when war had become endemic, his achievement was to delineate codes of justice for distinguishing a just war from an unjust war, for protecting innocent non-combatants, for discerning rights of persons and property, and for arranging procedures for truces, treaties, and the humane treatment of hostages and prisoners. In the face of the disintegration of the spiritual and legal unity of Christendom, Grotius developed a system of law governing the relations of independent states. His transformation of the basis of just war theory from a close connection with Christian ethics into one defined by natural law enabled it to continue to develop in the pluralistic environment of the modern world. He thus made a great contribution to the development of international law and a more just conduct of war.

The distinction between just and unjust wars was not originally conceived by Grotius. It can be traced to the legal tradition of early Rome, and was elaborated by Cicero (Draper 179). The Christian concept of the just war was formulated by Saint Augustine, who embraced Cicero's view that war should always be the last choice, but could be waged in order to preserve peace. The concept was adopted by Thomas Aquinas, who asserted that for a war to be righteous, it should fulfill three criteria: it should have just cause, be declared and conducted by the supreme public authority, and have a rightful intention. The Spanish Dominican theologian Francisco de Vitoria was the first to question the assumed right of his countrymen to wage war against Native Indians in order to conquer their territories. He insisted that the war of the Spaniards against the natives should have a just cause and castigated the inhumane practices of the invaders. His ideas were subsequently developed by such sixteenth-century scholars as Francisco Suarez, Balthazar Ayala, and Alberico Gentili, all of whom wrote about laws of war. Given that he was relying on a tradition that stretched from Cicero and Augustine to Vitoria and Gentili, it may seem that Grotius' ideas about international law were not strikingly original. However, it is the vast range of his learning, his well-developed arguments, and his ability to systematize existing knowledge of the subject that commands our attention. No one before him had attempted to treat the issue of just and unjust wars in its entirety. Unlike Vitoria, Suarez, Ayala, and Gentili, he had in view a complete system of international law, rather than mere fragments. Furthermore, unlike these scholastic writers, he wrote for Christians and non-Christians alike, setting an example of a systematic approach to international problems, emancipated from theology.

In 1648, three years after Grotius' death, the Thirty Years' War was ended by the Peace of Westphalia. This peace embraced the notion of state sovereignty, guaranteed to rulers the authority to choose which version of Christianity their people would follow, and secured for the Protestant creed free expression in many parts of Europe. It also marked the emergence of international society, the acceptance by states of rules and institutions binding on them in their relations with one another. It thus realized many of the ideas that Grotius had set forth in his writings. In this way, his influence overshadowed the greater fame of many of his predecessors. Between 1625 and 1773, before it fell into neglect for a long period pending its rediscovery in the early twentieth century, his *De Jure Belli ac Pacis* was edited or translated over sixty times. Posterity saw in him the initiator of a new era, the founder of the law of nations. Nonetheless, although admired, his work initially had little impact on the actual behavior of states. The sovereigns of the period following the Peace of Westphalia would not always consider themselves rigidly bound by international agreements and were rather unscrupulous in interpreting and applying them. They were thus followers of the doctrine of *raison d'État* and disciples of Machiavelli, whose *Prince* taught them to break any treaty when the advantages that had originally induced them to conclude it ceased to exist. In contrast, in his works, Grotius placed great emphasis upon the binding force of promises and the obligation of good faith in their fulfillment (*De Jure* II, ch. 11). It was, in fact, principally against Machiavellism that he directed his argument.

GROTIUS' ARGUMENT AGAINST *RAISON D'ÉTAT*

During Grotius' time, the influence of Machiavelli's ideas had spread, and there were in circulation numerous works advocating the politics of *raison d'État*. It is surprising that *De Jure Belli ac Pacis* does not contain any reference to the Florentine thinker. Nevertheless, although he does not mention Machiavelli by name, Grotius challenges the views of the adherents of the doctrine of *raison d'État*, who license rulers to disobey legal and moral norms whenever the vital interests of the state are at stake and thus introduce a double morality—private and public. Drawing attention to the desirability of having the relations between states governed by law, he writes: "Many hold, in fact, that the standard of justice which they insist upon in the case of individuals within the state is inapplicable to a nation or the ruler of a nation" (*Prol.* § 22). He tells us that there are those who regard international law with contempt, "as having no reality except an empty name" (*Prol.* § 3). Such writers consider that for a state nothing is unjust that is expedient and that the conduct of foreign policy cannot be performed without injustice. Powerful states can afford to pursue their policies without regard to law and with solely their own advantage in view. Grotius rejects these views. In humanist fashion, instead of attacking his contemporary opponents directly, he makes his argument against Carneades (215-129 B.C.E.), a critic of natural law and an ancient representative of the belief that in international politics nothing is unjust that is expedient.

Carneades' position can be summarized as follows: There is no universally valid natural law, discoverable by "right reason," which determines what is right and wrong. Natural law has no basis because all creatures, human beings and animals, are impelled by nature to pursue ends advantageous for themselves (*Prol.* § 5). Therefore, nothing is right or just by nature, and all laws are conventional. Human beings impose them upon themselves for reasons of expediency, and such laws vary among different peoples and change at different times. Justice is derived from utility and is based only upon calculation of the advantages of living together in a particular society. Such advantages are apparent in the case of citizens who, singly, are powerless to protect themselves. But since strong individuals or powerful states contain in themselves everything required for their own protection, they do not need justice (*Prol.* § 22). They need acknowledge no higher law than their own strength. The notion of justice is thus not applicable to relations between states, or if there is justice, "it is supreme folly, since one does violence to one's own interests if one consults the advantage of others" (*Prol.* § 5). In short, to use the phrase of Reinhold Niebuhr, Carneades is one "in the long line of moral cynics in the field of international relations" who know no law beyond self-interest (Niebuhr, 1960, 8).

To Grotius, justice is not folly. He defends natural law as follows. First, he attacks the view that every animal is impelled by nature to seek only its own good. Even animals can restrain their self-serving appetites to further the advantage of other animals, most obviously their offspring, but also other members of their own and other species (*Prol.* § 7). Sheep-dogs, for example, go in advance of their flocks, fighting to the death, if necessary, to protect the flocks and shepherds from harm. If this is the case with animals, it is even more so with humans, who are rational creatures. Humans can benefit not only themselves but also others through their ability to recognize others' needs. They can refrain, even at the cost of inconvenience to themselves, from doing harm to others (*De Jure* I, ch. 1, xi). They have been endowed with the faculties of knowing good and evil, and of acting according to general principles. What is characteristic of human beings is "an overwhelming desire for society; that is, for social life not of any and every sort, but peaceful, and organized according to the measure of intelligence" (*Prol.* § 6). They never were, nor are they now by nature wild, unsociable beings. On the contrary, it is the corruption of their nature that makes them so (*De Jure* I, ch. 1, xii). Further, if humans are naturally social, their natural sociability should be protected against acts that destroy peace in society, such as the violation of others' property. Laws established to provide order in society are thus not merely conventional but have their basis in human sociability. The law of nature, as it appears in the *Prolegomena*, is the law that is in conformity with the social nature of humans and the preservation of social order; it is the law that applies to all human beings. To its sphere belong such standards as the principle of not taking anything belonging to another, the restoration of damage, the obligation to fulfill promises, the reparation of injury, and the right to inflict penalties (*Prol.* § 6). It exists independently of any will and cannot be changed by any authority whatsoever, whether divine or human.

Human beings' natural inclination to one another, sociability or fellowship—in short, the social nature of human beings and not mere expediency—is the foundation of natural law: "a dictate of right reason which points out that an act, according to whether it is or is not in conformity with rational nature, has in it a quality of moral baseness or moral necessity" (*De Jure* III, ch. 11, xvi). Nevertheless, insofar as we have all been created weak, and lack many things needed to live properly, laws that have their ultimate source in human sociability are reinforced by expediency (*Prol.* § 16). Grotius divides law into natural law and volitional law. Positive volitional laws, which emanate from the power of the state but have their ultimate point of reference in natural law, have always some advantage in view. Insofar as they are based on citizens' choice and consent, the laws of each state have in view the benefit of the whole society. For this reason, he argues, it is wrong to ridicule justice as folly. A citizen who obeys the law is not foolish, "even though, out of regard for that law, he may be obliged to forgo certain things advantageous for himself" (*Prol.* § 18). By violating a law of his country in order to maximize utility and obtain immediate advantage, an individual destroys the common welfare, by which the advantages of himself and his posterity are secured. The same applies to international law, which has in view "the advantage, not of particular states, but of the great society of states" (*Prol.* § 17).

Grotius replaces the double standard of conduct, one for states and one for individuals, which is characteristic of the politics of *raison d'État*, with a clear-cut parallelism. There is one morality that is applicable to both nations and individual human beings. The "nation is not foolish which does not press its own advantage to the point of disregarding the laws common to all countries" (*Prol.* § 18). Although law is not founded upon expediency alone, no state can disregard the benefits of international cooperation. Grotius stresses mutual interdependence of states. In the mutually interdependent world, there is no state so powerful that it may not at some time need the help of others outside itself—for instance, for purposes of trade, or even to ward off the forces of foreign nations united against it (*Prol.* § 22). No state is free to act unlawfully. By disobeying the law of nations to gain temporary advantage for itself, a state alienates itself from international society and hence undermines the foundation of its own security.

Grotius thus challenges the view that laws are merely conventional and justice is a matter of mere expediency. He asserts the essential identity of the legal and moral rules governing the conduct of states and individuals, and traces the source of these rules to the law of nature. He does not identify international law (law of nations) with natural law, since the latter represents a body of moral rules recognized by all civilized human beings, while the former consists of a body of rules that have been accepted as obligatory by the consent of all or many states. However, the law of nature is for him the ever-present source that can be drawn upon to supplement the voluntary law of nations, and that serves as a standard to judge the latter's adequacy in the light of ethics and reason (*Lauterpacht* 21-22). Natural law provides criteria against which the mere will and practice of states can be measured. At the same time, Grotius draws our attention to the utility of international law. While the proponents of the doctrine of *raison d'État* argue that state interests override international norms, he attempts to demonstrate that this way of viewing national interest is the equivalent of looking into the wrong end of a telescope. He asserts it establishes a false dichotomy between the interests of particular states and the interests of the whole international community. Even if no immediate advantage were to be envisioned as a result of heeding the law, he says, it would be a mark of wisdom, not of folly, to allow ourselves to be drawn toward that to which we feel our nature leads us (*Prol.* § 18). Respecting international law and promoting international order can bring long-term benefits to all nations.

JUS AD BELLUM AND JUS IN BELLO

For adherents of the doctrine of *raison d'État*, ethical and legal norms are suspended by the necessities that states confront in international relations, such as the necessity to survive or to secure power. The stern necessities of the state justify doing evil. In the affirmation of "reason of state," the claim to an unrestricted right to war is thus the most important. War becomes the right of sovereign states and the very symbol of their sovereignty. Moreover, since war is always an instrument of state policy, as Carl von Clausewitz points out, it is limited insofar as policy is limited; however, once a state decides to pursue a policy of conquest and is no longer prepared to be bound by any established norms, it would fight a total and unconstrained war (Howard 6). Grotius disputes these views. For him, states are composed of individual human beings (*De Jure* II, ch. 1, xvii) and this is the basic reason why their behavior is not subject to impersonal forces of necessity but is ultimately dependent upon human decisions. States are not disorderly crowds, but political associations. As such, they are, as a rule, governed by individuals who are capable of forming judgments on strategic, legal, and ethical issues, and then make decisions after deliberations. Moreover, since states are collections of people, they are subordinated to natural law arising from the nature of man as a rational and social being (*Prol.* § 26). Hence, their behavior is subjected to limitations. To limit war is thus not inherently impossible. Grotius attempts to do so in two ways: first, by his just war doctrine, which puts severe limitations on the reasons for which war may be fought; and second, by putting legal restraints on its conduct (*Prol.* § 25). The two phrases, *jus ad bellum* (justice of war) and *jus in bello* (justice in war) refer respectively to these two cases.

Views concerning the legitimacy of war can be placed into one of three broad categories. First, there is the pacifist view that no act of war is legitimate. Second, there is the militaristic or Machiavellian view that any war that benefits the state is legitimate. Third, there is the legalistic or Grotian view that there is a distinction between just and unjust causes of war, and that some wars are therefore legitimate and others are not. The pacifist and militarist views can both be considered as inimical to international order. The former rejects the violence that is necessary to uphold the international order against attempts to subvert it; the latter admits violence of a sort that destroys international order (Bull, 1966, 54). For Grotius, the use of force is in no way dissonant with the social nature of humankind. "The right reason and the nature of society prohibit not all force," he says, "but only that which is repugnant to society, by depriving another of his right" (*De Jure* I, ch. 2, i). Convinced that there is a common law among nations, which is valid for war and in war, he attempts to provide an alternative to both extremes, pacifism and militarism, to counter the belief that either nothing is allowable or anything is (*Prol.* § 29). He denies the state the right to resort to war except in pursuance of a just cause: "No other just cause for undertaking war can there be excepting injury received" (*De Jure* II, ch. 1, i). He limits the justifiable causes of war to defense, recovery of property, and inflicting of punishment. In addition, he devotes an entire chapter of the *De Jure Belli ac Pacis* to an enumeration of various unjustifiable causes of war (Book II, ch. 12). He accepts as a just cause of war neither the desire for richer lands nor the desire to rule others against their own will on the pretext that it is for their own good. There is no just cause for war against those who merely refuse to accept our ideology or religion or those who err in its interpretation. Furthermore, in elaborating the right of self-defense, Grotius rejects the claims of the war of prevention. He argues that the notion that "the mere possibility of being attacked confers the right to attack is abhorrent to every principle of equity. Human life exists in such conditions that complete security is never guaranteed to us" (*De Jure* II, ch. 1, xvii). In another part of the book, he says plainly that to "authorize hostilities as a defensive measure, they must arise from the necessity which right apprehensions create: there must be a clear evidence, not only of the power, but also of the intentions of the formidable state, and such evidence as amounts to a moral certainty" (*De Jure* II, ch. 22, v).

In Book III of *De Jure Belli ac Pacis*, Grotius discusses what was considered to be just in war according to the customs of his day: wantonly killing and wounding enemies, devastating or plundering property, enslaving prisoners of war, and obtaining supreme governing power. However, he does not endorse these practices. In chapters 11–16, which include chapters setting out *temperamenta belli* (restraints on war), he aims to provide rules for minimizing bloodshed. First, he seeks to restrain the right to kill. He states that no one may be killed intentionally except as a just punishment or by necessity, when there is no other way to protect life or property. Next, he specifies the categories of people who may not be killed. These include non-combatants such as children, women (unless they are in fact combatants), old men, members of the clergy, men of letters, farmers, merchants, and artisans. He also states that the lives of those combatants who surrender unconditionally or beg for mercy, and thus no longer pose a threat, should be spared. Grotius' argument in respect to devastating and pillaging the enemy's lands is similar. Such means can occasionally be used to reduce the strength of the enemy. But devastation for devastation's sake is absurd and should be avoided. Grotius also insists that combatants should refrain from destroying works of art, especially those devoted to sacred purposes. He believes that reverence for things sacred requires that sacred buildings and their furnishings be preserved. To evaluate the usefulness of such *temperamenta,* he does not refer only to the law of nature. He also supports his stand regarding moderation in war by a prudential argument (*De Jure* III, ch. 12, viii). To refrain from indiscriminate killing, and from destroying and pillaging property, he argues, increases the likeness of one's own victory by depriving the enemy of the great weapon of despair.

De Jure Belli ac Pacis was read widely in the European intellectual circles of the seventeenth and the eighteenth centuries, and must then have exerted some influence on the process by which the severity of war in Europe was mitigated. Many rules and basic formulations of the law of war established in the late nineteenth and early twentieth centuries, especially by the Hague and Geneva conventions, correspond to Grotius' restraints on the conduct of war. Nevertheless, his just war doctrine was not accepted in his day, nor in the three centuries that followed. Prior to the changes introduced into international law in the aftermath of the First World War, states had the right to resort to war not only to defend their own legal rights but also to destroy the rights of other states. This idea of the unqualified prerogative of states to resort to war as an instrument of national policy was opposed by the just war tradition, which denied the absolute right to war and differentiated between wars that were, in law, just and those that were not. Grotius made a significant contribution to this tradition. In the Covenant of the League of Nations, established in 1919 by the Treaty of Versailles and dissolved in 1946, the extent of the lawful resort to war was diminished for the League's member states (Draper 202). International law on the right to resort to war was further developed by the Kellogg-Briand Pact of 1928, outlawing war as an instrument of national policy, and the U.N. Chapter of 1945. The provisions of the U.N. Chapter, aiming at providing a system of collective security, go beyond Grotius' position. However, they preserve his basic idea that states may use unilateral force only for the purpose of self-defense, and not for the pursuit of their foreign policy objectives.

THE UNIVERSALITY OF INTERNATIONAL SOCIETY

For Martin Wight, Hedley Bull, and other twentieth-century international relations theorists of the English School, Grotius has set forth one of the classic paradigms that has since determined both our understanding of inter-state relations and our ideas as to what constitutes right conduct therein (Bull, 1990, 71). This paradigm is "international society," or what Grotius calls "the great society of states" (*Prol.* § 17). In Bull's definition, international society "exists when a group of states, conscious of common interests and common values, form a society in the sense that they conceive themselves to be bound by a common set of rules in their relations to one another, and share in the working of common institutions" (Bull, 1977, 13). It involves a system of interacting states and a set of shared norms concerning their behavior, norms that are incorporated in international law. It differs from "cosmopolitan society" (or "world society"), whose members are not states but individual human beings, that is, members of the world's population.

Political philosophy offers two standard paradigms of international relations. On the one hand, in the tradition of realism, associated with Machiavelli and Hobbes, the sovereign states in their dealings with one another are in the state of nature, unrestrained by legal or moral rules in their relations with one another. Viewed from this perspective, the international environment is characterized by ongoing conflict. Placed in a situation of anarchy, with no ruler above them, states are caught in a continuous struggle for power and survival. In counterpart to this tradition, reflection on the conflictive character of inter-state relations can also lead to the alternative conclusion that peace among nations should be secured by bringing this international anarchy to an end. Thus, another paradigm, advocated as early as the middle of the thirteenth century by Dante Aligheieri in his *De Monarchia*, is the idea that states can be made subject to a world empire and thus escape from the state of nature. Advocates of this idea attempt a radical transformation of the existing international system. They believe that what is needed to ensure lasting peace is the transfer of the sovereignties of individual states to a central authority, one that would be sovereign over individual nations in the same way that such nations are sovereign over their respective territories. In contrast, Grotius neither approves of lawlessness in international relations, nor is he attracted by the idea of replacing individual sovereign states with a universal empire, "whose advantages are counterbalanced by still greater disadvantages" (*De Jure* II, ch. 22, xiii). He instead advocates a third paradigm, in which states in their dealings with one another are linked by mutual obligations, and thus form a society with one another, a "society without government" (Bull, 1995, 79). He subjects relations between sovereign states to the rule of law.

Grotius defines the sovereign power as one "whose actions are not subject to the legal control of another, so that they cannot be rendered void by operation of another human will" (*De Jure* I, ch. 3, vi). The distinguishing marks of sovereignty are for him the right of appointing magistrates, of enacting and repealing laws, and of making war and peace, to which he adds "the administration of justice, the supreme authority in the matters of religion, and the right of calling general councils" (Ibid.). He denies both the Machiavellian claim that there should be no limits whatsoever on individual state sovereignty, and the attempts in effect to eliminate it proposed by the advocates of a world empire. His idea is that sovereign states, like individuals, are equally subject to law and can recognize the common bonds of their society. They can still preserve their sovereignty even when they are enmeshed in a web of shared rules and norms, and particularly when they choose to become members of an international organization. "Many states," Grotius claims, "may be connected by the closest union ... , and yet, each of them can retain the condition of a perfect, individual state" (*De Jure* I, ch. 3, vii). Furthermore, in subjecting inter-state relations to the rule of law, he does not maintain that this is true only with respect to a certain class of states, such as Western or "civilized." He regards the formal equality of all states as a fundamental principle of international law. Although he acknowledges that "the rules of the law of nations can only be applied to those who are capable of political or commercial intercourse, and not to a people entirely destitute of reason," he adds that "it is a matter of just doubt whether any such is to be found" (*De jure* II, ch. 22, x). In his *Mare Liberum*, he regards Asian rulers as sovereigns capable of entering into diplomatic and treaty relations with European powers. Arguing against the imperialist theories of his time, he denies that some peoples can be subjected to conquest because of their religion or their alleged cultural and intellectual inferiority. All humans are capable of reason. Since Grotius grounds international rules in natural law, his international society is global and all-inclusive in its scope. It is applicable to all peoples, not only Christians or Europeans. He quotes the view of Themistius that "kings who measure up to the rule of wisdom make account not only of the nation that has been committed to them, but of the whole of human race" (*Prol.* § 24). He thus places the great society of states within the universal context of the great society of all humankind.

HUMAN RIGHTS AND INTERVENTION

Countering advocates of the doctrine of *raison d'État*, Grotius argues that "there is a common law among nations, valid for war and in war" (*Prol.* § 24). His contribution to international relations theory is the idea that the binding force of law can be preserved in an anarchic international system. Thus, he lays the foundation for a universal international order dedicated to peaceful cooperation between equal and independent sovereign states. Furthermore, in addition to promoting the rule of law in inter-state relations, Grotius sets before the international community another goal: that of protecting people from harm and of promoting the recognition of basic human rights. This leads him from the concept of international society to that of cosmopolitan society, and from the issue of the security of states to that of the security of populations within states. In the chapter "On Punishments," he says:

> The fact must also be recognized that kings, and those who possess rights equal to kings, have the right of demanding punishments not only on account of injuries committed, against themselves or their subjects, but also on account of injuries which do not directly affect them but excessively violate the law of nature or of nations in regard to any persons whatsoever (*De Jure* II, ch. 20, xl).

Central to Grotius' thought about war is the insistence that private war, violence between families, groups, or cities, is forbidden. "No war can be made but by the authority of the sovereign in each state" (*De Jure* I, ch. 3, v). Grotius thus disapproves of non-state violence, and has been criticized because of his denial of the right of resistance to oppression. He asserts that a rebellion in the form of a war of liberation is not permitted under natural law. To recognize a right of resistance is for him contrary to the purpose for which the state is formed, that is, the maintenance of public peace (*De Jure* I, ch. 4, ii-v). Nevertheless, he adds to his position a few important qualifications. The right of popular resistance exists in cases where rulers openly show themselves to be enemies of the whole people or attempt to usurp parts of the sovereign power that do not belong to them. Further, he upholds the legitimacy of non-violent struggle and defends such individual rights as the right to defend one's person and property, the right to refuse to carry arms in an unjust or even a morally doubtful war, and the right to purchase necessities of life, such as food, clothing and medicine, at a reasonable price (*De Jure* II, ch. 2, xix). Grotius is likewise also ahead of his time in discussing humanitarian intervention. Notwithstanding his reluctance to sanction wars of national liberation, he considers preventing a state from maltreating its own subjects to be a just reason for war.

Based on the notion of state sovereignty over its own territory, international law has traditionally opposed not only unilateral intervention in the domestic affairs of one country by another but also collective action, except in cases of grave threats to the peace and security of other states and of egregious and potentially genocidal violations of human rights. Addressing the dilemma of whether the sovereign rights of a state or the rights of the individuals within the state should take precedence, Grotius offers a basic principle upon which humanitarian intervention can be justified. He acknowledges the established rule that "every sovereign is supreme judge in his own kingdom and over his own subjects, in whose disputes no foreign power can justly interfere"

(*De Jure* II, ch. 25, viii). However, he argues that a state that is oppressive and egregiously violates basic human rights forfeits its moral claim to full sovereignty. When rulers provoke their people to despair and resistance by extreme cruelty, having themselves abandoned all laws of nature, they lose the rights of independent sovereigns and can no longer claim the privilege of the law of nations. Grotius thus regards humanitarian intervention as a kind of international equivalent of domestic law enforcement. He considers governments to be criminal if they engage in acts so egregious as to justify other states' intervention in their domestic affairs for humanitarian purposes. While he generally denies the oppressed the right of resistance, he permits a foreign state to intervene, through war, on their behalf. "Admitting that it would be fraught with the greatest dangers if the subjects were allowed to redress grievances by force of arms, it does not necessarily follow that other powers are prohibited from giving them assistance when laboring under grievous oppression."

Grotius' argument for intervention is based on the assumption of one common nature that all human beings have and that is in itself sufficient reason to oblige people to assist each other (*De Jure* II, ch. 25, vi). Human social and rational nature is the source of natural law, and a foundation of human rights. In connection with an individual human being, "right (*ius*) is a moral quality, annexed to the person, justly entitling him to possess some particular privilege, or to perform particular acts" (*De Jure* I, ch. 1, iv). Although Grotius' list of human rights violations and barbaric acts may be different from those of today, he asserts as a matter of principle that members of the international community are not obliged to respect the sovereignty of a state that engages in acts of cruelty and violates human rights. Whoever commits a crime, whether a criminal individual or a criminal nation, can by their very act be considered to fall to the level of a brute and thus can be regarded as inferior to anyone else (*De Jure* II, ch. 20, iii). Those human beings that break basic rules of humanity and renounce natural law are wild beasts rather than humans; a just war can be fought against them. "The most just war is against savage beasts, the next against men who are like beasts" (*De Jure* II, ch. 20, xl). However, Grotius does not license intervention everywhere to everyone, and qualifies his argument with prudential considerations. Since a state's own existence and preservation is an object of greater value than the welfare and security of other states, "no one is bound to give assistance or protection when it will be attended with evident danger" (*De Jure* II, ch. 25, vii). In Grotius, as in Cicero, national responsibility, the obligation of the government to its own citizens, is regarded as being of the foremost importance, taking precedence over the broader cosmopolitan responsibility for all human beings. Our common nature, Grotius suggests, tells us that, when possible, something should be done to stop human suffering on a mass scale wherever it occurs. But governments should always first protect their own people and avoid taking unnecessary risks with their welfare; only then may they try to help others. "No ally is bound to assist in the prosecution of schemes which afford no possible prospect of a happy termination" (*De Jure* II, ch. 25, iv). Intervention is justified only if the military risk is not high and there is a reasonable chance of success.

Political realists are critical of the concept of intervention, believing as they do that states act only when it is in their interest to do so. They argue that disregarding the rights of sovereignty of other states for the purpose of promoting human rights may lead to an undermining of peace and order. Grotius does not deny self-interest in international politics. However, he believes that states can identify their interests not only with narrow national goals but also with the greater task of preserving international order (*Prol.* § 17). Exercising cosmopolitan responsibility for other peoples and punishing rogue states (especially in situations where human rights violations result in grave threats to the peace of neighboring states) is not, in many cases, contrary to national interest. Nevertheless, Grotius cautions that "wars which are undertaken to inflict punishment are under suspicion of being unjust, unless crimes are very atrocious and evident" (*De Jure* II, ch. 20, xliii). The danger that humanitarian intervention can be used as the cover for ambitious designs, "by which no faults of kings but their power and authority will be assailed," cannot be completely removed. "But right does not lose its nature from being in the hands of wicked men" (*De Jure* II, ch. 25, viii). Grotius anticipates the idea, which underlies the system of collective security of the United Nations, that in a situation where, under a proposed humanitarian intervention, a single state might benefit from taking military action against another, the process of deciding whether or not to undertake such action must be multinational (Smith 291). Collectively approved action can reduce the risk of self-interested interventions covered by a thin cloak of humanitarianism.

OLD AND NEW CHALLENGES TO THE GROTIAN ORDER

Under Grotius' influence, international law changed from its old meaning of a set of customs that were discovered to be common to the juridical practice of many different peoples, to a body of rules regulating the relations between sovereign states. He posited the idea of the international rule of law, even in warfare, and thus provided the foundation for a universal legal order applicable to all nations, an order whose purpose was to encourage cooperation between states and reduce the risk of a conflict arising among them. Yet, just as his ideas were frequently discussed, quoted, and admired, they were also fiercely attacked and described as utopian or unrealistic. Challenges have been made to not only his notion of international legal order but also his concept of fixed moral standards derived from natural law, by which policies and political actions could be judged.

The initial challenge came from Thomas Hobbes, Grotius' younger contemporary. Although he does not mention Grotius by name, in his *Leviathan*, first published in 1651, Hobbes makes a formidable attack on the views underlying Grotius' lifework. He argues that there is no society among states because there is no common power, authority, and law; that states have an absolute and unlimited sovereign power and, as a matter of sovereign prerogative, are entitled to wage war; that their mutual relations appear to be those of perpetual conflict; that peace is only a breathing space; and that ethical norms do not hold during war and consequently war crimes do not exist. Hobbes joins the camp of those who dismiss the idea of international law based on universal moral principles derived from natural law. In different ways, Machiavellians, Hobbesians, Hegelians, and Marxists all agree.

In subjecting Grotius' ideas to criticism, Hobbes voiced the prevailing international practice of the governments of his day. In many cases, these ideas were read in a way that was contrary to Grotius' own intentions. Grotius was praised equally by hawks and doves. His ideas could gratify the high-minded because they sounded lofty and pointed out a reasonable way to a more peaceful world, while in practice, they could not restrain the struggle for power between European states and their endeavor to subject non-European people to their authority (Röling 297). Hard-liners and militarists were able to use his just war doctrine to justify the right to go to war. His theory of intervention provided all too readily a pretext for brigands of all kinds to subjugate foreign peoples.

The age in which Grotius lived was a time of national arms build-up, not arms restriction. Religious, dynastic, and colonial rivalries had brought about frequent wars in Europe. Yet even today, individuals and nations are contending with some of the same important questions that were faced in the seventeenth century. Under what conditions can states punish other states or undertake humanitarian interventions? Can the rules and norms of international society provide restraint against the potential egoism of states? Do they contribute to greater cooperation and peace among nations? Are international rules and norms merely the expression of national or class interests at a particular time?

The value of Grotius' work is not that it provides conclusive answers to all these questions. He is, nevertheless, an important voice in the debate about the character of international politics. He wrestled with problems that continue to concern us. It was his conviction that people do not conduct their foreign policies independently of their cultural values. The international order that he envisions is not compatible with societies in which the individual human being is not recognized as the primary principle, but is reduced to a member of a tribe, a nation, or a class; in which the essential elements that constitute human nature—human rationality and sociability—are not recognized; and in which natural law is either not acknowledged or not understood as a moral law. Those core values and norms of Western civilization have been under constant threat from militaristic ideologies. It is upon their sustenance that the future of the present Grotian global order, based on the rule of law in international relations, ultimately depends.

QUESTIONS

- What is the thesis of Carneades? How does he defend it? How might you object to it?
- How convincing is Grotius' argument in the defense of natural law? How might you criticize or support this argument?

- Grotius subjects the actions of states to the same moral rules as those that govern the conduct of individuals. Do you agree?
- Can international law have any effect without sanction, and if so, why?
- What are the differences among the militarist, pacifist, and Grotian views of war?
- When are wars legitimate, and how they should be conducted?
- What is "international society"? What is the difference between international society and other paradigms of international relations?
- Under what conditions is humanitarian intervention justified? When it is unlikely to take place?

GUIDE TO FURTHER READING

Translations of Grotius' Selected Political Works:

Grotius, Hugo. *The Rights of War and Peace.* Trans. A. C. Campbell. Westport, VA: Hyperion, 1993.

Grotius, Hugo. *Prolegomena.* Trans. Francis W. Kelsey. Rpt. in *The Theory of International Relations: Selected Texts from Gentili to Treitschke.* Ed. M. G. Forsyth, H. M. A. Keens-Soper, and P. Savigear. London: George Allen, 1970. 39–85.

Selected Readings:

Bull, Hedley, Benedict Kingsbury, and Adam Roberts, eds. *Hugo Grotius and International Relations.* Oxford: Clarendon, 1990.

Howard, Michael, ed. *Restraints on War: Studies in the Limitation of Armed Conflict.* Oxford: Oxford UP, 1995.

Keene, Robert. *Beyond The Anarchical Society: Grotius, Colonialism and Order in World Politics.* Cambridge: Cambridge UP, 2002.

Yasuaki, Onuma, ed. *A Normative Approach to War: Peace, War, and Justice in Hugo Grotius.* Oxford: Clarendon, 1993.

Hobbes: The Beginning of Modernity

Thomas Hobbes, regarded as a founding father of modern political thought, was born into a relatively poor family in Westport near Malmesbury in Wiltshire, England on April 5, 1588. His father was an undistinguished clergyman, an alcoholic who deserted the family when Thomas was sixteen. He was then supported by his uncle, a glove manufacturer. Hobbes' precocity was recognized at an early age, and was evidenced by his ability to master the humanist curriculum of a sixteenth-century grammar school. A talented linguist, he could speak and write Latin, Greek, French, and Italian, in addition to his native English. At the age of fourteen, he translated Euripides' *Medea* from Greek into Latin verse, and would continue to use his skills as a translator throughout his life. His first publication, in 1629, was an English rendering of Thucydides' *History of the Peloponnesian War*; among his last works was a translation of Homer's *Odyssey*.

Hobbes entered the University of Oxford when he was fifteen and received a bachelor's degree five years later, in 1608. He was subsequently invited to join the household of William Cavendish, Earl of Devonshire, as a tutor to the earl's eldest son, also named William. From then on, Hobbes remained closely connected with the Cavendishes, and for many years resided in their houses, either at Hardwick or in London. Like many other seventeenth-century scholars who lived as retainers of wealthy aristocratic families, he never married.

Hobbes spent most of his life tutoring members of the higher nobility, including the future King Charles II during his exile in France. He also acted as a secretary, financial agent, and close adviser to various noblemen. In addition, he accompanied young aristocrats on their tours of the Continent, traveling abroad in 1610–1605, 1629, and 1634–1637. These trips gave him a rare opportunity to meet leading politicians and scholars of his day. During his first tour of Germany, France, and Italy, which he undertook with young William Cavendish, he met Fulgenzio Micanzio and other intellectuals of the Venetian Republic, the sole surviving state from the grand days of Italian republicanism.

After returning to England, Hobbes continued to maintain contact with his Venetian acquaintances, who preached religious independence and advocated political realism. Around that time, he also met Francis Bacon, for whom he acted as secretary from 1618 to 1622. Under Bacon's influence, Hobbes became disillusioned with Aristotelianism, which was still taught at universities, and with scholasticism. During his later European tour, in 1634–1637, he met Galileo Galilei, and came into contact with the scientific circle of Marin Mersenne, which included René Descartes and Pierre Gassendi. It was under the influence of Galileo and Descartes (whom he would not personally meet until 1648) that Hobbes conceived the idea that permeates his political philosophy—the geometrical deduction of human behavior from abstract principles.

Hobbes' lifetime (like that of Grotius) was marked by turbulent political events, including wars for overseas possessions and wars of religion. As he stated in the Latin edition of *Leviathan*, he and fear were born twins. His mother gave birth to him prematurely, upon hearing the rumor of an impending foreign invasion. This rumor was based on fact: the sailing of the Spanish Armada, which the Catholic King Philip II of Spain had ordered with the goal of ousting the Protestant Queen Elizabeth I from the throne and restoring Catholicism in England. The Armada was defeated; however, the maritime war between England and Spain continued until Elizabeth died in 1603. The Tudor dynasty died with her, and upon the succession of a new dynasty, the Stuarts, the internal tensions already existing within English society became apparent.

The first Stuart ruler, Elizabeth's cousin James I (previously James IV of Scotland), did not fully appreciate English political traditions. He insisted that he was king by divine right, thereby rejecting the tradition of parliamentary rule that had originated in England in the middle of the thirteenth century. He attempted to govern without parliamentary approval, and also tried to enforce his own views on religion. He refused to make concessions to the radical Protestants, the Puritans, who wanted to "purify" the Church of England (also known as the Episcopal or Anglican Church) by eliminating elaborate religious ceremonies and establishing a representative form of church government to replace the bishops. He followed Elizabeth's policy of Crown supremacy in all matters, ecclesiastical and civil.

On the positive side, during the Jacobean reign there were virtually no wars. James I sought peace, and negotiated an alliance with Catholic Spain, which was to be cemented by the marriage of his son Charles to a Spanish princess. But the marriage negotiations subsequently broke down, and when James died in 1625, the son, who succeeded him as Charles I, sent forces against Spain. Not long afterward, England went to war with France as well. Needing funds for the war but facing opposition in the lower house of Parliament, which was dominated by the Puritans, the new king resorted to the unpopular step of collecting taxes without parliamentary consent. In 1627, Hobbes, acting as secretary to the Earl of Devonshire, helped to collect Charles' Forced Loan, which was widely considered an illegal levy. For eleven years, from 1629 to 1640, Charles ruled England without Parliament, and during this time once more raised money without its consent. Moreover, his religious views also caused discord. Charles I attempted to enforce universal observance of Anglican doctrine and forms of worship and church organization. In 1637, his government ordered the use of the Anglican service in Presbyterian churches in Scotland. This provoked widespread resistance.

Opposition to the religious policies of the king, and to his attempts to collect money for a campaign in Scotland, finally led to the Civil War of 1642-1646. There was a struggle between the mainline Anglican Protestant groups that supported the king and defended the idea that the monarch had absolute rights, including the power to raise and collect taxes, and the Puritans and other radical Protestant groups that supported parliamentary rule. In the end, the opposition won. The monarchy was abolished, the king was executed, the House of the Lords was dissolved, and a republic was declared under the leadership of Oliver Cromwell. Hobbes, however, escaped the bitter campaigns of the English Civil War. In November 1640, fearing for his life, he went to France, living in Paris until 1651.

The immediate reason why Hobbes left England was the essay *Elements of Law Natural and Politic*, which he had written in English for the Earl of Newcastle. This work, composed quickly in 1640, with contemporary political events very much in mind, had been widely circulated among Hobbes' friends and was intended for use in parliamentary debates in support of the royalists. But with opposition to the king growing, Hobbes feared that the essay might be used against him in some future prosecution.

Once settled safely in Paris, in 1642 he completed and published *De Cive* (*On the Citizen*), which was one section of his larger Latin work, *Elementa Philosophiae* (*Elements of Philosophy*). It included many ideas that were initially expressed in *Elements of Law*. The publication of the other two sections, *De Corpore* (*On Matter*) and *De Homine* (*On Humanity*), which were devoted to metaphysics and epistemology, was considerably delayed. This was partly the result of Hobbes' unfavorable financial situation, which in 1646 forced him to accept the position of mathematics tutor to the Prince of Wales, later Charles II, who, like other royalist exiles, had come to Paris. Another reason for the delay was the onset of illness, presumed to be Parkinson's disease, in 1647. *De Corpore* and *De Homine* were both published only after his return to England at the end of 1651 (in 1655 and 1658 respectively).

Although the illness, from which Hobbes would never completely recover, slowed his writing—he had to rely on secretaries to transcribe his words on paper—during this period he was nonetheless able to compose his most famous and most controversial work, *Leviathan*, first published in April 1651. This classic of English prose immediately ignited a controversy. It was regarded as the expression of a thoroughly materialistic and atheistic philosophy and gained Hobbes the reputation as the "Beast of Malmesbury." He began receiving threats from men who had once been his friends and supporters, but who regarded the new publication as treachery to the royal cause that Hobbes defended in the *Elements of Law* and *De Cive*. Royalists also saw *Leviathan* as an attack on the Anglican ecclesiastical order, which they supported, and a defense of "Independency," the idea that all religious congregations should be independent in doctrinal matters, with the state exercising a supervisory role over religion (Tuck 28).

It was during the last years of the regime of Cromwell—who supported Independency and fought against religious radicals as he had done earlier against the royalists—that Hobbes returned to England. There, he was for a time able to live relatively undisturbed, being little affected by Cromwell's despotic rule and his foreign and domestic military campaigns. Hobbes gained friends within the new regime and backed the Independents against the Presbyterians, who, like the Calvinists in Holland, wanted to establish religious control over political institutions.

Hobbes' situation changed drastically after the restoration of monarchy in 1660. Cromwell died in September 1658 and was succeeded by his son, Richard. The latter had none of his father's political talents and soon resigned. It was then that the uneasy and hastily constructed coalition of former enemies, Anglicans and Presbyterians, paved the way for the king's return. Their prize was the restoration of the Anglican order in England and the establishment of a Presbyterian government in Scotland. The Anglicans—among whom were two principal ministers of the new government, Edward Hyde and Gilbert Shelton—included many individuals who had admired Hobbes before he wrote *Leviathan,* but now detested him and wanted to punish him for his apparent treachery. Fortunately, King Charles II, a former pupil of Hobbes, aligned himself with some of his more tolerant courtiers, who favored loosening the restrictions on religious nonconformists and dissenters. Hobbes' "heresy" thus became an issue in the struggle within the government over religious freedom. Finally, in 1666, a bill was introduced into the House of the Commons with the intention of making heresy a crime. The committee preparing the bill was empowered to gather information about the atheistic implications of *Leviathan.* The bill failed in the House of Lords. However, it was repeatedly reintroduced in succeeding years, and Hobbes lived under the continual threat of being either imprisoned or again forced into exile for his beliefs.

In spite of such threats, in 1666, Hobbes published a Latin translation of *Leviathan* in which he dropped the section devoted to the defense of Independency and added an appendix defending materialism. In the following years, he composed six shorter works (including the historical work *Behemoth or the Long Parliament*), but none of them was published during his lifetime. He also found an influential protector in Henry Bennet, Earl of Arlington, who, as a minister in a newly formed government, vigorously promoted the cause of religious toleration. Arlington and other members of the government had a number of advisers, one of whom was John Locke. It is not known whether Hobbes and Locke ever met. Nevertheless, they were working for a common cause, with Hobbes writing papers on the issue of heresy for Arlington, and Locke composing speeches concerning the subject of toleration for the Earl of Shaftesbury. In 1672 the king issued a Declaration of Indulgence, removing the restrictions previously imposed on the non-Anglican Protestants. The legislation was what the country needed to enable it to settle down into a state of mutual tolerance; nevertheless, the House of Commons forced the king to withdraw his declaration and in 1673 passed the Test Act. This act, directed primarily against Catholics, required all officeholders to take an oath of allegiance to the Anglican Church. The king's brother, James, admitted to being a Catholic and resigned his office as Lord High Admiral; Sir Thomas Clifford gave up his post as Lord Treasurer. Their resignations were followed by those of many others in the military and the civil service of the Crown. The Anglican-dominated and anti-tolerationist Parliament called upon the king to dismiss Arlington. His government fell in 1674, consequently achieving no long-term change in policy concerning religious toleration. Locke went abroad and Hobbes left London to spend the rest of his life in the Cavendish house at Hardwick.

Hobbes' last contribution to the political debate concerning religion, which was at that time being fueled by allegations of a Popish plot to restore Roman Catholicism in England and also by the question of whether Charles' Catholic brother could be excluded from the line of succession to the throne, was a paper in which he argued that the sovereign could legitimately exclude his natural successor from following him to the throne, but could not be forced to do so by his subjects.

Hobbes lived to the age of ninety-one and died at Hardwick on December 3, 1679. He did not see a clergyman or take the sacrament, although his friends explained this by the suddenness with which his last illness overtook him (Tuck 39). His reputation as an atheist and purveyor of seditious opinions continued after his death. On July 21, 1683, *De Cive* and *Leviathan* were two of the more than two dozen books publicly burned at Oxford. In 1649 and again in 1703, all of Hobbes' books were placed on the Vatican's index of prohibited books. It was this unfavorable reputation that was responsible for his ideas not immediately gaining prominence. From the middle of seventeenth century to the middle of the eighteenth, English moral and political philosophy was marked by persistent attempts to refute Hobbes' doctrines. Although Locke, Pufendorf, Spinoza, the French Encyclopedists, and the English Utilitarians made use of some important parts of his thought, it was only gradually that the significance of his works became widely recognized, with *Leviathan* eventually hailed as "the greatest, perhaps sole, masterpiece of philosophy written in English language" (Oakshott 3). The impact of Hobbes' philosophy on the modern mind, and on modern political theory in particular, cannot be disregarded.

A NEW POLITICAL SCIENCE

During the late sixteenth and early seventeenth centuries, the Scientific Revolution was underway. The heliocentric theory of the universe put forward by Copernicus would gradually gain acceptance and replace Ptolemy's geocentric model. While Newton was developing the law of universal gravitation, other scientists were laying the foundations of the scientific study of anatomy, chemistry, biology, and physics. Hobbes, who like other seventeenth century scholars still made no formal distinction between "philosophy" and "science," treating the terms as synonyms, was the first thinker to draw radical social and political implications from the Scientific Revolution (Wolin 18). In an often-cited fragment at the beginning of *De Corpore,* he remarks that "natural philosophy" was then "but young, being no older than the research of Copernicus, Kepler, Galileo, and Harvey," and "civil philosophy" was still younger, "no older . . . than my own book *De Cive.*" What he means by this bold statement is that before *De Cive,* which he wrote in 1642, no genuine political philosophy or science of politics had existed. He claims that there was no political science in the works of Aristotle or any other ancient political writer. "Aristotle, Cicero, and other men, Greeks and Romans, . . . derived those rights [of commonwealths] not from the principles of nature, but transcribed them into their books out of the practice of their own commonwealths" (*Leviathan* XXI 9). He opposes classical political philosophy because he feels it was based on experience rather than on deductive reasoning; it was *prudentia* (prudence) rather then *sapience* (theoretical wisdom). To follow blindly such "vain philosophy" and to trust the authority of the classics, he argues, is "a sign of folly" (V 22). He states that Euclid founded geometry; Copernicus astronomy, which was then advanced by Kepler; Galileo, natural philosophy; and William Harvey, "the science of man's body" (*De Corpore,* Intro.). He credits himself with the discovery of a new kind of political philosophy, modeled after science, and suggests that only such a philosophy can tackle political problems and remove the most urgent social evils. He calls for the reconstruction of society on the basis of the new scientific thought.

Hobbes was a part of an intellectual movement whose goal was to free emerging modern science from the constraints of the classical and scholastic heritage. He follows Francis Bacon, who in *Novum Organon* insisted that the first requirement of scientific method was for us to purge ourselves from the prejudices and dogmas received from previous philosophers, "in order to become again as a child before nature" (Losee 65). His attempt to develop a new political science has, however, a deeper philosophical and historiographical basis. It rests on the sweeping claim that all past and contemporary political societies have been radically defective because they have never been free from social conflict and civil war.

In *Behemoth* and other historical writings, Hobbes investigates three types of societies that were for him exemplary of the civilized world: the ancient kingdoms of the Near East, the republics of ancient Greece and Italy, and the monarchies of Christian Europe (Kraynak 689). In the ancient kingdoms, he argues, authority was based on the coercive power of kings and the opinions of priests and prophets. The development of Western civilization, however, was characterized by the diminishing influence of coercive power and religion, and by the growing importance of philosophy. Consequently, Athens and Rome were much more unstable than the ancient kingdoms of the Near East. The invention of philosophy made politics a realm of dispute. Philosophical discussions "became the pastime of learned men who kept the republics in the state of constant turmoil" (695). With the advent of Christianity, philosophy was institutionalized in churches, schools, and universities. The practice of philosophy, including the disputation of established laws and doctrines, was now seen as the quintessence of a civilized way of life. This development had, in Hobbes' view, eventually led to the greatest human misery, as some priests and scholars began not only cultivating the art of rhetoric and disputative philosophy, but also popularizing and democratizing them. By endorsing the Reformation idea that anyone could interpret Scripture, they made every individual a practitioner of disputation. The result was religious sectarian warfare. Having arrived at a stage in which disputative philosophy dominated all aspects of life, Western civilization degraded into a series of bitter battles over opinions, as exemplified by the English Civil War. It is precisely at this stage, Hobbes contends, that a new kind of philosophy or universally recognized science becomes necessary, specifically, one that emancipates the human mind from the domain of opinion. This new philosophy or science, he believes, would create conditions for a commonwealth free from conflict and would inaugurate, for the first time in history, an era of perpetual civil peace.

As Hobbes himself acknowledges, Plato also held that civil society would never be free of "disorders of state and change of governments by civil war" until it was free from the domination of opinion (*Leviathan* XXXI 41). Nevertheless, his own position differs from Plato's considerably, for in the realm of opinion he includes not only pre-philosophical views but also authoritatively established opinions of philosophers whose approach was based on none other than the classical distinction between opinion and knowledge. He refers to the entire domain of authoritative opinion as the kingdom of "darkness from vain philosophy" (XLI). He wants to establish society on scientific grounds and free people from the influence of traditional authorities. Hence, rather than supporting a Platonic vision of a regime in which philosophers, who had knowledge, would rule, he advocates the reign of science upheld by the power of a sovereign. He argues that authoritative opinion should be replaced by a universally recognized and indisputable science as the basis of civil society. The model for such a science is for Hobbes not empirical science but, as it was for Galileo and Descartes, geometry. "The science of making and maintaining commonwealths," he says, "has definite and infallible rules, as does arithmetic and geometry" (XX 19). According to Hobbes, geometry and the political science he envisions both involve arbitrary or conventional definitions of terms and both are based on the process of deductive reasoning, by which we can arrive at "general, eternal, and immutable truth" (XLVI 2). They both refer to our own constructions. Geometry is demonstrable, Hobbes states, because the lines and figures from which we reason are drawn and described by ourselves; similarly, political science is demonstrable because we construct the commonwealth ourselves. For Aristotle and the classical tradition, the state as a form of human community, whereby it reaches self-sufficiency, is natural; for Hobbes, it is an artifact, and like the rest of politics, merely a human construct.

Following Galileo, Hobbes excludes teleological accounts from the range of scientific explanations. He attempts to ground his political philosophy in the modern mechanistic theory of nature and accepts the Galilean view of physical reality: namely, that the universe is nothing but a body in motion. He defines science as "the knowledge of consequences, and dependence of one fact upon another" (V 17). His new political science comprises knowledge of the consequences of the two accidents pertaining to bodies: motion and magnitude (IX). Measured by motion and magnitude, politics is no longer about virtue; it becomes the domain of passions and power.

THE REALITY OF CONFLICT

At the starting point of his inquiry in *Leviathan*, Hobbes, like Galileo and other seventeenth century scientists, adopts the technique of abstraction and idealization. In his highly abstract and materialist vision, "life is just a movement of limbs" (*Leviathan*, Intro.). He maintains that the phenomenon of life can be reduced to a simple principle of physical motion. "For what is the heart, but a spring; and the nerves, but so many strings, and the joints, but so many wheels, giving the motion to the whole body, such as was intended by the artificer?" The human being is like a machine; furthermore, the state is like an artificial person, although of greater stature and strength than the natural one. What animates both human beings and states are passions, which Hobbes describes—in contrast to mere vital animal motions, such as the circulation of the blood or the process of breeding—as "voluntary motions" (VI 1). The objects of passions—which are the things desired, feared, or hoped—may be different; yet passions, he claims, are common to and fundamentally the same in all members of the human race. All human beings are thus equalized and reduced to the lowest common denominator. Their behavior is determined by their drives and, like natural objects, they are subject to mechanical necessity. Moved solely by passions, they become one-dimensional.

Not surprisingly then, Hobbes denies any natural inequalities among human beings. He admits that there may be some individuals physically stronger, or more eloquent and learned than others. Yet, these differences have no political significance and should be disregarded. His argument for human equality goes as follows. First, he says, weaker individuals can always successfully oppose someone who is stronger, and even "kill the strongest either by secret machinations, or by confederacy with others that are in the same danger with himself" (XIII 1). Secondly, individuals are generally unwilling to acknowledge any intellectual superiority in others, "for they see their own wit at hand, and other men's at a distance" (XIII 2). Being relatively similar in their minds and bodies, and driven by the same passions, human beings are thus for him equal rather than unequal.

Still, rather than being a straightforwardly positive value, the equality of human beings is the reason for their enmity. For, "if any two men desire the same thing, which nevertheless they cannot both enjoy, they become enemies" (XIII 3). Equals, who do not recognize any superiority or natural hierarchy among themselves and who compete for goods that are scarce, are prone to conflict. Hence, conflict (and not cooperation) is the natural state of humankind. The state of nature, in which human beings live when a political society is absent, is for Hobbes the state of war.

The state of nature does not merely mean for Hobbes, as it does for Rousseau, a primitive condition in which human beings are deprived of manufactured goods. Rather, it is the situation of anarchy, understood etymologically as absence of government. This designation may refer either to pre-political times, in which a government has not yet been established, or to a point when, due to civil war or other domestic turmoil, a government loses effective control over its citizens (XIII 11). The Hobbesian argument that human relations in the state of nature are characterized by conflict is based on five assertions: (1) people are roughly equal in their mental and physical powers; (2) they are moved by passions, that is, by their appetites or aversions, which are similar for all members of the human race; (3) as egoistic utility maximizers, they are concerned solely with their own benefit; (4) they possess no innate notions of right or wrong; (5) they are not naturally social. All these assertions challenge the classical, particularly the Aristotelian, view of the nature of human beings.

In the classical tradition of moral and political thought, human beings differ in their natural capacities and some are more fit to rule than others. The notion of virtue is of key importance for this tradition, according to which, human beings, if virtuous, can control their passions by reason and can work for the benefit of others, even at the expense of their own benefits. The ability to rationally deliberate about what is beneficial and what is harmful, about what just and what is unjust, is what distinguishes humans from other animals. Therefore, for classical political thinkers, human beings are both rational and moral agents, capable of distinguishing between right and wrong, and of making moral choices. Finally, the prevailing view of the classical tradition is that human beings are naturally social.

With great skill and considerable force Hobbes attacks all these views. This attack begins on the first pages of *De Cive* and is continued in *Leviathan*.

> The greatest part of those men who have written aught concerning Commonwealths, either suppose, or require us, or beg us to believe, that Man is a Creature born for Society . . . and on this foundation they so build up the Doctrine of Civil Society" (*De Cive* I 2).

Hobbes denies that human beings have a natural desire for society. He claims that when they associate, it is solely for the sake of some mutual advantage. We come together, "not so much for love of our Fellows, as for love of our Selves." Hobbes also denies that there is any morality in the state of nature. The notions of justice or injustice have no application here (*Leviathan* XIII 13). His human beings, extremely individualistic rather than moral or social, are subject to "a perpetual and restless desire of power after power, that ceases only in death" (XI 2). They struggle for power. For Hobbes, power is a way to control others and to obtain goods; moreover, goods themselves are power (X 1). Everything that is commonly praised—reputation, success, eminence of faculties of body and mind, wealth, honor, and even knowledge and virtues—is power, and serves as a means to acquire more power. For Aristotle and the classical tradition, distinctively human activities are those that are in accordance with reason. For Hobbes, reason is dethroned, and passions take the dominant role. Since reason no longer concerns itself with the questions of right and wrong, it serves the passions by attempting to satisfy particular wants or desires. Reason becomes a mere instrument, a calculus of utilities, with rationality no more than a reckoning "of the consequences of things imagined in the mind" (IV 9), of desires, aversions, hopes and fears, or of possible gains or losses. The human being becomes a creature of interest. He finds satisfaction "in the never-ending process of making the world serve his insatiable needs" (Rapaczynski 64). Rather than stemming from some virtuous activity involving the exercise of reason, for Hobbes, happiness consists in "a continual satisfaction of desire, from one object to another" (*Leviathan* XI 1).

One of the most widely known concepts of Hobbes is the state of nature, seen as entailing a state of war—and "such a war as is of every man against every man" (XII 8). He derives his notion of the state of war from his views of both human nature and the condition in which individuals exist. The core of his argument is that the passions by which human beings are led and an environment of anarchy both diminish the possibility of cooperation.

According to Hobbes, there are three powerful motives by which individuals are driven: "first competition, secondly diffidence, thirdly glory" (XIII 6). Since in the anarchic state of nature there is no government and everyone enjoys equal status, every individual has a right to everything; that is, there are no constraints on an individual's behavior. Anyone may at any time use force, and all must constantly be ready to counter such force with force. Hence, driven by acquisitiveness, having no moral restraints, and motivated to compete for scarce goods, individuals are apt to "invade" one another for gain. Being "diffident," that is, suspicious of each other and driven by fear, they are also likely to engage in preemptive actions and invade one another to ensure their own safety. For, as Hobbes claims, "from this diffidence of one another, there is no way for any man to secure himself as reasonable as anticipation, that is, by force or wiles to master the persons of all men he can, so long till he see no other power great enough to endanger him" (XIII 4). Finally, individuals are also vain, driven by pride and a desire for glory. This leads them to fight for reputation, and to quarrel over matters as small as "a word, a smile, a different opinion, and any other sign of undervalue" (XIII 7). Whether for gain, safety, or reputation, power-seeking individuals will thus "endeavor to destroy or subdue one another" (XIII 3), leading to ongoing conflict. In such uncertain conditions argues Hobbes, where everyone is a potential aggressor, making war on others is a more advantageous strategy than peaceable behavior. Those who, satisfied with the extent of their power, might be tempted to relax their aggressive efforts, "would not be able, long time, by standing only on their defense, to subsist" (XIII 4). To survive, one needs to learn that domination over others is necessary for one's own continued survival.

Following Galileo, who attempted to describe the free fall of physical bodies in the void, Hobbes describes "idealized" human beings, all equals, moving in a moral void. By implying that both their passions and the actions that proceed from those passions "are in themselves of no sin" (XIII 10), he frees human beings from ties of responsibility for one another and from any moral considerations. He denies any community between them. Therefore, Hobbes' view of the state of war between individuals can be regarded as a deductive abstraction; he refers to this state as an "inference made from the passions" (XIII 10). Nonetheless, he does not see his use of abstraction and idealization as affecting the validity of his demonstration. He presents the conclusions of his reasoning as if they were true not only of human relations abstracted from the real world but also of empirical reality. He does not regard them as merely conventional or arbitrary.

Hobbes' description of human life in the state of nature, which he identifies with the state of war, resembles the portrait of archaic times presented in Book I of Thucydides' *History of the Peloponnesian War*, whose translation he published in 1628. Hobbes argues that even if there were no actual war and no constant fighting between individuals, people would still be haunted by fear of aggression as long as they lived in the state of nature. The threat of violence would always be present. In this condition of insecurity, few individuals would cultivate land, develop industry, or make long-term plans. Thus, in the state of nature, as in ancient Greece before civilization was established, there is no place for industry, agriculture, navigation, large-scale building, letters, arts, and sciences (XIII 9).

Hobbes does not consider human beings, whom he asserts in his theoretical model to be egoistic, antisocial, and driven by passions, and whose identities he thus constructs, to be capable of improvement. From the outset, he excludes the possibility of a religious or moral appeal to individuals that would make them more cooperative. His deterministic account of human behavior, which is grounded in the mechanistic view of modern science, does not allow for any meaningful moral choice. If, human beings cannot be changed, then the only way to escape the state of war is to change the conditions in which they exist. For Hobbes, individuals must of necessity transfer from the state of nature to civil society. The desirability of a powerful government is a matter of logic. Without a central authority having sufficient power to keep individuals in check, human life would be "solitary, poor, nasty, brutish, and short" (XIII 9), and the state of war would continue to be the prevailing condition of humankind.

SOCIAL CONTRACT

Hobbes' political theory revolves around two opposing poles: the state of nature and civil society. His logical validation of the need for civil or political society proceeds as a standard reduction to absurdity: if A (the state of nature), then B (absurdity, the state of war); not-B (peace, that is the contrary to B), therefore, not-A (civil society, that is contrary to A). The state of nature, which leads to the state of war, is a wretched condition that human beings should want to leave as soon as possible, so that peace can be achieved. Peace is not for Hobbes a matter of increased understanding among peoples or a product of human goodness. Human beings, subject to blind, mechanistic drives, are ruled by passions. It is by passions such as acquisitiveness, fear, and pride that they are driven to war against one another; it is also through passions, especially fear of violent death, and only partly through reason, that they at last achieve peace.

> The passions that incline men to peace are fear of death, desire of such things as are necessary to commodious living, and a hope by their industry to obtain them. And reason suggests convenient articles of peace, upon which men may be drawn to agreement (XIII 14).

Individuals living in the insecurity of the state of nature, afraid of being killed, and also desiring a better, more comfortable life, Hobbes suggests, come to the conclusion that war does not pay and peace is in everyone's real interest. In such a case, reason prescribes "articles of peace," rules according to which individuals are to limit their natural appetites and passions. Although Hobbes calls these rules "laws of nature," they are not the rules of classical natural law that dictates principles of right action. The sole source of justice and morality for him is the state (XIII 13). Rather than being moral laws, the Hobbesian laws of nature are "dictates of reason" or prudential rules that appeal to self-interest. They instruct human beings on how to obtain peace and are derived from and subordinate to the fundamental right of nature, the individual's right to self-preservation: "the liberty each man has to use his own power, as he will himself, for the preservation of his own nature, that is to say of his own life" (XIV 1). They teach self-interested individuals to give up the utility-maximizing approach and to follow a cooperative route instead.

In the Hobbesian state of nature, each human being has a right to anything he considers necessary for his preservation, "even to one another's body" (XIV 4). Furthermore, there is in fact nothing to which individuals have no right by nature. Every individual has the right to do whatever he likes. As long as this "right of every man to everything" (Ibid.) endures, there is either potential or actual war on the part of each and every individual against each and every other individual and security for no one. The first two laws of nature tell individuals in the state of nature to seek peace and be ready to give up as many of their rights as others are prepared to renounce for the sake of peace. Rights are laid aside either by renouncing them or by transferring them to some designated party (XIV 7). A mutual transferring of rights, made by each individual with each other individual, is called by Hobbes a "contract." A contract in which one of the contractors fulfills his contract obligation and leaves the other contractor to fulfill his obligations at some later, indeterminate time is called a "covenant" (XIV 11). The social contract, whereby all human beings lay aside their rights to all things, is a covenant. Individuals agree not to do any more what they had a right to do in the past, namely, not to invade one another for gain (XIV 6). The only rights that they never give up are those of resisting others who make an assault by force and other rights related to personal self-defense. That they cannot be renounced follows from the logic of Hobbes' system. Since individuals enter into the contract with the view of obtaining security and preserving their lives, they cannot transfer or lay aside the rights to save themselves from death, wounds, or imprisonment (XIV 29). The third law of nature is that individuals perform their covenants. For without their performance, "covenants are in vain, and but empty words, and the right of all men to all things remaining, we are still in the condition of war" (XV 1). All other laws, such as those decreeing that every person should strive to adjust himself to society or that one individual should not declare hatred or contempt of another, are to help ensure the performance of covenants made.

If Hobbes' view of the state of war between individuals can be regarded as a deductive abstraction, his social contract can be described as a thought experiment. He appeals to self-interested and rational individuals, that is, to those who ask what good to themselves will be obtained in any given outcome and who are able to calculate consequences. He suggests that in seeking peace, such individuals will obey the laws of nature out of enlightened self-interest and thus escape the state of war. However, he also admits that "bonds of words are too weak to bridle men's ambition, avarice, anger, and other passions, without a fear of some coercive power" (XIV 18). Human beings are self-interested creatures, ruled by passions, and there will always be "fools" who, by breaking covenants and invading others, will try to gain advantage over them, not seeing that by doing so, and by returning everyone to the state of war, they ultimately bring about their own destruction (XV 5). Instead of thinking in terms of their long-term interests and cooperating with others, such fools choose their immediate advantage. In the Hobbesian state of nature then, there is then a reasonable danger of nonperformance of a contract. "Covenants without the sword are but words" (XVII 2). Since the laws of nature are prudential rules, not moral imperatives, an individual is bound to comply with them only if others do the same and he can reach his desired end, which is self-preservation. Accordingly, there must be a coercive power, the sovereign, who can compel all contractors equally to perform. Fear is again the passion to be relied upon. The sovereign must ensure that the terror of punishment is a great enough to outweigh any advantage that could be expected from breaking of a covenant.

The Hobbesian social contract thus involves the act of transferring rights and the simultaneous creation of a party—the sovereign—to be the beneficiary of this transfer. The contract is between each individual and all other individuals in the state, and not between the people and the ruler. Hobbes' idea—that a contract between human beings forms the basis for the establishment of the state—is an old one, going back to Plato's *Republic* (359a). However, it was elaborated into a social contract theory only in modern times. Hobbes was, in fact, the first of three great modern political thinkers to use this device, with Locke and Rousseau being the other two. The three are called "social contract theorists" because they envision individuals establishing civil society by agreeing to a contract among themselves. But if the modern idea of the social contract is relatively simple, its implications are far reaching. It suggests the notion that governments should be viewed as if they were created by the people and evaluated according to whether they have served the purpose for which they were originally established. This novel idea provides an answer to the questions of authority and political obligation. It indicates that, contrary to King James' conviction, governments do not derive their authority from divine sanction. Governments have universal authority, that is, authority over each citizen of the state, only to the extent that, by entering into contract, individuals have chosen to live under them, and hence, consented to them.

With his theory of the social contract, Hobbes challenges the religious and patriarchal theories of society that supported absolute rule. Yet, at the same time, as he destroys the old absolutism based on a divine right to authority, he lays the grounds for a new, firmer and more extensive one.

ABSOLUTE SOVEREIGNTY

A common objection to contract theories is that the social contract is a historical fiction. History suggests that states have been established as the result of conquest and force, not as a result of a contract between individuals. Hobbes anticipates this objection. He acknowledges that a state, or as he calls it, a commonwealth, can come into existence either by *institution*, that is, by social contract, when individuals agree among themselves "to submit to some man, or assembly of men, voluntarily, on confidence to be protected by him against all others" (*Leviathan* XVII 15), or by *acquisition*, that is, by force, "when men singly (or many together by plurality of voices) for fear of death or bonds do authorize all the actions of that man or that assembly that has their lives and liberty in his power" (XX 1). However, he claims that the only distinction between those cases is that in the first instance individuals subject themselves to a sovereign because of fear of one another, and in the second they subject themselves to someone they are afraid of. In both cases they do this out of fear and on the basis of a covenant of subjection. Those who submit to a conqueror can become his subjects and acquire an obligation to obey him only if they promise obedience. It is, then, not conquest, or victory in war, or naked power that legitimates authority and gives it the right to rule over the vanquished, but rather the latter's submission to the victor, amounting to the consent to be ruled (XX 11).

Accordingly, it makes no essential difference for Hobbes whether we are dealing with a commonwealth by institution or by acquisition. The rights of sovereigns remain the same. The sovereign is solely responsible for prescribing laws; for apportioning punishment and reward; for determining honors and orders of precedence; for choosing all ministers, magistrates, and officers; for waging war and making peace; and for judging what opinions and doctrines are adverse to the state (XVIII 8-15). Hobbes insists that these rights are non-transferable and indivisible. The exercise of sovereign power must not be limited by institutional constraints. The sovereign must be absolute, "or else there is no sovereignty at all" (XX 14).

In the modern world we speak of "sovereign states" and say that a state is sovereign if it has supreme or final authority within the territorial boundaries that it demarcates (Raphael 52). The development of the concept of sovereignty is closely related to the evolution of the state in early-modern Europe, and particularly to the development of the theory of absolute government. Medieval rulers were supreme heads of the state, but they were a part of constitutional and normative structures that restricted their use of power. They were constrained by the nobles and ecclesiastical institutions, as well as by social and religious traditions and customs. Medieval and Renaissance political theories were influenced by the classical ideals of a government that was both mixed and limited. In the wake of the Reformation and the subsequent wars of religion, the strong and centralized authority of a secular state came to be seen as the most effective remedy for political disorder. The theory of absolute government was first outlined in the late sixteenth century by the political philosopher Jean Bodin, who argued in his *Les six livres de la République*—written at the height of the civil war between the French Catholics and the Huguenots—that to maintain order, the central authority should wield unlimited power. He defined sovereignty as "the most high, absolute, and perpetual power over the citizens and subjects in a commonwealth," unrestrained by law and therefore unlimited in extension and duration (*République* bk. I, ch. 8). But for Bodin, sovereigns still faced some limitations. Their powers over their subjects were subordinate to the "laws of God and Nature." Bodin referred to the common law of the land, as handed down by custom, suggesting that such law could not be changed even by the sovereign. It was left to Hobbes to sweep aside all limitations on sovereignty.

By the time Hobbes wrote *Leviathan*, there was a flourishing tradition of absolutist thinking in both continental Europe and England (Sommerville 81). Although he was influenced by this tradition and adopted many ideas from Bodin and other absolutists, his uncompromising view of sovereignty is more than anything else the outcome of his logic. "If there be no power erected, or not great enough for our security, every man will rely, and may lawfully rely, on his own strength and art for caution against all other men" (*Leviathan* XVII 2). Because of his view of human nature, Hobbes rejects the possibility of a more or less voluntary loyalty that leads individuals to obey with little or no compulsion. "The laws are of no power to protect them, without a sword in the hands of man, or men, to cause those laws to be put in execution" (XXI 6). To enforce the laws of the state, and ensure that its citizens will enjoy peace and security, the sovereign power must be strong.

For this reason, Hobbes removes all elements that can weaken the sovereign power. By means of the covenant made in the course of instituting or acquiring a state, he argues, individuals promise obedience to the sovereign and authorize him to act for them. Consequently, while in the state of nature everyone has a right to all things and to free use of their own power, in civil society only the sovereign, whether established by social contract or by conquest, possesses this right. Its exercise, in reference to matters that concern the common safety, is, like the exercise of individuals' rights in the state of nature, unlimited. The sovereign can do "whatever he shall think necessary to be done . . . for the preserving of peace and security," the end for which the state is established (XVIII 8). He may use the strength and means of all his subjects, as he thinks expedient, for their peace and common defense (XVII 13). He is bound by neither customary morality nor any laws. Since the sovereign is not subject to any external limit, his power is absolute.

Further, Hobbes denies that sovereignty can be divided. His ideas run counter to the constitutional theories that were dominant in England both before and after his times. The constitutionalists attempted to limit the sovereign power by arguing that power, no matter who holds it, should be subordinated to law. They also supported the doctrine of mixed government. Hobbes discards all these ideas. His argument is absolutist and anti-constitutional. Since individuals are impelled by a perpetual and restless desire for power upon power, any power that falls to a group would be used for its own advantage vis-à-vis other groups. Thus, a division of power would always have the potential to breed social conflict. "If there had not first been an opinion received of the greatest part of England, that these powers were divided between the King, the Lords, and the House of Commons, the people had never been divided and fallen into this civil war . . ." (XVIII 16). Guided by the same logic, Hobbes rejects the possibility that there can be a division of sovereignty between political and religious authorities. He denies any independence to the church. There must not even be an independent intellectual elite, exerting its influence over members of society by means of learning and persuasion. The state must have complete control over the beliefs and opinions of the citizenry. Once we accept as truth that the natural condition of humankind is a war of all against all and that individuals are engaged in a perpetual struggle for power, he contends, absolute and unified sovereignty is indispensable for political order. The sovereign power cannot be limited and divided without being rendered ineffective.

Absolute and unified sovereignty is for Hobbes the only practical alternative to anarchy. It is an essential condition for the maintenance of domestic peace. He rejects the claims of other organizations, particularly the church, to share in this supreme authority. Thus, he contributes to the idea of the modern sovereign and secular state (Andrew Gamble 50-51). Nevertheless, his discussion of sovereignty is not free from difficulties and ambiguities. He does not draw a clear distinction between the sovereign state and the sovereign organ within the state. Moreover, his argument for unlimited and undivided sovereignty, although it may perhaps be persuasive, is fallacious. Hobbes locates sovereignty in one organ, either a single individual or an assembly of individuals, endowed with supreme power. His thought is in opposition to the idea that the sovereign power of the state can be divided, as in the United States, among different agencies (the President, Congress, and Supreme Court), each with the ability to check and monitor the activities of the others. He fears that any division of power may lead to conflict within society. However, although such conflict may be a logical possibility, it is not a logical necessity. Hobbes does not prove that "the division of sovereign powers always leads to disagreement among those who hold them and that the disagreement cannot be resolved peacefully" (Goldsmith 776). Further, although he makes a convincing argument that, in order to ensure compliance with the law, the sovereign must possess coercive power, he does not demonstrate that this power must necessarily be absolute. Abuse can be defined as going beyond agreed upon limits. Since for Hobbes there are no logical limits to sovereign power, a theory of the abuse of power is wholly lacking in his works.

THE LOGIC OF DESPOTISM

Although Hobbes values history as a means of political education, his theory is not derived from a historical or factual study of society. His method is non-empirical. The kind of knowledge that is, for him, required in the science of politics is a demonstrable knowledge based on the model of geometry. He does not want merely to convince his readers; he wants to compel them to accept his ideas through rigorous deductive reasoning. Beginning with an abstract conception of life as motion and deriving from it a dehistoricized view of human beings, all driven by passions, Hobbes reasons consistently to arrive first at the idea of the social contract and then at a radical theory of obedience. In accordance with the covenant of subjection, whereby they renounce their former rights save that of self-preservation, individuals must obey whatever the sovereign commands—except when their lives are threatened, for "covenants not to defend a man's own body are void" (*Leviathan* XXI 11).

The logic of complete obedience to the absolute sovereign is, at least formally, Hobbes' solution to the problem of social conflict—the main focus of his political theory. No matter whether they live under a monarchic, an aristocratic or a democratic government, if the subjects obey, and thus are in concord, it logically follows that there will be peace (XXX 7). But there is more to his philosophy than this formal solution. In *De Cive*, he says:

> If any man . . . by most firm reasons demonstrate that there are no authentic doctrines concerning right and wrong, good and evil, besides the constituted laws in each realm and government; and that the question whether any future action will prove just or unjust, good or ill, is to be demanded of none, but those to whom the supreme had commanded the interpretation of his laws: surely he will not only show us the high way to peace, but will also teach us how to avoid the close, dark, and dangerous by-paths of faction and sedition (Preface 8).

Starting with Plato, political philosophers have regarded civil war as the greatest social danger, more dangerous even than war against external enemies. Hobbes wants solve this problem once and for all, and remove the causes of faction and sedition in society. The classical solution to the problem of social conflict is the institution of justice in the form of a correct political regime. Hobbes rejects this solution and the classical distinction between correct and deviant types of government. Classical political thinkers, he claims, have failed to lead people toward peace; their errors have in fact bred sedition and war. He regards the belief that words correspond to reality and that an analysis of words can reveal the essence or nature of things as the most fundamental error of classical political philosophy (*Leviathan* XLVI 15). Associated with this "error" is the conviction that there are absolute natural standards on which politics should be based. On the basis of these ideas, politics turns into a debate over words, opinions, and standards; into a battle over what is just and unjust, right and wrong. Hobbes attempts to demonstrate that there are no "authentic doctrines concerning right and wrong, good and evil, besides the constituted laws in each realm and government." He wants to contribute to the establishment of peace in society by removing debate from the realm of politics (XXIX 6). Hence, he argues that the character of truth is merely conventional and arbitrary. It is precisely the conventional nature of all standards that makes it possible to know them with certainty and makes Hobbes' new political science possible (Hanson 343). His position combines the nominalist ontological assertion that "there is nothing in the world universal but names" (*Leviathan* IV 6) with legal positivism. In the absence of absolute natural standards, what is right is constituted by the will of the sovereign and expressed in the positive laws of each country, of which the sovereign is the only interpreter.

For a nominalist, universal terms such as *justice* do not correspond to a reality, but are mere names used to classify things or ideas. Reality is admitted only to singular observable things (Watkins 139). Justice and injustice are then no more than words that people arbitrarily ascribe to different kinds of behavior. They do not refer to a moral standard that exists independently from individuals and their passions. Consequently, nominalism implies that there is no classical natural law or natural moral order. Hobbes uses the vehicle of nominalism to reject the classical view that we can, through a process of disinterested inquiry and impartial dialogue, arrive at a single, authoritative opinion on what is right or good. To hold such a conviction is, according to him, to cling to an illusion of intellectual vainglory. He argues instead that while the mental faculties of human beings are more or less equal, everyone is governed by his own reason and moved by passions. Moral terms denote only subjective feelings, which vary from one individual to another, and can never be made universal. Not just one, but many conceptions of the good exist.

In the Hobbesian state of nature, moral relativism and subjectivism thus reign supreme. There is no agreement concerning moral standards. "The notions of right and wrong, justice and injustice, have there no place" (*Leviathan* XIII 13). It is their common fear of death and their desire for a more ordered and comfortable life that impel individuals to create a sovereign. In so doing they accept not only absolute sovereign power over them, but also the sovereign's reason as an artificially created standard of right (Okin 794). The state becomes for Hobbes the sole source of justice and morality. Consequently, his political vision is a complete denial of the classical vision of politics. Whereas the classical vision implies a political community united by a common idea of the good, the Hobbesian vision implies an aggregate of separate individuals who cannot have a shared conception of the good. Whereas there is in classical political philosophy a natural standard of righteousness, and politics is subservient to it, for Hobbes, "right" is a mere arbitrary term whose meaning is shaped by the sovereign.

Ancient thinkers made the basic distinction between correct and deviant forms of sovereignty on the basis of whether the ruling party aimed at the common advantage or only at its own private interest. Tyranny was regarded as the worst of all depravities, and signified a mode of rule that was "absolute, willful, and illegitimate" (Wolin 16). Hobbes, who opposes the classical tradition of moral and political thought, rejects this distinction. In accordance with his nominalism, he denies the validity of the ancient political categories of good and bad, or correct and deviant; in accordance with his moral skepticism, he denies the possibility that human beings would ever rule others for the sake of interests other than their own. Hence, he regards the differences between monarchy and tyranny or aristocracy and oligarchy as based on a merely subjective preference. Whoever dislikes monarchy, he says, calls it "tyranny," and likewise, the detractors of aristocracy or democracy call them "oligarchy," or "anarchy" (*Leviathan* XIX 2). He thus legitimizes tyranny by giving it the same rights of authority as any other form of rule. The choice between monarchy, aristocracy, or democracy is for him merely a matter of convenience or suitability that is related to the state's overall goal: "to produce the peace and security of the people" (*Leviathan* XIX 4). All forms of government have a tyrannical, arbitrary element, so that for Hobbes, any government actually amounts to a "government of tyranny" (Arendt 613). He makes this clear in his concluding remarks in *Leviathan* when he says: "the name of tyranny signifieth nothing more nor less than the name of sovereignty."

The Hobbesian state, pictured as the awesome figure of the monstrous Leviathan, is a collective being of incomparable power to which each individual is subject. It appropriates God's omnipotence and omniscience. It is that "Mortal God" to which we owe "our peace and defense" (*Leviathan* XVII 13). It alone is the source of justice and honor. The power and prestige of the subjects vanishes in the presence of the sovereign (XVIII 18). They all become powerless when confronted with the all-powerful state. Their traditional class distinctions, as well as their ancient dignities, liberties, and privileges are removed. They all become equalized and their liberty lies only in those things that the sovereign has not forbidden.

What Hobbes considered indispensable to sovereign power can be summed up as complete control over "militia, money, and mind" (Hanson 349). It is, in particular, the control over mind—that is, education—that is crucial. "Common people's minds . . . are like clean paper, fit to receive whatsoever by public authority shall be imprinted in them" (*Leviathan* XXX 6). They can therefore easily be subjected to the Hobbesian program of indoctrination. Since the teaching of sound political doctrine is essential for the preservation of peace, the sovereign decides what should be taught at schools and universities. The classics and all forms of traditional theology must be abandoned as potential sources of intellectual ferment and sedition (XXIX 14). The key is to ensure that people are instructed in "their duty to the sovereign power" (XXIII 6). Moreover, the sovereign has the right of censorship and it is his task to examine all books before publication. He also presides over the church, appoints judges and interpreters of the canonical scriptures, and resolves all controversies in religion, controlling thus not only the words and deeds of his subjects, but also their consciences (XLII 80).

Hobbes believes that Galileo's success in determining the laws of the natural world can be repeated for the social world. By means of science, unaided reason can find solutions to cure all of humanity's political and social ills. In *Leviathan,* he denounces the classical thinkers for extinguishing the light of reason with what he sees as their vain and absurd philosophies. Nevertheless, at the same time as he frees individuals from the bonds of tradition, he subjects them to the absolute sovereign who claims absolute obedience, who cannot be resisted (except when he threatens their lives), and whose acts are not liable to punishment. The logic of Hobbes' reasoning and his new political science, by means of which he attempts to radically break with the classical tradition and remove conflict from politics, bring him paradoxically to affirm the desirability of a despotic, authoritarian state. Furthermore, he transforms the world into a secularized place of abstract space and time, and populates it with the human artifact: a mere body in motion. In his theory, human beings become "what the requirements of theory demand that they must be if its theoretical power is to be realized" (Wolin 31): They become artificial men. Hobbes replaces the traditional political community, whose members are bounded to each other by custom, with "a collection of self-interested individuals held together only by contractual ties" (Nelson 189).

Although his political ideas, and especially his authoritarianism, were initially rejected and he failed to find disciples in his own time and country, those ideas would make themselves felt in the modern age that followed Hobbes. His attempt to base social and political doctrines on science opened a new era characterized by materialistic and secularized thought, which, while conducive to the process of social and economic change, proved corrosive to traditional ways of life and, in its darkest incarnation, led to the development of totalitarian ideologies.

INTERNATIONAL RELATIONS AS A STATE OF WAR

While Hobbes is primarily concerned with the relations between individuals and the state, and his comments about relations between states are scarce, he has nonetheless made a substantial impact on the study of international relations. Along with Thucydides and Machiavelli, he is regarded as one of the main representatives of the realist tradition. The realist scholars maintain that what Hobbes says about the lives of individuals in the state of nature can also be read as a description of states in relation to one another. They deny that states together form any kind of the society in the way that Grotius envisioned, and instead view international relations as a state of war.

For Hobbes, international politics, like all politics, is rooted in what (perhaps inconsistently with his nominalism) he perceives as the correct view of human nature. He regards human beings as self-interested individuals who, moved by their passions, struggle for power. Once states are established, individual drive for power becomes the basis for the states' behavior, which manifests itself in their efforts to dominate other states and peoples. States, "for their own security," writes Hobbes, "enlarge their dominions upon all pretences of danger and fear of invasion or assistance that may be given to invaders, [and] endeavour as much as they can, to subdue and weaken their neighbors" (*Leviathan* XIX 4). Accordingly, as it would be later for Hans Morgenthau, who was deeply influenced by Hobbes and adopted the same view of human nature, the quest and struggle for power lies at the core of the

Hobbesian vision of relations among states. Further, as it would be later for the neo-realist Kenneth Waltz, international anarchy (the very fact that sovereign states are not subject to any common sovereign) is for Hobbes the defining element of international relations. He identifies anarchy with the state of nature, in which there is no place for the notions of right and wrong, and no government to provide security. In such an environment, in which other states might use force at any time, each state is responsible for its own survival and must be prepared to defend itself.

> . . . yet in all times kings and persons of sovereign authority, because of their independency, are in continual jealousies and in the state and posture of gladiators, having their weapons pointing and their eyes fixed on one another, that is, their forts, garrisons, and guns upon the frontiers of their kingdoms, and continual spies upon their neighbours, which is the posture of war. But because they uphold thereby the industry of their subjects, there does not follow from it that misery which accompanies the misery of individual men (XIII 12).

By subjecting themselves to a sovereign, individuals escape the war of all against all that Hobbes associates with the state of nature; however, this war continues to dominate relations between states. This does not mean that states are always fighting, but rather that they have a disposition to fight (XIII 8). States adopt the "posture of gladiators" for the same reason that individuals would take up arms if their government were no longer able to offer them its protection: They are insecure, always ready for a violent confrontation. "With each state deciding for itself whether or not to use force, war may at any time break out" (Waltz 101). The achievement of domestic security through creating a state is then paralleled by a condition of inter-state insecurity. One can argue that if Hobbes were fully consistent, he would agree with the notion that, to escape this condition, states should also enter into a contract and submit themselves to a world sovereign. Although the idea of a world state would find support among some realists, this is not a position taken by Hobbes himself. He does not propose that a social contract between nations be implemented to bring international anarchy to an end because the condition of insecurity in which states are placed does not necessarily lead to insecurity for individuals. As long as an armed conflict or other type of hostility between states does not actually break out, individuals can feel relatively secure. After the sentence comparing persons of sovereign authority to gladiators prepared for combat, Hobbes goes on to say that "because they uphold thereby the industry of their subjects, there does not follow from it that misery which accompanies the misery of individual men." In other words, although states may regard each other with suspicion and be ready for war, the lives of the people who live in them are not necessarily "solitary, poor, nasty, brutish, and short."

The denial of the existence of universal moral principles in the relations between states brings Hobbes close to the Machiavellians and the followers of the doctrine of *raison d'État*. His political theory, which assumes that independent states, like independent individuals, are enemies by nature, asocial and selfish, and that there is no moral limitation on their behavior, is a great challenge to the Grotian vision of human sociability and to the concept of the international jurisprudence that is built on it. Since for Hobbes law is the command of the government (*Leviathan* XV 41), states—all of which are sovereign and have no super-sovereign above them—are not subject to supranational legal or moral rules, except those to which they give consent and regard as their own. They all have a basic natural right to do whatever they believe is necessary to preserve themselves. The right to self-preservation is possessed by sovereign states in just the same way as by individuals in the state of nature. Indeed, "every sovereign hath the same right, in procuring the safety of his people, that any particular man can have, in procuring the safety of his own body" (XXX 30). In practice, this idea of the natural right of states to self-preservation has, as Hedley Bull asserts, frequently been used by radical realists "as a means of demolishing the claims of international society on its members" (Bull, 1981, 725), in order to weaken the sway of international law and to undermine international organizations. However, what separates Hobbes from Machiavellian *realpolitik* and associates him more with classical realism is his insistence on the defensive character of foreign policy. We do not find in Hobbes any glorification of war. As he repeatedly reminds us, his overriding concern is that peace be secured. Moreover, his political theory does not put forward the invitation to do whatever may be advantageous for the state. His normative approach to international relations is prudential and pacific: Sovereign states, like individuals, should be disposed toward peace that is commended by reason.

The purpose for which the office of the sovereign is established is "the procuration of the safety of the people" (*Leviathan* XXX 1). What Hobbes means by the word *safety* is not merely "a bare preservation, but also all other contentments of life, which every man by lawful industry, without danger or hurt of commonwealth, shall acquire to himself" (Ibid.). Hence, not only is war for the sake of conquest, which endangers people's safety, contrary to the purpose of sovereignty; the sovereign has a positive duty to ensure peace, as a general condition for promoting human industry. When peace exists, people can acquire and enjoy the products of their labor. Consequently, Hobbes, who witnessed how the economic and colonial rivalries of his time led to frequent wars in Europe, argues that the sovereign should recognize the imprudence of adventurous foreign policies. He warns against the insatiable appetite to enlarge dominions and against policies of expansionism that lead to incurable wounds, to vast expenses, and ultimately to commonwealths being weakened and destroyed (XXIX 22). Further, while states are in the state of nature, which is a state of war, Hobbes believes that they can still manage the situation to the general advantage. As large, bureaucratic, and purposive organizations, they are more likely than are individuals in the state of nature to be guided by reason, instead of relying on passions. They are thus more likely to follow the rules of prudence.

The "articles of peace," which Hobbes also calls the "laws of nature" and introduces in chapters 14 and 15 of *Leviathan*, prescribe the ways in which individual entities, whether human beings or states, can "avoid the condition of war" and establish peaceful relationship among themselves. He expressly identifies these prudential rules with the laws of nations (XXX 30). Interpreted as international rules of peaceful co-existence, they command that peace should first be sought, and only when it cannot be obtained is it permissible to resort to war; that nations must mutually recognize their equality and be prepared to engage in mutual self-limitation of their original rights by entering into pacts and agreements; that they should fulfill their promises; that in their dealings with one another they should display willingness to pardon when pardon is due, and avoid pride, arrogance, and hatred; and that they should respect the immunity of envoys and be willing to submit disputes to arbitrators (Bull, 1981, 728–729).

Although it is clear from his writings that Hobbes does not think international conflict can ever be eliminated, it nonetheless cannot be maintained that he believes states are engaged in the same blind and self-destructive struggle in which individuals are engaged in the original state of nature. What Waltz and other neorealist readers of his works sometimes overlook is that he does not perceive international anarchy as an environment without any rules. By suggesting that certain dictates of reason apply even in the state of nature, he affirms that more peaceful and cooperative international relations are a possibility. Neither does Hobbes deny the existence of international law. Taking guidance from the articles of peace, sovereign states can sign treaties with one another to provide a legal basis for their relations. At the same time, however, by consequently regarding international relations as a state of war from which there is no escape, a moral void in which the mistrust and the desires for gain and prestige rather than human sociability prevail, Hobbes seems to impose limitations on any international rules. Although he recognizes that such rules exist, in his view, they will often prove ineffective in restraining the struggle for power. Each state will interpret them to its own advantage, and so international rules will be obeyed or ignored according to the interests of the states affected. Hence, international politics will always be a precarious affair and require prudence: knowledge based on experience (*Leviathan* VIII 11). Unlike domestic politics, it cannot be subjected to and regulated by a political science. This grim and at the same time prudential view of international politics lies at the core of Hobbes' political realism.

For Hobbes, the human being is a creature of interest, always on the move and thoroughly preoccupied with the pursuit of power—a pursuit that has no end, but rather is an end in itself. His argument for peace, which stresses the advantage of keeping a country safe and prosperous, is not based on any ethical considerations. The Hobbesian state is born of war and is always ready for war. Consequently, Hobbes does not exclude the possibility of foreign wars in distant lands to obtain goods, raw materials, or other resources that a state desires for its industries but may be hindered from acquiring. Foreign commodities, he says, can be obtained either "by exchange, or by just war, or by labour" (XXIV 4). Presumably, in accordance with his "articles of peace," such a "just war" should be started only if peaceful attempts to obtain these commodities, by exchange or labor, have been exhausted. Nevertheless, nothing but the superior power of another state can prevent a state from getting what it wants. The Hobbesian conception of "a perpetual and restless desire of power after power" that is not moderated by any moral limits is an expression of "an explicitly indeterminate striving for absolute mastery of the world" (Rapaczynski 46). The idea of the mastery of the world is one of the most basic features of modernity. Hobbes argues for peace, and yet, paradoxically, his view of the human being as having no aim other than unending acquisition provides a theoretical basis for modern imperialism.

HOBBES' MODERNITY

Hobbes wrote his political works in response to the issues that dominated the politics of early seventeenth-century England. He supported absolute monarchy. He tried to refute ideas held by some of his contemporaries, such as the notion that monarchs should be subject to the laws of the land, or that they should never tax without consent. Arguing with exceptional force and presenting his views as conclusions based on irrefutable deductions, he attempted to answer various fundamental questions that had immediate practical relevance to the current debates: What was the origin of authority? Why should individuals obey the government? What rights did they have? The same can be said regarding his views of sovereignty. His arguments were "steeped in references to the concepts and claims of his contemporaries" (Sommerville 167).

Even if Hobbes did not intend to provide the foundation of anything like modernity, his radical rejection of classical political philosophy and the conclusions that resulted from his own thought were instrumental in the rise of a new era. His modern approach manifested itself in his most revolutionary stance—a total break with the past. He was called "the father of revolutionary philosophy" by Comte and "the father of us all" by Marx (Watkins 145). Unlike Machiavelli, another thinker who is sometimes regarded as the first modern, he no longer wanted to imitate the ancients. He set up a modern political philosophy, modeled on science, that was certainly modern, for it differed radically from the ancient and the medieval. His nominalism and mechanistic reductionism made him look at society as comprising a collection of isolated individuals rather then a natural community. Thus, he arrived at a radical individualism that depicts individuals as seeking their own interests rather than striving for religious goals or pursuing the common good. He also laid theoretical foundations for the development of the modern state, sovereign and secular. Based on the Hobbesian idea that social arrangements can be subjected to the absolute sovereign's will, this state has been increasingly used to remold societies "along certain preconceived lines, wrenching them from traditionalism towards modernization" (Andrew Gamble 49). Furthermore, in his concept of life as motion, Hobbes preconceived the rise of the *bourgeoisie*, the class composed of unceasingly active individuals, engaged in the unlimited endeavor of increasing their property and power. The spread of his thought was supported by a radical process of social transformation and the advent of a commercial society for which classical ideals would cease to be viable.

By rejecting the tradition of classical political philosophy and attempting to base his political theory on science, Hobbes sets up a new paradigm for studying politics. Although many subsequent modern political theorists, such as Locke, Harrington, Montesquieu, and particularly the American founders, were still to some degree influenced by classical ideas, there was no real return to the classics. The world would become increasingly modern. Capitalism as a process of accumulation and rationalization, along with the progressive colonization of various parts of the globe by the European powers, created a world in which the moral voice of the Western tradition would become faint and the Hobbesian discourse of interest and power would gain prominence. It would be the task of Locke to avert some of the unwelcome consequences of Hobbes' thought and to provide this modern discourse with a moral dimension.

QUESTIONS

- What is life? What is your reaction to the Hobbesian vision of life?
- How convincing is Hobbes' argument that all human beings are equal by nature? How might you criticize or support this argument?
- What is the state of nature? Can life in the state of nature be peaceful? Explain your answer.
- Why is there neither justice nor injustice in the state of nature, according to Hobbes?
- Why do human beings become enemies? Do you agree with the explanation given by Hobbes?
- How do you understand the Hobbesian statement, "Covenants without the sword are but words"? Can we apply this statement to any situations in the world today?
- What does Hobbes mean when he says, "in all times kings and persons of sovereignty, because of their independence, are ... in the state and posture of gladiators"?
- Hobbes rejects the Aristotelian division between correct and deviant forms of government. Do you agree or disagree with him on this issue?
- Would Hobbes support the view of Machiavelli that the best possible constitution is the mixed constitution? Explain your answer.

GUIDE TO FURTHER READING

Hobbes' Selected Political Works:

Hobbes, Thomas. *De Cive.* Ed. Howard Warrender. Vol. 3 of The Clarendon Edition of the Political Works of Thomas Hobbes. Oxford: Clarendon, 1983.
Hobbes, Thomas. *The Elements of Law Natural and Politic.* 2nd ed. Ed. M. M. Goldsmith. New York: Barnes and Noble, 1969.
Hobbes, Thomas. *Leviathan.* Ed. Edwin Curley. Indianapolis: Hackett, 1994.

The Complete Works in English:

The English Works of Thomas Hobbes. 11 vols. Ed. Sir William Molesworth. London: John Bohn, 1839–1845.

Suggested Readings:

Dietz, Mary, ed. *Thomas Hobbes and Political Theory*. Lawrence: U of Kansas P, 1990.

Newey, Glen. *Routledge Philosophy Guidebook to Hobbes and Leviathan*. New York: Routledge, 2003.

Rapaczynski, Andrzej. *Nature and Politics: Liberalism in the Philosophies of Hobbes, Locke, and Rousseau*. Ithaca, NY: Cornell UP, 1987.

Sommerville, Johann P. *Thomas Hobbes: Political Ideas in Historical Context*. New York: St. Martin's P, 1992.

Springborg, Patricia. *The Cambridge Companion to Hobbes's Leviathan*. Cambridge: Cambridge UP, 2007.

Tuck, Richard. *Hobbes*. Past Masters. Oxford: Oxford UP, 1989.

Locke: Liberty and Property

John Locke, a philosopher and political theorist who is often regarded as the father of liberalism, was born in Wrington, a village in Somerset, England, on August 29, 1632. He lost his mother early in his life. His father was a lawyer and small landowner who served as a cavalry captain in the parliamentary army during the English Civil War. But the violent conflict of 1642–1646, which split the nation apart, had no significant effect on the course of Locke's life. In 1646, he entered the elite Westminster school, and in 1652, he went to the University of Oxford, where he studied medicine and natural science, in addition to the classics.

In the 1650s, Oxford was the scientific center of England, and even of Europe. Locke's tutor was Robert Boyle, a leading member of the group of scientists who would establish the Royal Society in 1660. His teaching introduced Locke to the modern scientific view of the world and instilled in the young man an appreciation for the empirical method of acquiring knowledge. During the course of his study, Locke also became familiar with works of the philosophers of the early scientific revolution, particularly Pierre Gassendi and René Descartes, whose ideas made a deep impact on him and attracted him to philosophy.

After graduation in 1656 as a bachelor of arts, Locke continued his affiliation with Oxford. In 1659, he qualified for a master's degree and then became a university lecturer and a senior fellow of Christ Church College. He kept this post until 1684, when he was deprived of it by royal mandate. During the initial years of his teaching, he offered courses in rhetoric, moral philosophy, and ancient Greek. His first books, *The Two Tracts on Government*, written during 1660–1662, and *Essays on the Law of Nature*, written in 1663–1664, were both composed at Oxford. In the winter of 1665–1666, Locke's scholarly life was briefly interrupted when he had his first experience of public service. He traveled to Brandenburg as secretary to a special diplomatic mission. However, he declined a subsequent offer to go to Spain in a similar capacity.

Undoubtedly more gratifying to him, the importance of his research work was becoming recognized at about the same time, and in 1668 he was admitted to the Royal Society, which he joined together with Boyle and Newton.

Wishing to expand his already considerable scientific knowledge, he turned to the study of medicine. His interest in medicine and occasional practice of it led, in 1666, to an acquaintance with Lord Ashley (from 1672, Earl of Shaftesbury), a leading politician at the court of Charles II. This connection had an immediate effect on Locke's career and allowed him to gain first-hand experience of the political world. From then on, politics and philosophy would compete with each other for his primary attention and energy. Without severing his ties with Oxford, he became a close associate of Shaftesbury and a member of his household. He assisted the politician in domestic, commercial, and political matters, shared his changing fortunes, and even saved his life by skillfully performing a surgical procedure. When Shaftesbury was made Lord Chancellor of the Realm in 1672, Locke became his secretary for presentations to benefices, and soon after was made secretary to the Proprietors of Carolina and to the Council of Trade. But in 1673, when Shaftesbury was deprived of his high office because of his growing opposition to the king, Locke's life as a public official came to a sudden end.

It was probably on Shaftesbury's request that Locke wrote a subversive pamphlet, *A Letter from a Person of Quality to his Friend in the Country*, published anonymously in 1675. The House of Lords ordered this pamphlet to be burned and set up a committee to discover and punish its author (Ashcraft 434). Afraid for his safety, and also seeking a milder climate because of his poor health, Locke departed for France. A travel journal, which he wrote while there, contains detailed descriptions of places he visited as well as French customs and institutions. It also contains many of the reflections that afterwards took shape in *An Essay Concerning Human Understanding*. During this period, which lasted until his return to England in 1679, Locke spent most of his time in Paris and Montpellier.

The four years following his return comprise a time of obscurity in Locke's life. As Shaftesbury's most trusted adviser, he produced a number of political writings for his patron. It is plausible that his major political work, *Two Treatises of Government*, probably written around 1680–1681, was composed at Shaftesbury's request. Since at that time Shaftesbury had become the leader of the Whig party, which opposed Charles II and in the end attempted to overthrow and even assassinate him, Locke's close association with him became a hazardous enterprise. At last, the king won, and they were both forced into exile, where Shaftesbury died.

From 1683 to 1689, Locke lived in Holland, like many other Whig exiles. But even abroad he did not feel safe, and with good reason: The authorities had him under surveillance and attempted to get him extradited. Nonetheless, he maintained contact with the leading members of the English political opposition. He also had friends among French Protestant refugees and liberal Dutch theologians. In particular, he developed a close friendship with the theologian

Philip van Limborch, to whom he dedicated his *Letter Concerning Toleration*. This work was completed in 1685, but not published at that time. In 1688, he wrote *An Essay Concerning Human Understanding*, and its abstract was published in a renowned intellectual journal, *Bibliothèque Universelle*.

In February 1689, Locke was able to return to England in the wake of the "Glorious Revolution," when the Parliament deposed King James II, brother and successor of Charles II, replacing him with William of Orange and his wife Mary. Locke, who was very much in favor of the new regime, took an active part in the political discussions of the day, giving advice to leading politicians on the Whig side. He was offered the post of ambassador to either Berlin or Vienna, but declined. Instead, he was made Commissioner of Appeals in May 1689, and from 1696 to 1700 served as Commissioner of the Council of Trade and Plantations. More important, his books began to be published on a significant scale. In the single year of 1689, he had his three greatest works printed: *Two Treatises of Government*, *A Letter on Toleration*, and *An Essay Concerning Human Understanding*. His writings gained such wide acceptance that they became almost a national orthodoxy.

John Locke died in the country house of his friends, Lady and Lord Masham, at Oates in Essex, on October 28, 1704. His fame continued to grow after his death, and he exerted more influence abroad, especially in France and the United States, than any other English political thinker. He produced works in philosophy and wrote about a variety of other subjects, including education, medicine, religion, and economics. But he left his true legacy in the area of politics, where his ideas were both of his time and for all times in the future. They were an expression of the English political experience of which he was an interpreter—an experience that has significantly contributed to the development of liberal thought.

THE QUESTION OF TOLERATION

When, in 1660, Charles II returned from his exile in France and was restored to the English throne, one of the important questions dominating the political life of the country was that of religious toleration. Should religious doctrine and worship be a purely private matter, with each individual enjoying full liberty of conscience, or, to the contrary, should there be a single official religion imposed on everyone and supported by the authorities? In other words, should there be "universal liberty" in religious matters, or "absolute obedience" (*Essay on Toleration* I.0)?

This question, discussed by many writers at that time, was not without practical significance; in fact, it was splitting English society apart. Those who were against toleration and supported unity in the church argued that religious diversity would produce seditions and endanger peace. Indeed, although at that time virtually everyone in England was a Christian, there were many religious denominations and profound theological differences among them. The conflict between Catholics and Protestants, which produced fierce religious wars in continental Europe as well as antagonism between different

Protestant sects, was a constant threat to Britain as well. The rise of Puritanism and its opposition to the Church of England—which meant opposition to King Charles I as well—culminated in the Civil War of 1642–1646.

As a precaution against sedition and civil conflict, the Parliament had, as early as 1563, during the reign of Queen Elizabeth I, issued the first Test Act. This statute required an oath of allegiance to the English Crown and abjuration of the authority of the Pope by all holders of office, lay or spiritual (Green 383). In addition, the religious policy of Elizabeth rested on the Act of Supremacy, introduced by her father Henry VIII in 1533, and the Act of Uniformity of 1559. The first vested authority in all matters ecclesiastical and civil in the Crown, and ordered that the monarch should be the supreme head of the Church of England, while the second prescribed a course of doctrine and worship from which no variation was legally permissible, and stipulated that all clergy use the Anglican Book of Common Prayer.

On the positive side, the Elizabethan legal system, intolerant as it was, aimed at order and moderation, and forced on the warring religious factions a sort of armed truce. The main principles of Protestantism were accepted, but the zeal of the Protestant radicals was held at bay. Outward conformity, notably in the requirement of adherence to a common form of worship and prayer, was imposed upon all, but the political designs of religious zealots, especially the idea of an ecclesiastical government that would subject the state to the church, were resisted. On the other hand, the effect of this policy, aimed at excluding Catholics from office and promoting religious uniformity, led to the one-sided empowerment of mainstream Protestants. As a result, Catholicism, which was the religion of three-fourths of the country's people at the time of Elizabeth's accession, quickly lost adherents. By the close of her reign, the only parts of England in which the old faith retained some of its former vigor were the poorest and least populated areas in the north and extreme west (Green 406). Nonetheless, despite the apparent triumph of the Anglican church, a significant number of individuals still remained utterly hostile to the spirit of the Reformation. They hoped for a Catholic king who could undo the work of the Protestant revolution.

The question of religious toleration was one of Locke's most persistent intellectual concerns. Often regarded as its foremost champion, he presented arguments for toleration first in *An Essay on Toleration*, which he wrote in 1667, and then in a number of writings, including the *Second Treatise of Government* and *A Letter Concerning Toleration*. Nevertheless, it is precisely this issue that presents a problem regarding the coherence of his political theory. In his early and little-studied work, *Two Tracts on Government*, which he wrote between 1660 and 1662, Locke is decisively intolerant. He defends the view that a government can impose religious doctrine and a prescribed form of religious worship on its citizens. As exemplified in his statement that "the supreme magistrate of every nation . . . must necessarily have an absolute and arbitrary power of all indifferent actions of his people" (*First Tract* Preface), he adopts an absolutist stance that is strikingly similar to that of Hobbes. The "indifferent actions" to which he refers were, in seventeenth-century religious usage, regarded as those that were neither commanded nor forbidden by the Scriptures. Locke argues that "rulers must have full power of all things indifferent" (Ibid.). They can prescribe religious worship and doctrine. Hence, when writing *Two Tracts*, he was still supportive of the Tudors' and Stuarts' authoritarian policies of royal supremacy and religious uniformity. Like English monarchs from Henry VIII and Elizabeth I to Charles I, and like the great supporter of absolutism—Hobbes, Locke saw the church as an instrument for securing, through moral and religious influences, the political ends of the state. His primary concern at that time was not toleration, but rather religious unity and civic order. He was pleased with Charles II's "happy return" and the restoration of those religious laws that "the prudence and providence of our ancestors established" (Ibid.). It was only after 1666, when he became associated with Earl of Shaftesbury, that Locke radically revised his earlier position.

Shaftesbury, as a member of the republican Council of State under the Commonwealth who after Oliver Cromwell's death took an active part in promoting the king's return, was rewarded by Charles II with a peerage and promotion to the government (Royal Council). A friend of the religious dissenters, during his service in the Royal Council Shaftesbury initially represented the Presbyterian and Nonconformist party, and was the steady and ardent advocate of toleration. But he saw no hope of obtaining it from the Anglican-dominated Parliament, which promoted the principle of religious uniformity in the church, and, between 1661 and 1665, had enacted a series of laws directed against Presbyterians, Puritans, and Catholics, which resulted in thousands of non-Anglican priests being driven out of their parishes and many being sent to jail. His only hope was the king. But since Locke suspected that the king had Catholic and absolutist sympathies and Locke himself supported Protestantism and the supremacy of the Parliament, he was distrustful of the king as well. Like most of his compatriots at that time, he abhorred three things: "popery, France, and arbitrary power" (Clark 322). This explains why he wavered, at one point supporting the king, and later opposing him. He was for religious toleration, but not for a toleration that would extend its benefit to the Catholics, as Charles desired. In 1673, a secret treaty was concluded at Dover, in which Charles agreed to support Catholic France against Protestant Holland in return for annual subsidies from the French that would make him independent of the financing he received from Parliament. Once Shaftesbury learned about this treaty, he began to oppose the king openly. Like a large portion of the public, he suspected that a plot was afoot to reestablish Catholicism in England. He supported a new Test Act, which was introduced in order to remove the Catholics from official posts. He tried also to exclude the possibility of Charles' brother James, who was a Catholic, succeeding him to the throne.

Seen against the background of these events, Locke was not a detached philosopher, indifferent to the political issues of concern to his contemporaries. His contact with Shaftesbury certainly contributed to a radical change, not only in his political views but also in his way of life, transforming him from a scholar into an activist. Almost immediately after joining Shaftesbury, he wrote *An Essay on Toleration*, recommending toleration for religious dissenters, an issue with which his patron was initially politically identified (Ashcraft 21). In the 1667 *Essay* we no longer find any claim that the authorities should prescribe religious worship and doctrine. To the contrary, Locke now argues that differences in theological doctrine and style of worship should be tolerated. In support of his argument, he draws a distinction between public and private spheres, and identifies religious matters with the private sphere and civil matters with the public sphere. The government, he says, is concerned about public affairs in this world, and has nothing to do with "my private interest in another world" (*Essay* II.1). In addition, he contends that intolerance always breeds conflict, and therefore that social peace can only be obtained through toleration. His argument for toleration is, however, complicated by the fact that in both the *Essay on Toleration* and the *Letter Concerning Toleration*, he is not prepared to include Catholics and atheists within the scope of the toleration he is arguing for.

Unquestionably, Locke's writings on toleration were the products of historical and personal circumstances. His *Essay on Toleration* was composed in support of Shaftesbury's campaign to obtain toleration for religious dissenters, and his *Letter Concerning Toleration* (or, more precisely, its Latin original, *Epistola de tolerantia*) was written in the shadow cast by Louis XIV's revocation of the Edict of Nantes, that is, in an environment of growing religious intolerance. This has led some commentators to conclude that Locke's case for toleration is so deeply permeated by the realities of his own age that it is no longer relevant in our times. Despite their historical references, however, both the *Essay* and the *Letter* are important philosophical works. They signal the birth of liberalism, setting forth the essential liberal belief that governments are instituted for no purpose other than to secure the "civil peace and property" of the citizenry (*Essay* II.0). It is within this context of limited government that Locke strives to provide a general justification for toleration and to define its limits.

TOLERATION AND ITS LIMITS

Toleration is not an exclusively liberal or modern concept. We can find its ancient expression in Pericles' statement: "we are not offended by our neighbor for following his own pleasure" (Thucydides 2.37) or in Saint Thomas Aquinas' conviction that human beings need freedom to pursue activities related to personal self-perfection. Although toleration can certainly have a place in other streams of political thought, "it is in liberalism that that place is most exalted" (Mendus 3). What, then, is toleration?

Historically and legally, toleration can be described as allowing people to pursue the way of life that they choose. This is in contrast to intolerance, which can take many forms, such as religious, racial, or sexual intolerance. Problems concerning toleration arise in situations of religious, racial, ethnic, or sexual diversity, where the diversity is of such a nature as to give rise to attitudes of strong disapproval or dislike. Such problems do not occur in relation to diverse beliefs or practices that are believed to be good or morally neutral.

An argument for toleration is thus "an argument which gives a reason for not interfering with a person's beliefs or practices even when we have reason to hold that those beliefs or practices are mistaken, heretical, or depraved" (Waldron 63). Formal, legal toleration, based on the idea of "live and let live," is achieved through the state's noninterference in matters such as religion, morality, and sexual preference. However, today's liberal writers argue that this type of formal toleration is not enough to guarantee actual toleration in society. Not only tolerant laws but also a tolerant attitude among the populace must exist. The formal aspects of toleration must be supplemented by a positive welcoming of difference and affirmation of diversity.

Waldron and other influential interpreters of Locke have suggested that the Lockean argument for toleration can be boiled down to an attempt to persuade the authorities of the irrationality of intolerance and persecution. Indeed, in both the *Essay* and the *Letter*, Locke contends that human beings should not be forced to renounce their own beliefs because such compulsion cannot produce any real effect. It is incapable of inducing any genuine belief, and results only in external compliance. It does not make individuals into believers, but only turns them into hypocrites (*Letter* 395). We can refute this assertion by reference to historical examples of religious and ideological coercion that sooner or later were able to produce real effects and change people's beliefs. Furthermore, we can argue that since Locke focuses on the irrationality of intolerance rather than on its immorality, and addresses the potential disadvantages to the perpetrators of intolerance rather than the wrong done to its victims, his defense of toleration is unsatisfactory (Mendus 146).

Nevertheless, whatever the weaknesses of Locke's contention regarding the irrationality of intolerance might be, this does not seem to be his main argument for toleration. In fact, he makes the case for toleration on the basis of several arguments; the most crucial concerns the distinction between public and private spheres, and the liberal idea of limited government. Individuals, Locke claims, have private concerns of a non-political nature, such as religious speculation and worship; preservation of their health; raising children; working, selling, and conducting other economic activities; and so on. In all these matters they should be entitled to toleration, provided that they "do not cause greater inconveniences than advantages to the community" (*Essay* II.2). They must be able to pursue their non-political interests without the state's interference. For, says Locke, the government "has nothing to do with the good of men's souls . . . , but is ordained for the quiet and comfortable living of men in society" (II.3).

Locke thus achieves religious toleration, but only at the cost of making religion irrelevant to public life (Snyder 242). He secularizes public affairs and moves all of religion to the private realm. Since the government deals with public and not private concerns, and one's religion, morality, and lifestyle are private matters, his argument goes, the government cannot interfere in the latter. Further, since religious matters are private, the church is "absolutely separate" from the state. "The boundaries on both sides are fixed and immovable" (*Letter* 403). Churches have no jurisdiction in civil affairs. They should have no influence on education and law. Like individuals, they can use persuasion to spread their beliefs, but cannot resort to force, for it is the function of government, and not of private entities, "to give laws, compel obedience, and compel with the sword" (395). Hence, neither churches nor individuals can deprive other people who are not of their faith of either liberty or any part of their worldly goods on account of differences in religion (Ibid.).

The Lockean argument for toleration is not merely restricted to religious toleration, for, in addition to religious matters, Locke also discusses moral issues and private domestic affairs. Further, he stresses a moral dimension of toleration. Intolerance, and especially religious intolerance (which he focuses on due to his own historical circumstances), is wrong because it takes us away from the search for truth. Particularly in matters of religion, we can never be certain where the truth lies. Each religion and each sect portrays itself as representing the true faith (*Letter* 401). Because of this uncertainty of belief, toleration should then be allowed on moral grounds. Individuals must not be punished for their beliefs and practices, which may in fact be true and pleasing to God. Public officials who try to coerce individuals in religious matters not only display arrogance by attempting to impose on others their own personal beliefs—which may be mistaken—but also commit injustice by overstepping the bounds of their authority.

There are, however, limits to toleration that are a logical consequence of the argument that Locke employs. For, just as the public sphere cannot infringe on what is private, so also private matters cannot infringe on what is public. Whatever private individuals do, they should neither violate the rights of others nor "break the public peace of societies" (417). If a government, by laws or other regulations, endeavors to compel or restrain individuals in a way that is contrary to their consciences, they may nonviolently disobey, but at the same time they must be ready to quietly submit to the penalty for such an act of civil disobedience (*Essay* II.2). John Stuart Mill and later liberals would attempt to set the limit of personal liberty at the point where harm is done to others. They would be prepared to tolerate all opinions and to allow individuals to enjoy freedom in the areas of life that concerned their own good (Mill 86). Locke is more restrictive. Not only should individuals not cause harm to others but also they should not obstruct the work of the government.

The government is responsible for maintaining domestic peace and protecting citizens and their goods from the "fraud or violence of others," as well as for providing external security (*Essay* I.0; *Letter* 406). Going beyond these safety and security issues, it is also concerned with ensuring "the temporal good and outward prosperity of society" (*Letter* 423). While theoretical opinions cannot do any damage to the public good, practical beliefs, which directly affect the way people live, may be harmful. Therefore, Locke declares, "no opinions contrary to human society, or to those moral rules that are necessary to the preservation of civil society, are to be tolerated by the magistrate" (*Letter* 424). Vice, which is destructive to society's well-being, must never be established through an act of law (*Essay* II.3). Further, no political party that is a potential threat to the peace of the state should be allowed to exist; and if an outward manifestation, for example, a particular type of clothing, is used by members of such a party as a badge or political symbol, it should be prohibited. It is a central responsibility of the government to issue commands or prohibitions regarding matters that affect the peace, safety, and security of the people, with the aim of protecting society against potential threats.

From his own days up through the present, Locke's arguments have had the potential to provoke discussion of very controversial topics. They are clearly relevant to questions debated in some countries today. Is legalizing homosexual marriage equivalent to legislating vice? Is wearing a religious headscarf just a private matter, or is it a political statement—an opposition to secularism? Should it be allowed in public institutions, such as schools? Locke is not free from controversy, in that he denies toleration to atheists and Catholics: His argument concerning the latter is that the benefits of toleration cannot be enjoyed by those who refuse it to others and who deliver themselves up to the protection and service of another prince (*Letter* 426).

In his advocacy of toleration, Locke also does not subscribe to the current rhetoric of diversity. For Locke, being tolerant of others does not mean approving of their conduct or beliefs. Human life involves a search for truth, and so individuals are not obliged to accept something that they believe to be false or evidently wrong. As Locke plainly says, every human being "has commission to admonish, exhort, convince another of error, and by reasoning to draw him into truth" (395). Since in everyday life, in philosophy, in religion, and even in science is there no one single way to arrive at truth, it is necessary to allow a multiplicity of views to flourish. Toleration and diversity are thus not values in themselves, but they serve as preconditions for the pursuit of truth.

Inevitably, the religious, social, and political realities of seventeenth-century England, and especially the tensions between Protestants and Catholics, affected Locke's views on toleration. Even if we should, when examining the argument by which he denies toleration to Catholics, refer to the Pope as a prince, as Locke does, he would in fact be considered a prince only in the realm of religious doctrine, rather than in the political arena. And if Catholics have been loyal to the Pope in matters of faith, this does not mean that they have not been able to fulfill their obligations to the state as well, as examples from the history of traditionally Catholic countries such as Spain, France, Poland, and Ireland can demonstrate. Locke's denial of toleration to Catholics thus seems to be the product of his own, or perhaps Shaftesbury's, personal beliefs and prejudices, and cannot be approved. His argument against granting tolerance to atheists would also find little support today. However, what can still be considered as valid is Locke's general view of toleration—namely, that it should serve the pursuit of truth, but should also be limited by the good of society; it should not extend to what is commonly considered as vice; and it should not apply to those who, once in power, would deny it to others.

Contemporary theories of toleration are based on the Kantian idea of human autonomy, that is, on the conviction that human beings are able to make judgments and to choose what is best for themselves. In the writings of Kant's twentieth-century American followers, especially John Rawls and Ronald Dworkin, judging and making choices for oneself becomes a normative ideal.

In their theories, the individual takes center stage. In contrast, Locke regards both the individual and the state as having legitimate requirements, which can coexist within certain limits. The needs of private life determine the limits of government power; the demands of the public good determine the limits of individual freedom. Locke's balanced view of toleration occupies a middle ground between the two extremes of absolute obedience and complete freedom.

FREEDOM AND LAW

Locke's political writings are often interpreted as being directed primarily against the ideas of Sir Robert Filmer. At the beginning of Book I of the *Two Treatises*—usually referred to as the *First Treatise*—Locke says that Filmer's position is "that all government is absolute monarchy" and "that no man is born free." Locke's own position is exactly the opposite. He sets out to demonstrate that legitimate government is constitutionally limited and exists only by the consent of the governed, and that this is true because all human beings are naturally free.

Filmer's *Patriarcha* was composed during the 1640s to defend absolute monarchy and the divine right of kings. Although some portions had been printed earlier, it was first published in its entirety in 1680 during the Exclusion Crisis, when Shaftesbury attempted to exclude Charles II's brother James as the possible successor to the throne. The work was used by the King's supporters as an ideological justification of passive obedience to the Crown. The writings of Thomas Hobbes, perhaps the most famous absolutist and advocate of complete obedience to the sovereign, had materialistic implications and so could not serve as a manifesto for the royalists, who were mostly devoted Catholics or members of the Anglican church. Instead, they seized upon Filmer's work, and thus refuting Filmer became Locke's immediate aim. In the *First Treatise*, he argues against Filmer's absolutist views and in the first paragraph of the *Second Treatise*, he offers a summary of this argument. Nevertheless, insofar as he rejects Filmer's absolutism, he implicitly rejects the Hobbesian version as well. Although Locke seldom mentions Hobbes by name, his works provide a critique of many of the ideas found in Hobbes's *Leviathan*.

One such idea is the concept of freedom, which Hobbes identifies as the absence of restraint. Individuals are free if they are not opposed or hindered from doing what they have the will and ability to do (*Leviathan* XXI). To be sure, in Hobbes' view, freedom is not derived from our capacity to make choices and is not even an exclusively human phenomenon. Hobbes defines liberty in negative terms—not as a positive power of human beings, but as a negative feature of the environment in which they live, that is, as freedom from obstacles. The freedom of human beings is thus not unlike that of natural objects, such as water, which can "behave" more "freely" if there are no external impediments to their motion. In the Hobbesian state of nature, where there is neither justice nor injustice, human beings are free in the sense that they are not restrained by any common power over them or by any moral considerations. They move freely, driven by their passions, by their appetites and aversions.

Locke overtly rejects this view. In *An Essay Concerning Human Understanding*, he says that there cannot be any liberty where "there is no thought, no volition, no will" (2.21.8). Therefore, only human beings, and not natural objects or irrational creatures, can be free. He defines liberty in positive terms. For Locke, freedom is the ability or "power to act or forbear acting" according to one's choice or preference (2.21.24). When someone does not have such power, he is not at liberty; he is under necessity. Obviously, being subject to the will of another person is not the condition of freedom, but rather is its opposite. But freedom is also not being subject to one's own appetites or desires. While for Hobbes, will and desire are identical, Locke distinguishes between the two. Our desires may impel us to act, but ultimately we direct our actions by using our will; in addition, our liberty to act in accordance with our will is in turn grounded in reason and the power of judgment. In short, we are free only insofar as we are rational. For, before the will is directed to act and the action is done, "we have opportunity to examine, view, and judge, of the good and evil of what we are going to do" (2.21.47). As is evident from everyday experience, argues Locke, if we do not find it right, we have the power to suspend the execution of this or that desire, and in this lies our liberty.

According to Hobbes and other representatives of the legal positivist or voluntarist school, "a law is a law if it is enacted by an authoritative lawgiver and promulgated" (Tully, 1993, 293). Laws are good because a legitimate lawgiver *wills* them into being, and not because they conform to some independent, rational criteria of what is good and just. From the Hobbesian perspective, freedom, which refers to the absence of restraint, and law, which refers to obligation, are thus mutually exclusive (*Leviathan* XIV). Locke, on the other hand, contends that "where there is no law, there is no freedom" because freedom exists in a situation when one is "free from the restraint and violence of others," and this cannot be "where there is no law" (*Second Treatise* 6.57). Thus, for Locke, there is no real freedom in the Hobbesian state of nature, which is characterized by constant insecurity and violence. The essence of freedom for Locke lies not in the mere absence of restraint, but rather in our ability to make rational choices so that we can enjoy a happy life; such a life is possible only under secure and lawful social conditions. In a rationally ordered political community, law—of which the ultimate measure is provided by natural law—enlarges rather than curtails our freedom, and is "not so much the limitation as the direction of a free and intelligent agent to his proper interest" (Ibid.). Although a modern political thinker, Locke embraces the natural law tradition, in which laws are considered to be norms discoverable by reason, and not mere imperatives or commands.

THE STATE OF NATURE AND NATURAL LAW

Like Hobbes, Locke discusses the state of nature: an idealized era in the history of humankind before the establishment of political society. In the state of nature, as described in the *Second Treatise of Government*, individuals are perfectly equal, in the sense that they have similar faculties and also in that no one individual has any claim to jurisdiction over the others. They are also perfectly free, in the sense of being able "to order their actions, and dispose of their possessions and persons, as they think fit" (2.4). However, their liberty does not give them license to do whatever they want; nor does it consist of their not being "tied to any laws" (4.22). In contrast to Hobbesian individuals, Lockean individuals, although also self-interested and pleasure-seeking, are not driven by their passions without any restraint because for Locke the state of nature is not a lawless condition. It has, in fact, the "law of nature to govern it" and "reason which is that law, teaches all mankind, who will but consult it, that being all equal and independent, no one ought to harm another in his life, health, liberty, or possessions" (2.6).

There is an extensive scholarly debate concerning natural law, and in particular the Lockean theory of natural law. Although the notion of natural law as a moral law that is eternal and immutable and discoverable by reason has a long tradition traceable to Aristotle and Cicero, it has been rejected by many modern thinkers, who have come to regard this notion as obsolete. There are, however, other contemporary theorists who claim that one cannot dispense with natural law and in fact make it the basis of their legal theories. An additional dimension is brought to the discussion by those Locke interpreters who argue that his theory of natural law is actually incompatible with the older natural law tradition because, as textual evidence shows, natural law is for Locke a decree of God, a product of God's will rather than of reason. Still, other scholars claim that even if we agree that according to Locke natural law has a source in God's will, his legal theory is not voluntarist. Since Locke argues that "God himself cannot choose what is not good" (*Essay HU* 2.21.49), the foundation of natural law in God's will does not for him imply that the law is good merely because the supreme lawgiver wills it. God chooses only what is good, but what is good is established by right reason, not by will. God, Locke says, directs "our actions to that which is best" and guides us either indirectly, by the "light of nature," or directly, by the "voice of revelation" (2.28.8). Hence, it seems that like other traditional natural law theorists, Locke maintains that in contrast to the revealed divine law that is promulgated by revelation, natural law is known by reason in a natural way, without revelation.

The questions about whether moral principles can be known by reason and whether they have any basis other than the conventions of a particular culture are certainly difficult to answer. In Locke's view, natural law is rational and knowable. It is a moral law, which can be justified rationally, and is thus, although unwritten, universal and applicable to the whole human race. To be sure, the universality of natural law is not related to any innate ideas, since Locke denies the existence of such inborn knowledge. When he refers to natural law, he is not alluding to anything preexistent implanted in human minds, for he believes that all knowledge, including knowledge of moral principles, is ultimately derived from experience. Instead, he is referring to a rational consensus. Locke thinks that since human beings have reason and strive for happiness, there is sufficient uniformity among them and the conditions of their lives, and that consequently, they can all form the same basic views of good and evil, and of moral obligation (2.21.52). They can thus develop a sense of justice and injustice. He does not, of course, deny that there are rules of conduct—especially the laws of "opinion or reputation"—that are culturally bound, and by which one culture can be distinguished from another (2.28.7). It is a matter of fact that a particular custom approved in one society may not be considered favorably in another. But there are also rules that can be rationally recognized as universally binding in all societies and as representing the necessary moral foundation of every legal order. These are the prescriptions of natural law—such as the plea that "humankind ought to be preserved" or that "one should not harm another."

At the same time, however, Locke understands that the moral universality of natural law cannot be based on reason alone, and in this respect he departs from the traditional view of natural law. According to his strikingly modern notion of human beings, we are always impelled to action on the basis of desire. What commands our actions is always a desire, or an uneasiness related to an absent good (2.21.31). We all seek pleasure and try to avoid pain. Desires accordingly play a part equally important to that of reason in human life. We cannot free ourselves from them. When pursuing the overall goal of happiness, we can only suspend their execution and thus substitute one desire, which we conventionally call "higher," for another one, which we call "lower." An alcoholic, for example, may realize that his desire for a drink impoverishes him and ruins his family life (2.21.34). Desiring a better family life, he may attempt to stop drinking. If he succeeds, the "lower" desire for drink is replaced by a "higher" one for a better family life. Further, if we should put desires into a hierarchy, for Locke the highest of all would be the desire for eternal life (2.21.70). This longing for life to come in the hereafter shapes the lives of those who believe in God and puts their desires into a proper order. Therefore, natural law, although known through reason, has its ultimate basis in the existence of God. Like any law, it requires a lawmaker with sufficient power to enforce it (1.3.12). In this case, the law is enforced by divine sanctions, by rewards and punishments in the afterlife for compliance with or breach of it, respectively.

We can now understand why Locke argues that tolerance should not be granted to atheists. He thinks those who deny God are likely to lose sight of a higher purpose in life, and consequently to devote themselves to the continual pursuit of earthly goals, which they identify with the good. In effect, they turn into Hobbesian individuals, who employ reason not to distinguish between right and wrong, but merely as an instrument for getting what they want—a calculus of utilities. Such individuals, in endless conflict with one another, know neither moral law nor any limit; they only understand the law of force. "Promises, covenants, and oaths, which are the bounds of human society, can have no hold upon an atheist" (*Letter* 426).

Human beings who are rational and who believe in God can recognize that even in the state of nature, where there is no common public authority to judge between them, there is still a law of nature, a moral law that imposes limitations on their actions. Thus, while Locke agrees with Hobbes that the state of nature is a condition of perfect freedom, he does not agree that individuals in this condition have a right to everything. They cannot use their natural liberty to destroy one another. No one can harm another in his "life, health, liberty, or possessions" (*Second Treatise* 2.6). Hobbes' mistake, Locke suggests, was to mechanistically deduce a state of war from the state of nature. Hobbes failed to understand that in the state of nature individuals are constrained to obey natural law, and that as long human beings obey this law and recognize each other's rights, the state of nature can be peaceful. In short, for Locke, the state of nature is based upon the order of natural law, which, if observed and enforced, preserves peace. He refuses to accept the idea that the absence of government inevitably leads to conflict and to the Hobbesian "war of everyone against everyone."

THE LIBERAL CONCEPT OF INTERNATIONAL RELATIONS

Theoretical approaches to international relations come in a variety of forms. Two of these, idealism and liberalism, are usually placed in the same category, and contrasted with realism. They both stress international norms, interdependence between states, and international cooperation rather than conflict. There are, however, important differences between "early liberalism," which can be identified with idealism, and "neoliberalism," a liberal approach developed in the 1970s (Jackson, Sørensen 49). Whereas idealism or early liberalism emphasizes legal and ethical issues, and as a theoretical perspective is rooted in classical political thinking, neoliberalism emphasizes cooperation in the environment of international anarchy and is influenced by modern social science. Neo-liberals repudiate the ideas of earlier liberals, and especially their belief in human rationality and self-control, and they adopt the modern view of human beings as basically self-interested individuals. Rather than moralizing about how international relations should be conducted, they attempt to show that even in an environment of anarchy, cooperation can still be achieved between self-interested actors.

Although Locke devoted only slight attention to international relations, one can find in his writings a powerful argument in support of liberalism in both its early and neoliberal form. In contrast to the Hobbesian image of the state of nature as a state of war in which life is "poor, nasty, brutish, and short" (*Leviathan* XIII 9), the Lockean state of nature is characterized by "peace, good will, mutual assistance, and preservation" (*Second Treatise* 3.19). While one can make a general objection that individuals have never truly been in the state of nature since they have actually always lived in some sort of community, Locke argues that such an objection does not apply in the case of states. What ends the state of nature is an agreement to enter into a community, but with the exception of some agreements at a regional level—of which the most striking example today would be the European Union—no such international agreements have been made. Therefore, "princes and rulers of independent governments, all through the world, are in the state of nature" (2.14). Having no common superior to whom they can appeal, they find themselves in an anarchic environment. The state of nature—international anarchy—is thus a permanent condition in which states exist. If this is so, how can it be peaceful and characterized by mutual assistance?

First, as has been stated above, even in the state of nature we can find a law—the law of nature. In other words, we can discern some norms that are applicable to the behavior of individuals as well as states, and these norms can be eventually incorporated into international law. Peace results from obedience to these universally accepted norms. Whoever does not recognize them essentially admits to being prepared "to live by another rule than reason and common equity" (2.8)—namely, by force and violence—and thus can be resisted and destroyed. At this point, Locke seems to support the idealist or early liberal perspective, which can be associated with the tradition of classical political thought, and also with Grotius. Locke, however, is not a classical political philosopher but is instead a modern thinker. His modernity is evident not only in his attempt to use the new scientific methodology and to derive all knowledge from experience but also in his depiction of human beings as self-seeking individuals who, instead of developing virtue, seek pleasure and avoid pain. Like other modern thinkers, he emphasizes interest rather than morality. He regards human beings as being self-interested and competitive up to a point, but also believes that they can have shared interests and can thus engage in cooperative action, resulting in greater benefits for everyone. What individuals particularly want, in his view, is "a secure enjoyment of their properties" (8.95). By recognizing the importance of self-interest for cooperation and relating the latter to economic affairs, Locke lays a theoretical foundation for neoliberalism.

From a liberal perspective, conflict and war are not inevitable. They are an aberration from normal peaceful conditions, and not a norm. In contrast to realists, who perceive states as independent actors constantly preoccupied with power, liberals see states as constitutional entities that establish and enforce the rule of law, and uphold some fundamental rights, which can, using Locke's conceptual framework, be summed up as the rights to life, liberty, and property. Protecting individual rights and freedoms and promoting commerce are considered to be the main concerns of liberal states. Such states, committed to civilized behavior—guaranteed at least as much (if not more) internally, by the voice of public opinion, as enforced externally, by other states—respect each other and deal with each other in accordance with the norms of mutual recognition.

In the chapter in the *Second Treatise* that concerns property, Locke connects the origin of territorial political units—that is, states—to the growth of population, the usage of money, and the beginning of commerce. The emerging states then form leagues, whose members "either expressly or tacitly disowning all claim and right to the land in the others' possession" (5.45) settle questions regarding their territories peacefully by themselves. Locke suggests that leagues, or, as we would say today, security communities, can be formed among states that share common values, especially if they trade with one another. Because these states are connected by economic ties and are thus interdependent, they can recognize each other and maintain peaceful relations.

This Lockean argument was further expanded by Immanuel Kant, who thought that the establishment of a powerful league of mutually respectful and constitutionally limited states, which we would today call "democratic," could lead to perpetual peace in the world (Jackson, Sørensen 108). In short, Kant believed that democracies would not fight one another, and so a world consisting of liberal democracies would be a more peaceful one. But the premise that democracies do not fight one another, which is the classic basis of the democratic peace theory, does not mean that democracies do not go to war at all. States that have not become a part of the league are not immune to invasion. In fact, the theory implies that for the sake of perpetual peace, all nations should be transformed into reliable commercial partners—that is, liberal democracies—and if this transformation cannot be achieved by peaceful means, we can expect war. Suspicious about authoritarian states, which are perceived as being unpredictable and dangerous, modern liberals are thus far more supportive of conflict than the traditional and more ethically minded early liberals or idealists.

In the state of nature, individuals are their own masters, and, Locke insists, their consent is required if they are to be subjected to authority. Similarly, states remain free and independent in the international state of nature unless they voluntarily subject themselves to a superior power. The state of war is "a state of enmity and destruction" (*Second Treatise* 3.16) created by the usage of "force without right" (3.19). At the level of individuals, it comes through words or actions by which one person threatens to take another into his power and "take away the freedom that belongs to one" (3.17) in the state of nature. Translated into international terms, for Locke this means that national self-determination—the power of a country to take the course of its destiny into its own hands—is a fundamental value, encompassing the country's rights to political sovereignty and territorial integrity. Aggression, by means of which one state enters into a state of war against another, is an act of force or an imminent threat of force by one state against the political sovereignty or territorial integrity of another (Walzer 62). An act of aggression justifies resistance: a war of self-defense on the part of the victim, and a war of law enforcement on the part of the victim and of other states. Any state can use necessary force against the aggressor in order to aid the victimized state. Since there is no common authority in the state of nature, everyone has executive power to enforce the law of nature and can punish another for any evil he has done (*Second Treatise* 2.7).

A serious defect of the state of nature, as Locke points out, is the absence of institutions that can deter aggression and encourage cooperation. This explains why today's liberals attach a great importance to such international organizations as the United Nations, which help to build trust and improve relations between states. Beyond this, liberals also see the need for a hegemon, a leading economic and military power that can enforce international rules in the absence of a world government. However, as already Cicero has shown, this hegemon, whose status is bestowed by other states and rests on recognition by them, cannot use its privileged position solely for its own sake. It must protect international order and help sustain a worldwide liberal market economy for the benefit of all. If it does not properly perform those responsibilities, and particularly if it violates international law and disregards the voice of world public opinion, its hegemony turns into tyranny. It becomes a terrifying concentration of power—an instance of might without right.

A LIMITED GOVERNMENT

If, as Locke says, individuals in the state of nature enjoy rights and perfect freedom, and if this state can be a peaceful one, why would they want to leave it and subject themselves to a government? While Hobbesian individuals quit the state of nature out of *necessity*, because life in the Hobbesian state of nature is unbearable, Lockean individuals do it for the sake of *convenience*. They "unite into a community for their comfortable, safe, and peaceable living one amongst another, in a secure enjoyment of their properties" (8.95).

A more complete picture of the transition from the state of nature to a political society has to include the economic background of Locke's *Two Treatises*, which will be discussed in the following sections. At this point, it is sufficient to note that Locke recognizes that there will always be individuals who, by transgressing natural law and engaging in acts of violence against others, would disrupt the peace of the state of nature. In such a case, everyone has a right to punish the offender. However, since it can be dangerous to punish offenders by oneself, and since people biased by self-interest may be poor judges in their own cases, a fully secure life requires that there be impartial judges to decide disputes, as well as written laws, promulgated for the benefit of the people, and the public means to execute such laws (9.124-126). Briefly, there must be institutions such as courts, laws, and tools of enforcement—institutions that we would identify as constituent parts of a government. But, says Locke, "no rational creature can be supposed to change his condition to be worse" (9.131). Contrary to Hobbes, Locke argues that the purpose of entering into a political society is not to establish just any government, but only one that can ensure that our basic rights to life, liberty, and property are protected.

Locke, like Hobbes, sees the state as being established by means of a social contract, but his view of the act of contracting differs. Although he is not entirely clear on some points, his social contract appears to involve a two-stage process. First of all, there must be *consent on the part of every individual* to enter into a community, which will constitute "one people, one body politic, under supreme government" (7.89). To do this, individuals must be willing to give up their natural right to judge and punish offenders, and turn it over to the public. This brings them together into political or civil society. "Those who are united into one body, and have a common established law and judicature to apply to, with authority to decide controversies among them, and punish offenders, are [then] in *civil society* one with another; but those who have not such a common appeal . . . are still in the state of nature, each being, where is no other, judge for himself, and executioner" (7.87). Second, there must be *consent of the majority* concerning the general direction in which this society should move, particularly concerning the selection of the type of government that will rule society. The state is then established on the basis of the decision of the majority.

Accordingly, the Lockean social contract not only leads to the establishment of the state but also gives the ultimate power to the majority. As Locke says, "every man, by consenting with others to make one body politic under one government, puts himself under an obligation . . . to submit to the determination of the majority" (8.97). Although this point is not made in as many words, we can deduce that since at this stage of the contract no individual intrinsically possesses any authority over another, the decision-making procedure must take into account the choice of each person. However, as Locke clearly acknowledges, obtaining the consent of every individual concerning public affairs is practically impossible. Therefore, the only practical solution is substituting the consent of the majority, whose decision is now regarded as being the "act of the whole" (8.98). The majority, which represents the people, entrusts their power to the government, and the people consent to obey as long as the government performs the functions for which it was entrusted with power.

There are some important implications that follow from the two-stage social contract.

First, civil society is distinguished from the state and "retains supreme power" (13.149). Whereas in the Hobbesian social contract individuals irrevocably transfer their power to the government, which thus becomes identified with the sovereign, in the Lockean social contract the power that every individual gives to the community remains vested in that community; the power rests with the people. We can thus call Locke an exponent of popular sovereignty.

Second, the government exists as an agent or trustee of society, and not as its master. The majority, which represents the whole community, does not once and for all relinquish the community's power, but merely entrusts it to a particular government. To be legitimate, the government must be accountable to the people and rely on their continuing consent.

Third, if the government holds its power only in trust from the community, this means that it must be limited by its purpose, which is to advance "the peace, safety and public good of the people" (9.131). If it neglects or acts contrary to this end—for example, by violating citizens' liberties or by seizing their property—it abuses its power.

Fourth, to minimize the possibility of the abuse of power, Locke proposes that governmental power also be limited, and divided into legislative and executive branches, so that no individual or group can have too much of it (12.144).

Fifth, if a government does commit abuse, the power with which it was once entrusted can be revoked, and devolves "into the hands of those who gave it, who may place it anew where they shall think best for their safety and security" (13.149). In other words, the people have a right to resist the government and to revolt. The concept of limited government is used to justify revolution. In the Hobbesian model, the sovereign power is irrevocable and the removal of a government inevitably brings individuals back to the state of nature, but this is not the case with Locke. When a government is removed, power reverts to the community, which is then capable of entrusting that power to a new government.

As Hobbes bluntly says, "the name of tyranny signifieth nothing more nor less than the name of sovereignty" (*Leviathan* Conc.). Every government is a tyranny for him. In his attempt to prevent all social conflict and to impose order, he subjects society to unlimited, unchecked, and undivided governmental power—in short, to a government whose acts can be wholly arbitrary. In contrast, Locke sees such an absolute and in effect tyrannical government as lacking legitimacy—it can perhaps impose control but without commanding authority (*Second Treatise* 16.196). Although it may seem possible to have an enlightened ruler who would use absolute power for the public good, Locke contends that there is no reason to believe such a ruler would always behave in this way. Absolute monarchs, who make arbitrary decisions and commit acts of injustice against which there is no possibility of appeal, are inconsistent with his idea of political community. They remain in the state of nature, in opposition to the rest of society. "For where-ever any two men are, who have no standing rule, and common judge to appeal to on earth, for the determination of controversies of right between them, they are still in the state of nature" (7.91).

The government that Locke proposes, whether monarchic or democratic, is founded on consent and exercises its power in trust. It lays claim to its authority on the basis of both individuals' initial consent to be members of a political community and their subsequent consent to the way in which the established political institutions are operated. It is circumscribed by both its purpose and its limited power. It does not act in an arbitrary way, but rather in accordance with laws that in turn have their ultimate reference in natural law.

Locke thus rejects the Hobbesian idea that "right" is merely an arbitrary term whose meaning depends on the will of the sovereign. There is, he argues, a natural standard of right that is expressed in natural law and that should be incorporated in the positive laws of a society. "The law of nature stands as an eternal rule to all men, legislators as well as others" (Ibid.). The government that violates this standard and uses might without right, even when it seeks legitimacy by making an attempt to obtain the consent of its subjects for what it does, is a tyranny in what Locke considers the proper sense of the word: "Tyranny is the exercise of power beyond right" (18.199). A government is tyrannical if it transgresses fundamental principles of natural law and through its arbitrary and therefore lawless exercise of power impoverishes, enslaves, or destroys its own citizens. Locke's understanding of tyranny thus goes far beyond its classical definition as the rule of one individual for his own benefit. Any form of government, monarchy as well as democracy, can turn into a tyranny if arbitrary rule and disregard of what is right come into practice (18.201).

From the perspective of classical thought, living in a political community allows individuals to develop their full human potential: It makes a good life possible. The people are seen as a community bound together by a shared idea of the common good and by history, traditions, and customs. Tyranny is rejected because it is incompatible with virtue and the common good. In contrast, Locke, who puts stress on the individual rather than on the community, does not view society as introducing any fundamental change in human life. Society is a contractually established arena that allows human beings to pursue the same private ends that they had been pursuing in the state of nature. Even though he starts from theoretical assumptions that differ from those of classical political thinkers, Locke also rejects tyranny. He argues that to authorize tyranny or arbitrary rule that would prevent human beings from striving to attain the basic ends they are entitled to pursue on the basis of natural law, and that thus constitute their rights, would contradict the purpose for which the state was instituted.

The defining characteristic of a liberal type of government is, above all, the protection of individual rights, that is, what is rightfully due to a person. Since government exists to safeguard the rights and liberties of citizens who are considered the best final judges of their own interests, it must be limited in scope and must not overstep its purpose. It is constrained by its task, which is to ensure that citizens have the maximum degree of freedom possible in order to pursue their private goals. And human beings' chief end in "uniting into common-wealths, and putting themselves under government, is the preservation of their property" (9.124).

PROPERTY AND LABOR

The relatively short Chapter 5 of the *Second Treatise of Government*, which sets forth the Lockean theory of property, can be considered one of the most significant pieces of all modern political writing. The standard interpretation is that Locke wrote it to show that there were individual property rights, countering Filmer and other writers who were denying such rights. This interpretation has been challenged by Macpherson, who argued that Locke wanted to justify not only private ownership as such but also a transformation of the traditional, limited idea of property into a new concept that embraced the notion of unlimited accumulation. In Macpherson's view, Locke was not simply a defender of private property but also an ideologist of capitalism. Although it has been criticized by Dunn, Tully, and other more rigorously historical researchers who are concerned with recovering the "original" meaning of Locke, Macpherson's analysis has considerably influenced Lockean scholarship and inspired others to explore the ideological dimensions of Locke's thought.

To be sure, the word "property" as used by Locke does not refer merely to the goods one has, or to the right one has to those goods. He often uses it in the more general sense of "right." When he says that it is "lives, liberties, and estates, which I call by the general name, property" (9.123), he implies that our life, liberty, and property (ownership) together make up something that is properly our own, something to which we have a claim: They thus constitute our rights. They are natural rights because they have not been bestowed on us by any superior; instead, they can be discovered in the pre-political condition of the state of nature. Since natural law is a basic feature of the Lockean state of nature, all these rights are derived from and limited by natural law. There are thus two meanings of "property" in Locke's theory: one referring to rights and the other referring to the ownership of things or external objects.

For Locke, the fundamental natural law is that humankind is to be preserved (9.135). What follows from this law is that human beings have a right to life and a corollary right to their preservation (5.25). Consequently, they should be able to use the earth's natural resources for their subsistence; thus, these resources must not be assigned to any particular person, but should be available for use by all. Assuming, then, that the earth and its resources, or "fruits," were given to humanity in common, how could anyone claim property in anything? Locke's answer to this question is that even if the earth and its fruits are common to everyone, a part of this common heritage is already private property—we ourselves. Everyone has "a property in his own person: this no body has any right to but himself" (5.27).

That the human being has "property in his own person" means that in the state of nature he is his own master, that "no body has any right to [his own person] but himself," and hence that he is free. Further, since human beings have property in their own persons, whatever they do as free agents also belongs to them. Labor belongs to the individual who works: It is an extension of his personality and his freedom. "The labour of his body, and the work of his hands, we may say, are properly his" (Ibid.). By freely exercising their ability to work, human beings obtain property rights to those goods that are necessary to their preservation and that they have legitimately labored to obtain. It is, then, free labor that creates property in things. "For this labour being unquestionable property of the labourer, no one but he can have a right to what is once joined to, at least where there is enough , and as good, left in common for others" (5.27).

To further clarify this, Locke argues that when one labors, he adds "something that is his own" (Ibid.) to things he "mixes" his labor with, and thus he appropriates those things, and makes them his own—his property. This "something that is his own" is more than a mere physical or mental effort: It is his own personality. For Locke, labor is a purposeful and creative act: It is an embodiment of the individual's personality and an expression of his freedom. It is not merely an activity by means of which human beings provide for the sustenance of their lives; it is an operation through which they infuse things with value. This type of labor involves the initiative of the free agent, who introduces something new—his own person—into the natural environment. Hired labor, on the other hand, which is established on the employer's initiative and executed at his command, is not free, and thus, is not labor in the proper sense of this word, but mere work. Although Locke does not formally introduce the issue of hired labor, he plainly says that the work of employees creates property rights for their employer. "The turfs that my servant has cut, . . . where I have a right to them in common with others, become my property. . . . The labour that was mine, removing them out of the common state they were in, had fixed my property in them" (5.28). In short, wage-laborers work but do not labor, and therefore they do not obtain any title to property through their work.

Embedded in freedom, the concept of private property based on labor implies that there must be a natural law limit to individual appropriation. Since everyone has a right to preservation, it must be ensured that there is "enough, and as good, left in common for others" (5.27). Human beings may appropriate only what they can mix with their labor and only as much as they can use before it "spoils," for "nothing was made by God for man to spoil or destroy" (5.31). This stipulation effectively confines private property, in the early stages of economic development, to a rather small amount, leaving a plentiful portion of common resources for appropriation by others. In the original state of nature, people live a simple life, "confining their desires within the narrow bounds of each man's small property" (8.106). Taking whatever they need from the earth or engaging in a primitive form of agriculture, they do not limit the supply of resources to anyone else. They initiate few conflicts and have no great temptations to enlarge their properties.

The introduction of money as a means of exchange radically changes this picture. People develop the "desire of having more" (5.37). Money (or currency of some other kind such as gold or silver) as a form of property that does not spoil allows for unlimited appropriation and leads to creation of unequal possessions (5.50). Once people consent to its use, they can acquire wealth by selling the products of their labor. They can also enlarge their estates by hiring others to work for them. Natural law loses its appeal to many who are "no longer strict observers of equity and justice" (9.123). An increase in population, growing scarcity of land, and a greater number of disputes about property finally cause humankind to reach a point where the advantages of living in the state of nature are outweighed by the disadvantages of living without impartial judges, written laws, and the public means to execute such laws. The state of nature becomes "full of fears and continual dangers" (Ibid.). In such circumstances, individuals agree to enter into political society "for the mutual preservation of their lives, liberties, and estates" (Ibid.).

The state of nature, which Locke treats historically in his chapter on property, is thus divided into two hypothetical stages. Whereas the first stage displays conditions of perfect equality, "without subordination or subjection" (2.4), the second stage is characterized by hired labor, unlimited appropriation, and "disproportionate and unequal" possessions (5.50). The way in which Locke set forth his historical explanation led Macpherson to argue that although the more advanced economic system based on money and commerce destroys the natural equality of humankind by creating differences in property holdings, Locke is prepared to justify it as more productive, and thus capable of providing subsistence to more people. Hence, he provides not only a theory of limited government but also a justification for the emerging capitalist system. According to Macpherson's analysis, in tracing the transition from the first to the second of these historical stages, Locke shifts his view of rationality, which he no longer relates to natural law, but to an ability to calculate how best to acquire and safeguard unequal amounts of property. In addition, he reads back into the state of nature a class division between owners and wage-laborers, and by his social contract institutes a class state that is established for the protection of social inequalities.

This argument would perhaps be persuasive if all Locke meant was that appropriation should not deprive others of the right to their own preservation, understood as the right to subsistence. However, by saying that one can appropriate resources only so long as there is "enough, and as good, left in common for others" (5.27), Locke seems to imply that a sufficient amount must be left for others, so that they can also appropriate a share. It is unlikely that those resources would be land. When money is introduced and states are founded, any land that is still held in common is generally replaced by private and public property. At the same time, however, money allows people to save and accumulate wealth in the form of capital, which then becomes the primary form of property. In an advanced economic system, such as the one already in place in England during Locke's time, the available resources are no longer land but capital, which can be employed for different projects in an almost infinite number of ways. There is thus no shortage of things to which labor can be productively applied. The source of scarcity does not lie in the limitation of resources as much as in the limitation related to the human potential of any given individual. The extent to which an individual can live a life of dignity, by adding something of his own to the resources he employs, does not depend "on how much he can snatch away from the grip of his fellows, but on the degree of his [individual] diligence and perseverance" (Rapaczynski 211). The world is given "to the use of the industrious and rational . . . and not to the fancy or covetousness of the quarrelsome and contentious" (*Second Treatise* 5.34).

Locke's belief that the world belongs to the "industrious and rational" is a reflection of what the sociologist Max Weber would later call the "Protestant ethic": a value system that emerged among the Puritan middle class around Locke's time. Its central theme is the doctrine of the "calling." Human beings are called by God to fill a particular role and discharge it with their full energy. The quality of a human life is judged by the effort expended during its course (Dunn 227). The differences between people are the consequence of their deeds. While Locke does not deny that property produces social divisions, he does not support any rigid class system. Anyone who is hard working and who makes proper life choices can achieve success and reach the upper levels of society. Hence, Locke would almost certainly not accept Macpherson's conclusion that his writings offer a defense of social inequality. In his view, the state is not established to protect any inequalities, but rather to provide equal opportunities for all. There should be no privileges: One rule should apply "for rich and poor, for the favourite at Court and the country man at plough" (*Second*

Treatise 11.142). All individuals should have the same rights: They should be free to determine the course of their lives and to acquire possessions. When Locke says that human beings unite into commonwealths for the purpose of the "preservation of property," he does not mean merely the protection of their economic interests but also the protection of their freedom, which is a condition for their ownership of things.

CIVIL SOCIETY AND STATE BUILDING

Economic liberalism emerged as a critique of the political control of economic affairs. Its beginnings can be associated with Locke and his idea that the sphere of politics should be separated from the private sphere of life.

Locke views human beings as self-interested individuals who conduct their lives in an area that is independent from any political interference, and who look to government primarily to protect their private lives, liberties, and properties. Society and state are separated, and two forces are at play. There is a realm of private activity, which provides scope for the expression of individual freedom and for economic pursuits. Later termed "civil society," this realm represents an economic force based on the right of property. The other realm is that of government, whose main function is to uphold citizens' rights and to act for the sake of the public good. It represents a political force. Ideally, those two forces reinforce one another in a positive feedback loop, rather than interfering with each other. As Locke says, "riches and power . . . beget each other" (*Political Essays*, "Trade"). Economic strength adds to a country's political power, and political power enhances its economic growth.

The independence of civil society from the state is conductive to commercial activities. It allows individuals to freely acquire property at home or abroad wherever and whenever any opportunity arises. However, this new social arrangement is not in itself sufficient to transform a traditional agricultural society, ruled by customs and organized hierarchically, into a new commercial society of equal and independent individuals. The new society must break down the old ideas and customs, and re-educate citizens so that they are "industrious and rational," and thus fit for their new social role.

During Locke's time, an intensive debate was going on regarding how to change the behavior of a populace that "appeared to have little interest in changing their conditions and seemed to be voluntary idle, a view supported by the frequent observance of various saint days and feasts" (Hundert 4). Locke entered this debate and in "An Essay on the Poor Law," which he wrote in 1697 as Commissioner of the Council of Trade and Plantations, contended that the state should make people more industrious by rewarding hard work and severely punishing idleness. He recommended that work schools for children above the age of three be established in each parish to instill the habit of industry into them. He also proposed that population growth should be stimulated by imposing fines on unmarried persons over a certain age, and that only those immigrants who did not live upon the labor of others, but could enrich society through their diligence or wealth, should be accepted into the country. From his notes on "Trade" in 1674, through to his articles on the employment of the poor and the naturalization of immigrants composed in the 1690s, Locke's writings argued in favor of what mercantilists saw as the twin pillars of national strength: the advancement of trade and the enhancement of the labor force.

For Locke, the liberal state is limited, but powerful within its proper sphere. It provides an effective framework of law and order for the market economy. And, in line with his mercantilist view, it also takes an active role in promoting commerce. It aims to achieve a favorable balance of trade, leading the country to economic prosperity measured in terms of "plenty of silver and gold" ("Trade"). Locke lists "freedom of trade, easy naturalization, freedom of religion, register or certainty of property, small customs" among the policies that serve to enhance national wealth, but he also adds: "fashions suited to your own manufacture, suitable manufacturers to the markets whose commodities we want, . . . new manufacturers at home" (Ibid.).

Today, because of the influence of the ideas of Adam Smith (1723–1790), economic liberalism is often contrasted with mercantilism, and the latter is associated with the subjection of the economy to political control. Locke's views, however, represent a prudent synthesis of these two perspectives, showing that at least during the seventeenth century, they were not necessarily seen as incompatible. The economy, as a domain of private activity, is separated from politics, but this does not mean that the state cannot enhance the economy by means of appropriate policies. The fact that the liberal state is limited by both its function and the principle of the separation of power does not mean that it should be weak. On the contrary, it must be able to effectively execute the tasks necessary to achieve its end, which is "the peace, safety and public good of the people." In order to do this, it must be a "substantial political-economic organization" (Jackson, Sørensen 24). It must have efficient political and legal institutions, an industrious and unified citizenry, and a sound economic basis.

LIBERTY, ECONOMY, COLONY

Examples of civil societies from which the state had withdrawn in order to allow them to produce wealth had already come into existence before Locke began to write his works. Private entities, including the Virginia Company and the Massachusetts Bay Company, transferred thousands of settlers to North America. The English government vigorously supported the establishment of colonies and overseas outposts around the world. The conquest of Jamaica was completed in 1660, establishing an important commercial and naval base in the Caribbean (Clark 317). An active rivalry with the Dutch was played out in both western and eastern seas. In 1665, Shaftesbury, a great enthusiast of overseas ventures, and other like-minded government ministers allowed the disputes with the Dutch to grow into armed encounters and then into a full-scale war. England gained the New Netherlands, with its port of New

Amsterdam, which was renamed New York. Finally, the Glorious Revolution of 1688 served as a crucial step in the process that allowed civil society to obtain autonomy from state. It resulted in the Bill of Rights. A few years after the Revolution, Locke became Commissioner of the Council of Trade and Plantations. He was developing the Western system of commerce in practice and justifying it in theory. Although this aspect of his thought is less often discussed by scholars than some of his other ideas, in his chapter on property, Locke in fact provides notable justification for colonial expansion.

As was discussed above, Locke regarded the introduction of money as a key step in the evolution of the world's economic and political systems. Yet another crucial change comes, he contends, with the enclosure of land. As population increases, large parts of the globe are divided into territories that belong to different states (*Second Treatise* 5.45). When they are founded, whether by contract or in some other way, the right of property, having had its foundation in labor, becomes regulated by law. Further, as states emerge, they form leagues and divide the world's land among themselves. Even so, Locke notes, "there are still great tracts of ground to be found, which (the inhabitants thereof not having joined with the rest of mankind, in the consent of the use of their common money) lie waste, and are more than the people who dwell on it do, or can make use of, and so still lie in common" (Ibid.). Such "waste" land, he explains, is land whose inhabitants are not engaged in commercial exchange and that is uncultivated by agriculture (5.42); thus, according to his labor theory of property, it is vacant for appropriation and settlement.

Locke sees the outstanding example of such uncultivated land as being found in America. For him, the hunting and gathering way of life practiced by many Native American communities represents the earliest stage of economic development. He claims that the system of private property, based on labor, not only uses the land far more productively but also results in everyone being economically better off. "Several nations of the Americans," he says, "are rich in land and poor in conveniences of life" (5.41). Since they do not improve their land by labor, they "have not one hundredth part of the conveniences we enjoy; and a king of a large and fruitful territory there, feeds, lodges, and is clad worse than a day-labourer in England" (Ibid.). By making the claim that the low-paid English laborers were more affluent than Native American rulers, Locke supports his contention that the value created in a modern commercial system is so great that all members of the community, even those at the bottom of the economic ladder, are more prosperous than the most privileged would be in a economic system that does not encompass private property. Consequently, he suggests that Native Americans should adopt Western ways of production and commerce.

One problem that European settlers faced was that Native Americans regarded themselves as being organized into nations that had some jurisdiction over their territories. Many Europeans thus concluded that the only legitimate way to settle in America was "to gain consent of the Aboriginal nations by means of nation to nation negotiations, as a Royal Commission concluded in

1665, fifteen years before Locke wrote the *Two Treatises*" (Tully, 1995, 71). But since the negotiations were a difficult process and the Native American inhabitants were often unwilling to cede the land the settlers wanted, "a justification was required for taking land and establishing European sovereignty without the consent of the native peoples" (Ibid.). Locke's labor theory of property helped to provide such a justification: It implies that since the Native Americans do not cultivate land, and thus do not thus appropriate it by labor, it is common. Examples that Locke uses throughout his chapter on property suggest that what rightly belongs to Native Americans are the fruits they gather or the animals they hunt, but not the land. "The fruit, or venison, which nourishes the wild Indian, who knows no inclosure, and is still a tenant in common must be his" (*Second Treatise* 5.26). Further, although he acknowledges that Native Americans are organized in nations or communities, Locke denies to those entities the status of states because states are born at the historical stage when money is introduced and commerce develops (5.45); in America, "no such thing as money was any where known" (5.49). Given money as a criterion, it then becomes obvious that Indian nations do not have equal status to European nations, and thus cannot be partners to agreements. They are not a part of the "democratic league" and are therefore not protected against invasion. Locke tries to show that America, in that it is at an early stage of economic development and does not use money, in fact represents a state of nature, even though it has kings. It is not a land divided into territorial political entities, but a vacant land lying waste.

Starting from such premises, Locke makes the following argument. If America is a state of nature, and if money is still unknown there, the right to property in land comes solely through labor, which in this case is understood in agricultural terms such as "pasturage, tillage, and planting" (5.42). Any European settler may appropriate the uncultivated American soil through labor and without the consent of its inhabitants, even if they have lived there for generations. Uncultivated land can "be looked on as waste, and might be the possession of any other" (5.38). If Native Americans try to prevent Europeans from settling down and cultivating land, they are invading "their neighbor's share," for they have no rights to it beyond its agricultural use (5.37). They are committing an offense against the common law of nature and the colonists or their government may punish them. The government is entitled to intervene, for "the controversies that happen between any man of the society with those that are out of it [in the state of nature] are managed by the public, and an injury done to a member of their body, engages the whole in reparation of it" (12.145). This argument advanced against Roger Williams and other European defenders of Native Americans' rights to the land provided a major justification for the appropriation of land in North America on the basis of individual property rights. While its premises—especially the idea that America was a state of nature—can be questioned, it provided a useful paradigm for various later justifications of land appropriation as well. It forwarded the process of subduing native peoples and helped to spread the Western system of commerce to the American continent and to other parts of the world.

COMMERCE AND THE QUESTION OF ETHICS

John Dunn, a renowned interpreter of Locke, has portrayed him as a man deeply concerned with matters of religion, his last major work being *The Reasonableness of Christianity as Delivered in the Scriptures*, first published in 1695. He has also emphasized the importance of Locke's religious concepts for his political theory, particularly in regard to the ethical dimensions of his thought. And yet, despite his own religious convictions, Locke—whom Dunn calls a "tragic" thinker—undermines the basis for religion by means of his modern epistemology. What commands our actions, Locke states (following Hobbes), is always some desire or uneasiness related to an absent good (*Essay HU* 2.21.31). In his catalogue of human desires, the desire for eternal life, while perhaps important to most individuals, is only one among many competing desires. In the milieu of civil society—the social arrangement that Locke proposes—desires are not only *unlimited* in scope but also *structured* to lead to economic success. In such an environment, of which today's secularized Western societies could serve as a case in point, there is increasingly less place for a genuine religious belief.

Natural law has, for Locke, its basis in the existence of God. Consequently, as Dunn observes, if the religious foundations "were to be removed from Locke's theory, the purpose of individual life and of social life would both be exhausted by the goal of maximization of utility" (Dunn 250). Without religious belief, individuals would no longer see their happiness as "happiness in another world" (*Political Essays*, "Thus I Think") and, accordingly, would not order their desires properly. They would devote themselves to the continual pursuit of earthly goals, and in particular to unlimited acquisition, which they would identify with the ultimate good. They would thus turn into Hobbesian individuals who are no longer constrained by natural moral law and who do not employ reason to distinguish between right and wrong, but merely as an instrument to get what they want.

The argument that Locke was essentially Hobbes in disguise was once advanced by two well-known scholars, Macpherson and Strauss; both of them, for different reasons, have identified Locke with the "spirit of capitalism" and have related his concept of rationality to the Hobbesian rationality of unlimited desire. However, both were mistaken. There is no reason to believe—and in this respect Dunn is certainly right—that Locke has ever changed his view of rationality by separating it from natural law. It was not he, but rather members of the subsequent secularized generations, who became Hobbesian. Post-Lockean liberalism, as represented by its prominent exponents Jeremy Bentham (1748–1832) and his disciple James Mill (1773–1836), aiming at a rationalist ethics, dispensed with the notion of natural law as obsolete and replaced it with the principle of utility. The utilitarians accepted the Hobbesian view, which Locke also adopted, of human beings as self-interested, pleasure-seeking individuals, but they denied the Lockean idea that our highest pleasures could be related to the expectation of happiness in another world. They regarded pleasure and pain as sensations quantifiable by their intensity, duration, and so on, as, for example, the pleasure of eating or the pain of stomachache. Working on the basis of the principle that human beings should maximize pleasure and minimize pain, they declared that property was the chief source of pleasure. They melted Hobbes and Locke together by asserting that desire for property demanded a liberal model of government.

The development of liberal thought does not, of course, end with the utilitarianism of Bentham and James Mill. The ideas that all pleasures are quantifiable and all politics can be organized according to the principle of utility were subjected to scrutiny by successive great liberal thinkers, such as Alexis de Tocqueville (1805–1859), John Stuart Mill (1806–1873), T. H. Green (1836–1882), and John Rawls (1921–2002). Early utilitarianism, based on the problematic equation between the ethical and the pleasurable, was supplied with some additional moral dimensions. However, returning to Locke, it can be seen that he had a more traditional view of ethics—a view that many still probably share. According to him, the moral goodness or badness of an action depends on its conformity to a law, and this law presupposes a lawmaker, who is God (*Political Essays*, "Of Ethics in General"). Again, although natural law, the law of reason on which ethics is founded, can be justified by purely rational means, it has for Locke its ultimate basis in the existence of God. If God is removed from the domain of human life, natural law no longer holds.

Locke has not changed his view of rationality by separating it from natural law. He has not reduced natural law to the set of rules for self-preservation, as in Hobbes, or to a rationale for individual hedonism, as in Bentham. In his view, this natural standard of right and wrong is preserved after government is instituted. Political decisions, including those of the majority, would be for him wholly arbitrary and tyrannical if they did not refer to natural law. Nevertheless, by separating civil society from the state, Locke has constructed the social environment in which individuals are likely to lose their religious beliefs, natural law is disobeyed, and rationality is no longer identified with the law of reason but with unlimited desire and unrestrained acquisition. By permitting or even encouraging individuals to focus on their own interests, he has opened the Pandora's box and released the limitless pursuit of individual desires. While Hobbes, in his unrelenting drive to impose order, suppresses human appetites through the power of absolute government, Locke releases them from all restraint, and directs them toward whatever riches the world has to offer.

Locke's political and economic writings are closely associated with the development of commerce, which in the eyes of his contemporaries had moral as well as economic significance. Commerce was seen not as an activity that took place in a separate sphere from moral life but rather as a pursuit that had the potential to enrich the human personality. By freeing individuals from vassalage and allowing them to enter into new types of relationships, commerce was regarded as contributing to sociability and liberty, and even to the development of virtue and more polite manners (Pocock 493). At the same time, however, it was also believed that if individuals were not educated in the value of frugality, commerce could easily corrupt them. According to widely held opinions whose origins were attributed to Cicero and Polybius, republics were transformed into empires by virtue, and subsequently corrupted and destroyed by luxury. The environment Locke grew up in was still penetrated by the rhetoric of virtue, classical concepts, and belief in God. And yet, by adopting a line of thought that followed that of Hobbes and ultimately resulted in the release of human desires from restraints, Locke created the modern human being: a man without God and without manners. He contributed to the concept of liberal democracy, the idea we so much cherish, and at the same time to the inherently unstable and dangerous domestic and international conditions in which we live today: a state of affairs in which egoism is seen as a rational choice.

LOCKE'S LIBERALISM

Locke's liberalism, built around such concepts as natural rights, popular sovereignty, limited government, and private property, has exerted an enormous influence on the world. The American Revolution was carried out, even if indirectly, in the name of Locke. The Declaration of Independence not only uses the language of natural rights but also implicitly conveys the idea that King George III violated the terms of the social contact. The constitutional structure of today's liberal democracies is built around the Lockean concept of a limited government whose power is legally circumscribed and divided. But the main impact of his thought can be related to the spread of Western civilization all around the globe. His idea that individuals have a right to accumulate private property, and that they have a chance for success if they are industrious and rational, has mobilized enormous social forces. The Lockean civil society from which the state has withdrawn, endowing it with institutions needed for wealth creation, has proven itself to be the most efficient social arrangement for commercial and political expansion, far more effective than the Hobbesian authoritarian state or any traditional type of social organization.

Western civilization is no longer defined by classical concepts, and it is no longer an exclusive property of the West. It has become universal because it has undermined and rejected traditional values—beginning with its own classical ones—and replaced the diversity of humankind with a uniform picture of self-interested individuals. Locke, one of the foremost thinkers of modernity, contributed to this process whereby human beings and their societies have been transformed to fulfill the requirements of the modern age. As a man who was deeply concerned with religious matters, he certainly would not have anticipated or intended that this transformation would produce "an economic and political plenum, and, in the same breath, a social and spiritual void" (Toynbee 207). The presence of this spiritual vacuum seems to indicate that the notion held by some that liberal democracy is the end of history is probably wrong. Lockean liberal thought, and indeed the whole heritage of modernity, calls for revision. Marxism, also constructed on modern foundations, cannot serve as an alternative, nor can any other stream of today's critical or post-modernist thought. Rather, a rethinking of liberalism suggests a classical solution—returning to the origins of Western civilization and restating the question of virtue.

QUESTIONS

- What is toleration? Should there be any limits to it?
- Should individuals be permitted to wear garments or ornaments symbolizing their private religious beliefs in public institutions such as schools?
- Locke makes a distinction between freedom and license. Do you agree or disagree with him on this issue?
- What are the differences between the Hobbesian and Lockean perceptions of the state of nature? By which main feature are they distinguished? Which picture of the state of nature looks more true to you?
- Do you think that states can cooperate in the environment of international anarchy? What conditions could stimulate international cooperation?
- What arguments can you make for and against the democratic peace theory?
- What are the main features of Lockean constitutional government?
- Do you think that private property can be justified on moral grounds? What arguments can you make in support of private property?
- Do we need to protect our domestic market? Can economic liberalism and mercantilism be reconciled?
- What reasons can you give for why commerce can or cannot be regarded as a moral activity?

GUIDE TO FURTHER READING

Locke's Selected Works:

Locke, John. *A Letter Concerning Toleration.* Ed. John Horton and Susan Mendus. *Routledge Philosophers in Focus Series.* London: Routledge, 1991.

Locke, John. *An Essay Concerning Human Understanding.* Ed. Gary Fuller, Robert Stecker, and John P. Wright. *Routledge Philosophers in Focus Series.* London: Routledge, 2000.

Locke, John. *Political Essays.* Ed. Mark Goldie. Cambridge: Cambridge UP, 1997.

Locke, John. *Second Treatise of Government.* Ed. C. B. Macpherson. Indianapolis: Hackett, 1980.

Locke, John. Two Treatises of Government. Ed. Peter Laslett. *Cambridge Texts in the History of Political Thought.* Cambridge: Cambridge UP, 1988.

Suggested Readings:

Dunn, John. *Locke.* Past Masters. Oxford: Oxford UP, 1990.

Josephson, Peter. *The Art of Government: Locke's Use of Consent.* Lawrence: UP of Kansas, 2002.

Macpherson, C. B. *The Political Theory of Possessive Individualism, Hobbes to Locke.* Oxford: Clarendon, 1962.

Rapaczynski, Andrzej. *Nature and Politics: Liberalism in the Philosophies of Hobbes, Locke, and Rousseau.* Ithaca, NY: Cornell UP, 1987.

The Classics and the Moderns

Western political thought is usually seen as a continuous intellectual tradition that begins around the time of Plato and extends up to our own time. Indeed, some fundamental questions, such as the question of justice or the question of the best form of government, have pervaded Western political philosophy from its beginnings. As we reflect on politics, we still frequently think in classical terms, for example, by evoking the notion of virtuous action or judging international events in moral terms. We discuss a number of reoccurring themes, such as justice in war, ethics and politics, human nature, rationality, and self-government, but these are precisely the themes around which great controversies have developed. Morality in politics has been denied, virtue undermined, human nature reconstructed, and self-government restricted. It is less frequently noticed that despite the common themes that run through the intellectual history of the West, that history is characterized by disputes, tensions, and radical transformations. Christianity challenges the classical world while assimilating some aspects of it, and is in turn challenged by the thinking of modernity. Modernity overturns the ideas and values of the traditional (classical and Christian) culture of the West, and, once it becomes global, leads to the erosion of other traditional cultures. The further destruction of traditional thinking and ways of life is brought about by post-modernity, which represents a challenge to modernity, but at the same time is a radical continuation of the modern project.

When the first modern republic, the United States, was founded, extensive debates about virtue, commerce, and corruption took place. It is clear that the classics exerted a formative influence upon the founders, including James Madison, Alexander Hamilton, John Adams, and Thomas Jefferson, as well as other key American intellectuals of that time. The questions as to whether commerce would lead America to corruption and whether some kind of fundamental decay was inherent in the idea of commercial society were framed in the traditional language of classical politics. And yet, despite the common

215

cultural background of those who joined the debate, different answers were given. On the one hand, the positive aspects of commerce were stressed. The founders, like many of their contemporaries, believed that commerce could actually contribute to virtue; that it stimulated the habits of industry, frugality, and self-restraint; that it had a liberating aspect, in that it allowed an increasing number of people to seek to improve their lives, releasing them from economic and class servitude; and, that it had a certain civilizing influence that promoted culture and made people less warlike (Vetterli, Bryner 211–218). On the other hand, there was a fear that the rise of modern commerce would lead to the growth of monied interests and the decline of virtue, and consequently engender financial and military corruption. Some, most prominently Jefferson, distrusted the potential effects of the development of industry and sought to preserve the agricultural way of life (Richard 238). They believed that virtue was the one sure foundation on which a republic could be built and maintained. They considered political institutions, such as the separation of powers and the checks and balances, insufficient to maintain order in societies whose members were motivated purely by self-interest and factious ambitions.

Whether the era of classical politics came to an end as early as the close of the founding period, as Gordon Wood and some other scholars argue, or in some later period, is not a question to be addressed in detail here. It is enough to say that the founders, like subsequent generations of Americans, were equally inspired by classical and modern ideas, and "believed that republican virtue and liberal individualism . . . [were] both compatible and interdependent" (Vetterli, Bryner 8). They did not fully conceptualize the profound tensions that exist between classical and modern political thinking. The former has its origin in an organic picture of the world, and the latter, in a mechanistic view; the former sees natural differences among people, and the latter assumes social homogeneity; the former stresses reason and virtue, and is interested in ethical questions and the common good, while the latter emphasizes desire and interest, and is concerned with individual rights and the questions of power. When these tensions finally became apparent, there was a shift from the classical to the modern paradigm in American political theory. It was declared that "virtue of the individual was no longer a necessary foundation of free government" (Pocock 526). Although traditional ways of thinking never disappeared from the American mind, classical education was gradually removed from the school curriculum. With the behavioral revolution in social sciences in the 1950s, America became a bastion of modernity. Modernity's unchanged hegemony did not last out the century, however. While Marxism had never been successful in profoundly influencing Americans, the intellectual circles were more hospitable to other critical strains of thought, such as feminism, critical theory, existentialism, and postmodernism, which took root there in the 1980s and led America to post-modernity.

Locke declared that "in the beginning all of the world was America" (*Second Treatise* 49). We may follow in this line of thought by saying that, in the end, all of the world will be America again. But, if this is to be so, America will obviously change. The beginning to which Locke refers is a world without money and commerce, a state of nature that he, perhaps wrongly, identifies with the American continent of his time. The end, as things stand at present, appears to be the global triumph of commerce and interest over virtue. But America is not merely a continent or a country. It is a symbol and embodiment of the world's transformation, of the Western ideas and Western techniques that have dominated the world as had no other civilization before it. This is why America can be the subject of philosophical inquiry. Although the process does not proceed smoothly, and occasional resistance is encountered, the world is being transformed according to one model. This model was not derived from classical political philosophy or from Christian culture. It is based on the notion of self-interested, pleasure-seeking individuals that we have inherited from modern political thought: individuals who are not perfected, or even tempered, by virtue. In Gamble's words, "the reason why the West has towered over the modern world and has undermined the traditional culture of other civilizations is because it first of all undermined and steadily rejected its own" (Andrew Gamble 4). In the process of transforming the world, the West has transformed itself. It has freed itself from the traditional restraints that kept human appetites in check, and has allowed individuals the unlimited pursuit of individual desires.

J. G. A. Pocock regards the decline of virtue in America as a "Machiavellian Movement." With the departure from the classical tradition, virtue is replaced by *virtù* and the latter is identified with the dynamics of commerce. As long as geographical extension is possible, the corruptive effects of commerce can be mitigated. Under the influence of this idea, which Pocock attributes to Machiavelli but also in part to the founders themselves, the American republic turns into an empire. Expansion is initially identified with the moving frontier. However, once the national boundaries reach the Western shore and the reservoir of land is exhausted, it becomes global commercial expansion. As the result of a curious mixture of classical and modern ideas, this commercial activity is seen as not merely an economic, but also a liberating endeavor. The opening up of world markets "is a part of the vision of America as 'redeemer nation'" (Pocock 542). The ultimate rejection of America by Asia "is seen as leading to a profound crisis in self-perception, in which the hope of renewed innocence and recovered virtue is felt . . . to have gone forever" (544).

However, this interpretation, which to some may look quite plausible, can be questioned. Jefferson would perhaps approve of the view that the development of industry should be balanced by the growth of agriculture, but neither he nor Madison nor any other founder who advocated a geographically large republic would identify territorial or commercial expansion with a means to stop corruption. The idea that war and expansion can contribute to the moral health of a nation can in fact not even be attributed to Machiavelli himself, but rather to the post-Machiavellian thinkers of *raison d'état*, such as Treitschke and Hegel. The American founders, whose main sources of inspiration were "the classical [tradition], the Enlightenment, English common law, New England Puritanism, and the radical English Whigs" (Vetterli, Bryner 10), were clearly not influenced by such ways of thinking. Therefore, the decline of virtue in America would perhaps be better described as a Hobbesian, rather than a Machiavellian movement. This "Hobbesian Movement" leads from the classics to Locke and then to Hobbes, but it does not stop there. It eventually undergoes a metamorphosis, developing into critical strains of thought. These include, most recently, modes of thought that can be associated with post-modernity.

The Federalist is a series of essays by Hamilton and Madison (with a small contribution by John Jay) that were written immediately after the 1787 Constitutional Convention. The pen name "Publius," with which the authors chose to conclude every *Federalist* paper, testifies to their intention to establish a clear link with the classical tradition (Thomas Pangle 21). The name comes from Plutarch's life of Publius Valerius Publicola, who was one of the founders of the Roman republic. More substantially, however, the link between the classics and the American Constitution can be seen in the authors' call for a revitalization of virtue. It is expected of the elected officials that they will be virtuous, that is, as the *Federalist* No. 51 argues, they should be possessed of "enlightened views and virtuous sentiments." The virtue of the people consists in their ability to rise above their selfish concerns and elect from themselves leaders of virtue and wisdom, "the purest and noblest characters" that society contains (Ibid.). A country whose inhabitants have no virtue, the founders contend, cannot be prosperous. "Is there no virtue among us?" Madison asks. "If there be not, we are in a wretched situation. No theoretical checks—no form of government can make us secure. To suppose that any form of government will secure liberty or happiness without any virtue in the people, is a chimerical idea" (qtd. in Thomas Pangle 22). For, as *Federalist* No. 68 says, the only firm basis for the whole political system is "the manly spirit which actuates the people of America—spirit which nourishes freedom and in return is nourished by it." Like Athens in the glorious times of Pericles, America exemplifies for the founders a civilized political community, whose members do not merely follow their self-interest, but also display virtuous qualities and are ready to contribute to the common good.

Nevertheless, while inspired by the classics, Hamilton and Madison also express criticism of classical republicanism. They contend that even the most successful republics of Greece and Italy were inherently unstable and short-lived because of flaws in their political design (*Federalist* 9). While it is possible to learn from these states by examining their history to identify various perennial political problems, the American republic must be a new project, combining liberty with stability, and virtue with commerce. It has to be built on principles that are "wholly new discoveries" and by which "the excellences of republican government may be retained and its imperfections lessened or avoided" (Ibid.). The Constitution, therefore, is an "experiment" (*Federalist* 14), a new political design arrived at through "reflection and choice" (Ibid.). The political theory set forth in *The Federalist* relies on the traditional understanding of rationality as deliberation about what is beneficial and harmful, just and unjust. If people cannot rely on deliberation, on reflection and choice, then they are "forever destined to depend for their political constitutions on accident and force" (Ibid.). They are subjected to anarchy (accident) or tyranny (force). The work of deliberative reason allows them to establish government that is "settled and stable; when it changes, it does so deliberately by design and for a definite purpose" (Mansfield 414). Such government is conceptually opposed to populist democracy and absolute monarchy, both of which are governments not of deliberative reason, but rather of capricious will. When framing the Constitution, the founders wished to avoid the excesses of anarchy and tyranny, but also to go beyond the ancient idea of a mixed constitution that gives different social classes separate powers. The mixed system, advocated by John Adams, was rejected as being incompatible with the idea of a modern republic, in which there were no fixed social classes. Departing from the now-obsolete, class-based view of the people as the many or the majority and instead identifying them with the whole society—with individuals who have become politically indistinguishable through sharing the same rights—the founders turn to Locke and declare that "the people are the only legitimate fountain of power" (*Federalist* 49).

Locke's influence on eighteenth-century Americans, and on the framers of the Constitution in particular, was "massive" (Huyler 249). He supplied the founders with a number of political concepts, such as natural rights, popular sovereignty, limited government, government by consent, separation of powers, and private property. Moreover, through the strikingly moral content of his philosophy, he offered them a hope that classical republican and modern liberal political paradigms could meet in the American republic—that liberty and property could be brought together with virtue and the common good. That this was possible seemed to follow from Locke's view that human desires and immediate interests could be suspended and subjected to the judgment of reason, and ultimately redirected from the pursuit of passing pleasure to the quest for true and lasting felicity (Ibid. 232). What this meant was that individual self-interest, if rightly understood, did need not to be inimical to the general interest or the common good. The idea of enlightened self-interest was indeed crucial to a modern republican system, if the freedom and individualism that it promoted were not to succumb to anarchy and factionalism. However, such a system required a society whose members had their passions contained by morality and religion. Hence, while supporting religious liberty and drawing the distinction between church and state, the founders, like Locke, considered religion as indispensable element of a good political order. "Our Constitution," John Adams declared, "was made only for a moral and religious people. It is wholly inadequate for any other" (qtd. in Vetterli, Bryner 70). In short, the synthesis between classical and modern political ideas seemed possible because, in the founders' vision, modernity could have an ethical dimension, without which it would in any case have little worth. They interpreted Locke in moral terms. Accepting his distinction between license and liberty, they agreed with him that individuals must be encouraged to pursue their chosen ends, but not by indulging wayward inclinations or unchecked passions; that all being the work of a common maker, they should enjoy certain fundamental liberties, including those of life, liberty, and property; and that coming into the world with specific needs, they also have the ability to satisfy those needs through virtuous, that is, rational and industrious, conduct (Huyler 305–306).

This moral interpretation of Locke's political thought is perfectly legitimate and is probably true to his own intentions. The view that Locke was Hobbes in disguise and had a hidden agenda aimed at "destroying the traditions of natural law and Biblical Christianity" (Thomas Pangle 39) is not convincing. It is more likely that Locke, like the founders, was not fully aware that the introduction of new ideas would erode traditional ideas, and that classical and modern paradigms of thought could not exist in concert but were, rather, alternative moral and political universes. In the modern fashion, Locke attempted to derive ethics from desires, by putting the latter in a hierarchy, and the founders looked to produce civic virtue on the basis of individual ambition and political arrangements (Vetterli, Bryner 243). Yet neither of these attempts could be successful. Just as it is implausible that what Locke considers the supreme desire—the desire for eternal life—can prevail in an environment of plurality and competition among desires, so also it is unlikely that interest or ambition in combination with some institutional system of checks and controls would lead to virtue rather than vice. For any behavior to be truly virtuous, it must already have virtue as its foundation. It is virtue that must come prior to interest and not otherwise. Once modern political thinking has reached the point where attention shifts from virtue to interest, and from reason to desire, interest and desire become predominant. Consequently, virtue diminishes and deliberative rationality is replaced by instrumental rationality. Only through what Machiavelli describes as a return to the original condition—namely, through the resolute and creative repetition of classical moral and political thinking—can virtue be restored. Although there have been scholars who continued to think and talk in classical terms (Alasdair MacIntyre and Martha Nussbaum, among others), the history of modern thought has not witnessed such a repetition. On the contrary, there is a growing gulf between modernity, which has by now become radicalized, and the classical tradition.

In the assumption that all human beings are fundamentally the same— self-interested, pleasure-seeking individuals, whose behavior is modified neither by virtue nor by natural law nor by religious belief, with the same cause having the same effect on everyone—the ideas of Hobbes come to the fore. Neither Locke nor the founders make such an assumption. It grows out of a more purely modern strain of thought. We can find it in the utilitarianism of Bentham and his followers and in today's positivist or behavioral social science. In such systems of thought, an attempt is made to reduce the complexity of the classical view of politics to a single, simple principle, whether it be desire, power, or interest. The constitutional character of political institutions is preserved, but politics is no longer about morality or religion. It becomes a power game or a play of interests—an exercise in collective bargaining. Moreover, this view of human beings as self-interested, passion-driven individuals is not confined to the realm of theory. With a model of education in place that is no longer based on classical ideas but increasingly dependent on positivist assumptions and methodology, such a picture is internalized during many years of schooling. It therefore influences both thinking and, ultimately, actual human behavior. Subject to social engineering, and convinced that "desires, and other passions of man, are in themselves no sin" (*Leviathan* XIII 10), individuals make their goal the maximization of utility: They just want to get what they want without paying attention to any restraints. They shift their focus from the law of nature to the laws of economics. In Jefferson's words, they "forget themselves, but in the sole faculty of making money" (qtd. in Huyler 308). If such individuals cannot achieve their goals at home, they look for expansion abroad. America's territorial and commercial expansion is not, as Pocock seems to think, the result of an idea that was superimposed on the American people. Rather, it is the result of a movement from within, a consequence of their social conditions and the liberty they have enjoyed in civil society—a liberty that has unleashed an unbounded commercial and economic zeal, impelling people to look for profit even in the most remote corners of the world. But at the same time, this social arrangement, which has stimulated human expectations and desires to a degree unknown before, has eroded the traditional sense of what is virtuous, just, and proper. It has also divided the inhabitants of the globe into those who possess extreme wealth and those who are sunk in dire poverty.

Today, modernity is challenged by post-modernity. It is quite obvious that once modernity separates itself from morality, it invites a critique. And the common people, involved in daily toil, unlike many of their leaders and professors, never forget to ask questions regarding what is just and unjust. Post-modernity thus can partially be regarded as an attempt to reintroduce an ethical discourse into modernity, but since its critical discourse is structured in terms of the dialectics of oppression, it is no longer a classical universalistic ethics. It divides the world into the oppressors and the oppressed. Traditional society, based on the idea of naturally differentiated human beings, was challenged by modernity, which replaced it with an artificial construct—a group of homogeneous individuals melted by social contract into a unity, into "one people, one body of politic, under one supreme government" (*Second Treatise* 7.89). Post-modernity in turn deconstructs the modern concept of unity through its notion of division. This term "diversity" is often used in reference to this division. However, diversity in the post-modern sense by no means refers to qualitatively dissimilar persons, divided into traditional social groups or classes. The existence of any such persons, especially of an aristocracy, is excluded from the modern project and certainly from post-modernity, its radicalization. The American founders' idea of a natural aristocracy, individuals of high moral standards and outstanding personal qualities, who would be selected during the electoral process and whose already excellent character would be further formed as they carried out the duties of their offices, can be seen as a sign of their link to the classical tradition rather than an aspect of their modern political thinking.

Modernity and post-modernity do not rely on anything "natural." Like modern social unity, a product of indoctrination and identity construction, post-modern diversity is to a substantial degree an artificial undertaking. It is a result of exploring potential tensions in, and introducing divisions into, the body of a modern or traditional society. Marxism, with its stress on class domination and oppression, could be considered a first step toward post-modernity. But it was still embedded in modern ontological concepts, and its failure can be associated with its production of a terrifying unity, rather than a real diversity. Today's critical thinkers go beyond Marxism to explore other forms of domination and oppression, which they identify with gender, sovereignty, and even with rationality, objectivity, or any kind of essentialist and foundational thinking (Theresa Lee 158). As a result, the essential institutions of both traditional and modern societies, such as family and state, are made problematic. Uprooted from any foundations and basically homeless, post-modern individuals find themselves floating in a boundless universe that offers freedom but no orientation. Thus, post-modernity brings modern individualism to an extreme: Freed from family and country, individuals become *singles*—isolated units, atoms detached from even that smallest of social structures, the nuclear family. The price is solitude, homelessness, and the weakening and final deconstruction of Western societies.

There is, however, a Hobbesian element in post-modernity as well. The critical thinkers of post-modernity share one central concern with modern theorists: power (Booth 339). However, unlike the moderns, they do not ask how to obtain and secure power, and what its limits are. The post-moderns want rather to know who will get what, and how much. Obsessed with the questions of power, they regard all knowledge of significance as power knowledge. This is why post-modernity can be considered a radicalized modern project—one that raises power, interest, and desire to positions of predominance. It is, in effect, a part of the Hobbesian Movement.

One cannot live by power or desire alone. Human beings are not one-dimensional, as Hobbes tried to make us believe, but in fact have many dimensions and many needs. The classical tradition reveals some of them. It speaks to us of community and friendship; virtue and corruption; self-interest and self-control; justice and order; freedom and law; happiness and sorrow; the purposes of life and the dangers of war. I have tried to bring forward some of those issues in this book and to show that the questions the classical authors ask and the answers they give are relevant for us. Those thinkers, who inspired the American founders, can still teach us many things. If nothing else, they remind us of the ancient simplicity—a simplicity that made the distinction between right and wrong seem clearer than it does today, helping to strengthen people in the courage of their convictions. And that, in itself, is a great deal—more than enough to make us realize that their ideas require serious reconsideration.

The Great Debate Concerning Justice, Law, Human Nature, and International Politics

Main Speakers:	**Main Speakers:**
The Athenians at Melos, Thrasymachus, Carneades, Machiavelli, Hobbes	The Melians, Socrates, Aristotle, Aquinas, Grotius, Locke
Justice is a matter of expediency. It is used instrumentally to one's own advantage. Where there is no law that a sovereign can enforce, there is neither justice nor injustice.	Justice is independent from the notion of positive, human law. To be just is to be fair toward others, to give everyone their proper due. Justice derives from the law of nature. It is unchangeable.
Positive laws are merely conventional and related to a particular constitution.	Positive laws are founded upon the law of nature.
Human beings can be described in terms of their passions. They act only for their own advantage. They have no moral sense.	Human beings are social animals, unable to live alone. They are rational and have a moral sense of what is right and what is wrong. They can see that they gain not only immediate but also long-term advantages by behaving justly toward others.

(continued)

Main Speakers:	**Main Speakers:**
Social peace can be maintained only by a coercive superior power that keeps individuals in awe.	Social peace can be maintained not only by coercion but also by good faith and mutual trust among people.
International politics is international anarchy, a state of war of all against all. Any system of international laws or international organizations is a fiction. Each state pursues its own interest and struggles for power.	Sovereign and independent states can form a society of nations. They can cooperate and establish international laws, which will be respected even without sanctions.
The only feasible solution to international anarchy is the establishment of a world state.	The struggle for power ends in war. The best solution is an international society organized on a cooperative basis. The establishment of a world government will end in corruption and a soulless despotism.
Conflict, war, and violence are permanent features of international affairs. War is a means to achieve political ends. The only response to violence is violence.	War should always be the last resort for civilized people. Violence is a means characteristic of wild beasts. International anarchy and violence should be countered with humanity.

WORKS CITED

Adcock, F. E. *Roman Political Ideas and Practice*. Ann Arbor: U of Michigan P, 1964.

Aquinas, St. Thomas. *On Politics and Ethics*. Ed. and trans. Paul E. Sigmund. New York: Norton, 1988.

Aquinas, Saint Thomas. *Political Writings*. Ed. and trans. R. W. Dyson. Cambridge: Cambridge UP, 2002.

Arendt, Hannah. "Expansion and the Philosophy of Power." *Sewanee Review* 54 (Nov. 1946): 601–616. Rpt. in *Hobbes*. Vol. 1. Ed. John Dunn and Ian Harris. *Great Political Thinkers; 8*. Cheltenham: Edward Edgar, 1997. 241–256.

Aristotle. *The Athenian Constitution*. Trans. P. J. Rhodes. London: Penguin, 1984.

Aristotle. *Nicomachean Ethics*. Trans. Terence Irwin. 2nd ed. Indianapolis: Hackett, 1999.

Aristotle. *Politics*. Trans. C. D. C. Reeve. Indianapolis: Hackett, 1998.

Aron, Raymond. *Peace and War: A Theory of International Relations*. Trans. Richard Howard and Anette Baker Fox. Garden City, NY: Doubleday, 1966.

Ashcraft, Richard. *Locke's Two Treatises of Government*. London: Unwin Hyman, 1987.

Augustine. *Political Writings*. Ed. Henry Paolucci. Washington, DC: Regnery Gateway, 1987.

Augustine. *Political Writings*. Ed. Ernest L. Fortin and Douglas Kries. Indianapolis: Hackett, 1994.

Augustine. *The City of God*. Trans. Henry Bettenson. London: Penguin, 1984.

Berlin, Isaiah. "The Originality of Machiavelli." *Against the Current: Essays in the History of Ideas*. Oxford: Clarendon, 1979. 25–79.

Bodin, Jean. *Les Six livres de la République: un abrégé du texte de l'édition de Paris de 1583*. Ed. Gérard Mairet. Paris: Librairie Générale Française, 1993.

Booth, Ken. "Dare Not to Know: International Relations Theory versus the Future." *International Relations Theory Today*. Ed. Ken Both and Steve Smith. Cambridge: Polity, 1995. 328–350.

Boucher, David. *Theories of International Relations: From Thucydides to the Present*. Oxford: Oxford UP, 1998.

Bozeman, Adda B. "On the Relevance of Hugo Grotius and *De Jure Belli Ac Pacis* for Our Times." *Grotiana* (1980): 65–124. Rpt. in *Grotius*. Vol. 1. Ed. John Dunn and Ian Harris. *Great Political Thinkers; 7*. Cheltenham: Edward Edgar, 1997. 531–590.

Brown, Chris. *Understanding International Relations*. London: Macmillan, 1997.

Bull, Hedley. "The Grotian Conception of International Society." *Diplomatic Investigations: Essays in the Theory of International Politics*. Ed. Herbert Butterfield and Martin Wight. London: Allen and Uwin, 1966. 51–73.

Bull, Hedley. *The Anarchical Society: A Study of Order in World Politics*. New York: Columbia UP, 1977.

Bull, Hedley. "Hobbes and the International Anarchy." *Social Research* 48.4 (1981): 717–738. Rpt. in *Hobbes*. Vol. 2. Ed. John Dunn and Ian Harris. *Great Political Thinkers; 8*. Cheltenham: Edward Edgar, 1997. 338–359.

Bull, Hedley. "The Importance of Grotius in the Study of International Relations." *Hugo Grotius and*

International Relations. Ed. Hedley Bull, Benedict Kingsbury, and Adam Roberts. Oxford: Clarendon, 1990. 65–93.

Bull, Hedley. "Society and Anarchy in International Relations." *International Theory: Critical Investigations*. Ed. James Der Derian. London: Macmillan, 1995. 75–93.

Burnell, Peter. "The Problem of Service in Unjust Regimes." *Journal of the History of Ideas*, 54.2 (April 1993): 177–188.

Burns, J. H, ed. *The Cambridge History of Medieval Political Thought c.350–c.1450*. Cambridge: Cambridge UP, 1988.

Carr, Edward Hallet. *The Twenty Years' Crisis, 1919–1939: An Introduction to Study International Relations*. 2nd ed. New York: St. Martin's P, 1946.

Cawkwell, George. *Thucydides and the Peloponnesian War*. London: Routledge, 1997.

Chadwick, Henry. *Augustine*. Past Masters. Oxford: Oxford UP, 1986.

Cicero. *On Duties*. Ed. M. T. Griffin and E. M. Atkins. Cambridge: Cambridge UP, 1991.

Cicero. *On the Commonwealth and On the Laws*. Ed. James E. G. Zetzel. Cambridge: Cambridge UP, 1999.

Clark, Sir George. *English History: A Survey*. Oxford, Clarendon, 1971.

Clarke, M. L. *The Roman Mind: Studies in the History of Thought from Cicero to Marcus Aurelius*. New York: Norton, 1968.

Clay, Diskin. "Reading the Republic." *Platonic Writings: Platonic Readings*. Ed. Charles L. Griswold, Jr. New York: Routledge, 1988.

Colish, Marcia. "Cicero's *De Officiis* and Machiavelli's Prince." *Sixteenth Century Journal*, 9.4 (1978): 81–93.

Coll, Alberto R. "Normative Prudence as a Tradition of Statecraft." *Ethics and International Affairs*. 2nd ed.

Ed. Joel H. Rosenthal. Washington, DC: Georgetown UP, 1999. 75–100.

Corwin, Edward S. *The "Higher Law" Background of American Constitutional Law*. Ithaca: Cornel UP, 1979.

Coyle, Martin, ed. *Niccolò Machiavelli's The Prince: New Interdisciplinary Essays*. Manchester: Manchester UP, 1995.

Cross, R. C. and A. D. Woozley. *Plato's Republic: A Philosophical Commentary*. London: Macmillan, 1964.

Dallmayr, Fred, ed. *From Contract to Community: Political Theory at the Crossroads*. New York: Marcel Dekker, 1978.

Davies, Brian. *The Thought of Thomas Aquinas*. Oxford: Clarendon P, 1993.

Dean, Herbert A. *The Political and Social Ideas of St. Augustine*. New York: Columbia UP, 1963.

Donnelly, Jack. *Realism and International Relations*. Cambridge: Cambridge UP, 2000.

Draper, G. I. A. D. "Grotius' Place in the Development of Legal Ideas about War." *Hugo Grotius and International Relations*. Ed. Hedley Bull, Benedict Kingsbury, and Adam Roberts. Oxford: Clarendon, 1990. 177–207.

Dunn, John. *The Political Thought of John Locke: An Historical Account of the "Argument of the Two Treatises of Government"*. Cambridge: Cambridge UP, 1969.

Dunn, John. *The History of Political Theory and Other Essays*. Cambridge: Cambridge UP, 1996.

Ferrari, Leo C. "Some Surprising Omissions from Augustine's 'City of God'." *Augustiniana* 20.1–2 (1970): 336–346.

Finnis, John. *Aquinas: Moral, Political, and Legal Theory*. Oxford: Oxford UP, 1998.

Fitzgerald, L. P. "St. Thomas Aquinas and the Two Powers." *Angelicum* 56.4 (1979): 515–556.

Forde, Steven. "Morality and Power in Thucydides." *Thucydides' Theory of International Relations: A Lasting Possession*. Ed. Lowell S. Gustafson. Baton Rouge: Louisiana State UP, 2000. 151–173.

Fortin, Ernest L. *Political Idealism and Christianity in the Thought of St. Augustine*. Villanova, PA: Villanova UP, 1971.

Fox, Marvin. "Maimonides and Aquinas on Natural Law." *Studies on Maimonides and St. Thomas Aquinas*. Ed. Jacob I. Dienstag. New York: KTAV, 1975. 75–106.

Gamble, Andrew. *An Introduction to Modern Social and Political Thought*. London: Macmillan, 1981.

Gamble, Richard M. "Savior Nation: Woodrow Wilson and the Gospel of Service." *Humanitas* 14.1 (2001): 4–22.

Gelinas, Elmer T. "*Ius* and *Lex* in Thomas Aquinas." *American Journal of Jurisprudence* 15 (1970): 154–170.

Geyl, Pieter. "Grotius." *Transactions of the Grotius Society* 12 (1927): 81–97. Rpt. in *Grotius*. Vol. 1. Ed. John Dunn and Ian Harris. *Great Political Thinkers; 7*. Cheltenham: Edward Edgar, 1997. 5–21.

Gilson, Etienne. *The Spirit of Medieval Philosophy*. Trans. A. H. C. Downes. New York: Charles Scribner's Sons, 1940.

Golding, Martin P. "Aquinas and Some Contemporary Natural Law Theories." *Proceedings of the American Catholic Philosophical Association* 48 (1974). 238–247.

Goldsmith, M. M. "Hobbes's 'Mortall God': Is There a Fallacy in Hobbes's Theory of Sovereignty?" *History of Political Thought* 1.1 (1980): 33–50. Rpt. in *Thomas Hobbes: Critical Assessments*. Vol. 3. Ed. Preston King. London: Routledge, 1993. 768–786.

Green, John Richard. *A Short History of the English People*. London: Macmillan, 1947.

Grotius, Hugo. *Prolegomena*. Trans. Francis W. Kelsey. Rpt. in *The Theory of International Relations: Selected Texts from Gentili to Treitschke*. Ed. M. G. Forsyth, H. M. A. Keens-Soper, and P. Savigear. London: George Allen and Uwin, 1970. 39–85.

Grotius, Hugo. *The Rights of War and Peace*. Trans. A. C. Campbell. Westport, VA: Hyperion, 1993.

Gunnel, John. *Political Theory: Tradition and Interpretation*. Lanham, MD: UP of America, 1987.

Hanson, Donald W. "Thomas Hobbes's 'Highway to Peace'." *International Organization* 38.2 (1984): 329–354. Rpt. in *Hobbes*. Vol. 2. Ed. John Dunn and Ian Harris. *Great Political Thinkers; 8*. Cheltenham: Edward Edgar, 1997. 487–512.

Harbour, Frances V. *Thinking about International Ethics: Moral Theory and Cases from American Foreign Policy*. Boulder, CO: Westview, 1999.

Hobbes, Thomas. *De Cive*. Ed. Howard Warrender. Vol. 3 of *The Clarendon Edition of the Political Works of Thomas Hobbes*. Oxford: Clarendon, 1983.

Hobbes, Thomas. *Leviathan*. Ed. Edwin Curley. Indianapolis: Hackett, 1994.

Howard, Michael, ed. *Restraints on War: Studies in the Limitation of Armed Conflict*. Oxford: Oxford UP, 1995.

Hrezo, Margaret. "Thucydides, Plato, and the Kinesis of Cities and Souls," in Lowell S. Gustafson (ed.), *Thucydides' Theory of International Relations*. Baton Rouge: Louisiana State UP, 2000. 42–63.

Huyler, Jerome. *Locke in America: The Moral Philosophy of the Founding Era*. Lawrence: UP of Kansas, 1995.

Jackson, Robert and Georg Sørensen. *Introduction to International Relations: Theories and Approaches*. Oxford: Oxford UP, 2003.

Johnson, Curtis N. *Aristotle's Theory of the State*. New York: St. Martin's P, 1990.

Kayser, John R. and Ronald J. Lettieri. "Aquinas's Regimem Bene Commixtum and the Medieval Critique of Classical Republicanism." *Thomist* 46(1982): 195–220.

Keene, Robert. *Beyond The Anarchical Society: Grotius, Colonialism and Order in World Politics*. Cambridge: Cambridge UP, 2002.

Kirk, Russell. *The Roots of American Order*. Washington, DC: Regnery Gateway, 1992.

Knowles, David. *The Evolution of Medieval Thought*. London: Longman, 1988.

Kocis, Robert A. *Machiavelli Redeemed: Retrieving His Humanist Perspectives on Equality, Power, and Glory*. Bethlehem: Lehigh UP, 1998.

Kraynak, R. P. "Hobbes on Barbarism and Civilization." *Journal of Politics* 45.1 (1983): 86–109. Rpt. in *Thomas Hobbes: Critical Assessments*. Vol. 3. Ed. Preston King. London: Routledge, 1993. 686–708.

Kretzmann, Norman and Eleonore Stump, eds. *The Cambridge Companion to Aquinas*. Cambridge: Cambridge UP, 1993.

Kristeller, Paul Oscar. "The Moral Thought of Renaissance Humanism." *Renaissance Thought and Arts: Collected Essays*. Princeton: Princeton UP, 1990. 20–68.

Lauterpacht, H. "The Grotian Tradition in International Law." *British Yearbook for International Law* 23 (1946): 1–53. Rpt. in *Grotius*. Vol. 1. Ed. John Dunn and Ian Harris. *Great Political Thinkers; 7*. Cheltenham: Edward Edgar, 1997. 396–448.

Lee, R. W. "Hugo Grotius." *Proceedings of the British Academy* 16 (1980): 219–279. Rpt. in *Grotius*. Vol. 1. Ed. John Dunn and Ian Harris. *Great Political Thinkers; 7*. Cheltenham: Edward Edgar, 1997. 213–273.

Lee, Theresa Man Ling. *Politics and Truth: Political Theory and Postmodernist Challenge*. Albany, NY: State U of New York P, 1997.

Locke, John. *A Letter Concerning Toleration*. Ed. John Horton and Susan Mendus. *Routledge Philosophers in Focus Series*. London: Routledge, 1991.

Locke, John. *An Essay Concerning Human Understanding*. Ed. Gary Fuller, Robert Stecker, and John P. Wright. Routledge Philosophers in Focus Series. London: Routledge, 2000.

Locke, John. *Political Essays*. Ed. Mark Goldie. Cambridge UP, 1997.

Locke, John. *Second Treatise of Government*. Ed. C. B. Macpherson. Indianapolis: Hackett, 1980.

Locke, John. *Two Treatises of Government*. Ed. Peter Laslett. Cambridge Texts in the History of Political Thought. Cambridge: Cambridge UP, 1988.

Losee, John. *A Historical Introduction to the Philosophy of Science*. 3rd ed. Oxford: Oxford UP, 1983.

Machiavelli, Niccolò. *The Discourses*. 2 vols. Trans. Leslie J. Walker. London: Routledge, 1975.

Machiavelli, Niccolò. *The Prince*. Trans. Harvey C. Mansfield, Jr. Chicago: Chicago UP, 1985.

MacKendrick, Paul. *The Philosophical Books of Cicero*. London: Duckworth, 1989.

Macpherson, C. B. *The Political Theory of Possessive Individualism, Hobbes to Locke*. Oxford: Clarendon, 1962.

Mansfield, Harvey C. "Social Science and the Constitution." *Confronting the Constitution*. Ed. Allan Bloom. *AEI Studies 496*. Washington, DC: AEI, 1990. 411–436.

Meinecke, Friedrich. *Machiavellism: The Doctrine of Raison d'État in Modern History*. Trans. Douglas Scott. New Brunswick, NJ: Transaction Publishers, 1998.

Mendus, Susan. *Toleration and the Limits of Liberalism*. Atlantic Highlands, NJ: Humanities P, 1989.

Mill, John Stuart. *On Liberty and Other Essays*. Ed. John Gray. Oxford World Classics. Oxford: Oxford UP, 1998.

Minogue, Kenneth. *Politics: A Very Short Introduction*. Oxford: Oxford UP, 1995.

Morrall, John B. *Political Thought in Medieval Times*. Toronto: U of Toronto P, 1980.

Morgenthau, Hans J. *Politics among Nations: The Struggle for Power and Peace*. 2nd ed. New York: Alfred A. Knopf, 1956.

Nelson, Brian R. *Western Political Thought: From Socrates to the Age of Ideology*. Upper Saddle River, NJ: Prentice Hall, 1996.

Nichols, Mary P. *Citizens and Statesmen: A Study of Aristotle's Politics*. Savage, MD: Rowman and Littlefield, 1992.

Niebuhr, Reinhold. "Augustine's Political Realism." *The City of God: A Collection of Critical Essays*. New York: Peter Lang, 1995. 119–134.

Niebuhr, Reinhold. *The Children of Light and the Children of Darkness: A Vindication of Democracy and a Critique of Its Traditional Defense*. New York: Charles Scriber's Sons, 1960.

Oakshott, Michael. *Hobbes on Civil Association*. Oxford: Basil Blackwell, 1975.

Okin, S. M. "'The Sovereign and His Counsellours': Hobbes's Reevaluation of the Parliament." *Political Theory* 10.1 (1982): 49–75. Rpt. in *Thomas Hobbes: Critical Assessments*. Vol. 3. Ed. Preston King. London: Routledge, 1993. 787–810.

Osmond, Patricia J., "Sallust and Machiavelli: From Civic Humanism to Political Prudence." *Journal of Medieval and Renaissance Studies*. 23 (1993): 407–438.

Pangle, Lorraine Smith. "Friendship and Self-Love in Aristotle's Nicomachean Ethics." *Action and Contemplation: Studies in the Moral and Political Thought of Aristotle*. Ed. Robert C. Bartlett and Susan D. Collins. Albany, NY: State U of New York P, 1999. 171–202.

Pangle, Thomas L. "The Philosophic Understanding of Human Nature Informing the Constitution." *Confronting the Constitution*. Ed. Allan Bloom. *AEI Studies 496*. Washington, DC: AEI, 1990. 9–76.

Parel, Anthony. *The Machiavellian Cosmos*. New Haven: Yale UP, 1992.

Parkes, Henry Bamford. *The Divine Order: Western Culture in the Middle Ages and the Renaissance*. London: Victor Gollancz, 1970.

Pieper, Josef. *Guide to Thomas Aquinas*. San Francisco: Ignatius P, 1986.

Plamenatz, John. "In Search of Machiavellian Virtù," *The Political Calculus: Essays on Machiavelli's Philosophy*. Toronto: Toronto UP, 1972. 157–178.

Plato. "Alcibiades I." *The Roots of Political Philosophy: Ten Forgotten Socratic Dialogues*. Ed. Thomas L. Pangle. Ithaca: Cornell UP, 1987. 175–221.

Plato. *Republic*. Trans. G. M. A. Grube (revised by C. D. C. Reeve). Indianapolis: Hackett, 1992.

Plato. *The Laws*. Trans. Thomas L. Pangle. Indianapolis: Hackett, 1992.

Pocock, J. G. A. *The Machiavellian Movement: Florentine Political Thought and the Atlantic Political Tradition*. Princeton: Princeton UP, 1975.

Polansky, Ronald. "Aristotle on Political Change." *A Companion to Aristotle's Politics*. Ed. David Keyt and Fred Miller, Jr. Oxford: Blackwell, 1991. 323–345.

Polybius. *The Rise of the Roman Empire*. Trans. Ian Scott-Kilvert. London: Penguin, 1979.

Popper, Karl. *The Open Society and Its Enemies*. London: Routledge and Kegan, 1945.

Price, Russell. "The Theme Gloria in Machiavelli." *Renaissance Quarterly*, 30 (1977): 588–631.

Rahe, Paul A. "Thucydides' Critique of *Realpolitik*." *Security Studies* 5 (1995/1996): 105–141.

Rapaczynski, Andrzej. *Nature and Politics: Liberalism in the Philosophies of Hobbes, Locke, and Rousseau*. Ithaca, NY: Cornell UP, 1987.

Raphael, D. D. *Problems of Political Philosophy*. 2nd ed. London: Macmillan, 1990.

Richard, Carl J. *The Founders and the Classics: Greece, Rome and the American Enlightenment*. Cambridge, MA: Harvard UP, 1994.

Röling, B. V. A. "Are Grotius' Ideas Obsolete in an Expanded World?" *Hugo Grotius and International Relations*. Ed. Hedley Bull, Benedict Kingsbury, and Adam Roberts. Oxford: Clarendon, 1990. 281–299.

Rommen, Heinrich A. H. *The Natural Law: A Study in Legal and Social History and Philosophy*. Trans. Thomas R. Hanley. Indianapolis: Liberty Fund, 1998.

Rudkowski, Victor Anthony. *The Price: A Historical Critique*. New York: Twayne Publishers, 1992.

Russell, Greg. *Hans J. Morgenthau and the Ethics of American Statecraft*. Baton Rouge: Louisiana State UP, 1990.

Rzadkiewicz, Arnold L. *The Philosophical Basis of Human Liberty According to St. Thomas Aquinas: A Study in Social Philosophy*. Washington, DC: Catholic U of America P, 1949.

Schall, James V. "Human Rights as an Ideological Project." *American Journal of Jurisprudence* 32 (1987): 47–61.

Schofield, Malcolm. "Cicero's Definition of *Res Publica*." *Cicero the Philosopher: Twelve Papers*. Ed. J. G. F. Powell. Oxford: Oxford UP, 1995. 63–83.

Sigmund, Paul E. "Thomistic Natural Law and Social Theory." *Calgary Aquinas Studies*. Ed. Anthony Parel. Toronto: Pontifical Institute of Medieval Studies, 1978. 67–76.

Skinner, Quentin. *The Foundations of Modern Political Thought*. Vol. 1. Cambridge: Cambridge UP, 1978.

Smith, Michael J. "Humanitarian Intervention: An Overview of the Ethical Issues." *Ethics and International Affairs: A Reader*. 2nd ed. Washington, DC: Georgetown UP, 1999. 271–295.

Snyder, David C. "John Locke and the Freedom of Belief." *Journal of Church and State* 30.2 (Spring 1988): 227–243.

Sommerville, Johann P. *Thomas Hobbes: Political Ideas in Historical Context*. New York: St. Martin's, 1992.

Strauss, Leo. *What Is Political Philosophy? And Other Studies*. Chicago: Chicago UP, 1988.

Sullivan, Michael P. *International Relations: Theories and Evidences*. Englewood Cliffs, NJ: Prentice-Hall, 1976.

Tessitore, Aristide. *Reading Aristotle's Ethics: Virtue, Rhetoric, and Political Philosophy*. Albany, NY: State U of New York P, 1996.

Thompson, Kenneth W. *Moral and Political Discourse: Theory and Practice of International Relations*. Lanham, MD: UP of America, 1987.

Thucydides. *On Justice, Power, and Human Nature: The Essence of Thucydides' History of the Peloponnesian War*. Ed. and trans. Paul Woodruff. Indianapolis: Hackett, 1993.

Toynbee, Arnold. *Civilization on Trial*. Oxford: Oxford UP, 1948.

Tuck, Richard. *Hobbes*. Past Masters. Oxford: Oxford UP, 1989.

Tully, James. *An Approach to Political Philosophy: Locke in Contexts.* Cambridge: Cambridge UP, 1993.

Tully, James. *Strange Multiplicity: Constitutionalism in an Age of Diversity.* Cambridge: Cambridge UP, 1995.

Vetterli, Richard and Gary Bryner. *In Search of the Republic: Public Virtue and the Roots of American Government.* Totowa, NJ: Rowman and Littlefiled, 1987.

Viroli, Maurizio. "Machiavelli and the Republican Idea of Politics." *Machiavelli and Republicanism.* Eds. Gisela Bock, Quentin Skinner, and Maurizio Viroli. Cambridge: Cambridge UP, 1990.

Vlastos, Gregory. *Studies in Greek Philosophy.* 2 vols. Princeton: Princeton UP, 1993.

Vogelin, Eric. *The World of the Polis.* Baton Rouge: Louisiana State UP, 1957.

Waldron, Jeremy. "Locke: Toleration and the Rationality of Persecution." *Justifying Toleration: Conceptual and Historical Perspectives.* Cambridge: Cambridge UP, 1988. 61–86.

Waltz, Kenneth. *Theory of International Politics.* Reading, MA: Addison-Wesley, 1979.

Walzer, Michael. *Just and Unjust Wars: A Moral Argument with Historical Illustrations.* New York: Basic Books, 1977.

Watkins, J. W. N. "Philosophy and Politics in Hobbes." *Political Quarterly* 5.19 (1955): 125–146. Rpt. in *Hobbes.* Vol. 1. Ed. John Dunn and Ian Harris. *Great Political Thinkers; 8.* Cheltenham: Edward Edgar, 1997. 314–335.

Wight, Martin. *International Theory: Three Traditions.* Leicester: U of Leicester P, 1991.

Wight, Martin. "Why Is There No International Theory?" *International Theory: Critical Investigations.* Ed. James Der Derian. London: Macmillan, 1995.

Williams, Mary Frances. *Ethics in Thucydides: The Ancient Simplicity.* Lanham, MD: UP of America, 1998.

Winton, Richard. "Herodotus, Thucydides and the Sophists." *The Cambridge History of Greek and Roman Thought.* Ed. Christopher Rowe and Malcolm Schofield. Cambridge: Cambridge UP, 2000. 89–121.

Wolin, Sheldon S. "Hobbes and the Culture of Despotism." *Thomas Hobbes and Political Theory.* Ed. Mary G. Dietz. Lawrence: UP of Kansas. 9–36. Rpt. in *Hobbes.* Vol. 3. Ed. John Dunn and Ian Harris. *Great Political Thinkers; 8.* Cheltenham: Edward Edgar, 1997. 420–447.

Wood, Gordon S. *The Creation of the American Republic 1776–1887.* New York: Norton, 1969.

Wood, Neal. *Cicero's Social and Political Philosophy.* Berkeley: U of California P, 1988.

Yasuaki, Onuma, ed. *A Normative Approach to War: Peace, War, and Justice in Hugo Grotius.* Oxford: Clarendon, 1993.

Zeitlin, Irving. *Plato's Vision: The Classical Origins of Social and Political Thought.* Englewood Cliffs, NJ: Prentice-Hall, 1993.

GLOSSARY

Absolutism. A system of government in which the power of the ruler is not limited by constitutional or other restraints; despotism. *See* Tyranny.

Anarchy. (1) Absence of a ruler. (2) International anarchy—absence of a world authority that can exercise an effective power over states.

Aristocracy. (1) Individuals of high moral standards and outstanding personal qualities, as in natural aristocracy or individuals who are born into noble families, as in hereditary aristocracy. (2) Upper class, nobility. (3) Government by the upper class with a vision of the common good, as contrasted with an oligarchic rule. *See* Oligarchy.

Authority. (1) Right to act, command, enforce obedience, or make decisions. (2) Person or group possessing and exercising such a right. If the government has authority, this means that it has the right to issue orders to citizens. Political authority can be justified by knowledge, as in Plato; by divine right, as in Sir Robert Filmer; and by consent of the governed, as in Locke. Legitimate power. *See* Legitimacy.

Balance of Power. An International System in which states or alliances of states have relatively equal power and no one of them is able to become dominant. *See* Power.

Civic Virtue. Public Virtue. Willingness to sacrifice individual concerns for the benefit of society as a whole. Patriotism. *See* Virtue.

Civil Society. (1) Political society. In the classical conceptualization that stretches from Aristotle to early modern times, the term "civil society" is used as a synonym for "political society" or "political community." Locke still uses this language. However, by radically separating public and private spheres of life, he contributes to a new meaning of the term as (2) A realm of private activity, which provides scope for the expression of individual freedom, and particularly for economic pursuits, and is independent of the state. The modern distinction between "civil society" and "the state" was further elaborated by Hegel. *See* Political Society.

Civilization. A stage of human society characterized by a complex level of social, political, economic, moral, and intellectual development. When the moral and intellectual development fades, civilization declines into barbarism.

Classical Tradition. The tradition of moral and political thought that begins with Socrates and Plato, and ends in modern times, challenged first by Machiavelli, and then by Hobbes and his followers. *See* Modernity.

Collective Security. An idea of international security that lies behind the United Nations, namely, that aggression by one state against another is aggression against all and should be defeated collectively.

Common Good. Public interest or general interest. Whatever benefits the whole society or general public. It can be contrasted with a particular interest of an individual, class, or faction. *See* Self-Interest.

Common Law. A body of law based on custom, usage, and court decisions, as distinct from statutory law, that is, law based on statutes.

Constitution. (1) A system of fundamental principles according to which an association or a political entity is governed. (2) Written document containing these principles. (3) In ancient philosophy, a political regime. Aristotle mentions six basic constitutions: kingship, contrasted with tyranny; aristocracy, contrasted with oligarchy; and polity, contrasted with democracy.

Corruption. Abandonment of expected standards of behavior, as in moral corruption. In political terms, extreme self-interest: acting without a due respect for the common good, and particularly, misusing the public office for a private gain. *See* Self-Interest, Common Good.

Critical Theory. A post-Marxist strain of critical thought, which questions the status quo, reveals the power interests behind it, and regards knowledge as an instrument of social change. Critical theorists believe that traditional theories do not question the political and social order, but have the effect of legitimizing it. The most influential thinkers are Theodor Adorno, Herbert Marcuse, and Jürgen Habermas.

Democracy. "Government of the people, by the people, for the people." (1) In ancient philosophy, the rule of the citizen body with a view of the common good, as in polity. (2) Also, a deviant regime in which the poor people (*demos*), constituting the majority of society, exercise power in their own interest as against the interests of the aristocratic and wealthy minorities. (3) In modern political thought, a political system based universal suffrage, regular and free elections, and civil and political liberties. (4) The right of all to decide about matters of general concern. *See* Polity.

Democratic Peace Theory. A view that democratic states do not go to war against one another. This view is criticized by the realists.

Determinism. Doctrine that the same effects produce the same causes, and that every fact in the universe is guided entirely by law. Hobbes applies this doctrine to human affairs. A mechanistic view of the universe.

Distributive Justice. Just or fair principles of distribution of goods within a society. Distributive justice is one of the most extensively debated subjects, and has given birth to libertarian, socialist, liberal, communitarian, and feminist concepts of justice. *See* Justice.

Dogma. Rigid belief, accepted on authority without the support of demonstration or experience.

Epistemology. Theory of cognition. The branch of philosophy that seeks to investigate the origin, structure, methods, and validity of knowledge.

Equality. (1) State of being equal. Having the same faculties, abilities, privileges, rights, and duties. (2) Moral exhortation that in public matters all persons should be treated equally. (3) Belief that everyone has the right and equal capacity to participate in a collective decision-making process. (4) Equality of social conditions. (5) Equality before the law. (6) Equality of opportunity.

Equity. *See* Fairness.

Ethics. (1) A normative discipline that deals with right and wrong human actions. (2) Morality. *See* Morality.

Existentialism. Anti-essentialist and anti-foundational thinking that can be associated primarily with Jean-Paul Sartre and Martin Heidegger. Heidegger's critique of metaphysics and his opposition to technological world domination have been embraced by leading theorists of post-modernity, such as Derrida, Foucault, and Lyotard. While rejecting traditional values and any foundations on which one can stand beyond the elusive being, which is not a thing and which he makes the main subject of his inquiry, Heidegger leaves the post-modern individual with nothing—with the nothingness from which he tries to derive being.

Fairness. Equity or fairness is frequently contrasted with equality. Fair shares, for example, do not need to be the same as equal shares. They may depend on merit or need, which are usually not equally distributed. The idea of justice is often considered to be roughly equivalent to the idea of fairness or equity. *See* Justice, Equality.

Feminism. (1) The belief that in most existing societies there is an imbalance of power and benefits between women and men. (2) More specifically, for feminists such as Nancy Hartsock or Carol Gilligan, the central issue is to investigate the consequences of the claim that women's' lives differ structurally from those of men. Male domination, oppression, and exclusion of women are stressed. Since "masculine" reason is contrasted with such "feminine" characteristics as intuition and emotion, the Western traditional emphasis on rationality is sometimes regarded as exclusionary of women. Justice may also be considered a gender-biased category and is contrasted with care. Philosophy, science, and politics have been seen as male-dominated.

Freedom. (1) Self-mastery, lack of subjection. (2) In Hobbes, absence of restraint. (3) In Locke, the ability to act or forbear acting according to one's choice or preference.

Good Life. A complete life. Material prosperity and moral excellence. In Aristotle, the highest normative goal of a political community as contrasted with its mere life or survival. This implies that once the conditions of physical survival are met and basic prosperity is achieved, a political community becomes potentially an area of good living, an environment in which the mind can be enlarged and virtue can develop. *See* Politics.

Happiness. (1) In Aristotle, well-being or *eudaimonia*, flourishing of the most distinctive human capacities for reason and speech, exercise of complete virtue. (2) In Locke, no fixed model of life, but a complex ideal that causes one desire to be suspended in the name of other considerations, such as a calculation of present and future satisfactions or an idea of what a life worth living might be.

(3) In Hobbes, a continual satisfaction of desire, from one object to another. (4) In utilitarianism, pleasure and absence of pain.

Hedonism. Pursuit of pleasure as a way of life. A theory that pleasure is the highest good.

Hegemon. Hegemonic leader. A state with preponderant influence and authority over all others. A leading economic and military power, which, in the absence of a world government, enforces international rules.

Human Nature. (1) Permanent and universal characteristics of human beings. (2) In Aristotle, natural human capacities for reason and speech rather than any fixed characteristics. To develop fully these capacities in virtuous acts is an important end of human life.

Human Rights. Natural rights. Rights that all human beings have in virtue of their specifically and universally human characteristics. The doctrine of natural rights was developed in treatises and documents, of which the most important is The Universal Declaration of Human Rights of the United Nations. *See* Right.

Idealism, Political. The theoretical perspective in the discipline of International Relations that emphasizes the cooperative side of international politics. The idealists attach importance to moral and legal norms and to cooperative values. Both the League of Nations and the United Nations are products of idealist thinking. *See* Collective Security, Liberalism.

Ideology. Pseudo-theory. There are similarities between political theory and political ideology. They both contain assumptions about the nature of the social and political world. They both provide explanations of phenomena and recommend some norms of behavior. The main difference between theories and ideologies is that whereas the former are open ended and growing, the latter tend to be dogmatic. An ideology is fixed, closed, and finished because those who support it believe that they have already discovered answers to all problems that interest them. The point now is not to inquire further into problems in the social world, but to change it. By contrast, a theory is open ended and can be modified or discarded upon substantial evidence or force of a convincing argument. *See* Dogma.

Individualism. Pursuit of private interests. The view that looks at individuals as concerned with their private interests rather than with any community goals. *See* Self-Interest.

International Society. A society of states that presupposes that the member states share some common values and are prepared to cooperate. The United Nations Organization is a practical expression of this concept, but international society can also assume other forms. The idea of international society is usually associated with Grotius and is today strongly supported by the English school of international relations, whose intellectual founders were Martin Wight and Hedley Bull.

Justice. Justice concerns our relations with other people. Considered as a virtue, it consists in giving people what is due to them. Two main kinds of justice are retributive justice and distributive justice. They have their place, respectively, in the fixing of penalties and rewards for bad and good actions, and in distributing goods between the possible recipients. From the perspective of the natural law tradition, justice is the foundation and limitation of all law. But it can also be understood as conformity with law. *See* Distributive Justice, Natural Law.

Laissez-faire. Doctrine of minimal government intervention in the market transactions of civil society. *See* Civil Society.

Law. (1) Rules that forbid or require certain conduct or activities, established

by custom, as in common law, or by official adoption, as by a legislature, and applying to all members of a community. (2) In legal positivism, rules that must be obeyed and followed by citizens, subject to sanctions and legal consequences. *See* Common Law, Legal Positivism, Natural Law.

Legal Positivism. Voluntarism. "Whatever pleases the prince has the force of law." A legal theory that defines law in terms of commands of a sovereign or any generally recognized authority, and without reference to natural law or any moral considerations. *See* Natural Law.

Legitimacy. To be legitimate means to be authorized or sanctioned by something, and to have an adequate rationale. What makes a government legitimate is whether it has authority and pursues proper ends and observes due limits. *See* Authority.

Liberal Democracy. Modern democracy, which includes such institutions as representative government, universal suffrage, and regular and free elections, and which upholds fundamental individual, civil, and political rights. These rights include rights to freedom of thought, expression, and association; the right to freedom of religion; the right to political participation; and the right of legal due process. Central to liberal democracy is the requirement that the state and civil society, that is, politics and economics, are separated. Described in Aristotelian philosophical terms, liberal democracy represents two key values: freedom and wealth. It is thus, in contrast to populist democracy, a correct constitution; a modern equivalent to the ancient polity. *See* Liberalism, Constitution, Polity.

Liberalism. (1) A political doctrine that regards society as composed of individuals, rather than social classes, and considers liberty as the primary social good. This liberty is defined by some fundamental rights, such as Locke's "life, liberty, and property." The liberal government is instituted for a limited purpose, primarily for maintaining domestic peace and providing external security, and should not be concerned with the private sphere of human life, which includes commercial activities. In practice, the liberal doctrine has never been fully realized. (2) In International Relations, liberalism is a theoretical perspective that emphasized a cooperative character of international politics. Early liberalism, of the interwar period of 1919–1939, also known as liberal internationalism or utopianism, can be associated with idealism. A later version of liberalism, especially as developed by Robert Keohane and Joseph Nye in the late 1970s, is known as neorealism. *See* Idealism, Neorealism.

Liberty.   Freedom that is delimited by some legal or moral norms. *See* Freedom, License.

License.   Complete or unrestrained freedom. Living as one likes without regard for any norms.

Mercantilism.   Economic policy aimed at protection of domestic industry and commerce against foreign intrusion. Economic activities are subordinated to state building, to the increase of the state's power.

Militarism.   Glorification of war. National policy that emphasizes forceful territorial expansion, conquest, or other militaristic goals.

Mixed Constitution.   A constitution in which different social classes, as well as the interests and values of different social classes, are represented.

Modernity.   An intellectual current that can be related to the ascendancy of modern science and the ideas of the Enlightenment, a cultural and scientific movement (from the eighteenth and nineteenth centuries) whose goal was to foster material and social progress, and make reason the absolute ruler of human life. In contrast to a traditional political community, which is a product of a natural historical development, the modern state is a rational construct. Its institutions are a result of a rational design and its citizens are considered to be atomistic, rational agents whose interests are prior to society, and whose identities have been fabricated and molded into cultural homogeneity. As Hegel noticed, modern individuals can give their alliance to political institutions that they recognize as conforming to rational principles. Traditional political institutions, such as hereditary rule, guilds, and social classes, are considered not to pass rational criteria and consequently are rejected. Modernity is thus a challenge to the traditional (classical and Christian) culture of the West. *See* Post-Modernity.

Morality.   A system of conduct embodying principles of right and wrong that is accepted in a given society.

Nation.   People who identify themselves with each other by sharing the same history, language, and culture. In this sense, there are states that have within their borders members of different nations, and there are nations that lack their own state. *See* Nation-State.

Nation-State.   State formed by a nation. Nation organized as a political association. *See* State, Nation.

Natural Law.   Law of Nature. (1) A moral law that is unchangeable and universally valid, and discoverable by reason. A "higher" law on which, according to the natural law tradition, positive laws of a state should be based. (2) In Hobbes, who breaks with the natural law tradition, laws of nature are not moral but rather prudential rules, which guide human beings on how to survive in the state of nature.

Necessity.   A state of affairs is said to be necessary if it cannot be otherwise than it is—if there is no choice. In Machiavelli, necessity is identified with compulsion. The concept of necessity is employed by realists to justify certain courses of action, especially in war. The critics argue that in human affairs there are no situations without choice, and that the realist "necessities" are actually "masked choices."

Neoliberalism. A theoretical perspective in the discipline of International Relations. Neo-liberals emphasize that states cooperate in the anarchic international system because it is in their self-interest to do so. There are branches of neoliberalism, such as sociological liberalism, interdependence liberalism, institutional liberalism, and republican liberalism. *See* Liberalism.

Neorealism. A scientific reinterpretation of political realism. Neo-realists regard states as egoistic actors and try to deduce their behavior from the anarchic international system. *See* Anarchy, Realism.

Nominalism. In Hobbes, the theory that general terms have no real existence, but are mere words or names. Reality is admitted only to actual physical particulars.

Norms; Normative. Standards suggesting what something should be. Ethical standards of action. Normative political theory deals with ethical issues.

Oligarchy. Rule of the wealthy upper class in its own interest. A deviation from aristocracy. *See* Aristocracy.

Ontology. Theory of reality. The branch of philosophy that deals with the nature of being.

Participation. Citizens' involvement in public life. The ancient city-state was based on the idea of self-government and extensive participation of citizens in public life. For John Stuart Mill, a modern proponent of participation, it must at minimum involve selecting representatives during the electoral process. *See* Representative Government.

Polis. Ancient city-state. Self-governed community.

Politeia. *See* Polity.

Political Culture. Fundamental beliefs and values, the foci of identification and loyalty, which are the product of the specific historical experience of a nation or a political community.

Political Obligation. Citizens' duty to obey laws of the state.

Political Society. Politically organized society. Political community. State.

Politics. (1) Management of public affairs. (2) In the classical tradition, an art by means of which human beings build their social and political institutions for the more perfect realization of a good life. (3) In modern political thinking, a struggle for power. *See* Good Life.

Polity. (1) Constitution, a political regime. (2) Mixed Constitution. (3) In Aristotle, government of the majority with a view of the common good. A correct form of democracy. *See* Mixed Constitution.

Positive Laws. Human or human-made laws as contrasted with natural law. *See* Natural Law.

Postmodernism. The most influential postmodernist thinkers are Gilles Deleuze, Jacques Derrida, and Michael Foucault. Postmodernism is a very broad movement that can be traced to the philosophy of Martin Heidegger but is much more political and radical. The relationship between knowledge and power is emphasized. History is seen as a series of power dominations and an endless power struggle. The social world is a "text" to be interpreted. Deconstruction is a method of interpretation that shakes any establishment, whether a text or theory or political institution, by exposing its internal tensions. *See* Post-Modernity.

Post-Modernity. (1) The post-modern condition: a state of affairs following on from the decline of modernity, marked by social and cultural fragmentation. (2) An intellectual current that challenges modernity and leads us to the post-modern era. It explores internal tensions and contradictions in the rational moral project and unveils power interests behind it. Modern ideas such as the cultural identity, national unity, state sovereignty, rationality, and progress related to science are questioned as leading to potentially oppressive practices. The main focus is social change: liberation from all kinds of domination and oppression. Yet, while post-modernity attempts to replace identity by difference, it is not a return to traditionalism. By creating new social divisions, it deconstructs both modern and traditional societies. By undermining the institutions of state and family, it challenges Western societies. Critical strains of thought, such as feminism, critical theory, existentialism, and postmodernism can all be associated with the post-modern challenge. *See* Critical Theory, Existentialism, Feminism, Postmodernism.

Power. (1) Ability to do or effect something. (2) Ability to command, control, or impose will on others. (3) Sovereignty. (4) A state that possesses or exercises influence or control over others. (5) Political, military, economic strength of a state. Power can exist without authority. A government may have power and yet it may lack authority if it lacks legitimacy. *See* Authority, Legitimacy.

Prudence. Ability to judge political action by its possible alternative political consequences. The key virtue of a political leader. While being prudent, leaders must be concerned with the interests of the states for which they are responsible, but they must take seriously into consideration the interests of other states and not ignore them.

Raison d'État. Reason of state. A post-Machiavellian doctrine based on separation of politics from ethics, according to which states can do whatever is necessary to promote their own interests (including engaging in armed conflicts) irrespective of any human cost or moral consequences. The popularity of this doctrine in Germany has led the West into two world wars. *See* Realpolitik.

Rationality. (1) In the Classical Tradition and Locke, deliberative rationality—a reflection about what is beneficial and harmful, just and unjust, and the making of right judgments and choices. (2) In Hobbes and his followers, instrumental rationality, using reason in a purely instrumental way to get what one wants, by maximizing benefits and minimizing costs. (3) Commitment to certain ends—the Enlightenment's idea of reason and the rational modern society as contrasted with a traditional society. *See* Modernity.

Realpolitik. As an extreme form of realism, *realpolitik* has much in common with the practice of *raison d'État* in the nineteenth and twentieth centuries. It denotes politics based on force, reliance on naked power, ruthlessness, and fraud. Moral considerations are excluded for the sake of a geopolitical and strategic gain. War, conquest, nation's honor, and destiny are glorified. The term was coined by Ludwig von Rochau in *Gründsatze der Realpolitik* (1853). If, by its glorification of war and conquest, *realpolitik* is basically an immoral position, by its stress on prudence, realism, especially classical realism, is rather amoral. Classical realism does not deny morality, but, by defining politics as an autonomous sphere, asserts the supreme value to successful political action based on prudence. *See* Realism, Prudence.

Realism. Political realism. A theoretical perspective in the discipline of International Relations that emphasizes the conflicting character of international politics and stresses the importance of power and security issues. *See* Neorealism.

Representative Government. The whole citizenry exercise control over their country's affairs through representatives periodically elected by themselves.

Republic. (1) In the classical tradition, the republic is associated with the ancient idea of a mixed constitution, on which, for example, the political system of the Roman republic was based. (2) The modern republic asserts sovereignty of the people and is based on modern political institutions, such as separation of powers and representative government. *See* Mixed Constitution, Sovereignty of the People, Separation of Powers, Representative Government.

Right. (1) Objective right refers to something that is just: what is rightfully due to a person; subjective, to a right that a person claims or possesses. (2) Having a right to do something means not having any obligation to refrain from doing it. Legal or moral liberty. (3) Having a right to receive something is a right against someone else who has an obligation to provide that to which the person is said to have a right. (4) Claim to something due against someone else. Human rights are a species of claim-rights: for example, the right to hold opinions without interference; the right to life, liberty, and security of a person; the right to own property. *See* Human Rights.

Right Reason. Moral judgment, the ability to distinguish right from wrong. In the natural law tradition, positive or human laws have their foundation in natural law and are based on right reason. *See* Natural Law.

Self-Interest. Private or particular interest, as opposed to general interest. *See* Common Good.

Separation of Powers. The division of government institutions into executive, legislative, and juridical with a goal to create checks and balances between them.

Social Classes. Main social groups, such as the nobility, the wealthy, and the common people in a traditional society, or the haves and have-nots in a commercial society.

Sovereignty. (1) Supreme controlling power. (2) State sovereignty. The authority of the state, based on recognition by other states, to govern matters within its own borders that affect its own people, economy, and security. The modern state is a sovereign state. It enjoys supremacy over the territory it controls and it is recognized as sovereign by other states. Post-modernity erodes the idea of state sovereignty. *See* Post-Modernity.

Sovereignty of the People. Popular Sovereignty. The supreme controlling power is vested in the entire aggregate of the community, in the whole citizenry; it rests with the people.

State. (1) In Aristotle, political association or political community. (2) A territorially based political unit, recognized by other states, that has a stable population and a government to which the population owes allegiance. (3) A set of political institutions within this unit—government. *See* Nation-State.

State of Nature. (1) An era in the history of humankind before the establishment of political societies. (2) Anarchy. *See* Anarchy.

Totalitarianism. A total domination of civil society by the state as exemplified by Nazi Germany and the Stalinist Soviet Union. State's complete control of political, social, and economic activities, monopoly of the flow of information, suppression of opposition.

Tyranny. (1) In Aristotle, rule of one individual for his own benefit. (2) In Locke, arbitrary and lawless exercise of power, especially if natural law is disregarded. (3) The tyranny of the majority—unchecked rule of the majority. *See* Natural Law.

Utilitarianism. Doctrine that all moral obligations depend on their utility for promoting pleasure or happiness for the greatest number of people. Utilitarians generally adopt the Hobbesian view of human beings as pleasure-seeking individuals. *See* Happiness.

Utility. (1) Benefit. Pleasure. (2) In Utilitarianism, the principle that holds that actions are right in proportion as they tend to promote happiness (pleasure), wrong as they tend to produce the reverse of happiness (pain). *See* Utilitarianism.

Virtù. Ability or vigor, a quality displayed by successful leaders, but also by the body of citizens as a whole. Machiavellian reinterpretation of classical virtue. *See* Virtue. Civic Virtue.

Virtue. Moral and intellectual excellence; a quality that can be associated with the individual and with the public. Classical virtues, such as such as wisdom, courage, moderation, and justice, were in a later period supplemented by Christian virtues of faith, hope, charity, and benevolence. Modern virtues, mentioned by John Stuart Mill in *Considerations on Representative Government*, include industry, integrity, activity, and originality.

INDEX

Note: Definitions in the Glossary are indicated by **emboldened numbers**